Great Places™
MONTANA

*A Recreational Guide to Montana's Public Lands and Historic Places
for Birding, Hiking, Photography, Fishing, Hunting, and Camping*

Titles Available from Wilderness Adventures Press, Inc.™

Flyfishers Guide to™

Flyfisher's Guide to Alaska

Flyfisher's Guide to Arizona

Flyfisher's Guide to Chesapeake Bay

Flyfisher's Guide to Colorado

Flyfisher's Guide to the Florida Keys

Flyfisher's Guide to Freshwater Florida

Flyfisher's Guide to Idaho

Flyfisher's Guide to Montana

Flyfisher's Guide to Michigan

Flyfisher's Guide to Minnesota

Flyfisher's Guide to Missouri & Arkansas

Flyfisher's Guide to New York

Flyfisher's Guide to New Mexico

Flyfisher's Guide to Northern California

Flyfisher's Guide to Northern New England

Flyfisher's Guide to Oregon

Flyfisher's Guide to Pennsylvania

Flyfisher's Guide to Saltwater Florida

Flyfisher's Guide to Texas

Flyfisher's Guide to Utah

Flyfisher's Guide to Virginia

Flyfisher's Guide to Washington

Flyfisher's Guide to Wisconsin & Iowa

Flyfisher's Guide to Wyoming

Flyfisher's Guide to Yellowstone National Park

Best Fishing Waters™

California's Best Fishing Waters

Colorado's Best Fishing Waters

Idaho's Best Fishing Waters

Montana's Best Fishing Waters

Oregon's Best Fishing Waters

Washington's Best Fishing Waters

Anglers Guide to™

Complete Anglers Guide to Oregon

Saltwater Angler's Guide to the Southeast

Saltwater Angler's Guide to Southern California

On the Fly Guide to™

On the Fly Guide to the Northwest

On the Fly Guide to the Northern Rockies

Field Guide to™

Field Guide to Fishing Knots

Field Guide to Retriever Drills

Field Guide to Dog First Aid

Fly Tying

Go-To Flies™

Great Places™

Great Places™ Montana

Great Places™
MONTANA

*A Recreational Guide to Montana's Public Lands and Historic Places
for Birding, Hiking, Photography, Fishing, Hunting, and Camping*

Chuck Robbins

Great Places™ Series

Wilderness
Adventures
Press, Inc.™

Belgrade, Montana

Great Places™ Series

Published by Wilderness Adventures Press, Inc.™
45 Buckskin Road
Belgrade, MT 59714
866-400-2012
Website: www.wildadvpress.com
email: books@wildadvpress.com

First Edition

Printed in China

ISBN 978-1932098-59-4 (1-932098-59-3)

Dedication

For Gale, who somehow stoically manages to keep our projects (and me) on a somewhat-even keel. And for wild lands, wildlife, healthy habitat, clean air, clean water and good soil.

Acknowledgements

Thanks to all the U.S. Fish and Wildlife Service refuge managers and staff, Montana Fish Wildlife and Parks biologists and personnel, the helpful folks at the various Bureau of Land Management offices scattered throughout the state, and the U.S. Forest Service. Thanks to all the birders who willingly shared their considerable expertise in hopes of somehow enlightening perhaps one of the sorriest wannabes on the planet. And to all our many photographer friends who encouraged us to keep on shooting despite a once-upon-a-time feeling we might actually be drowning in throw away shots. Thanks also to publishers, Chuck and Blanche Johnson and last, but hardly least, editor Josh Bergan who somehow managed to turn my brand of twisted prose into something that readers might actually find lucid.

Cabinet Mountains

Table of Contents

Dedication v
Acknowledgements v
Introduction. 1
REGION 1 13
   Glacier National Park. 15
   Lake Mary Ronan State Park 26
   Lost Trail National Wildlife Refuge. 30
   National Bison Range National Wildlife Refuge 37
   Ninepipe National Wildlife Refuge. 42
   Pablo National Wildlife Refuge 47
   Swan River National Wildlife Refuge 50
   Wild Horse Island State Park 54
REGION 2 57
   Blackfoot-Clearwater Wildlife Management Area 58
   Lee Metcalf National Wildlife Refuge 63
   Council Grove State Park 68
   Lost Creek State Park. 76
   Painted Rocks State Park. 80
   Warm Springs Wildlife Management Area 83
REGION 3 89
   Canyon Ferry Wildlife Management Area 91
   Humbug Spires Wilderness Study Area. 99
   Mount Haggin Wildlife Management Area. 105
   Missouri Headwaters State Park 113
   Red Rock Lakes National Wildlife Refuge. 116
   Robb-Ledford/Blacktail Creek Wildlife Management Area 127
REGION 4 133
   Beartooth Wildlife Management Area. 135
   Blackleaf Wildlife Management Area. 141
   Benton Lake National Wildlife Refuge. 150
   Ear Mountain Outstanding Natural Area 159
   Giant Springs Heritage State Park. 165

Freezeout Lake Wildlife Management Area 168
Sluice Boxes State Park 179
Sun River Wildlife Management Area 182
Upper Missouri Breaks National Monument. 186
War Horse National Wildlife Refuge 189
REGION 5 193
Bridger Waterfowl Production Area. 195
Haymaker Wilderness Management Area 200
Hailstone National Wildlife Refuge 203
Halfbreed National Wildlife Refuge 207
Lake Mason National Wildlife Refuge 211
Pryor Mountains Wild Horse Range 215
REGION 6 227
Bowdoin National Wildlife Refuge 229
Black Coulee National Wildlife Refuge 239
Creedman Coulee National Wildlife Refuge 241
Hewitt Lake National Wildlife Refuge 243
Lake Thibadeau National Wildlife Refuge 246
Brush Lake State Park 249
Charles M. Russell National Wildlife Refuge 253
UL Bend National Wildlife Refuge 269
Medicine Lake National Wildlife Refuge. 273
Bitter Creek Wilderness Study Area (WSA) 282
Fox Lake Wildlife Management Area 284
Fort Union Trading Post 286
REGION 7 289
Elk Island Wildlife Management Area 291
Hell Creek State Park 297
Isaac Homestead Wildlife Management Area 299
Lamesteer National Wildlife Refuge. 307
Makoshika State Park. 317
Medicine Rocks State Park 323
Pirogue Island State Park 327
Seven Sisters Wildlife Management Area 331
Nature Conservancy Sites. 337
Northern Prairies of Montana 337
Lindbergh Lake Pines - Swan Valley 338
Dancing Prairie Preserve 338
Safe Harbor Marsh Preserve - Flathead Basin 340
Crown Butte Preserve - Simms 342

South Fork Madison Preserve 344
Swan River Oxbow Preserve - Swan Valley. 345
Comertown Pothole Prairie Preserve 347
Pine Butte Swamp Preserve 348
Lewis and Clark 351
In Montana 351
OTHER PLACES OF INTEREST. 353
Great Montana Birding and Nature Trail 354
Bridger Raptor Festival 354
Holter Museum of Art 355
Lewis and Clark National Historic Trail Interpretive Center 356
C.M. Russell Museum 357
Montana's Museum 358
Museum of the Rockies. 359
Historic Battlefields 361
Bear Paw and Big Hole Battlefields 361
Little Bighorn Battlefield. 365
Bureau of Land Management (BLM). 370
Wilderness Study Areas 371
Wilderness Montana 374
Montana Bird List. 375
Montana Wildlife List 393
Montana Specialty Bird List 395
Optics and Gear 397

Introduction

Officially nicknamed the Treasure State; though perhaps better known by handles such as Last Best Place, Big Sky Country, High Plains and Shining Mountains, one thing I think most would agree upon is that Montana is indeed high, wide and handsome. Above all, in this increasingly shrinking modern world of ours, Montana is a mecca for wildlife and wildlife lovers alike.

It seems Montanans as a whole are more likely to rave about our mountain man-cum-cowboy roots than talk about the ravages that the cut-and-run mining industry wreaked upon the landscape and left behind for future generations, as happens way too often. But as a whole, it seems we are most proud of our incredible wildlife heritage; everything from grizzly bears and bison to tundra swans and relic sage grouse. Yes, we Montanans like our wild lands and wildlife. Most of us spend far more time outdoors than indoors and, judging those I know best, dream constantly all that outside stuff we are surely missing, when forced indoors. Something like one in four of us hunt and an even higher percentage are licensed to fish. While I can't prove it, I'd bet the farm the great majority who don't do either, place watching wildlife (birding) high on their list of preferred ways to wile away free time.

With that in mind, comes Great Places Montana, an in-depth book written solely for wildlife lovers, birders, wildlife watchers, photographers, hunters, fishers, hikers, campers, picnickers, or those who want to kick back, relax, and take it all in. It is my sincere hope you will find the information not only helpful, but key to opening up a whole new, heretofore largely untapped, world of enjoyment, entertainment and adventure.

The lands described in the book are (and I really believe this) the very best of the best for wildlife, and people too. Think about it: Wildlife depends on habitat. No habitat, no wildlife. In a nutshell, that's it. The same goes for people: As our population continues to explode our "habitat" if you will, continues to shrink at an alarming rate actually. As such, open spaces, undeveloped land becomes more and more valuable, not just in real dollars but to our overall well being. There is not room to discuss at length here (I'm not smart enough anyway), but population-wise we've about reached a code-red situation. Yet the lands described here are, believe it or not, virtually protected from human encroachment forever. Forever. Think about that for a moment. Put simply, these lands are going to be there for wildlife and for us, if even for just a few fleeting hours or days. A wild life, tomorrow, next week, next month, next year, next life. Imagine that. Especially considering how easy, and how too often, we forget wildlife and wild lands in our haste to tame the landscape, grab the brass ring, or bank the almighty dollar.

Our National Wildlife Refuges, State Wildlife Management Areas, Waterfowl Production Areas, and Wetland Management Districts continue to provide the sort of diverse, healthy habitat upon which wildlife depends, and in some instances, despite what some special interest groups would have us believe, are the only games in town. Thank goodness for the clear thinking, dedication and hard work of good folks whose goals aren't swayed by the numbskulls of society, the greedy land grabbers and, too often it seems, even greedier politicians.

"There's a growing concern about the increased rate at which valuable wildlife habitats are being lost to changing land uses," Jeff Herbert, of Montana Fish, Wildlife and Parks said in a recent conversation. "Recently we've seen an influx of people moving into what have been important areas of big game winter range and creek bottom habitats. At the same time we've seen conversion of native grasslands to

Bighorn sheep (ram)

intensively farmed croplands and other developments that have removed these lands from the habitat base. For the future welfare of our many species of wildlife, we will need to look toward conserving habitat whenever we can."

With that in mind, sportsmen's groups, conservation organizations, and others coerced the 1987 Montana Legislature to pass House Bill 526, a landmark conservation law setting aside a portion of hunting license revenues for acquisition of important and threatened wildlife habitats; not just game species habitat but all wildlife and encourages use of conservation easements and leases as preferred alternatives to fee title acquisition. The years since have resulted in over 40 parcels, — purchases, lease agreements and conservation easements — more than 268,000 acres and $37.6 million worth of prime habitat protected forever. That, to me, is the really good news.

In addition, Montana boasts 21 National Wildlife Refuges within its far-flung borders. Administratively, eight are staffed. Benton Lake, Lee Metcalf, Lost Trail and Red Rock Lakes stand alone, while Bowdoin, Charles M. Russell, Medicine Lake and National Bison Range all administer satellite refuges. The Bowdoin staff administers Black Coulee, Creedman Coulee, Hewitt Lake and Lake Thibadeau NWRs, the Charles M. Russell staff administers UL Bend, Hailstone, Halfbreed, War Horse and Lake Mason NWRs; the Medicine Lake staff administers Lamesteer NWR, and the National Bison Range staff administers Ninepipe, Pablo, and Swan River NWRs. Montana NWRs range in size from tiny Lamesteer (110 acres) to the sprawling CMR (1,100,000 acres).

The Bowdoin, CMR, Medicine Lake and National Bison Range staffs oversee Montana's five Wetland Management Districts.

Benton Lake Wetland Management District (WMD) encompasses 25,000 square miles in ten counties of north-central Montana. It includes the western-most extension of the glaciated prairie pothole habitat of the Northern Great Plains and the Blackfoot River valley, a glaciated intermountain valley west of the continental divide. The 21 Waterfowl Production Areas (WPAs) in the district are extremely varied in habitat types and include prairie grasslands, fresh and saline wetlands, riparian and montane forests, and rivers. Habitat conservation easements protect both wetlands and upland habitat in the WMD from conversion to uses incompatible with wildlife. The primary role of the WMD is conservation of habitat for waterfowl, but a wide variety of other species benefit, including sandhill cranes, bald eagles, grizzly bears, deer and elk. Management practices include reseeding grasses and forbs on former cropland and restoring drained wetlands. Occasionally prescribed burning, haying and grazing are used as tools to stimulate growth of vegetation or to manage weeds.

Nearly all WPAs are open to public hunting in accordance with state regulations.

The Bowdoin WMD is located in Valley, Phillips, Blaine, and part of Hill Counties in northern Montana. The District varies from glaciated-end-moraine pothole con-centrations to glacial outwash plains with many manmade reservoirs subject to severe soil erosion. Most WPAs and wetland easements are located in glaciated areas. Predominant land use is ranching, with considerable amounts of cultivated land converted to Conservation Reserve Program (CRP) lands. Waterfowl Production Areas within the District were established under the Migratory Bird Conservation Act primarily for migratory bird protection.

McNeil Slough WPA, a large acquisition on the Milk River, rivals many NWRs for resource values and management complexity. A flow-through water system provides management potential, essentially nonexistent on other units. Pearce WPA, located adjacent to Bowdoin NWR, is similarly managed and included in Bowdoin surveys. Beaver Creek WPA, located just east of Bowdoin, contains the main outlet canal for moving Bowdoin water to Beaver Creek.

Other WPAs are located distant from Bowdoin and do not receive as much management effort or public use. Most are open to public hunting (subject to state regulations).

The CMR Wetlands Management District (CMR WMD) includes 20 counties in southeastern Montana and encompasses 52,834 square miles. Included are three WPAs: Clarksfork WPA, Tews WPA and Spidel WPA. A wetland manager located at CMR NWR headquarters in Lewistown administers the district.

The WMD is outside the Prairie Pothole Region and contains few fee title easement properties. Since 1988, most of the WMD workload has involved the Partners for Wildlife program consisting of wetland projects, landowner assistance, Food Security Act activities, FmHA (Farmers Home Administration) conservation easement fee title inspections and other Department activities. Granted some of these are off limits to

Snowcrest Range in Robb Ledford/Blacktail Creek Wildlife Management Area

John Q. Citizen, but the wildlife benefits; and remember there are few critters out there bound by something as trivial as property lines.

The Medicine Lake Wetland Management District (WMD) is located in the extreme northeastern corner of Montana. Heavily glaciated, it is part of the prairie pothole region. The WMD lies within the transition zone between the mixed and short grass prairie. Over 80 percent of Montana's threatened piping plover population nests within the many alkali lakes. Waterfowl production rates are among the highest in the prairie pothole region.

Privately owned wetland acres are protected from drainage, burning, leveling and filling by perpetual wetland easements. Perpetual grassland easements are also being acquired throughout the district, which prohibits the landowner from "breaking" the native prairie. The WMD has an active 'Partners for Wildlife' program, which encourages landowners to implement wildlife habitat projects compatible with their farming and ranching operations.

The Northwest Montana WMD encompasses Lake and Flathead Counties in northwestern Montana. Lake County WPAs are located in glacial and lakebed soil deposits, part of numerous glacial kettles formed during the 100,000-year Wisconsin glaciation. Flathead WPA consists of seven miles of lakeshore and uplands at the

Fish, Wildlife, and Parks: Regions

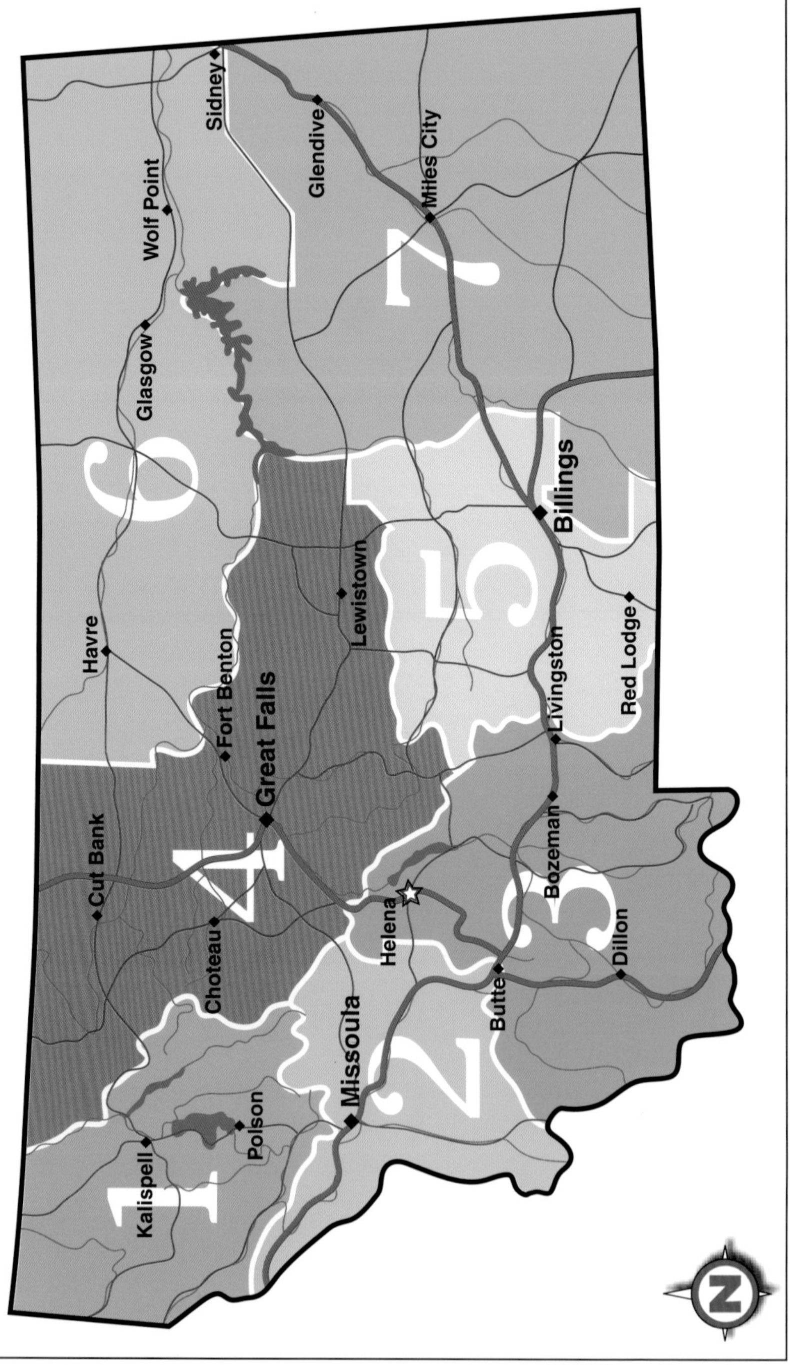

Sidney
Glendive
Miles City
Wolf Point
Glasgow
7
Billings
6
Lewistown
5
Havre
Fort Benton
Great Falls
Livingston
Red Lodge
Cut Bank
4
Bozeman
Choteau
Helena
Dillon
3
Butte
Kalispell
Polson
Missoula
2
1

north end of Flathead Lake. Included are remnants of "delta" islands at the mouth of the Flathead River.

Several other WPAs are scattered throughout the valley. Most are small tracts of wetlands acquired for waterfowl production, while associated uplands provide habitat for a variety of wildlife. Management plans provide for the preservation and enhancement of wetlands, with emphasis on nesting cover, and establishing food plots on the uplands. All are open to public hunting subject to state regulations.

Montana Fish, Wildlife, and Parks owns (for the most part), manages and administers over 60 Wildlife Management Areas (WMAs), encompassing approximately 260,000 acres of diverse wildlife habitat. As a reminder: A State Lands Recreational Use Permit is required to recreate on state lands. Many WMAs provide critical winter habitat for big game and, as such, human visitation is restricted part of the year; however, the rest of the year all are afforded free public access. Wildlife viewing and birding opportunities abound. For example, visit the Kootenai River WMA in fall and you might find as many as 175 bald eagles sharing the view. Visitors to Wall Creek WMA (Madison River south of Ennis) in winter can focus binoculars or spotting scopes on hundreds of wintering elk, and not leave the main highway. Other activities include photography, hunting and fishing, picnicking and camping. Even motor vehicles are often allowed seasonally on designated roads. Trapping is allowed on many WMAs, though usually by permit only. Of course not all activities are allowed (or possible for that matter), so it pays to check in beforehand.

In this book you will find descriptions and viewing information for some of the more dynamic WMAs. In addition, I've included information regarding some of our more unique State Parks, especially those affording a good chance to observe wildlife.

As with the NWRs, topography ranges from rolling sagebrush and grasslands, to timbered foothills and rugged bad lands, to lakes and lush riparian corridors and marshlands. While no one parcel encompasses all, nearly every species of native and alien fauna and flora occurs somewhere within the WMA system: native and introduced grasses, shrubs, trees and wildflowers, mega fauna — grizzly and black bear, mountain lion, gray wolf, elk, moose, mountain goat, bighorn sheep, mule and white-tailed deer, pronghorn—and lesser critters such as wolverine, bobcat, Canada lynx, coyote, red fox, badger, marten, otter, beaver, fisher, weasel, marmot, several rabbits, porcupine, skunk, pica, several ground squirrels and prairie dogs. You name it, WMAs are likely places to find it.

The Montana Bird List (see the Appendix) comprises about 400 bird species — native and introduced upland birds, songbirds, birds of prey, waterfowl, shorebirds and wading birds. The Montana Wildlife List (Appendix) boasts nearly 150 species, moose to mice, regal mountain goats to creepy-crawlies — bull snake, rattlesnake, lizard...I'm sure you get the point. When it comes to wildlife and birdlife, Montana might not have it all, but close enough, don't you think? More than enough, it would seem to keep even the most dedicated enthusiast from running out of marks anytime soon.

The book is arranged according to the seven (management) regions employed by Montana FWP. Each region is prefaced by a map that shows the general location of individual sites. There is also a section on Nature Conservancy sites, which includes an overview of these unique parcels scattered throughout Montana. Each, by the way, affords great birding and wildlife viewing opportunities.

A brief word on how to peruse the book: Beneath the title line, the size of the particular parcel of land is noted and a brief statement as to location is included. The narrative section follows and here you will find the meat, so to speak, of the subject; not only birding and wildlife viewing prospects, but in many cases a little history lesson as well. Following the narrative is a section called Nearby Restaurants and Accommodations. This is in no way meant to be all inclusive, but rather a brief overview of where you might find a bite to eat, or a bed in which to sleep. Wherever possible we've included only those of which we have prior knowledge, either personally or from friends and acquaintances. Bear in mind a lot of these are in small towns, where resident wildlife often outnumbers resident people and keeping a business solvent can be tough. In other words what we found yesterday you might not today. With that in mind we rarely leave home without first tossing in the camp outfit, food, whatever, prepared to wing it for at least a day or two.

In the Fast Facts section you will find contact information, specific directions to the site and, in brief, everything a particular site has to offer. However, should you have a specific check-off in mind, such as a Baird's sparrow for example, before heading to Refuge X, check the various bird lists in the book…just where might Baird's sparrows indeed occur, then using the Contact Information contact those sites—refuge and other administrative staff are more than capable, willing in almost every case to offer valuable assistance. Timing, as they say, is everything. This game is no different. Use the book, do your homework, check out the possibilities, formulate a game plan and then go for it.

About the Montana Bird List

The bird lists are the most up to date available, for many sites there just aren't any; in such cases use a list from a similar site, but keep in mind since it isn't site specific it may not be 100-percent accurate. Still, to my way of thinking, any list is better than none. If all else fails, consult the State Bird List. Another thing: Dedicated birders are forever coming up with new additions, so there are no guarantees any of the lists are 100-percent accurate. Use your birding skills, consult your Field Guide to Upland Birds and Waterfowl (by Christopher Smith) and if it's a bird new to the area, contact the appropriate office and report it. Like the bird list, the Wildlife List is as inclusive as I could make it, with apologies for any oversights.

The optics and gear section suggestions are, I'm afraid, heavily biased. Based on my having spent at least a half century staring down binoculars and spotting scopes, weathering the elements, beating around the bush, wasting more time as it were, than any man should be allowed. Sorry, but this is the stuff that works for me, I'm sure it will for you too, but, by all means, feel free to experiment.

Montana falls within the Central and Pacific Flyways. During spring and fall migrations hundreds of thousands of birds migrate through. Winging overhead, resting, breeding, nesting, rearing their brood, feeding, etc. You might spy a twenty-pound-plus trumpeter swan one minute and a miniscule tenth-of-an-ounce calliope hummingbird the next; perhaps a foraging 600-pound grizzly bear or a six-ounce pika.

While thousands visit our wildlife refuges, management areas and state parks each year hoping to catch a glimpse, crowding is seldom a problem; when you do find a crowd, usually you can just go around the corner, hike a ways off the beaten path and have the birds and wildlife all to yourself. Birding by the seat of your pants works, but getting out and beating the brush works better — at the very least, it's healthier.

Diverse is the one word I would choose to describe the wild lands of Montana. From the near-rain forest conditions of the northwest to the arid plains of the east to the alpine tundra of the south, it's difficult to argue diversity. You might hear the call of chestnut-backed chickadees at elevations of just above 1,800 feet near the Kootenai River, or watch black rosy finches feeding at the edge of a receding snowfield at 11,000 feet on the Beartooth Highway in July. An experienced birder, one willing to spend a couple weeks traveling the state in early summer, should easily tally 200 bird species or more and enjoy countless wildlife encounters, grizzly bears to ground squirrels and who can say what else in between. Montana is also huge: the fourth largest state,

Western meadowlark

500-plus miles east to west, 300-plus miles north to south, over 147,000 square miles in area. Beaverhead County, Montana's largest, is bigger than some eastern states.

Then too Montana offers plenty of unique birding or wildlife viewing opportunities. For example visit the Bridger Mountains near Bozeman in late September, early October and witness the highest concentration of migrating golden eagles in the lower 48 states. If you can handle the two-hour walk and 8,600-foot elevation, just go, I guarantee you won't be disappointed. Visit Freezeout Lake in late March and early April and share space with thousands upon thousands snow geese and other water birds as well. Visit the CMR Refuge in September and observe one of nature's finest spectacles — rutting bull elk. And the beat goes on and on...

Seasonal gathering points attract birders from all over the world. Medicine Lake in the northeast to Ninepipe in the northwest to Red Rock Lakes in the south, Montana is well known for its many hotspots, and should be on every serious birder's must-do list. Inside this book you will find the necessary information to make it happen.

Be aware Montana is rife with sudden elevation changes and such break points usually mean bird and wildlife species sightings are apt to change just as suddenly. A sudden change in habitat and elevation, such as from Ninepipe to the Bison Range and Mission Mountains, is typical of many of the best birding areas, especially in the western half of the state. Of particular note are mountain ranges rising abruptly up out of the prairie, wide river valleys separating steep mountain ranges; in other words what you find at the bottom of the canyon is not likely the same as at the top. Such abrupt elevation changes create spectacular updrafts and raptors, especially, take advantage. A prime example is the Kevin (Kee-vin) Rim where sandstone cliffs rise dramatically from the mixed grass prairie north of Great Falls. The world's highest nesting density of ferruginous hawks is found here; these regal buteos hunt the ground squirrel colonies dotting the countryside to the south and east. Golden eagles, prairie falcons, American kestrels and red-tailed hawks share this abode as well. Watch for great-horned owls and a potential merlin too. And its appeal is not lost on birds such as McCowan's and chestnut-collared longspurs as well as horned larks and Sprague's pipits that pirouette over the lands bordering these cliffs. Such sites exist throughout Montana, and are as easy to find as getting in your vehicle and taking a drive — actually the hardest part might be coming up empty.

For your information

Nickname: Treasure State, aka, Big Sky Country; Land of the Shining Mountains; Mountain State; Bonanza State and Headwaters State (Depending, our rivers flow to the Pacific, Atlantic and Arctic Oceans)
State Animal: Grizzly Bear
State Bird: Western Meadowlark
State Dance: Square Dance
State Fish: Black-spotted Cutthroat Trout
State Flower: Bitterroot

State Fossil: Duck-billed Dinosaur *(Maiasaura Peeblesorum)*
State Gemstones: Sapphire & Agate
State Grass: Bluebunch Wheatgrass
State Tree: Ponderosa Pine
State Butterfly: Mourning Cloak
State Song: "Montana" – written one night by a Montana newspaper editor and famous songwriter in 1910.
State Ballad: "Montana Melody" – Montana is one of few states to have a state song and ballad.
Admitted to the Union: Nov. 8, 1889, the 41st state.
Population: 926,865, 6.2 persons per square mile, the 44th most populous state.
Capital City: Helena – population, 26,718
Largest City: Billings – population, 95,220
State Name: "Montana" is from the Latin word for "mountainous region"
Size:
    147,046 square miles in total area
    145,556 square miles in land area
    1,490 square miles in water area
    94,109,440 total acres
Public land comprises 28% within Montana
Fourth largest state in the union
Greatest distance from east to west boundary: approximately 550 miles
Greatest distance from north to south boundary: approximately 320 miles
Geographic Center: Fergus County, about 11 miles west of Lewistown
Number of Counties: 56
Highest Point: 12,799 feet (3,901 meters) above sea level at summit of Granite Peak in Park County near south-central boundary
Lowest Point: 1,820 feet in Lincoln County in the northwest corner where the Kootenai River enters Idaho
Mean Elevation: 3,400 feet
Time Zone: Mountain Standard
Area Code: 406
Postal Abbreviation: MT
Resident: Montanan
Motto: Oro y Plata (Spanish for "gold and silver")

So there you have it, turn the pages of the book, enjoy, and here's to great birding and wildlife viewing.

Chuck Robbins
Dillon, MT
2008

Fish, Wildlife, and Parks: Region 1

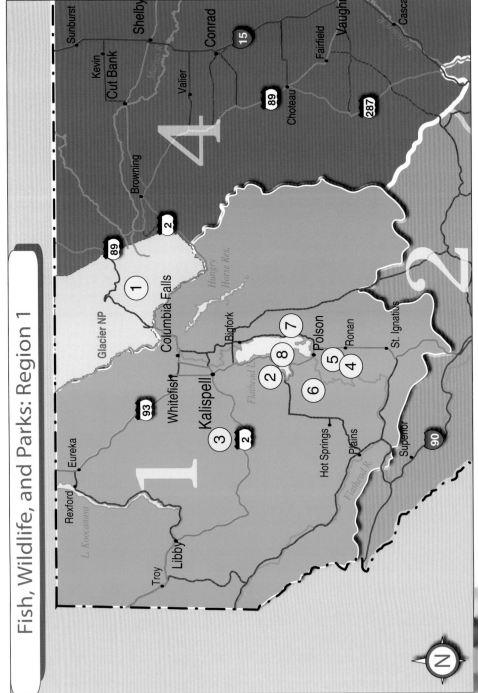

REGION I

1. Glacier National Park 15
2. Lake Mary Ronan
   State Park 26
3. Lost Trail National Wildlife
   Refuge 30
4. National Bison Range National
   Wildlife Refuge 37
5. Ninepipe National Wildlife
   Refuge 42
6. Pablo National Wildlife
   Refuge 47
7. Swan River National Wildlife
   Refuge 50
8. Wild Horse Island State Park 54

Glacier National Park

1,000,000 ACRES; NORTHEAST OF KALISPELL

Some call it the Shining Mountains; others refer to it as the Backbone of the World, most of us know it simply as Glacier National Park (officially it is designated Waterton-Glacier International Peace Park). Whatever you call it, the park encompasses more than a million acres — including glaciers, forests, alpine meadows, lakes, rugged peaks and valleys — of prime wildlife habitat that is home to over 70 species of mammals including the grizzly bear, wolverine, gray wolf, lynx, bobcat, fisher, mountain lion, mountain goat, bighorn sheep, moose, elk, mule deer and white-tailed deer. To date 272 species of birds have been observed, from harlequin ducks to dippers, awesome eagles to tiny neotropical migrants such as Calliope hummingbirds.

A wildlife viewer, birder and hiker's paradise, GNP is crisscrossed by 151 maintained hiking trails totaling 743 miles. It owes its climate variation to its extreme elevation swing (3,150 feet at the confluence of the Middle and North Forks of the Flathead River, to 10,466 feet atop Mount Cleveland) and the fact that it sits at the headwaters of rivers run to three oceans (Pacific, Atlantic and Arctic). All of that gives rise to one of the world's most diverse habitats, supporting a dizzying array of wildlife, bird and plant species — more than 1,800 species actually, including 25 major tree species.

The park is named for its prominent glacier-carved terrain and remnant glaciers (although in recent drastic decline, only about 50 remain active, 37 of which are named) that descended from the ice ages of 10-12,000 years ago. Bedrock and deposited materials exposed by receding glaciers tell a story of ancient seas, geologic uplifting and faults, and the appearance of giant slabs of the earth's ancient crust overlaying younger strata. The combination of spectacular geology, 762 glacial lakes and 563 streams tumbling for over 1,000 miles results in some of the most spectacular scenery on the planet. By the way, park lakes and streams contain 23 fish species; in other words for those of you so inclined, be sure to pack along a rod and reel. Beyond natural wonders and wildlife the park is also rich in cultural history, with over 400 archeological sites, including more than 50 vision quest sites, sacred to native peoples for eons.

In 1932 Glacier National Park and Waterton Lakes National Park, across the border in Canada, were designated Waterton-Glacier International Peace Park — celebrating the long-standing peace and friendship between the two nations. Both parks have since been designated International Biosphere Reserves and together were recognized in 1995 as a World Heritage Site. If any spot in Montana deserves of world-class recognition this is it.

From a wildlife standpoint the best thing about the park is it's so big and there are no roads, relatively speaking anyway. One road, Going-to-the-Sun Highway, bisects it from West Glacier across Logan Pass (6,680 feet) to St. Mary, and two other roads penetrate the east boundary for short distances — Two Medicine and Many Glacier. Along the west boundary there is the Camas Road (aka, Inside North Fork Road) and US 2 more or less skirts the other side. As far as roads go, those are it. The roads of course lead to many trailheads, and from the trailheads, foot power rules.

Most visitors do Glacier seat of the pants style, vehicle touring the Going-to-the-Sun, been there done that. And it is indeed a spectacular drive. Completed in 1932, the highway offers a scenic overview of what the park has to offer: gushing streams, unmatched alpine vistas, spectacular alpine lakes, old growth forest and wildlife including, if you are lucky, grizzly bears, mountain goats and perhaps even a white-tailed ptarmigan or two. The drive is almost worth it just to gawk at glacial Lake McDonald and the gushing whitewater rapids of McDonald Creek where you have to be extremely unlucky not to glimpse a water ouzel (American dipper) and a harlequin duck or three.

If you are really on top of your game, the check-off list could very well include varied thrush, Wilson's, MacGillivray's and Townsend's warblers, black bear, pikas, mountain goats, bighorn sheep, black swifts, varied thrushes, winter wrens, chestnut-backed chickadees, blue grouse, American pipit, gray-crowned rosy finches, white-crowned and fox sparrows, wildflowers... At times it looks like the work of a gardener gone mad. Bear grass is particularly prevalent up toward the pass and one of the few spots in the lower 48 where you actually might catch a glimpse of a wolverine.

Ascending Logan Pass, the road carves a path through towering mountain peaks, avalanche chutes and glaciers — a rush in itself. By the way, check the road report beforehand. This is major snow country and the road often opens late and closes early — drifts in excess of 50 feet are not at all uncommon come spring.

All the above is also possible along Inside North Fork Road, but bears and elk are most common and this is the best spot in Montana to view and hear the rare LeConte's sparrow. In the burned area look for red-naped sapsuckers, three-toed and black-backed woodpeckers and northern hawk owls (which nest here but might take a bit of sleuthing on your part to find). Gray wolves live here too, but good luck seeing one (although there is a decent chance of hearing their hackle-raising howls).

By now, I'm sure you realize how much I like this place, but stay with me. There is more...

To narrow the park's birding experience a bit further: Soaring bald and golden eagles and perching, strutting blue grouse are common sights anywhere on the Going-to-the-Sun Highway. The Red Eagle Valley, southwest of St. Mary, is a good place to spot yellow warblers, Swainson's thrushes and red-naped sapsuckers, tree swallows, golden-crowned kinglets and a variety of woodpeckers. In spring, Red Eagle Lake is a good spot to observe loon chicks hitching a ride on parents' backs. To the west, Two Dog Flats is home to a variety of raptors including prairie falcons, white-crowned sparrows and MacGillivray's warbler. Higher up look for sharp-shinned hawks, calliope hummingbirds, olive-sided flycatchers, white-tailed ptarmigan, mountain bluebirds, Townsend's solitaires, gray-crowned rosy finches, American pipits and the rare, diurnal and much coveted check off, northern hawk owl. On the southern flanks, especially in the Firebrand Pass area, look for common snipe, spotted sandpipers, red-tailed hawks, harriers and flickers. Waterfowl abounds: stunning harlequin ducks are common on MacDonald Creek, and ponds throughout the park are likely to hold, mallards, cinnamon and blue-winged teals, lesser scaup (bluebills), wigeon, goldeneye and common mergansers.

A park highlight is the Walton Goat Lick, which lies right off US 2, near Essex about halfway between East and West Glacier. An exposed bank of the Middle Fork Flathead River, mountain goats and other animals come to lick the mineral laden soils. From the parking area a short trail leads to an overlook. The lick looks unimpressive, just gray clay, but is actually laden with minerals and salts animals, especially goats, crave. There are four other known licks within the park but none receive the traffic Walton Goat Lick does.

Many Glacier Hotel

In geology speak, the lick is an exposure of the Roosevelt Fault comprised of gypsum, kieserite and sulfates. The craving for sodium and the shift to green vegetations each spring prompt goats to visit the lick. Calcium, potassium and magnesium found in the lick may help replace elements lost from bones during the long, grueling winter. Or it may just be goats have an acquired taste for salts, perhaps for digestive acids. Or maybe it's just a goat social. Except for the goats no one really knows for sure.

Park goats travel as far as four miles to the lick, while other goats scattered about the Flathead National Forest travel perhaps three times as far. April through August sees the most traffic, although some use continues year round. During late June and July dozens of goats are typically at the lick — 95 to 120 park goats and 20-45 Flathead NF goats. Elk and deer are also frequent visitors. The way to the lick is passed down from old goat to young goat. One of the most well-worn, traveled trails traverses the crest of Running Rabbit Mountain.

Goats are crepuscular critters; as such the most activity occurs in the twilight hours of dawn and dusk. A goat typically licks for about 24 hours, in five to six hour intervals during his first visit. After the first day more time is spent feeding and napping. Competition for the best spots is fierce so aggression and size rule, although goats adhere to a strict pecking order, which tends to keep serious injuries to a minimum. At the lick adult billies and nannies with kids share top billing within the hierarchy, followed by barren nannies, sub adults and yearlings. Interestingly, away from the lick nannies with kids are the lynch pins, followed by adult billies and so forth.

Keep your eyes peeled for:

Aggressive encounters

Occasional accidental falls into the river

Goats often swim the river to reach the lick

Interaction between goats and other animals, particularly black bears and elk

Most of us view our world bottom up, but the mountain goat views his upside down, literally. In other words, the highest pinnacles, the very heights that instill such fear in many humans, mountain goats find most comforting. To navigate precarious heights the goat sports a specialized hoof pad, soft and spongy inside surrounded by a hard outer ring, an almost perfect anti-skid device further enhanced by extra long dewclaws. To dodge the almost constant wind and extreme cold, especially in winter, the goat wears a luxurious coat, which is made up of thick fleece underneath a long (nearly six inch) guard-hair overcoat. Shaggy is perhaps an understatement when the goat decides to shed his winter hair.

Goats on high are fairly safe from predators, but as with most high lifestyles it comes with a price. While goats might mock most agility tests, falls do occur with some frequency. But falls pale in comparison to the real goat killers: avalanches. So much so that avalanche chutes are often the first place winter-starved bears head for in spring and wolverines have long associated the roar of sliding snow with gourmet goat dinners.

Both sexes wear horns, although billies' are generally thicker and more swept back. From a distance billies appear more yellow and dirty looking (imagine that) than nannies. The real giveaway, however, is that nannies and kids are nearly inseparable — if you see one, the other is almost sure to be close by. The flip side of course, billies tend toward being aloof and hanging out alone; even in bachelor groups, the oldest, biggest billy is often found off by himself.

Like all goats, mountain goats are eclectic eaters. As herbivores, goats munch pretty much whatever plant species they happen to stumble upon, including shrubs, mosses, lichens, forbs, grasses, sedges and rushes, and their winter range is usually separate from their summer range. A single kid, weighing six to eight pounds, is born in May following five to six-month gestation period. Kids are quite precocious as they are able to keep up with mom after just a few hours. Weaning occurs at about six weeks but kids graze grass and other plants just a few days after birth. Both sexes mature at two and a half years and nannies mate every other year.

Nearby Restaurants and Accommodations

Whistle Stop Restaurant, East Glacier, 7am-9pm
Eddie's Restaurant, Apgar Village, Open June-October, breakfast, lunch, dinner
Snowgoose Grille, St. Mary, breakfast, lunch, dinner, open year around. Six lodging facilities in GNP, phone 730-2544.
There are 13 campgrounds in the park, and with a backcountry permit you can camp almost anywhere in the backcountry; phone: 406-888-7800; online: www.nps.gov/glac.
Polebridge, one of the more remote outposts in the state, somewhat surprisingly boasts to very popular eateries, Polebridge Saloon and Mercantile, open year round but the two roads (Camas and North Fork), that lead there often are not — wildland fires having shut them down several times in recent summers.

Fast Facts

Contact Info: Glacier National Park; phone: 406-888-7800; online: www.nps.gov/glac
Getting There: US 2 west of Kalispell, entrances via West Glacier, East Glacier and St. Mary.
Activities: Wildlife viewing, birding, photography, hiking, fishing, camping.
Principle Mammals: Except for perhaps bison, just about every mammal found in Montana lives in the park.
Mammals of Special Interest: Grizzly bear, mountain goat, bighorn sheep, wolverine, lynx and pika.
Principle Birdlife: See below.
Birds of Special Interest: Harlequin duck, white-tailed ptarmigan, many lesser birds.

Habitat Overview: Glaciers, forests, alpine meadows, lakes, rugged peaks and valleys, elevations range from just over 3,000 feet, to nearly 10,500 feet.

Flora of Special Interest: more than 1,800 species actually, including 25 major tree species and wildflower displays to die for...

Best Wildlife Viewing Ops: Look for grizzlies in the avalanche chutes, from the Granite Park Chalet overlook; on Logan Pass: white-tailed ptarmigan, mountain goats, bighorn sheep and pikas.

Best Birding Ops: See above narrative for an overview of what might be seen in some of the park's many habitats.

Best Photo Ops: Wildlife and scenic opportunities abound throughout.

Hunting Ops: None.

Fishing Ops: No license required, check Park HQ for particulars.

Camping Ops: 13 campgrounds within the Park; backcountry permit required to camp in the backcountry.

Boating Ops: Lake Macdonald is primo; other opportunities exist, check with Park HQ.

Hiking Trails: 151 trails, totaling nearly 750 miles.

Motor Trails: Going-to-the-Sun Highway, Camas Road and Many Glaciers inside the Park; US 2 skirts the southern edge; US 89 skirts the east flank.

GNP Bird List

Loons and Grebes

Common loon
Red-throated loon
Arctic loon
Red-necked grebe
Horned grebe
Eared grebe
Clark's grebe
Pied-billed grebe

Pelicans

American white pelican

Cormorants

Double-crested cormorant

Herons

Great blue heron
Great egret
Black-crowned night heron
American bittern

Waterfowl

Tundra swan
Trumpeter swan
Canada goose
White fronted goose
Snow goose
Ross' goose
Mallard
Gadwall
Pintail
Green winged teal
Blue winged teal
Cinnamon teal
European wigeon
Northern shoveler
Wood duck
Redhead
Ringnecked duck
Canvasback
Greater scaup
Lesser scaup

Common goldeneye
Barrow's goldeneye
Bufflehead
Oldsquaw
Harlequin duck
White winged scoter
Surf scoter
Ruddy duck
Hooded merganser
Common merganser
Red-breasted merganser

Vultures

Turkey vulture

Hawks

Northern goshawk
Sharp-shinned hawk
Cooper's hawk
Red-tailed hawk
Red-shouldered hawk
Broad-winged hawk
Swainson's hawk
Rough-legged hawk
Ferruginous hawk
Golden eagle
Bald eagle
Northern harrier
Osprey

Falcons

Prairie falcon
Merlin
Gyrfalcon
American kestrel

Upland Game Birds

Blue grouse
Spruce grouse
Ruffed grouse
Willow ptarmigan
White-tailed ptarmigan
Sharp-tailed grouse
Ringnecked pheasant

Hungarian partridge

Cranes

Sandhill crane

Rails and Coots

Sora rail
Coot

Plovers

Killdeer
Semi-palmated plover
Black-bellied plover

Sandpipers

Black turnstone
Common snipe
Long-billed curlew
Upland sandpiper
Spotted sandpiper
Solitary sandpiper
Willet
Greater yellowlegs
Lesser yellowlegs
Pectoral sandpiper
Baird's sandpiper
Least sandpiper
Sanderling
Long-billed dowitcher
Marbled godwit
American avocet
Wilson's phalarope
Red-necked phalarope

Gulls and Terns

Glaucous gull
Glaucous winged gull
Herring gull
California gull
Ring-billed gull
Franklin's gull
Bonaparte's gull
Black-legged kittiwake

Forster's tern
Common tern
Caspian tern
Black tern

Pigeons

Band-tailed pigeon
Rock dove
Mourning dove

Owls

Western screech owl
Great horned owl
Snowy owl
Northern hawk owl
Northern pygmy owl
Burrowing owl
Barred owl
Great gray owl
Long-eared owl
Short-eared owl
Boreal owl
Northern saw whet owl

Goatsuckers

Common nighthawk

Swifts

Black swift
Vaux's swift
White throated swift

Hummingbirds

Black-chinned hummingbird
Broad-tailed hummingbird
Rufous hummingbird
Calliope hummingbird

Kingfisher

Belted kingfisher

Woodpeckers

Northern flicker

Pileated woodpecker
Redheaded woodpecker
Lewis' woodpecker
Yellowbellied sapsucker
Williamson's sapsucker
Hairy woodpecker
Downy woodpecker
White-headed woodpecker
Black-backed woodpecker
Three-toed woodpecker

Flycatchers

Eastern kingbird
Western kingbird
Scissor-tailed kingbird
Ash-throated kingbird
Say's phoebe
Willow flycatcher
Least flycatcher
Hammond's flycatcher
Dusky flycatcher
Western flycatcher
Western wood pewee
Olive-sided flycatcher

Lark

Horned lark

Swallows

Violet green swallow
Tree swallow
Bank swallow
Rough-winged swallow
Barn swallow
Cliff swallow

Jays

Gray jay
Blue jay
Stellar's jay
Clark's nutcracker

Crows

Black-billed magpie
Common raven
Crow

Tits, Nuthatches and Tree Creepers

Black-capped chickadee
Mountain chickadee
Boreal chickadee
Chestnut-backed chickadee
White-breasted nuthatch
Red-breasted nuthatch
Brown creeper

Dippers

American dipper

Wrens

House wren
Winter wren
Marsh wren
Rock wren

Mimids

Northern mockingbird
Gray catbird

Thrushes

American robin
Varied thrush
Hermit thrush
Swainson's thrush
Veery
Eastern bluebird
Western bluebird
Mountain bluebird
Townsend's solitaire

Kinglets

Golden-crowned kinglet
Ruby-crowned kinglet

Wagtails and Pipits

Water pipit
Sprague's pipit

Waxwings

Bohemian waxwing
Cedar waxwing

Shrikes

Northern shrike
Loggerhead shrike

Starlings

European starling

Vireos

Solitary vireo
Red-eyed vireo
Warbling vireo

Warblers

Black-and-white warbler
Tennessee warbler
Orange-crowned warbler
Nashville warbler
Yellow warbler
Cape May warbler
Yellow-rumped warbler
Townsend's warbler
Bay-breasted warbler
Ovenbird
Northern waterthrush
MacGillivray's warbler
Common yellowthroat
Yellow-breasted chat
Wilson's warbler
American redstart

Old World Weavers

House sparrow

New World Blackbirds

Bobolink
Western meadowlark

Yellow-headed blackbird
Red-winged blackbird
Northern oriole
Rusty blackbird
Brewer's blackbird
Common grackle
Brown-headed cowbird

Tanagers

Western tanager

Grosbeaks

Black-headed grosbeak
Evening grosbeak
Pine grosbeak

Sparrows and Finches

Indigo bunting
Lazuli bunting
Lark bunting
Snow bunting
Cassin's finch
House finch
Rosy finch
Common redpoll
Hoary redpoll
Pine siskin
American goldfinch
Red crossbill
White-winged crossbill
Green-tailed towhee
Rufous-sided towhee
Savannah sparrow
LeConte's sparrow
Vesper sparrow
Lark sparrow
American tree sparrow
Chipping sparrow
Clay-colored sparrow
Brewer's sparrow
Field sparrow
Harris' sparrow
White-crowned sparrow

Fox sparrow
Lincoln's sparrow
Song sparrow
Dark-eyed junco
McCowan's longspur
Lapland longspur
Chestnut-collared longspur

GNP Mammal List

Pygmy shrew
Masked shrew
Vagrant shrew
Montane shrew
Northern water shrew
Little brown bat
Long-eared bat
Long-legged bat
Big brown bat
Silver-haired bat
Hoary bat
Bobcat
Lynx
Mountain lion
Raccoon
Black bear
Grizzly bear
Red fox
Coyote
Gray wolf
Striped skunk
Badger
River otter
Wolverine
Least weasel
Short-tailed weasel
Long-tailed weasel
Mink
Marten
Fisher
Pika
Snowshoe hare
White-tailed jackrabbit
Porcupine

Beaver
Northern pocket gopher
Yellow-bellied marmot
Hoary marmot
Least chipmunk
Yellow pine chipmunk
Red-tailed chipmunk
Golden-mantled ground squirrel
Columbian ground squirrel
Thirteen-lined ground squirrel
Richardson ground squirrel
Northern flying squirrel
Red squirrel
Western jumping mouse
Bushy-tailed wood rat

Deer mouse
Muskrat
Northern bog lemming
Red back vole
Montane heather vole
Water vole
Long tailed vole
Meadow vole
White-tailed deer
Mule deer
Elk
Moose
Bighorn sheep
Mountain goat

Red-Winged blackbird

Lake Mary Ronan State Park

120 ACRES; SOUTHWEST OF KALISPELL

Lake Mary Ronan State Park is just seven miles west of Flathead Lake, yet far enough off the beaten path to dodge most of the summer crowds. The park is forested with Douglas fir and western larch, with several trails leading into the surrounding Flathead National Forest. These trails abound in wildflowers and wildlife — moose, elk, white-tailed deer, black bears, mountain lions, lesser mammals such as red squirrels and chipmunks, wild turkeys and a host of forest dwelling songbirds, ruby crowned kinglet, a variety of woodpeckers, chickadees, nuthatches and a whole host of warblers, and many of the 14 owls known to nest in Montana. Not only is the park a popular birding destination, it provides opportunities to pick huckleberries, hunt mushrooms, photograph wildflowers and wildlife, and is a good spot for just taking a hike and enjoy whatever comes along.

The lake, 1,500-plus acres, offers excellent fishing opportunities for rainbow trout, pumpkinseed, yellow perch, kokanee salmon and largemouth bass — some of which grow quite large. Ronan Creek, a small, pleasant mountain stream, contains brook and bull trout. Bull trout are of course protected, so be sure you know the difference before creeling a meal.

Nearby Restaurants and Accommodations

Lake Mary Ronan Lodge, restaurant, bar, casino, rustic cabins, camping and marina; phone: 849-5483

Mountain Meadows Resort, camping, lodging, restaurant, and the world's worst golf course in the last best place, when you're on the greens you're in the rough; phone: 849-5459

Camp Tuffit, cabins, store, campsites; phone: 849-5220.

Fast Facts

Contact Info: Lake Mary Ronan, 490 North Meridian Kalispell, MT 59901; phone: 849-5082.

Getting There: U.S. 93 south of Kalispell, turn west at Dayton on MT 352, 7 miles northwest.

Activities: Wildlife viewing, bird watching, photography, fishing, boating, camping, mountain biking, picnicking. Open year around, day use only in winter.

Principle Mammals: Moose, elk, deer, black bear, mountain lion, furbearers, pine squirrels and chipmunks.

Mammals of Special Interest: Moose, elk, black bear and mountain lion.

Principle Birdlife: Waterfowl, including loons, bald eagles, osprey, and dippers in the creek, songbirds abound, as do owls.

Birds of Special Interest: Loons, a variety of owls, bald eagles, osprey.

Habitat Overview: Lake surrounded by Douglas fir, western larch forest.

Flora of Special Interest: Huckleberry bushes, western larch are especially colorful in fall.

Best Wildlife Viewing Ops: Several trails leading to the surrounding Flathead NF, and the lake itself.

Best Birding Ops: Lake and surrounding national forest lands.

Red (pine) squirrel

Best Photo Ops: Year around opportunities for a variety of wildlife and birds, wildflowers abound in spring and early summer.

Hunting Ops: None.

Fishing Ops: Kokanee salmon, rainbow trout, largemouth bass, pumpkinseed and yellow perch; popular ice fishing spot. Closed February 28 to third Saturday in May.

Camping Ops: Developed sites, with hookups and a camp host; day use only in winter.

Boating Ops: Standard boating regulations apply.

Hiking Trails: Several trails around the lake and into the National Forest.

Motor Trails: None.

Great blue heron

Lost Trail National Wildlife Refuge

7,885 ACRES; IN THE WEST-CENTRAL PORTION OF FLATHEAD COUNTY APPROXIMATELY 25 AIR MILES WEST OF KALISPELL

Lost Trail NWR is Montana's newest National Wildlife Refuge and among the more recent in the entire system. Officially established on August 24, 1999 it is the 519th refuge in the NWR system; a system that comprises over 93 million acres and some of the country's most fertile and productive wildlife habitat.

Located in the serene and picturesque mountain drainage known as Pleasant Valley (20 miles north-northwest of the small, rural town of Marion), the refuge's mission statement is "to manage for migratory birds, incidental fish and wildlife-oriented recreational development as well as the protection of natural resources and/or the conservation of endangered or threatened species."

The mountain drainage known as Pleasant Valley was formed during the Pleistocene Period by glacial and sedimentation activity. Wetland habitats consist of sub-irrigated wet meadows composed primarily of non-native reed canary grass. Upland areas are a mosaic of prairie grasslands dominated by a variety of cool season native and non-native grasses. Surrounding wooded slopes are composed of a variety of indigenous coniferous and deciduous timber species.

The refuge encompasses the 160-acre Dahl Lake, a partially drained shallow lacustrine wetland system maintained by several watersheds. Water levels within the lake are subject to seasonal fluctuations. Elevations vary from 3,488 feet to 4,600 feet.

The refuge is bordered by Plum Creek Timber Company and two private ranches and four separate School Trust land tracts totaling 1,440 acres. These tracts are managed by the MT Department Natural Resources Conservation (DNRC) and are open to recreational uses according to state law.

The diverse habitat supports a wide variety of wildlife species. At least 14 species of migratory and breeding waterfowl utilize wetland areas — mallard, gadwall, cinnamon teal, green-winged teal, lesser scaup (bluebill), wood duck, redhead, common goldeneye and Canada geese. Various species of marsh and shorebirds are present during the summer months, including grebes, herons, gulls, killdeer, sandhill cranes, dowitchers, sandpipers, common snipe, bitterns and black terns.

Upland game bird species include spruce grouse, blue grouse and ruffed grouse. The refuge lies within the historic range of the Columbian sharp-tailed grouse; although none are known to exist anywhere nearby today.

Raptor species such as bald eagles, northern harriers, red-tailed hawks, Swainson's hawks, American kestrels and great-horned owls are common.

During the summer months, this intermountain grassland supports vesper and savannah sparrows, mountain bluebirds and western meadowlarks. Sandhill cranes, black terns, horned, eared and red-necked grebes, among others, nest around the shores of Dahl Lake. In the spring and fall the lake hosts thousands of migrating waterfowl. Snipe are common sights in the wet meadows and along Pleasant Valley Creek, as are willow flycatcher, western tanager, warbling vireo, yellow warbler and red-naped sapsucker.

Refuge headquarters is located at the western end of the refuge off Lost Prairie Road.

Resident mammal species include white-tailed deer, mule deer, elk, moose and black bear, as well as furbearers muskrat, badger, fisher, pine martin, lynx, wolverine and bobcat; Columbian ground squirrels inhabit the drier uplands.

Both grizzlies and gray wolves are seen occasionally and known to inhabit the Pleasant Valley area.

Prior to acquisition, refuge lands were privately owned and managed as the cattle and horse ranch known as Lost Trail Ranch, whose long and diverse cattle ranching history dates back to the late 1800s.

Cinnamon teal

In 1996, LTR was purchased by the Montana Power Company (MPC) to partially satisfy a mitigative settlement order. This order was issued by the Federal Energy Regulatory Commission (FERC) between MPC, the Department of Interior and the Confederated Salish and Kootenai Tribes to mitigate for wildlife losses and impacts on the Flathead Waterfowl Production Area attributed to past and future operations of Kerr Dam (Flathead Lake). In 1999, MPC conveyed approximately 3,100 acres of the ranch to the USFWS. The service purchased the remaining acreage from MPC under the authority of the Migratory Bird Conservation Act.

A mix of wetlands, grasslands and timberlands, the refuge is a haven for waterfowl, upland game birds, raptors and a variety of mammal species including a wintering herd of about 160 elk. One downside to converting a working cattle ranch to a wildlife sanctuary is what to do with all that barbed wire. In this case about 80 miles of five-strand barbed-wire fence posed a hurdle for both young and adult elk and moose that frequently get caught in the wire while trying to cross — some end up dead. In July 2004, Rocky Mountain Elk Foundation volunteers decided to do something about it. With the U.S. Fish and Wildlife Service's blessing, the group set up camp and went to work.

Working with manager Ray Washtak and other refuge employees, the volunteers removed the top wire and the fourth wire down along several miles of the boundary fence where animals were known to cross most frequently. They also removed all the barbed wire from a few interior fences to allow animals to roam more freely within the refuge.

Altogether the group removed and rolled about 17 miles of barbed wire. Almost before the dust settled, refuge personnel reported elk and moose crossing the altered fences without a problem.

More fence was removed in spring 2005 and the group vows to keep coming back until it's all gone.

An invasive weed control program is helping to reduce and eliminate common tansy and spotted knapweed and restore native plants.

Among wildlife lovers elk rank right up there. Obviously hunters adore them but folks who would never think of picking up a gun flock to places just for the chance of catching a glimpse — for proof just spend a day at Yellowstone National Park (or anywhere, for that matter, where elk are known to congregate). Rocky Mountain elk are descendents of Asian red deer that crossed the Bering Land Bridge thousands of years ago. Anthropologists theorize the red deer probably entered Montana from Canada via the Old North Trail, near Choteau, perhaps as long ago as 120,000 years — even before man made the crossing. Most biologists now agree North American elk, or wapiti, and Asian and European red deer are not just related, but the same species. Wapiti is a Shawnee name that means "white rump."

People have been hunting elk for as long as the two have coexisted. Archeologists have uncovered prehistoric sites that clearly show the lengths ancients were willing to go for a taste of wapiti. Apparently one of the most popular (efficient) methods was to herd elk along natural features such as cliffs and lakeshores, even man-made rock walls, to waiting hunters.

The fact that elk were important fare is portrayed in pictographs (paintings on rock) and petroglyphs (drawings chipped into rock) by the ancient Anastazi and Fremont people.

Besides food, elk parts provided a variety of tools, hides provided clothing and shelter, even boats were constructed of stretched elk hide — Kootenai, Cree, Ojibwa and Pawnee appear to have used elk bone and antler to fashion harpoons and other fishing gear.

On the Great Plains, elk were considered a dominant spirit, associated with love, passion, strength, courage, persistence and swiftness — which was especially strong medicine amongst the Ogallala Sioux whose elk-dream cults shared visions, danced in steps and uttered cries to mimic elk.

Lewis and Clark journals left no doubt how important elk were to the success of the expedition — where elk thrived, the expedition lived fat and happy; where scarce, they nearly starved to death. When Europeans first landed, elk thrived pretty much all across the northern half of North America. Westward settlement pushed the elk further and further toward the Rocky Mountains and so decimated their numbers that as early as 1785 some people, such as Thomas Pennant, were voicing alarm. In his book Arctic Zoology, he noted the apparent decline, and a century later the elk were all but gone from North America. Loss of habitat and market hunting were the main culprits, but unregulated sport hunting played a role also.

Their demise occurred at a time when naturalists, hunters and other concerned citizens were just starting to realize the importance of natural resources; that unless something was done to stop the skid, elk and other wildlife might be lost forever. Thank goodness the enlightened conservation movement that followed turned things around. The advent of regulated hunting seasons, state wildlife areas, national wildlife refuges, national parks and national forests, along with a new discipline called wildlife management eventually led to the recovery of elk and other wildlife populations. Actually elk, along with white-tailed deer and wild turkeys are today near, at, or above historical highs in many parts of the country.

Lost Trail NWR is managed as a satellite of the National Bison Range Complex, which administers over 40,000 acres of land in both Flathead and Lake Counties. USFWS is bound by law to identify and protect archeological tribal resources. As such any existing archeological and historical resources, as well as those uncovered in the future will be protected and managed as cultural resources subject to exclusion from other management policies and programs as deemed appropriate. Prime examples are the Indian pictographs located within refuge boundaries.

Activities are wildlife viewing, birding, hiking, photography and environmental interpretation. Portions of the refuge are open to hunting of elk, deer, mountain grouse (ruffed, spruce, and blue), and wild turkey in accordance with state regulations. Shotgun hunting for turkey and mountain grouse is limited to nontoxic shot. Vehicle access is permitted on designated roads only (no off-roading) and parking is in designated areas only. The first week of archery deer and elk season and the first week of the general deer and elk season is Youth Hunting Only; open to youths 12 to 14 years of age accompanied by an adult and/or guardian who is at least 21 years of age. Hunters with disabilities, in possession of a FWP permit to hunt from a vehicle, are provided with limited access to refuge management roads and trails. There are no viable game fish species, so obviously no fishing.

Nearby Restaurants and Accommodations

In Marion, check out the
Hilltop Hitchin' Post, 854-2442
Moose Crossing, 854-2070
The Middle Fork Motel, 387-5900
Lake B&B, 858-2456.
Camping abounds in the nearby Flathead and Kootenai National Forests.

Fast Facts

Contact Info: Lost Trail NWR, 6295 Pleasant Valley Road, Marion, MT   59925
  E-mail: bisonrange@fws.gov Phone: 644-2211

Getting There: US 2, west of Kalispell, turn north at Marion, on Pleasant Valley Rd., refuge is approximately 20 miles.

Activities: Wildlife viewing, birding, hiking, cross-country skiing, snowshoeing, and designated roads are open to horseback and mountain biking. No hiking, skiing, snowshoeing, horseback, mountain biking during hunting season, Sept. 1-Dec. 1.

Principle Mammals: White-tailed and mule deer, elk, moose, black bear, muskrat, badger, fisher, pine martin, lynx, wolverine and bobcat, Columbian ground squirrels; while rare, both grizzlies and gray wolves have been observed.

Mammals of Special Interest: Elk, moose.

Principle Birdlife: Waterfowl, forest and marsh dwelling songbirds, upland game birds (blue, spruce and ruffed grouse) and raptors.

Birds of Special Interest: Marsh and shorebirds such as grebes, herons, gulls, killdeer, sandhill cranes, dowitchers, sandpipers, common snipe, bitterns and black terns.

Habitat Overview: A mix of wetlands, grasslands and coniferous forest.

Flora of Special Interest: Noxious weeds, native plants.

Best Wildlife Viewing Ops: Elk, deer and moose, year around; early and late in day.

Best Birding Ops: Spring and fall migration, wet meadows and riparian zones.

Best Photo Ops: Dahl Lake for waterfowl, spring and fall migration; big game opportunities exist year around, especially for deer and moose.

Hunting Ops: Elk, deer, mountain grouse, wild turkey in accordance with state regulations.

Fishing Ops: None.

Camping Ops: None on refuge; camping abounds in nearby Kootenai and Flathead National Forests.
Boating Ops: None.
Hiking Trails: No developed trails.
Motor Trails: Driving on designated roads only.

Newborn calf elk

National Bison Range National Wildlife Refuge

18,500 ACRES; LOCATED AT MOISE, SOUTH OF POLSON AND FLATHEAD LAKE

Established in 1908, the National Bison Range NWR is one of the oldest wildlife refuges in the nation. As its name implies, the refuge's main goal is to maintain and support 350 and 500 head of American bison. Other mega fauna includes elk, white-tailed and mule deer, pronghorn antelope, bighorn sheep and black bear. Mostly open grasslands, along with a mix of forest and riparian habitats, the range is a popular spot for wildlife observation and photography.

Douglas fir and Ponderosa pine forest dominates the hilltops of the Bison Range and surrounding landscape. Forests are complex ecosystems. Forest type (coniferous, hardwoods, mixed) as well as age (old growth, regenerative) in large part determines the plants and wildlife. Normally forests develop wherever the average temperature is greater than 50 degrees in the warm season and the annual rainfall exceeds about 13 inches. The Bison Range teeters on the edge of too dry, as evidenced by the tree-growth patterns: The only trees in the refuge exist where the microclimate is cooler and wetter, such as north facing slopes or where depressions tend to gather moisture.

Birds are adapted to different habitat types — grasslands, wetlands, forest, etc. Forest dwellers tend to eat the pine nuts, new tree buds, seeds, berries and insects that live in bark or burrow into the wood. Since many of these items are available all year, many forest birds such as chickadees, jays, and woodpeckers do not migrate. Over 200 species have been listed (see end of chapter). Golden eagle, Lewis' woodpecker, mountain bluebird, western meadowlark, clay-colored and grasshopper sparrows, western tanager, red crossbill, and blue grouse are possibilities. Few snakes are observed but garter, gopher, rubber boa, and prairie rattlesnake live here. Other animals use the forest for shelter and food, like deer and elk that hide in the trees and browse on woodland plants.

American bison (bull)

Grasslands are one of nature's better ideas: A rich and diverse ecosystem of specially adapted plants and animals. The grasslands here are native Palouse prairie (primarily Idaho fescue, rough fescue, and bluebunch wheatgrass) bunch grasses. Bunch grasses are specially adapted to dry, semi-arid conditions and grow in clumps with the crown shading their roots. While most plants grow from the tips of their branches or stems, bunch grasses grow from the base of the stem, enabling growth to continue with the tops grazed off. Bunch grasses are well adapted to the harsh, unsheltered environment of the open prairie; conditions ranging from subzero temperatures to blistering heat, winter blizzards to driving summer thunderstorms and wind...always wind. Another special adaptation is when leaves die back; the withered dense crown protects the roots over winter. In the summer the long slender vertical leaves present fewer surfaces to the sun's rays and prevent overheating.

Palouse prairie grasslands also contain other broader-leaved plants called forbs (wildflowers), which also have defenses against the weather extremes. Many are perennials that winter under the snow as tiny flat rosettes of green leaves. In summer their leaves are small and have deep indented margins to minimize surface area or curl to reflect the heat, and many are covered with insulating hairs.

The grassland ecosystem is not complete without large ungulates (hoofed animals) to periodically graze and keep the plants thrifty. Native grazers such as bison and pronghorn, and rodents such as mice, ground squirrels, and prairie dogs fit the scheme perfectly. In an ideal world, coyotes, raptors and snakes would keep the rodents in check, and large predators such as bears, mountain lions and wolves would maintain a balance among larger ungulates (bison, elk, deer, pronghorn). These days, of course, maintaining the status quo usually requires the hand of the man.

Grassland birds are usually plentiful but consist of fewer species than would be found in wetlands and riparian zones. The birds too, are specially adapted to this environment of extremes. Their backs are streaked so they can nest unseen on the ground in the shade of an overhanging grass clump. They can be seen defending their own patch of turf by singing from song perches, usually tall weeds, around their territorial boundaries.

Several streams course through the Bison Range, most notably Mission Creek along the refuge's north side and the Jocko River on the south side. Both drain a large area and flow year round. Others are seasonal, draining only small open areas with little vegetation to hold the moisture. The lush vegetation, or riparian zone, along both Mission Creek and the Jocko River create micro ecosystems. Compared to the dry uplands, very different plants grow here that are attractive not only to most year-round residents of the range, but to migrants and summer residents as well. Riparian zones also created their own microclimates, very different in temperature due to increased shade and very different humidity due to the constant moisture. Combined, the two generally result in increased air movement. To live in shade, leaves of trees and other associated plants tend to be broad and flat, and spread on wide branches to maximize solar collection.

Where the streams wander and bend, marshes and wetlands are created, further diversifying the overall habitat. Permanent healthy streams create habitat for fish, aquatic plants and insects — mayflies, caddis, stoneflies, midges, etc. As a rule of thumb, the faster the flow, the fewer the aquatic plants.

Riparian zones in general, here too, contain a far more diverse wildlife population (songbirds, deer, small mammals, furbearers etc.) than the dryer uplands.

Like riparian zones, wetlands produce lush nesting and protective cover. Plants such as cattails and rushes, called emergents, are rooted near shores and grow up out of the water. Waterweeds grow mostly under water with their roots in the silt, blooms on the surface. Plants, such as duckweed, float on the surface with their roots hanging down, drawing all their nutrients from the water alone. These plants are the green, vegetative cover that characterize most wetlands.

Insects abound in wetlands. Larvae and pupae develop in water then crawl up the stems of aquatic vegetation, molt and emerge as winged adults. Insects fuel both adult birds and growing chicks — songbirds and waterfowl alike. Aquatic insects provide sustenance for turtles, fish, snakes and other creatures. Numerous species of birds, not just water birds, nest in and around wetlands to take advantage of the feast. Swooping swallows, a prime example, are a most common sight.

Technically speaking, American bison are not buffalo and are not related to the true buffalo — Africa's Cape buffalo and Asia's water buffalo. The bison's only relative is the wisent, another bison species that survives in small numbers on reserves in Europe; sort of a moot point considering our "bison" has been called "buffalo" from the beginning.

Call him what you will, bison are well adapted to life on the open grasslands of the High Plains. Heavy coats protect them from both summer sun and winter winds — the proof is in the many images of bison covered in snow — with zero heat loss and no snow melt. Bison are strong, hardy beasts, suffer few diseases, and adults have few enemies — even the ferocious gray wolf would rather tangle a bull elk than a bull bison. The brucellosis attributed to bison herds today is really a cattle disease, which was transmitted to bison in some areas. The Bison Range herd is vaccinated against this and other cattle diseases and is certified brucellosis free.

Bison are unpredictable and very dangerous. They appear slow and docile but really are quite agile and can run as fast as a horse (no human can outrun a charging bison). A bison's tail is often a handy warning flag. When it hangs down and is switching naturally, the animal usually is unperturbed. If it extends out straight and droops at the end he/she is becoming mildly agitated. If the tail is sticking straight up, they are ready to charge and you should get somewhere else....but do not run.

Bison bulls top out around 2,000 pounds, sport heavy horns and a large hump, which supports the enormous head and thick skull. Bison wear a thick coat of hair from about the midway point forward, even in summer. More than a mere adornment, the heavy coat enhances the bull's size and protects them in battles — which during rut, can be frequent and savage beyond imagination. Bulls are especially ill tempered during the breeding season (mid-July through August) and their loud roars enough to make the hackles stand out, believe me.

Cows weigh about half as much as bulls and wear narrower, slightly curved horns. The older the cow the more curved — those of ancient matrons often meet, or nearly so. Cows have smaller humps and a lighter, smoother summer coat. Calves are born in mid-April and May and, unlike the dark brown, almost black adults, calves are a bright rust-red color for the first month or so. Cows are extremely protective, even more dangerous than bulls, with a calf in tow.

The Red Sleep Mountain Drive opens the first Saturday in May, weather permitting, and closes for the year in late October, depending on weather. The drive is 19 miles on a one-way gravel road. Elevation gain is about 2,000 feet and takes about two hours to complete. Since it travels from the valley grasslands up to the timberline and along Mission Creek, visitors have the opportunity to see a wide range of animals and birds, including bison as well as deer, elk, pronghorn and eagles. Wildflowers abound and, of course, in early May the highlights are the newborn baby (calf) bison—as sure a sign of spring as any.

The Visitor Center is open from 8 a.m. to 6 p.m. weekdays and 9 a.m. to 6 p.m. weekends. The main gate will open daily by 7 a.m. and closes at 9:30 p.m. Morning and evening hours provide the best wildlife viewing opportunities. Plan enough time to enjoy the drive at a leisurely and safe pace. Visitors need to start the Red Sleep Mountain Drive no later than 6 p.m. to finish the loop before the main gate closes at dark. Large vehicles over 30 feet in length, trailers and other towed units are not allowed on the Red Sleep Mountain Drive and parking is available at the Visitor Center.

The shorter, graveled West Loop and Prairie Drives are open for trailers, buses and large motor homes. These drives also offer views of bison, elk, deer and pronghorn and take about 30 minutes.

A $4-per-car fee is charged. There is no charge for the Visitor Center, day use areas or for educational groups. You can obtain a Bison Range season pass for $10. Golden Park Passes and Federal Waterfowl Stamp are accepted for admission. All are available at the Visitor Center.

Visitors are asked to stop at the Visitor Center to pay fees, check current conditions and pertinent wildlife information and a complimentary copy of the Field Guide to the Bison Range. Large groups are asked to pre-register to avoid potential conflicts.

Nearby Restaurants and Accommodations

Mission Mountain Restaurant and Lounge, Ronan, 676-4653
Ranch House Restaurant, Ronan, 676-0500
Twin Creeks B&B, Ronan, 676-8800
Lumi-Vista B&B, Ronan, 676-7877
The Timbers B&B, Ronan, 676-4373
Zeraphath Inn B&B, Ronan, 676-4351
Starlite Motel, Ronan, 676-7000
Diamond S RV, Ronan, 676-3641

Fast Facts

Contact Info: National Bison Range, 132 Bison Range Road, Moiese, MT 59824; phone: 644-2211; e-mail:bisonrange@fws.gov

Getting There: Located off MT 212 at Moiese, Montana. MT 212 can be accessed off US 93 south of Kalispell/Polson at Ronan. Coming north on US 93 out of Missoula, take MT 200 at Ravalli to MT 212. From the west, take MT 135 out of St. Regis to MT 200 to MT 212, just past Dixon.

Activities: Wildlife viewing, birding, environmental education, nature exhibit, photography, picnicking, sightseeing, auto tour.

Principle Mammals: American bison, elk, white-tail and mule deer, pronghorn antelope, bighorn sheep and black bear.

Mammals of Special Interest: Bison.

Principle Birdlife: See below.

Birds of Special Interest: Bald eagle, peregrine falcon; large and nationally significant numbers of rough-legged hawks, short-eared owls, and northern harriers frequent and/or nest in the grasslands.

Habitat Overview: Mix of grasslands, coniferous forest, riparian zones and wetlands.

Flora of Special Interest: None.

Best Wildlife Viewing Ops: Three drive routes afford visitors ample opportunities; early and late in day is best. Drive routes are open May to late October, check for dates.

Best Birding Ops: Three drive routes afford visitors ample opportunities; early and late in day is best. Drive routes are open May to late October, check for dates.

Best Photo Ops: Three drive routes afford visitors ample opportunities; early and late in day is best. Drive routes are open May to late October, check for dates; bison calves are born mid-April and May.

Hunting Ops: None.

Fishing Ops: Trout fishing in Mission Creek and Jocko River; some of which is on Flathead Indian Reservation; check with Tribal HQ for information.

Camping Ops: None.

Boating Ops: None.

Hiking Trails: None. Vehicle Access only.

Motor Trails: Three drive routes; vehicle restrictions apply, check in first.

Ninepipe National Wildlife Refuge

2,000 ACRES; ONE MILE EAST OF CHARLO IN LOWER FLATHEAD VALLEY

Established in 1921, Ninepipe NWR is located in the south-central part of the Flathead Valley in western Montana. Primarily for waterfowl, the 2,000 acres includes a 1,672-acre reservoir, surrounding marshes and grasslands. The refuge sits in the shadow of the rugged Mission Mountains. The valley itself was shaped by glacial activity, which ended about 12,000 years ago and is the center of a terminal moraine — rolling grasslands, interspersed with numerous potholes and marshes, many of which remain wet year round. The reservoir is managed by the Flathead Indian Tribe as part of the BIA Flathead Irrigation Project for irrigation and flood control.

The refuge uplands consist of a narrow band of grasslands and marsh surrounding the reservoir. Surrounding the refuge proper are 3,420 acres of the Ninepipe WMA, approximately 3,000 acres of tribal lands and 2,000 acres of USFWS conservation easements. There are no developments or facilities on the refuge.

The reservoir is managed primarily for irrigation water storage, as such drawdowns during the irrigation season result in wide fluctuations of the water level. For waterfowl the saving grace is numerous glacial potholes in the vicinity that hold water throughout the year and provide excellent habitat for nesting and brood rearing.

Waterfowl numbers peak in spring and fall. From late March to early May as many as 100,000 birds may be observed. Fall numbers often peak in excess of 200,000 birds in early October to late November. Primary nesting season is from April to July. Mallards, northern shovelers, gadwalls, redheads and ruddy ducks, along with Canada geese are the primary nesters.

Red-necked grebes and the valley's only nesting western grebe colony nest on the refuge. Other common nesters include song sparrows, yellow-headed and red-winged blackbirds, American bitterns, sora rails and ringnecked pheasants. Ospreys nest on platforms along the south shore of the reservoir. And there are active rookeries of great blue herons and double crested cormorants.

Grizzly bears are seen occasionally, although you are much more likely to spot muskrat, striped skunk, mink, badger, field mouse, meadow vole or porcupine.

The reservoir, a popular fishing hole, contains yellow perch and largemouth bass, as well as pumpkinseed and brown bullhead. Fishing is allowed only from shore, no boats or other watercraft allowed. Ice fishing is, however, allowed.

The refuge is located on Tribal Trust Lands of the Confederated Salish and Kootenai Tribes. As such, the refuge is operated as an easement; USFWS owns the rights to manage the wildlife and habitat only. The tribes own all other rights, but management must comply and be compatible with the operation and purpose of the refuge. A 1948 Act of Congress reimbursed the Tribes $400,000 for all past and future uses of certain reservation lands for physical works and facilities of the Flathead project irrigation and power systems and for national wildlife refuges. The payment included $50,644 for the permanent easement at Ninepipe National Wildlife Refuge. Tribal members continue to harvest native plants for food and medicinal uses. Cattle grazing on a rest-rotation system is carried out by the tribes within the guidelines of the overall management plan of USFWS.

Other activities include photography, wildlife viewing and birding. There is a short accessible Interpretive Nature Trail and a Watchable Wildlife Viewing Area off US 93. Portions of the refuge are closed in spring to minimize disturbance of nesting

Immature Least Bittern

waterfowl and other birds. The refuge is closed to hunting, but the adjoining WMA is open to hunting under state regulations. Many feel the refuge closure actually enhances the quality of hunting in the Flathead Valley by providing a sanctuary, and holds over more birds for a longer period of time.

Ninepipe, along with nearby Pablo NWR, attracts a wide diversity of bird species. Long- and short-eared owls, as well as great-horned owls, are common, as are grassland nesters and of course waterfowl. Six species of grebes are known to nest within the refuge boundaries — western, clark's, red-necked, eared, horned and pied-billed. American avocets and bald eagles nest in the area and trumpeter swans have recently been re-introduced.

One late-April visit resulted in this impressive (for us) check off: All six grebes mentioned above, double-crested cormorant, great blue heron, turkey vulture, Canada goose, gadwall, wigeon, blue-winged and cinnamon teals, northern shoveler, redhead, ring-necked duck and pheasant, mallard, common and Barrow's goldeneye, hooded and common merganser, osprey, bald eagle; northern harrier, Cooper's, red-tailed and kestrel hawks; sora rail, coot, sandhill crane, killdeer, ring-billed and California gulls; great-horned, long-eared, short-eared and great gray owls; northern flicker, magpie, crow, raven, barn, tree and cliff swallows, black-capped chickadee, red-breasted nuthatch, house and marsh wren, dipper, starling, cedar waxwing, song sparrow, chipping sparrow, spotted towhee, junco, red-winged and yellow-headed blackbirds, western meadowlark, house finch, house sparrow and robin. We also spied Columbian ground squirrel, fox squirrel, muskrat, white-tailed deer and the largest striped skunk you can imagine.

NINEPIPE WILDERNESS MANAGEMENT AREA
3,142 acres; surrounding Ninepipe NWR, in Flathead Valley, one mile east Charlo

The Ninepipe WMA surrounds the Ninepipe NWR. At approximately 3,000 feet above sea level, the property consists of rolling, open grasslands and numerous prairie potholes, or kettle ponds. There are remnants of native rough fescue grasslands but today, the area vegetation is mostly introduced grasses and croplands. The area is owned by Montana FWP and lies within the exterior boundaries of the Flathead Indian Reservation. The WMA was established through a complex series of transactions (28 in all). Parcels were acquired between 1953 and 1962, in 1974, and in 1993, with the management goal to conserve and enhance upland and wetland habitats for a variety of wildlife species, and to provide quality upland bird and waterfowl hunting and viewing opportunities.

Opportunities abound for viewing songbirds, upland game birds, and waterfowl, especially in spring. Winter raptor viewing is nationally acclaimed. Numerous mammal and reptile species are commonly seen. A wildlife viewing and interpretative site with special features for people with disabilities has recently been added.

Excellent pheasant and waterfowl hunting is available. A joint state/tribal license and a Flathead Reservation bird stamp are required of all hunters who are not members of the Confederated Salish and Kootenai Tribes. A federal migratory waterfowl stamp is required to hunt waterfowl. Regulations are formulated by the Flathead Reservation Fish and Wildlife Advisory Board and approved by the Tribal Council and the Montana FWP Commission.

Carved up as it is by US 93, MT 212 and several county roads, visitors are required to park in the designated parking areas and to refrain parking alongside roads.

Nearby Restaurants and Accommodations

Ninepipes Lodge, Charlo, 644-2588
Port Polson Inn, Polson, 883-5385
Flathead Lake State Park, 752-5501
Swan Hill B&B, Polson, 853-5292
Countryside Café, Charlo, 644-2823
Ranch House Restaurant, Ronan, 676-0500.

Fast Facts

Contact Info: Ninepipe NWR, 132 Bison Range Rd., Moiese, MT 59284; phone: 644-2211; E-mail: bisonrange@fws.gov
Getting There: One mile east of Charlo, in lower Flathead Valley.
Activities. Wildlife viewing, birding, photography, hiking, fishing (restricted to shore and ice fishing), picnicking, Watchable Wildlife Viewing Area, Accessible Interpretive Nature Trail.
Principle Mammals: White-tailed deer, muskrat, occasional grizzly bear observed.
Mammals of Special Interest: Grizzly bear.
Principle Birdlife: Waterfowl, shorebirds, wading birds, birds of prey, songbirds.
Birds of Special Interest: Waterfowl, raptors.
Habitat Overview: Lake, wetlands, grasslands and croplands.
Flora of Special Interest: Marsh and native grasslands.
Best Wildlife Viewing Ops: Watchable Wildlife Viewing Area, Interpretive Nature Trail, year around opportunities.
Best Birding Ops: Spring and fall migration, summer nesting and brood rearing period; winter raptor viewing is a highlight.
Best Photo Ops: Bird numbers peak spring through fall, year around opportunities do exist.
Hunting Ops: None on the refuge itself, but hunting is allowed on the surrounding WMA.
Fishing Ops: Largemouth bass, yellow perch, pumpkinseed and brown bullhead; fishing from shore only, no boats, ice fishing, however, is allowed.
Camping Ops: None
Boating Ops: None
Hiking Trails: Interpretive Nature Trail
Motor Trails: Watchable Wildlife Viewing Area off US 93.

Pablo National Wildlife Refuge

2542 ACRES; TWO MILES SOUTH POLSON, IN FLATHEAD VALLEY

Like its sister just down the road, Pablo NWR nestles in the shadow of the imposing Mission Mountains. It was established in 1921 as a refuge for waterfowl and other birds and wildlife. It is located on Tribal Trust Lands of the Confederated Salish and Kootenai Tribes and subject to reservoir uses at the request of the tribes. The refuge is operated as an easement only, meaning only rights pertaining to management of wildlife and their habitat were purchased. The tribes retain all other rights subject to compatibility with the purpose of the refuge. As such, tribal members continue to harvest plants throughout the reservation for food and medicinal uses. A 1948 Act of Congress reimbursed the tribes $400,000 for all past and future uses of certain reservation lands for physical works and facilities of the Flathead irrigation project and power systems and for wildlife refuges. The payment included $68,712 for the Pablo easement.

The refuge is centered around the 1,850-acre Pablo Reservoir amid 602 acres of rolling uplands, grasslands, wetlands and potholes that were carved by the receding ice cap 12,000 years ago. That many of the wetlands and potholes remain wet throughout the year makes Pablo particularly attractive to water oriented birds and wildlife. The lake itself is managed for irrigation and flood control as part of the Flathead Irrigation Project and water levels fluctuate a great deal seasonally.

Pablo reservoir is extremely brushy (willows) along the south and west shorelines, while a stand of cottonwoods marks the north shoreline. The trees and brush attract numerous bird species not normally attracted to your typical prairie pothole/lake environment — several species of warblers, vireos, robins, thrushes and other species are known to nest there. Numerous waterfowl species in large numbers use the refuge; during almost any visit you can count on observing blue-winged, green-winged and cinnamon teals, mallards, pintails, wigeons, common mergansers, coots, shovelers, redheads, ruddy ducks, gadwalls and several species of grebes. In addition, 19

Canada goose

trumpeter swans were released in 1996, thanks to a joint effort of the Confederated Salish and Kootenai Tribes, MTFWP and USFWS to establish a breeding flock. There is an active bald eagle nest, which fledges young most years. One to three loons are observed each season, hanging out from spring to fall, but to date no nest has been found.

White-tailed deer, muskrat, striped skunk, mink, badgers, field mice, meadow voles and porcupines are common residents.

The lake is popular among anglers for largemouth bass, yellow perch, pumpkinseed and brown bullhead. Like Ninepipe fishing is allowed only from shore, no boats are allowed but ice fishing is. Other activities include wildlife viewing, birding, photography, picnicking and hiking. Some portions of the refuge are closed in spring to protect nesting birds from undue human disturbance. There is vehicle access along roads across the dam and along the north side of the refuge. No hunting is allowed on the refuge but is allowed on the WMA surrounding the refuge. Many feel the closure of Pablo enhances the quality of hunting by providing a sanctuary, which tends to keep more birds in the area for a longer period of time. The uplands surrounding the reservoir are used by tribal members for farming and grazing under permits issued by the BIA in conjunction with a Memorandum of Understanding with USFWS.

There are no facilities on the refuge.

Nearby Restaurants and Accommodations

Ninepipes Lodge, Charlo, 644-2588
Port Polson Inn, Polson, 883-5385
Flathead Lake State Park, 752-5501
Swan Hill B&B, Polson, 853-5292
Countryside Café, Charlo, 644-2823
Ranch House Restaurant, Ronan, 676-0500.

Fast Facts

Contact Info: Pablo NWR, 132 Bison Range Road, Moise, MT 59284; phone: 644-2211; e-mail: bisonrange@fws.gov

Getting There: From Polson, follow MT 354 or US 93 south to refuge; less than five miles.

Activities: Wildlife viewing, birding, photography, fishing, hiking, picnicking.

Principle Mammals: White-tailed deer, muskrat, striped skunk, mink, badgers, field mice, meadow voles and porcupines.

Mammals of Special Interest: None.

Principle Birdlife: Waterfowl, upland game birds, birds of prey, shorebirds, songbirds, wading birds.

Birds of Special Interest: Bald eagle, trumpeter swan.

Habitat Overview: Lake, with surrounding marsh, wetlands and uplands.

Flora of Special Interest: Marsh and wetland plants.

Best Wildlife Viewing Ops: Year around, early and late in day.

Best Birding Ops: Bird numbers peak during spring and fall migrations; numerous year around residents.

Best Photo Ops: Year around, early and late in day provides best light.

Hunting Ops: None on refuge, surrounding WMA lands open to hunting according to state law.

Fishing Ops: Largemouth bass, yellow perch, pumpkinseed, brown bullhead, from shore only, no boats; ice fishing is allowed.

Boating Ops: None allowed.

Motor Trails: Motor vehicle access with restrictions as posted; no off-road travel.

American avocet

Swan River National Wildlife Refuge

3,700 ACRES; LOCATED IN NORTHWEST MONTANA, AT THE SOUTHERN TIP (UPPER END) OF SWAN LAKE

Established in 1973 under the Migratory Bird Act as an "inviolate bird sanctuary and a refuge for migratory birds", the refuge consists of 1,568 acres in addition to a USFS inholding managed by USFWS under a Memorandum of Understanding. The refuge lies within the floodplain of the Swan River, next to Swan Lake and between the Swan Mountain Range to the east and the Mission Mountain Range to the west. It is not only an important habitat for resident and migrant birds it serves as a vital cog for grizzly bears moving between the two mountain ranges and for other wildlife as well.

Twelve hundred years or so ago, glacial ice poured down the steep slopes of the Mission Range and scoured out Swan Lake, leaving the valley relatively flat, though narrow and steeply rising to the surrounding mountainsides. Today the flood plain (the refuge itself) is largely composed of canary grass and old growth cottonwood trees giving way to old growth fir, spruce, cedar and larch on the forested slopes. The river once carved a meandering path down the center of the floodplain but since has been shoved to the west side by deposits of silt, leaving a series of oxbow sloughs which in general characterize the floodplain and the refuge itself.

To date, 171 bird species have been observed. Waterfowl such as Canada geese, mallards, cinnamon teal and common goldeneye nest here, as do a pair of bald eagles, several pairs of ospreys, sandhill cranes and the elusive black tern, among many others. Northern harriers (marsh hawks), Swainson's and red-tailed hawks are frequently observed, as are great horned owls, although we probably hear the big owls hooting more than we see them. Sora and Virginia rails and American bitterns (mud hens) frequent the marshy area, although, as with the great horned owls, we hear more mud hens. Marsh wrens, winter wrens, song sparrows, yellow-headed and red-winged blackbirds are almost automatic check offs.

White-tailed deer abound, but elk, moose, beaver, coyote, muskrat, raccoon, bobcat and black bear are far from uncommon. And keep at least one eye peeled for grizzlies; they do show up occasionally, especially in spring. The refuge, and the surrounding Swan and Mission ranges have been designated as an "A" Habitat

Corridor for grizzlies, so...

A canoe trip through the refuge in spring is an especially productive and enjoyable way to view birds and other wildlife. Bog Road (not maintained and not recommended for vehicles) traverses the refuge east to west. The road is open for wildlife observation, photography, and provides access to the interior portion of the refuge.

Management schemes are largely restricted to periodic haying and livestock grazing, carried out by private ranchers under supervision and direction of USFWS staff.

Both Swan Lake and Swan River are popular fishing spots. Game fish include yellow perch, bull trout, northern pike, kokanee salmon, largemouth bass, cutthroat trout, brook trout and mountain whitefish. Fishing is allowed on the lake and those portions of Swan River that flow through the refuge according to state law; Spring Creek, within the refuge, is closed from March 1 through July 15.

Nearby Restaurants and Accommodations

Swan Lake Trading Post and Campground; phone: 886-2303
El Topo Cantina, Bigfork; phone: 837-2114
Big Fork Espresso: phone: 837-2114
BuggNBagels, Bigfork, phone: 837-2899
Double Arrow, Seeley Lake, phone: 677-2900
Lindey's Landing, Seeley Lake, phone: 677-9229.

There are of course other restaurants and motels in Bigfork and Seeley Lake as well as several private campgrounds.

Immature wood duck drake

Fast Facts

Contact Info: Swan River NWR, 132 Bison Range Rd., Moiese, MT 59824; phone: 644-2211; e-mail:bisonrange@fws.gov

Getting There: Just off MT 83 between Bigfork and Seeley Lake.

Activities: Wildlife viewing, birding, photography, hiking, canoeing, fishing.

Principle Mammals: White-tailed deer are most common; elk, moose, black bears, the occasional grizzly bear, and a variety of furbearers and predators frequent the area.

Mammals of Special Interest: Grizzly bear.

Principle Birdlife: Waterfowl, songbirds and birds of prey abound.

Birds of Special Interest: Bald eagle, black tern, sandhill crane.

Habitat Overview: Flood plain consists largely of canary grass and old growth cottonwood forest, old growth fir, cedar, spruce and larch forest dominates the mountainsides.

Flora of Special Interest: Wildflowers associated with marshy, flood plain habitats.

Best Wildlife Viewing Ops: Spring through fall, early and late in the day.

Best Birding Ops: Bird numbers peak in spring and fall during migration; broods are most evident soon after hatching in early summer.

Best Photo Ops: Canoeing the river or hiking the Bog Road offers a variety of opportunities.

Hunting Ops: No hunting allowed.

Fishing Ops: Fishing is allowed according to state law; Spring Creek within refuge closed March 1 to July 15.

Camping Ops: No camping allowed; surrounding Flathead NF offers unlimited opportunities; many USFS developed campgrounds within the Seeley-Swan corridor.

Boating Ops: Boating is allowed, both on the lake and the river.

Hiking Trails: None developed, but Bog Road is open to hiking.

Motor Trails: None.

Porcupine

Wild Horse Island State Park

2164 ACRES; IN FLATHEAD LAKE'S BIG ARM

There are five designated landing sites on Wild Horse Island, from which trails loop through the backcountry. The island's flora and fauna is surprisingly diverse, bighorn sheep roam the rocky high country, osprey, bald eagle, black-capped chickadee, red-breasted nuthatch and yellow-rumped warblers nest in the trees. Black bears frequent the island, swimming out from the mainland to munch forest goodies and graze fields of wildflowers, arrow leaf balsamroot, owl clover, larkspur, yarrow and nodding onion. Coyotes are common sights as are mule deer; while the island's wild horses — all four of them, one black, one brown, one buckskin and a paint — can prove elusive. The island has a long history of feral: First, local Indian ponies were stashed on the island to elude theft by raiding Blackfeet. Later, the island was populated by escaped horses from area ranching operations, which were removed during the homesteading boom of the late 1800s. In the 1980s FWP decided to restore feral horses to the namesake island, adopted several from BLM herds in Oregon and set them free—the idea apparently was the island's rolling Palouse prairie resembled the horses homeland, so why not...

Nearby Restaurants and Accommodations

Papa Don's Grill, 883-1297
Lake City Bakery and Eatery, 883-5667
Cove Deli, 883-0334;Circle P Ranch, 249-1939
Mission Mountain Ranch, 883-1883
Home on the Range B&B, 849-5500
Big Sky RV and Eatery, 844-3501
Arrowhead RV, 849-5545
Flathead KOA, 883-2151.

Fast Facts

Contact Info: Wild Horse Island, 490 North Meridian, Kalispell, MT 59901; phone: 752-5501.
Getting There: Accessible by boat only.
Activities: Wildlife viewing, birding, photography, swimming, picnicking.

Principle Mammals: Bighorn sheep, feral horses, mule deer, yellow bellied marmot, red squirrel.

Mammals of Special Interest: Bighorn sheep, feral horses (four).

Principle Birdlife: Waterfowl, shorebirds, songbirds, birds of prey, wading birds.

Birds of Special Interest: Bald eagles, osprey, double-crested cormorants.

Habitat Overview: Palouse native prairie, coniferous forest, rocky cliffs.

Flora of Special Interest: Native prairie grasses.

Best Wildlife Viewing Ops: Feral horses can be difficult to find, due to low number (four) bighorn sheep and mule deer are common.

Best Birding Ops: Numbers peak in spring and fall, a large variety nest on island in various habitats. For a more complete listing see Safe Harbor Marsh Preserve in the Nature Conservancy Chapter.

Best Photo Ops: Year around opportunities for both mammals and birds; early and late in the day provide best light.

Hunting Ops: None.

Fishing Ops: Excellent fishing in Flathead Lake primarily for lake trout and lake whitefish.

Camping Ops: Day use only; camping is available at the State Parks on the mainland.

Boating Ops: Unlimited boating opportunities on Flathead Lake.

Hiking Trails: Five designated landings lead to trails which loop through the backcountry.

Motor Trails: None.

Bald eagle

Fish, Wildlife, and Parks: Region 2

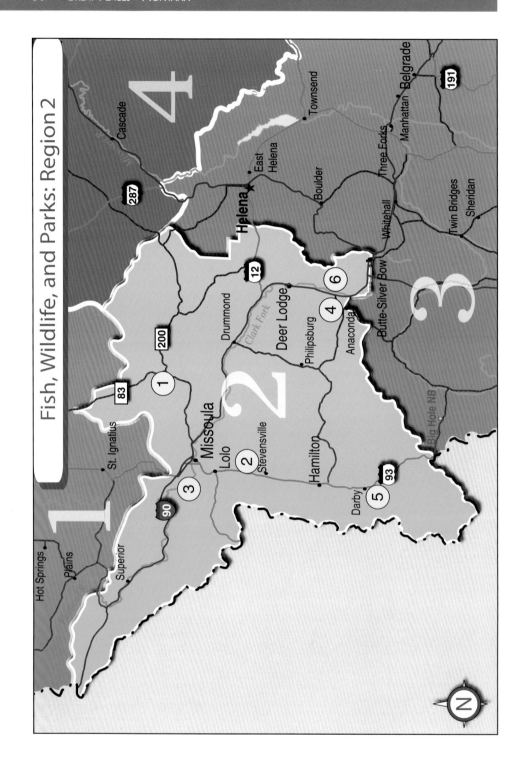

REGION 2

1. Blackfoot - Clearwater Wildlife
   Management Area 58
2. Lee Metcalf National Wildlife
   Refuge 63
3. Council Grove State Park 68
4. Lost Creek State Park 76
5. Painted Rocks State Park 80
6. Warm Springs Wildlife
   Management Area 83

Blackfoot-Clearwater Wildlife Management Area

67,000 ACRES; LOCATED JUST NORTHEAST OF CLEARWATER JUNCTION BETWEEN THE BLACKFOOT AND SWAN RIVERS.

Montana's largest WMA, about 1,000 elk, 1,000 mule deer and 1,000 whitetails winter on the 67,000-acre plot, a mix of grasslands and low mountains. The WMA was established in 1948 when MTFWP purchased the Boyd Ranch, a large ranching operation running as many as 6,000 sheep and 1,400 cattle, a buy made possible through funds derived from hunting license sales and federal Pitman-Robertson dollars collected from excise taxes on firearms and ammunition. Deriving its official name from the confluence of the Blackfoot River and Clearwater River, to locals the WMA is known simply as "the game range."

Purchasing the 10,936-acre Boyd Ranch established a wintering area for wild populations of elk, mule and white-tailed deer, part of a statewide effort to restore wildlife populations that were decimated by market hunting and other factors around the turn of the century. The original purchase price was $160,000. Along with the original fee-title purchase, MTFWP assumed grazing leases on an additional 44,000 acres.

Since 1956, FWP has completed an additional 50 transactions, purchases, disposals or exchanges, an ongoing effort to match the boundaries of critical winter habitat with FWP property ownership or control. Major acquisitions include Ovando Mountain (1957), Dreyer Ranch (1989) and Blanchard Flats (1995). By 1998 FWP owned 18,000 acres, leased approximately 36,000 acres from Plum Creek and leased another 13,000 acres from the Montana Department of Natural Resources. In total this allowed FWP to exclude livestock from key winter game range but granted no authority to manage other uses on leased lands. In 1999, MTFWP struck a deal with Plum Creek to purchase 7,800 acres of inholdings. In 2004, the deal was completed, with the final 3,834 acres purchased at a price of $3.3 million. FWP's purpose for purchasing the land is to ensure the continued availability of important winter range for elk and deer populations by preventing the possibility of future residential or other development within the BCWMA.

At the time of the original purchase, only about 200 elk used the game range, and also wintered on private ranches located further to the east, along Monture Creek. In the 1950s, to lure elk off private land and onto the game range, FWP personnel established "bait trails." Once most of those elk migrated to the game range, the bait trails were discontinued. Additional elk were trapped and transferred from Yellowstone National Park to speed population recovery and growth. With livestock removed, overwintering elk thrived on the abundant natural forage and more liberal hunting regulations were needed to keep elk numbers in balance with the capacity of the range.

Winter elk numbers on the range increased to a high of about 1,200 animals in 1988, with the highest rate of growth occurring in the 1980s. FWP purposely reduced elk numbers in the 1990s to address problems with dispersal onto private ranches. This action, in combination with poor calf survival caused by the severe winter of 1996-1997, dropped the population to about 760 animals in 1998. The herd has since rebounded to about 1,000 animals.

Bull elk, bugling

In order to maintain the current productivity of the land, emphasis is placed on preventing any potential degradation to the land. Thus management schemes aimed at controlling or eliminating noxious weeds, eliminating off-road vehicle traffic and the use of prescribed fire and cattle grazing treatments as warranted.

Still the "game range" isn't just for wildlife; people often use it too. The WMA is open between May 15 and November 10 and a State Lands Recreational Use permit is required. Activities include, wildlife viewing, bird watching, hunting, fishing, hiking, dog training, target shooting (please no glass and pack out what you plink) picnicking and shed hunting. Motorized vehicles are allowed on any established road, but if you choose to park on the road's shoulders please leave room for others to pass. Group use also requires a permit.

Unlike elk and deer, which tend to use the entire area, birds are fairly predictable. For example, likely spots for sandhill cranes, upland sandpipers, vesper and savannah sparrows and long-billed curlews are along the fence lines and associated grasslands. For brown-headed cowbirds, dippers, belted kingfishers, MacGillivray's warblers, redstarts, willow and dusky flycatchers, robins, warbling vireos, northern waterthrushes and yellow throats check out the riparian areas beside Cottonwood Creek — for dippers (water ouzels) fast water sections are better than slow. In 1991, a forest fire swept a part of the WMA creating a hot spot for checking off birds such as the three-toed black-backed woodpecker, Lazuli bunting and mountain bluebird. Marshy areas and ponds attract such species as bald eagle, tree and barn swallows, redstart, loon, bittern, great blue heron, wigeon, snipe, red-naped sapsucker, marsh wren, yellow warbler, northern waterthrush song and fox sparrows. Pileated woodpeckers, the largest woodpeckers in North America, nest primarily in large dead trees, ponderosa pine, western larch and black cottonwood. They chop new nest cavities each spring; old nest holes are quickly taken over by other cavity-nesters such as western screech owls and northern flying squirrels. Other tree lovers to keep an eye peeled for are Vaux's swift, red-breasted nuthatch, ruby- and golden-crowned kinglets, winter wren, Cassin's vireo, yellow-rumped and Townsend's warblers, western tanager and black-capped chickadees.

Nearby Brown's Lake is a good spot to catch a glimpse of the Brewer's sparrow; a small, brown-streaked sparrow with two distinct subspecies, one that nests at timberline in willows and stunted conifers, and another that nests only in sagebrush habitat. The sagebrush variety is in sharp decline across its range, primarily due to loss of habitat, conversion of sagebrush to cropland. Other common species are red-tailed hawk, sandhill crane, killdeer, long-billed curlew, clay-colored sparrow, vesper sparrow, savannah sparrow, bobolink, red-winged blackbird, western meadowlark, yellow-headed blackbird. On and around the lake itself look for red-necked grebes, great blue herons, cinnamon teal, shoveler, wigeon, bluebill, Barrow's goldeneye, bald eagle, black tern, marsh wren, common yellowthroat and the ubiquitous red-winged and yellow-headed blackbirds.

Nearby Restaurants and Accommodations

There are developed camping units at Clearwater Crossing, a mile west of
Clearwater Junction on MT 200 and at Harper's Lake just up the road on MT 83.
There is unlimited camping in Lolo National Forest and on the WMA itself. Cabin
rentals are available at Krutar Homestead (793-5607); Motel and restaurant
facilities are available at Clearwater Junction and throughout the Seeley-Swan
area.

Fast Facts:

Contact Info: Blackfoot-Clearwater WMA, MTFWP, 3201 Spurgin Rd., Missoula,
MT 59801; phone: 542-5500

Getting There: Via I-90 and MT 200, 45 miles east of Missoula the game range
borders the junction (Clearwater Junction) of MT 200 and 83. From the north,
follow MT 83, 15 miles south of Seeley Lake. To reach the headquarters, turn left
(north) on Woodworth (105) road and take the first left and follow it for about a
mile to the Old Boyd Ranch, and current WMA headquarters.

Activities: Wildlife viewing, bird watching, hunting, fishing, hiking, dog training,
target shooting (please no glass and pack out what you pack in to shoot at)
picnicking and shed hunting. Motorized vehicles are allowed on any established
road. Group use requires a permit.

Principle Mammals: Elk, mule, white-tailed deer.

Mammals of Special Interest: Elk.

Principle Birdlife: A variety of species, songbirds, waterfowl, upland birds, birds of
prey in a variety of habitats.

Birds of Special Interest: Brewer's sparrow.

Habitat Overview: Grasslands, woodlands, riparian zones, wetlands and ponds,
low elevation mountains.

Flora of Special Interest: Noxious weeds, for example, leafy spurge has spread
across 31,000 acres, nearly half the WMA's 67,000 acres.

Best Wildlife Viewing Ops: WMA is closed to visitation from the end of big game
season to May 15.

Best Birding Ops: May 15 to start of hunting in September; species are habitat
specific (see above).

Best Photo Ops: Early and late in day provide best light; spring and summer are
primo.

Hunting Ops: Big game, upland birds (mountain grouse) and limited waterfowl.

Fishing Ops: Limited opportunities within WMA, primarily Cottonwood Creek,
nearby opportunities abound, Blackfoot River, Clearwater River, a variety of
lakes and smaller tributaries.

Camping Ops: Camping is allowed on WMA and surrounding Lolo National Forest;
numerous developed campgrounds in area.

Hiking Trails: None developed, but hiking opportunities abound.

Motor Trails: No off road travel but motor vehicles are allowed on designated
roads.

Lee Metcalf National Wildlife Refuge

2800 ACRES, BESIDE THE BITTERROOT RIVER JUST OUTSIDE STEVENSVILLE

It's early March, and although officially still winter, spring is in the air. For at least here in the Bitterroot Valley, spring has apparently sprung early. Signs of the new season are evident: snow-free valley floor, bare in the foothills all the way up to black timber. Paired Canada geese and mallards pass by overhead where just last week huge white flocks plied the airspace. And the river is running clear and free of ice — even the bank ice is gone. And judging by the loud background music, geese and ducks are not the only birds to feel the change. But perhaps the surest sign of all is the number of rigs lined up at the fishing access sites. The big question for us: fish first, then check out the refuge or just the opposite. After much debate, we choose the latter although the vote is far from a landslide.

Pulling off the highway, we head first for the big pond beside Wildfowl Lane. The pond is about two-thirds open water and at least half is wall-to-wall waterfowl. A quick scan with binoculars reveals a ton of northern pintails but a good mix of others too. While I do the check off, Gale studies the flock through the spotting scope.

"Mallard, common goldeneye, hooded merganser, ruddy and ring-necked duck, blue-winged teal, Canada geese, and, oh, there, just beyond the cattails are, one, two, at least six, snow geese!"

As the flock feeds back and forth in the shallow water, we find it easy to separate puddlers from divers simply by noting dining technique. Puddlers, such as pintail, mallard and teal, being vegetarians at heart, graze the bottom for goodies by tipping head-down, butt in the air. While the divers, ring-necked, golden eye and merganser, the meat-eaters of the duck world, dive and chase down dinner.

Panning the camera, shooting a group of flying pintails, I notice several white-tailed deer bedded down in the brown grass beyond the pond.

"Can you see those whitetails bedded in the grass?"

Nesting ospreys

Gale, still glassing, replies, "Yes, and the more I look the more there are, must be 25, 30 heads out there."

Since I hadn't noticed anywhere near that many, I refocus the big 600mm lens from the pond to the deer. What jumps into view is sort of amazing. Ears and heads poke up just about anywhere I point the lens. I've no idea how many, but I'm sure 25, 30 is on the conservative side.

The valley's defining natural icons are, of course, the Bitterroot River and namesake jagged and picturesque mountain range, the top of which denotes the Montana-Idaho line. The river and the mountains were named for the pink blossoms of the bitterroot plant, which, by the way, is Montana's state flower. The valley is the ancestral home of Salish (Flathead) Tribe and a favorite spot for gathering the starchy roots of the succulent plant — a staple of their diet.

On Sept. 4, 1805, Lewis and Clark's Corps of Discovery expedition, after crossing Lost Trail Pass, camped near the present site of Sula, where they met a party of Salish. In his journal Clark remarked on the event: "These people received us friendly. I was the first white man on the water of this river." Later the expedition marched on downriver past the present site of Lee Metcalf NWR to eventually camp at Traveler's Rest at the mouth of Lolo Creek. The next leg in the trek to the Pacific took them over the Bitterroots into present day Idaho via Lolo Pass.

Later in the century, white settlement began in earnest; in many cases signs of the hard work remain even today. A good example is the Whaley Homestead: A weathered, white house on Wildfowl Lane within the refuge. Built in the late 1800s by Peter Whaley, an Irish immigrant who, in 1877, along with his wife, came looking for gold. Failing to strike it rich, he and his family finally settled down to a life of farming and livestock ranching. In 1988, the refuge assumed ownership and the old homestead is listed in the National Register of Historic Places.

Lee Metcalf NWR was established in 1963, primarily to provide and protect habitat for resident and migratory birds. Located along the meandering Bitterroot River and surrounded by majestic towering mountains (the rugged Bitterroots to the west and the Sapphires to the east), the Lee Metcalf National Wildlife Refuge offers spectacular viewing opportunities of the landscape and wildlife.

The refuge was named in honor of the late U.S. Senator Lee Metcalf, a local high school graduate and a lifelong champion of wise conservation. Its mission, along with providing habitat for wildlife, migratory birds and endangered and threatened species, is to provide compatible human benefits associated with wildlife and wild lands.

The diverse blend of habitats (fertile marshes, wet meadows, forested river bottom dominated by a mix of ponderosa pine and cottonwoods) blend well with uplands and croplands. The river flows along the western border of the refuge, and while the valley floor is increasingly populated, there remains a surprisingly healthy mix of rangelands, croplands and orchards. To the west lies the 1.2 million-acre Selway-Bitterroot Wilderness area, a unique complexity of dark timber, jagged peaks, steep canyons, mountain streams and lakes. To the east, grassy foothills and brush lands give way to forested slopes of the rugged Sapphire Mountains. All-in-all, a healthy blend of diverse wildlife habitats.

The valley is noted for its relatively mild winters; the valley's average elevation is about 3,300 feet and the annual precipitation averages about 12 inches. The water is abundant, a series of man-made impoundments feeding a chain of ponds and sloughs is the main attraction for a variety of wildlife and birds on a year-round basis.

To date 235 species of birds, 111 confirmed nesters, 41 species of mammals and 17 species of reptiles and amphibians have been noted. The most common sightings include white-tailed deer, muskrats, bald eagles, ospreys and, of course, waterfowl and legions of lesser birds.

Of note, a pair of bald eagles has established a nest within the refuge. Several osprey pairs nest here also and one of the highlights of a trip to the refuge is watching these master-class fishers do their thing.

The refuge is bordered its entire length by the Bitterroot River, an important and dynamic link in the overall ebb and flow. Though the real heart and soul are the connecting ponds and surrounding wetlands. Just about every critter that frequents western mountain riparian corridors shows itself here at one time or another.

For a different perspective and a wonderful wildlife and birding experience, take to the Bitterroot in a canoe, drift boat or raft. Put in at the Stevensville Bridge (east side the river) and float to and take out at Florence, just upstream of the bridge on the left. This is actually a leg of the recently completed Bitterroot Birding and Nature Trail and a fascinating 11-mile trip. June features western tanagers, bank swallows, honking Canada geese, mergansers and all sorts of waterfowl; stalking great blue herons and dancing mayflies add to the show; as do backwater eddies thick with tadpoles of Columbia spotted frogs or western toads. Fall floats feature dazzling, colorful displays of bankside willows and stately cottonwoods, ospreys and bald eagles and all sorts of waterfowl wheeling overhead, all set to a backdrop of deep blue skies carved by the jagged white splashed peaks of the tall Bitterroots.

The river grows in stature and strength on the downstream journey, gathering the icy flows of numerous tributaries coming from the Bitterroots to the west and the Sapphires to the east. The broad floodplain is a mix of irrigated croplands, wetlands and forests, dominated by cottonwoods in the bottomlands and ponderosas in the uplands.

The Salish knew the river as Spitlem Seukn or "waters of the bitter root."

Watch for wildlife on the water, at the edge, in the bushes, treetops and in the skies overhead. Summer floats are great for observing butterflies and dragonflies.

At normal flows allow at least three to four hours to float.

Nearby Restaurants and Accommodations

Good eateries in the Bitterroot Valley are springing up faster than wildflowers. They might be an easier find than even the ubiquitous whitetails and Canada geese. In Stevensville, check out the fresh-baked goodies and have a more-than-passable cup of Joe at the Olde Coffee Mill (777-2939). At The Broad Ax (821-3878), seven miles from Sula, one of the dinner sides offered is "wildlife viewing" (bighorn sheep and other wildlife) — no charge for the binoculars. In Darby, check out the Bear's Lair (821-2218) for great homemade lasagna, while adventurous pizza lovers will flat out drool over such unique offerings as The River Runner: grilled salmon, onion, spinach and a "delectable garlic parmesan sauce." Sounds yummy, huh? Should you hanker for a brew after a long day of wildlife viewing, tool up to Hamilton and saunter to the bar at Bitter Root Brewing (363-7468). You'll find a whole bevy of ales and seasonal brews to slake most any thirst.

Triple Creek Ranch (821-4408) is about as uptown as you'll find anywhere. Stay in a private luxurious cabin with a hot tub and enjoy gourmet dining and drinks all for one (rather steep) price. But considering what is included and that it is, after all, only money...hell, go for it. For the more frugal campers in the audience both developed and primitive campsites abound in the nearby Bitterroot NF. The closest developed USFS campground is on Bass Creek (turn off on Bass Creek Rd., just a few miles south of Stevensville on US 93).

Fast Facts

Contact Info: Lee Metcalf NWR, 4567 Wildfowl Lane Stevensville, MT 59870; Phone: 777-5552; Fax: 777-4344; E-mail: leemetcalf@fws.gov

Getting There: US 93, south of Missoula, turn off at Stevensville, follow signs to refuge; refuge headquarters is located in Stevensville; 3rd Street, Kohl Office Building, Suite 107, behind Valley Drug Store.

Activities: Wildlife viewing, photography, hunting, fishing, environmental interpretation.

Painted turtles

Principle Mammals: White-tailed deer, common muskrat, American beaver, northern pocket gopher, red squirrel, yellow-pine chipmunk, yellow-bellied marmot, striped skunk, meadow vole, Columbian ground squirrel, deer mouse.

Mammals of Special Interest: White-tailed deer, American beaver.

Principle Birdlife: waterfowl, marsh birds, shorebirds, raptors, pheasants and songbirds.

Birds of Special Interest: Bald eagle, osprey, wood duck, pheasant and various songbirds.

Habitat Overview: Bitterroot River, connecting ponds and surrounding wetlands.

Flora of Special Interest: Cottonwoods, cattails and marsh grasses.

Best Wildlife Viewing Ops: Wildfowl Lane, nature trail, various ponds and sloughs and river itself. Early and late in day year round.

Best Birding Ops: Spring and fall migration, spring through fall for residents, early and late in day.

Best Photo Ops: Year around, first and last hours of daylight; spring and fall migration are highlights.

Hunting Ops: Excellent opportunities for hunting white-tailed deer (archery only), pheasant and waterfowl.

Fishing Ops: Access to Bitterroot River, a blue-ribbon trout fishery.

Camping Ops: No camping on the refuge; several USFS campgrounds nearby (see Accommodations above).

Boating Ops: Bitterroot River

Hiking Trails: 2.5 miles within Wildlife Viewing Area; ½ mile paved; handicap accessible.

Motor Trails: Wildfowl Lane.

Council Grove State Park

187 ACRES; 10 MILES WEST OF MISSOULA ON CLARK FORK RIVER

In the Salish language, Council Grove is known as chilmeh — the place of tall trees with no limbs. A long besieged battleground where Blackfeet and mountain tribes fought to control the passageway through the Rockies, Indians called it the Gates of Hell. Here, in 1855, Issac Stevens negotiated the Hellgate Treaty between the United States and the Salish, Kootenai and Pend Oreille Indians and created the Flathead Reservation. This day-use-only park, rich in both cultural and natural history is a popular destination for western Montana birders these days. Council Grove State Park was created in 1978 when FWP acquired 187 acres of bottomland from the George Duseault family.

For wildlife viewers and birders, the park houses a prolific white-tailed deer herd and the riparian bottomlands attract a large variety of birds, both seasonal and year-round residents. Facilities include drinking water, vault toilets, picnic tables and fire rings (pack out what you pack in).

Nearby Restaurants and Accommodations

Elkstrom's Lodge, Campground and Restaurant, Clinton, 825-3183
El-Mar RV, 549-0881
Rowdy's Cabin Restaurant, Missoula, 543-800
Scotty's Table Restaurant, Missoula, 544-8691
Goldsmith Inn B&B, Missoula, 721-6732
Gracenote B&B, Missoula, 721-6732
Greenough B&B, Missoula, 728-3626
Hubbard's Ponderosa Lodge, Missoula, 543-3102

Fast Facts:

Contact Info: Council Grove, 3201 Spurgin Road Missoula, MT 59804; phone: 542-5500.

Getting There: In Missoula take the I-90 Reserve St. Exit, go two miles south on Reserve St., then ten miles west on Mullan Rd.

Activities: Wildlife viewing, birding, photography, picnicking, bicycling, hiking, horseback riding, interpretive programs.

Principle Mammals: White-tailed deer, a variety of furbearers, including muskrat and beaver.

Mammals of Special Interest: None.

Principle Birdlife: A variety of waterfowl, songbirds and birds of prey.

Birds of Special Interest: Osprey, bald eagle, pileated and other wood peckers associated with old growth forest.

Habitat Overview: Old growth ponderosa pine forest, riparian zone beside the Clark Fork River.

Flora of Special Interest: Old growth ponderosa pine forest.

Best Wildlife Viewing Ops: Year around opportunities, best early and late in day.

Best Birding Ops: Numbers peak during spring and fall migrations, but a large number of species are year around residents, attracted to the riparian bottomland habitat.

Best Photo Ops: Year around opportunities, best light is early morning and late afternoon.

Hunting Ops: Bowhunting for white tailed deer and waterfowl hunting.

Fishing Ops: Fishing opportunities abound on the Clark Fork River; no boat launch.

Camping Ops: Day use only.

Hiking Trails: Interpretive trail.

Mallard hen

Least chipmonk

Other Birding Hotspots in the Missoula Area

Kelly Island Fishing Access

Kelly Island Fishing Access is a 631-acre undeveloped island owned by MTFWP, at the confluence of the Bitterroot and Clark Fork Rivers. Cottonwood bottoms, open meadows and ponderosa pine forest characterize its habitat. It is accessible by boat and can be forded during low water periods. It has good birding throughout, including the access points. To reach Kelly from Reserve St. in Missoula, turn west on Spurgin Road and go to the end; a second access is 1 block north of Spurgin at the end of North 7th St. West; a third access is located north of the river off Reserve St., turn west on Mullan Rd. to Cote Lane and follow the signs. Look for pileated and Lewis' woodpeckers, a variety of warbler species, hummingbirds, Vaux's swift, Cooper's hawk, turkey vultures and bald eagles.

Maclay Flat Trail

Maclay Flat Trail is reached from US 93 south of Missoula, by turning right on Blue Mountain Road (at the traffic light near the fitness center), and after two miles is a signed parking lot. The trail is circular, two miles end to end consisting of Bitterroot River riparian zone, ponderosa pine plantation and several marshes. Spring and summer residents include wood duck, cinnamon teal, pileated woodpecker, western wood pewee, nuthatches, black-headed grosbeak, warbling vireo, western tanager, American kestrel, and chipping sparrow. Winter birds include chickadees, nuthatches, woodpeckers, northern pygmy, barred and great horned owls, bald eagle, red crossbill, redtail hawk, American kestrel and Clark's nutcracker. Blue Mountain Road itself is worth a shot, climbing quickly from the valley it weaves through Douglas fir and western larch forest, where Clark's nutcracker, ruby-crowned kinglet, dusky and Hammond's flycatchers, Townsend's solitaire, a variety of warbler species, chickadees and nuthatches live.

Rattlesnake National Recreation Area

To reach the main trailhead off Broadway, go 4.5 miles north on Van Buren and Rattlesnake drives, turn west at the trailhead sign to the parking lot. Common spring and summer residents include cordillerean flycatcher, American dipper (water ouzel) warbling vireo, American redstart, a variety of warbler species, ruffed grouse, woodpeckers (including pileated) chickadees, nuthatches, ruby-crowned kinglet, Hammond's flycatcher, Cassin's vireo, western tanager, Vaux's swift and spotted towhee. Two other trailheads to the RNRA worth checking out are Sawmill Gulch trailhead (1.5 miles west of the main parking lot) and Woods Gulch trailhead to Sheep Mountain (a half mile east of Rattlesnake Drive on Woods Gulch Road, staying right all the way to trailhead.)

Mount Jumbo

Mount Jumbo is city owned, mostly open space, a mix of grassland, shrub, and dry forest habitats. The south side overlooks Hellgate Canyon (reached via Cherry Street or Poplar Street just north of the freeway). Follow the trails up to the "L" or along the south face. Look for spotted towhee, warblers, hummingbirds, flycatchers and rock wren. The saddle is reached via Lincoln Hills Drive. Look for western and mountain bluebirds, Lazuli bunting, yellow warbler, vesper sparrow, redtail hawk, western tanager, warbling and Cassin's vireos, pine siskin, and Cassin's finch.

Greenough Park

Located along Rattlesnake Creek, the 42-acre city park is easily accessible from town and heavily used by pedestrians, nonetheless it harbors a large and diverse bird population. The parking lot is on Monroe Street where a circle trail takes off encompassing the entire park. Residents include American dipper, chickadees, brown creeper, red-breasted nuthatch, pileated woodpecker, Bohemian and cedar waxwings, golden-crowned and ruby-crowned kinglets, western screech, great horned and northern pygmy owls, juncos, American kestrel, Veerys and Swainson thrush, warbling, red-eyed and Cassin's vireos, yellow, yellow-rumped and MacGillivrays warblers, orange-crowned and American redstart warblers, willow flycatcher; black-headed grosbeak, Lazuli bunting; spotted towhee, Bullock's oriole, Vaux's swift, chipping and song sparrows.

Riverfront-Kim Williams Trail

A former railroad bed heads at the Orange Street Bridge in downtown Missoula and follows the Clark Fork River upstream through the university for about three miles, includes several islands, a riparian zone and associated Douglas fir forest. Nashville warbler, Lazuli bunting, Bullock's oriole, American redstart, willow and cordilleran flycatchers, osprey, calliope hummingbird, cliff and violet-green swallows and western tanager are common spring and summer. In winter look for bald eagle, Bohemian waxwing, common goldeneye, common merganser and American dipper. Hellgate Canyon Trail accesses higher ground and different habitat, marked by a sign 1.5 miles from the start.

Clark Fork River, I-90 East

Milltown Superfund Site

Take Exit 110 to Bonner. Where Hwy 200 turns north into Bonner, go east 0.2 mile on the frontage road to the orange Milwaukee Railroad caboose. Park there and follow the trails down to the river for good riparian birding.

Rock Creek

Take Exit 125. The slough on the north side of I-90 is good for wood ducks, Lazuli buntings, and warblers. On the south side, follow Rock Creek several miles to Valley of the Moon Campground. Look for bighorn sheep, wood ducks, hummingbirds and other mountain species.

Beavertail Hill State Park

Take Exit 130 and turn south. A mile or so past the park is a hotspot for wild turkeys. In the park, look for American dippers, five species of swallows, woodpeckers including red-naped sapsucker, American redstart, Nashville warbler, black-headed grosbeak and cedar waxwing. Check out the ponds north of I-90 too.

Bearmouth Canyon

Exit at the Rest Area (about MP 144) and look for white-throated swifts which nest in the canyon just east of the Rest Area. Take Exit 138 to the Bearmouth Chalet and follow the frontage road into Bearmouth Canyon and on to Drummond for some interesting birding.

Pattee Canyon

Featuring miles of trails through mature ponderosa pine, western larch and Douglas fir, the canyon is reached via Higgins Avenue, south past Dornblazer Field, turn east on Pattee Canyon Drive and go 4.5 miles to the trailhead. All the trails are good as is the Picnic Area. Look for varied and hermit thrushes, western tanager, red crossbill, black headed and evening grosbeaks, Townsend's, orange-crowned and MacGillvray's warblers, pygmy, barred and flammulated owls, pileated and hairy woodpeckers and occassionally even a Williamson's sapsucker shows up.

Lolo Pass

From Missoula, US 93 south to Lolo, then west on US 12 for 33 miles. Watch for American dippers along Lolo Creek especially in winter. At the pass, take Packer Meadow Road, which winds through Montana and Idaho, eventually back to US 12. A Lolo National Forest map shows the entire loop.

Look for Steller's and gray jay, winter wren, mountain and chestnut-sided chickadee, hairy and three-toed woodpeckers, ruby-crowned kinglet, Townsend's and yellow-rumped warblers, Hammond's flycatcher, rufous hummingbird, Swainson's thrush, Lincoln and white-crowned sparrows, Clark's nutcracker and a variety of hawks. Wildflowers abound in spring and early summer, especially in the open areas.

Bitterroot Canyons

US 93 south of Missoula is bordered on the west by the Bitterroot Mountains, characterized by jagged, imposing peaks, swift mountain streams tumbling down dramatic canyons, many of which afford excellent birding trails; Bass, Larry and Kootenai are particularly interesting. Dippers, rock canyon wrens, peregrine and prairie falcons, golden eagles, turkey vultures and white-throated swifts, western screech owls, pileated woodpeckers, red-eyed vireos, red-naped sapsuckers, American redstarts and MacGillvray's warblers are among the highlights.

Teller Wildlife Refuge

Public access is permitted from the Woodside Fishing Access Site (east side of the bridge crossing the Bitterroot River on the Corvallis Cutoff Road between Hwy 93 and Corvallis). Please stay on the main trail to the north or to the river (west) side of that trail. Access to the area east of the trail requires permission from the Refuge Manager (961-3507). River bottom habitat dominated by cottonwoods and ponderosa pines over a dense understory of hardwood shrubs attracts a variety of birds, including white-breasted nuthatch, yellow and MacGillvray's warbler, pileated, downy and Lewis' woodpeckers, warbling vireo, gray catbird, red-naped sapsucker, osprey and great blue heron (there's a rookery south of the Woodside Bridge, visible until leaf-out in April). Best birding is in spring and summer.

Kiwanis Park, Hamilton

Located behind Westview Junior High on Main Street, west of downtown Hamilton. A mix of young and old cottonwood forest, cattail marsh and shrub stands, and of course the river (and backwaters) provides an interesting and diverse habitat. Typical of river bottoms it attracts a large variety of species such as Lewis' woodpecker, great horned owl, belted kingfisher, osprey, Bullock's oriole, wood duck, Wilson's warbler, western wood peewee, pileated woodpecker and gray catbird. Unusual vagrants sometimes show up here. It's a good spot year round, but spring and summer are best.

Coyote Coulee Trail

From Hamilton go nine miles south on US 93, turn west on Lost Horse Creek Rd., for 2.5 miles, turn right onto Forest Road 496 (at the end of pavement) go a half mile to the trailhead. The trail crosses several small creeks and goes through a mix of aspen-dominated riparian areas and second-growth ponderosa pine and Douglas fir habitats before it reaches the cool, coniferous riparian zone along Camas Creek. Look for chickadees, nuthatches, kinglets, woodpeckers, warblers, redstarts, vireos, sparrows, juncos, as well as deer and elk, which are common.

Lake Como

From Darby take US 93 north for five miles, turn west onto Lake Como Road, follow the signs past the beach to the campground and Lake Como National Recreation Trail. The trail passes through old growth ponderosa pine and Douglas fir for much of the seven-mile trip that circles the lake. Chickadees, nuthatches, kinglets, western tanager, Cassin's vireo and yellow-rumped warbler; pileated woodpecker, mountain bluebird and olive-sided flycatcher are typical, the latter three especially in the burn area. Dippers nest above the bridge over Rock Creek at the head of the lake. Many species of waterfowl appear briefly on Lake Como during the late spring and fall migrations, and both osprey and bald eagles frequent the lake.

Bitterroot River Fishing Access Sites

There are nine official fishing access sites along the Bitterroot River between Lolo and Conner, with signs marking each site. Most provide a mix of cottonwood and ponderosa pine with riparian shrub understories that hold many birds. Expect typical river-bottom birds such as killdeer, spotted sandpiper, belted kingfisher, pileated, Lewis' and downy woodpeckers, western wood peewee, gray catbird, warblers, sparrows, Bullock's oriole, black-headed grosbeak, osprey and a variety of waterfowl. Dippers are common on the river during winter.

Lost Creek State Park

500 ACRES AT 6,000 FEET ELEVATION, NEAR ANACONDA

Grey limestone sprinkled with pink and white granite cliffs tower 1,200 feet above the canyon's narrow floor. Scanning the vertiginous rock faces hoping for a glimpse of mountain goats or bighorn sheep (the park's two premier critters) is a neck-craning experience. But today, despite carefully glassing every nook and cranny, none show up; they've apparently gone off somewhere else for the day. We'll have to be satisfied with a single soaring golden eagle and several croaking ravens as our reward for enduring the neck-pain.

Lost Creek State Park is, perhaps, not the best place in Montana to view goats and sheep. But it is our favorite, especially in winter since most days we have the whole park to ourselves. The first time we came here, a cold early April morning maybe 10 years ago, we hit the goat jackpot, so to speak. The windfall started off with a bang when less than a hundred yards from the truck Gale spied a big band of yearlings and nannies working their way along the top of the cliffs. A few hundred yards further up-canyon, three reclusive billies sunned themselves on a narrow ledge. How they got there (or got off) will forever remain a mystery. Despite glassing their precarious position from several angles to us there just was no way — up down or horizontal seemed to involve navigating vertical sheer rock. Obviously the goats knew something we did not.

Last time we missed out on goats but found a big band of sheep, a mix of ewes and lambs, with several rams tagging along behind — young rams with horns barely half-curl and old timers with heavy broomed full curls. The stuff trophy hunters dream about. In all our visits I can recall just two complete goat or sheep busts but there's always something to gawk at, be it soaring eagles, hawks, ravens, chattering pine squirrels, marmots, at least one moose, deer, always there are dippers and chickadees, woodpeckers, nuthatches, and Clark's nutcrackers. Then too, Lost Creek Falls, a 50-foot cascade in the park's northwest corner, isn't exactly a booby prize.

Mountain goats and bighorn sheep (Montana's only wild sheep) often occupy the same mountain, but in truth are but passing acquaintances on those mountains. Goats are more eclectic eaters, seemingly defying gravity as they forage vertiginous rock gardens where lichens and shrubs often outnumber lush grasses, while sheep tend to graze the more rolling, folded terrain at the periphery while using the vertical cliffs for resting and sleeping, and as sanctuaries from predators. Subtle dining preferences aside, both are well adapted for negotiating an up-and-down landscape perhaps best known by golden eagles and rock rabbits.

Both wear specialized hooves for clinging to slick rock surfaces and take agile, graceful climbing to the next level. While sheep usually migrate to lower elevations during winter, goats tend to go higher; a trait that sometimes gets them in trouble in avalanche prone areas. For an animal so at home in the roughest mountain terrain, a surprising number meet their makers falling and by being overwhelmed by avalanches. Sheep are susceptible to periodic die-off. A disease similar to pneumonia is the biggest culprit, often wiping out entire populations. Especially prone are wild sheep living in close proximity to domestics.

Nearby Restaurants and Accommodations

Hickory House Inn, B&B, 563-5481
Mill Creek, B&B, 560-7666
Brown Derby Bar, Restaurant and Motel, 563-5788
Celtic House Inn, 563-2372
New China Café, 563-5871
Donovan's Family Restaurant, 563-6241
Daily Grind and Mesquite Grill, 563-2393
All listed are in Anaconda or nearby and of course there are many other options.

Fast Facts

Contact Info: Lost Creek, 3201 Spurgin Road Missoula, MT 59804; phone: 542-5500.

Getting There: From I-90 take MT 1 toward Anaconda; two miles east of town take Galen Road, follow signs to park.

Activities: Picnicking, hiking, camping, photography, wildlife viewing, fishing.

Mammals of Special Interest: Bighorn sheep and mountain goats.

Principle Birdlife: Golden eagle, owls, ravens, forest dwelling songbirds, woodpeckers, blue grouse, dippers, northern waterthrush.

Birds of Special Interest: Golden eagle, dipper, blue grouse.

Habitat Overview: Small, willow-choked mountain creek, coniferous forest and sheer rock cliff, soaring 1,200 feet above the canyon floor.

Flora of Special Interest: Wildflowers abound in spring and early summer.

Best Wildlife Viewing Ops: Goats and sheep can be seen year around; winter especially.

Best Birding Ops: Year around opportunities, numbers peak spring and summer.

Best Photo Ops: Year around, to photograph sheep and goats, bring a big lens.

Hunting Ops: No hunting in Park, hunting according to state law in surrounding National Forest and the Lost Creek WMA.

Fishing Ops: Small stream contains brook, brown and threatened westslope cutthroat and bull trout.

Camping Ops: 25 sites, vault toilets, grills/fire rings, picnic tables, drinking water and interpretive displays. RV/trailer size limited to 23' with 14-day stay limit. No fee.

Boating Ops: None

Hiking Trails: Semi-developed trail leads uphill into the National Forest at the end of the road.

Motor Trails: None.

Black-capped chickadee

Painted Rocks State Park

323 ACRES; ON WEST FORK BITTERROOT RIVER ABOVE CONNER

For starters, I don't know if we've ever been to Painted Rocks and not seen bighorn sheep; the dam seems to be a popular crossing. Forest-dwelling bird species abound and there is almost always a loon or two on the reservoir. Bald eagles and ospreys are common as are numerous neotropical migrant species. Our check-off list includes northern goshawk, kestrel, coot, killdeer, mallard, common merganser, least sandpiper, common snipe, Wilson's phalarope, mourning dove, great horned owl, belted kingfisher, hairy and downy woodpeckers, northern flicker, western wood peewee, willow flycatcher and eastern kingbird, cliff, tree and barn swallows, Clark's nutcracker, Stellar's jay, raven, black-capped chickadee, mountain chickadee, red- and white-breasted nuthatch, marsh wren, American dipper, ruby-crowned kinglet, robin, mountain bluebird, assorted warblers and waterfowl, numbers and species of which vary widely according to season.

The reservoir contains brook, rainbow, westslope cutthroat and mountain whitefish. The West Fork Bitterroot River is an excellent cutthroat fishery, and also contains brook, brown and rainbow trout and mountain whitefish. The West Fork has been identified as critical bull trout habitat.

Hiking and mountain biking are pretty much limited by your imagination and endurance as there are miles of Forest Service roads and trails in the area; ditto for the camping.

Nearby Restaurants and Accommodations

Bud and Shirleys, Darby, 821-4031
Café de las Senoritas, Darby, 821-3020
Montana Café, Darby, 821-1931
The Edge, Hamilton, 375-0007
The Grubsteak, Hamilton, 363-3068

Alta Meadow Ranch, 349-2464
Wildlife Adventures, B&B, 642-3262
In addition are numerous Forest Service campgrounds, motels, restaurants, cafes, saloons, you name it the Bitterroot Valley has it.

Fast Facts

Contact Info: Painted Rocks, 3201 Spurgin Road Missoula, MT 59804; phone: 542-5500.

Getting There: From Hamilton, 17 miles south on US 93, then 23 miles SW on MT 473.

Activities: Wildlife viewing, birding, boating, fishing, camping, bicycling, picnicking.

Principle Mammals: Elk, moose, bighorn sheep, deer, black bear, furbearers, pine squirrel and chipmunk.

Mammals of Special Interest: Elk, moose, bighorn sheep.

Principle Birdlife: Waterfowl, songbirds, wading birds, shorebirds and birds of prey.

Birds of Special Interest: Loon, bald eagle, osprey, warblers.

Habitat Overview: Lake, surrounded by dense coniferous forest amid steep, rugged mountains.

Flora of Special Interest: Huge, old growth ponderosa pines, some of which are called "Indian Pines"; look for bark scars about shoulder height, where Indians stripped bark to get at the sweet, gum-like cambium layer.

Best Wildlife Viewing Ops: Bighorn sheep, especially in spring and summer months.

Best Birding Ops: Neotropical migrants peak during spring and summer.

Best Photo Ops: Year around opportunities, Painted Rocks is an especially scenic area.

Hunting Ops: Hunting for big game, waterfowl and mountain grouse, outside the park itself.

Fishing Ops: Reservoir contains brook, rainbow, westslope cutthroat and mountain whitefish; West Fork Bitterroot is an excellent cutthroat fishery, also contains brook, brown and rainbow trout and mountain whitefish. The West Fork has been identified as critical bull trout habitat.

Camping Ops: Campsites with community drinking water, vault toilets, pack out what you pack in.

Boating Ops: Boating allowed, in accordance with standard Montana boating law.

Hiking Trails: None developed but opportunities abound in the surrounding Bitterroot National Forest.

Motor Trails: None within the park but countless miles exist within the national forest.

Warm Springs Wildlife Management Area

6,000 ACRES; OFF I-90 AT WARM SPRINGS EXIT EAST OF ANACONDA

When it comes to bird and fish life, the nation's largest (worst) Superfund (an environmental program established to address abandoned hazardous waste sites) site is sort of an oxymoron. Not just some birds, but legions of waterfowl, wading birds, shorebirds, birds of prey and songbirds, even upland game birds; and not just a few trout, there are monster trout, rainbows and browns that routinely top 10 pounds. What's up with that; this is a Superfund site, right? Right.

Past environmental ravages aside, and considering all that wildlife and all those big fish, what's even more puzzling is the location — right next to busy I-90, right up the street, so to speak, from industrial Anaconda and less than 20 miles from Butte. Collectively, not exactly what one thinks of as attractive, conducive habitat to harboring wildlife and giant trout. The hub of the WMA, the wildlife and the fish is the Warm Springs (Anaconda) Settling Ponds, designed to absorb the toxic-metals waste from mining activities carried out over more than a century ago. There are also seven more ponds established by Ducks Unlimited in the 1980s, located across the interstate behind the state hospital. While there is overlap of species, generally speaking puddle ducks prefer the shallower DU ponds, while divers prefer the deeper water at the settling ponds. The settling ponds are owned and maintained by Arco, but managed by MTFWP as part of the WMA.

The settling ponds' history is a story in itself. For over a century, extensive copper-mining activities in Butte and smelting activities in Anaconda lay waste to Silver Bow Creek and nearby Warm Springs Creek. Toxic metals, such as zinc, copper and arsenic were flushed into the tributaries and eventually downstream to the Clark Fork River. Tremendous environmental damage is evident to this day, despite the ongoing effort at cleanup.

Initially, the area around the settling ponds was nothing but a mine-tailings wasteland, barren and essentially lifeless. At tremendous cost (currently over $200 million and counting), the wasteland is slowly but surely coming back to life. The settling ponds now catch and treat all water coming down from Silver Bow Creek, and the water-quality turnaround is nothing short of amazing. Once it leaves the settling ponds the creek shows virtually no traces of toxic metals or wastes. As part of the remediation process planting trees, bushes, cattails and other aquatic and upland vegetation has created a surprisingly healthy and productive wildlife habitat — wetlands, uplands and riparian zones. Overall, the project included planting 1,000,000 cattails, 500,000 bulrushes, 100,000 willows, in addition to building six settling ponds with islands and completely rebuilding the stream itself.

And did it work?

Well, if over 100 pairs of nesting geese, over 200 pairs of nesting ducks, over 300 pairs of songbirds, regular catches of trout weighing in excess of 10 pounds, legions of bugs, daily sightings of just about every species of wildlife known to inhabit the area are proof, it would sure seem so.

According to Dave Dziak, MTFWP manager, the WMA hosts more than 140 bird species. Records show hunting pressure averages between 28 and 48 hunters daily during the waterfowl season which typically runs from the first Saturday in October through mid-January. Hunters on average spend a combined 100 hours per day, bagging on average 60 assorted ducks and nine geese. In addition to hunting the WMA provides valuable count information on waterfowl populations (counts are performed in January, April and September on approximately the same date each year).

"While opportunities vary widely according to season, weather conditions and time of day, generally the best times are periods of low light and wind; and of course numbers peak during spring and fall migrations," Dziak said.

Nearby Restaurants and Accommodations

Anaconda, once little more than a ravaged industrial center, albeit one with a rich history and heritage, these days is renowned in many circles as a recreation hub. While the "Big Stack" still stands as stark testament to its dark past, immediately behind loom the tall peaks of the Pintlar Range, the Continental Divide, towering well beyond 10,000 feet in some instances. Camping abounds in the area and is allowed on the WMA, although it has no developed sites as yet anyway. We've enjoyed great meals at the Barclay II, 563-5541; Granny's Kitchen, 563-2349; and the Daily Grind Deli and Mesquite Grill, 563-2393 but there are a whole host of others. Fairmont Hot Springs Resort is a popular place to bed down for the night, 797-3241; as is Fairmont RV Park, 797-3505; B&Bs include the popular Hickory House Inn, 563-5481; the Marcus Daly Motel, 800-535-6528 is friendly, clean and reasonable.

And last but not least Anaconda boasts the Jack Nicklaus-designed Old Works Golf Course, 563-5827. In 1883, an Irish immigrant, Marcus Daly backed by J.B. Haggin and others purchased the land on which the city of Anaconda and the Old Works were to be built. In September 1884, the Upper Works began production, with a capacity to treat 500 tons of ore daily. (Remnants of the Upper Works can be seen today when playing the front nine at Old Works.) In 1886, installing updated equipment increased capacity to 1,000 tons per day. The need for more smelting capacity from the Butte mines resulted in construction beginning on the Lower Works in 1887, one mile east of the Upper Works. Shortly after completion, the Lower Works were destroyed by fire. The rebuilt Lower Works were operational by 1889 with a capacity to process 3,000 tons of ore daily. To keep up with the ore supply, a third smelter was planned across the valley. Marcus Daly never saw these Reduction Works in operation; he died in New York in 1900.

The new, more modern Washoe Smelter had the capacity to process all of the ore from the Butte mines, resulting in the dismantling and closure of the Old Works. The location lay idle until 1983 when it became a Superfund cleanup site. In 1989, Anaconda citizen's formed a group to promote the construction of a "world-class" golf course on the site. Through hard work and cooperation between the community, ARCO, state and federal agencies along with golf legend Jack Nicklaus, ground was broken on May 26, 1994. The rest is of course history.

Who said Superfund sites were all bad...

Barrow's goldeneye

Fast Facts

Contact Info: MTFWP, Warm Springs Office, 693-7395

Getting There: I-90 between Butte and Deer Lodge, get off at Warm Springs exit.

Activities: Auto tour route, hiking, biking, wildlife viewing and bird watching, photography, picnicking, fishing, hunting (waterfowl and upland birds), trapping (by permit only), dog training (Aug 15-Mar 31).

Principle Mammals: White-tailed deer, muskrat.

Mammals of Special Interest: None.

Principle Birdlife: Waterfowl, wading birds, shorebirds, song birds, birds of prey, upland birds (Huns).

Birds of Special Interest: None.

Habitat Overview: Ponds surrounded by a mix of wetlands, uplands and riparian areas.

Flora of Special Interest: Cattails, bulrushes, wetland plants and willows.

Best Wildlife Viewing Ops: Numerous walking trails and ponds provide ample opportunities to view whitetails, muskrats and other wildlife.

Best Birding Ops: Auto tour route, numerous walking trails and the ponds offer nearly unlimited birding opportunities. Spring, summer and early fall are best for migrants.

Best Photo Ops: Access to wetlands and ponds makes for great photo ops. Early and late in day provide best lighting. Spring and fall for migrants.

Hunting Ops: Waterfowl and upland birds, check for special regulations and restrictions.

Fishing Ops: Clark Fork River, Warm Springs Creek and several ponds afford a variety of opportunities; special regulations are in effect, so be sure to check in first.

Camping Ops: Allowed in some areas; no developed camp sites.

Boating Ops: No motors, and some ponds and all streams are restricted, check before launching.

Hiking Trails: Numerous trails offer access to just about the entire WMA.

Motor Trails: Auto tour route with interpretive information.

White-tailed deer fawn

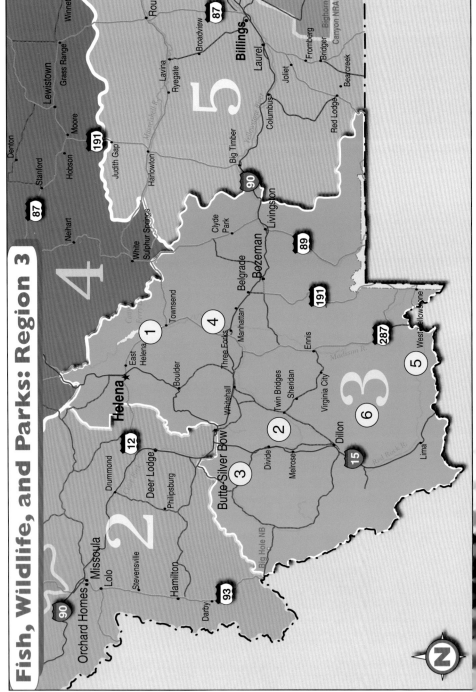

Fish, Wildlife, and Parks: Region 3

REGION 3

1. Canyon Ferry Wildlife
   Management Area 91
2. Humbug Spires Wilderness
   Study Area 99
3. Mount Haggin Wildlife
   Management Area 105
4. Missouri Headwaters
   State Park 113
5. Red Rock Lakes National
   Wildlife Refuge 116
6. Robb-Ledford/Blacktail Creek
   Wildlife Management Area 127

Canyon Ferry Wildlife Management Area

5,000 ACRES; IN BROADWATER COUNTY, ONE MILE NORTH OF TOWNSEND

At the lower (south) end of Canyon Ferry Reservoir

Amid the brushy thickets of Canyon Ferry WMA it's easy to lose sight of the fact that this is, indeed, southwest Montana, where there's typically more high and dry semi-desert than lush riparian bottomland. Waterfowl wheel overhead, roosters cackle and everywhere you look (step) is white-tailed-deer sign. But the reality check comes in the form of a yearling bull moose, gracefully (yes, in this case, full of grace actually) high stepping through a small opening in the Russian olives. From the tiny, ruby-crowned kinglet, to rooster pheasants and Canada geese, white-tailed deer and bull moose to Richardson's ground squirrel, striped skunk and northern chorus frog, the WMA at the south end of Canyon Ferry Lake is a rich, diverse habitat for a variety of species.

Canyon Ferry Dam is about 17 miles northeast of Helena. Meriwether Lewis and William Clark led their famous expedition up the Missouri River and past the dam site in 1805. The expedition paved the way for later settlement in Montana.

In 1862, the discovery of placer and lode gold near the town of Bannack fostered a mining rush to the area. Miners involved in the rush soon encountered even more gold, as well as silver and lead near the present site of York. The Homestead Act of 1862 encouraged settlement of the area, but crop farming advanced slowly.

Then in 1865, John Oakes began operating a ferry across the Missouri River. Oakes established the ferry to directly connect the city of Helena, ten miles west, with mining operations on the east side of the Missouri. J.V. Stafford bought Oakes's ferry in 1866, and built a general store and a post office on the east side of the river. The future dam took the name of the ferry in the canyon.

Red fox

The earliest agriculture in the area consisted of gardens and small dairy operations. In 1866, stockmen brought the first cattle herd from Texas to Montana over the Bozeman Trail, many of them to ranches in the Helena area. Open-range cattle operations dominated the scene until about 1908 when open range largely gave way to barbed wire. Then the farming began picking up. But in the 1920s, successive years of bad weather and drought forced many farmers out but, for the large majority of survivors, the Great Depression and drought in the 1930s sealed it. Those that hung on depended on irrigation water backed up by the original Canyon Ferry Dam, a rock-filled, masonry-cored timber crib, completed in 1901. It stood 47 feet high and stretched 300 feet; at full pool it contained something less than 40,000 acre-feet of water. The Army Corps of Engineers first studied Canyon Ferry in 1929, but took no action toward development. The existing reservoirs irrigated 623,000 acres of land. A further 196,300 acres needed a supplemental supply of water. The Bureau of Reclamation (BOR) estimated the area had another 311,900 acres of irrigable land. Such development necessitated seasonal and long-term carry-over storage, but at the time found insufficient finances budgeted for such a large-scale investigation. BOR engineers then met with representatives of Montana Power and the Montana State Water Conservation Board. Montana Power pledged $50,000 in cash, and the state of Montana offered $25,000 worth of personnel time to match equal funds contributed by BOR for the necessary studies, and Canyon Ferry received approval as part of the Missouri River Basin Project in the 1944 Flood Control Act. BOR engineers visited the original Canyon Ferry site and a newly proposed site in August 1944 and July 1945 and eventually chose the new (present) site. BOR studied the possibilities of both earth-fill and concrete dams for the site. The earth-fill dam design required 3.4 million cubic yards of fill, and would stand 173 feet high. Instead, BOR chose to build a concrete dam because of unspecified, simplified spillway requirements. Construction began with road relocation work in fall 1947. Canyon Constructors, a California-based construction company with Texas ties was awarded the dam construction contract on April 20, 1949, for $11,896,425. Dam construction began May 28, 1949 and was completed in 1954.

BOR built up the marsh areas of Canyon Ferry Lake as habitat for upland game birds and waterfowl. Montana informed the USFWS in 1950, that the state Fish and Game Department did not want to operate the refuges. The declaration forced the Feds to reduce the wildlife development to 400 acres. In spite of their refusal to operate the refuges, Montana asked the National Park Service to consider recreation development in the wildlife area in 1951. The request was denied and BOR continued to administer wildlife related activities. In 1957, MTFWP accepted wildlife management responsibilities under a memorandum of understanding.

The WMA changed character dramatically in the 1970s when BOR built a series of dikes designed to mitigate a severe dust problem created when winter drawdown exposed fine silt beds to the area's notorious gale-force winds. Silt dredged from the delta created four basins which were then permanently flooded creating four ponds, each about 400 acres; about 325 small islands were created during the dredging to serve as nesting sites for waterfowl, shorebirds and other birds as well. Thanks to the dike system, natural and manmade islands and lush riparian cover, in addition to a sound management program, productive wildlife habitat has increased at least ten-fold. As proof that the system is working, about 40 to 50 pairs of Canada geese nested there prior to the construction, and these days the annual count runs closer to 600 pairs. Duck production is right on track with the geese.

The WMA has become a haven for white-tailed deer, typically supporting between 200-300 head. The drier thickets teem with ringnecks and non-game species abound throughout the WMA: Double-crested cormorants, white pelicans and Caspian terns are particularly numerous, as are songbirds of every color and description. Recently established wild turkeys are frequently sighted as are moose, although hunting them is not allowed as of yet. Mourning doves, however, are hunted and following the summer nesting season doves are one of the WMA's most familiar residents. Large flocks swarm the surrounding wheat fields to glean spilled grain, following harvest. One late August outing, we spotted the following not so common (to us) species: Buff-breasted sandpiper, Jaeger (unable to confirm species), Bonaparte's gull, Franklin's gull, Sabine's gull, black and white warbler, pinyon jay, Canada warbler,

Nesting Canada Goose

yellow-bellied flycatcher among many other familiar species. A mountain lion was reported sighted the same day nearby, alas we missed it. On a Block Management Area that borders the WMA, Katie has pointed Huns on several occasions.

Waterfowl abounds during migration but not that many species nest here.

"About a half dozen species, Canada geese, mallards, two teals, gadwall and wood ducks," according to Tom Carlson, an area biologist. Redheads, canvasbacks, shovelers and pintails are common visitors. Thanks to an aggressive nest box program, the WMA produces a fair number of wood ducks; sloughs and interior pockets of water are the places to find them. Dawn is the best time to observe whitetails moving from nearby alfalfa and grain fields. The grassy meadows hidden between the river and Highway 287 and along the WMA's western edge are also good bird and wildlife viewing locations at dawn. Overall, as a wildlife viewing area, the WMA gets high marks. Carlson emphasizes Canyon Ferry is "an exceptional wetland and river bottom area...a good place to see migrating waterfowl and many nesting birds..."

Nearby Restaurants and Accommodations

Developed campgrounds surround Canyon Ferry. In nearby Townsend:
  Horseshoe Café, 266-3800
  China Wok Restaurant, 266-3981
  Mustang Motel, 266-3491
  Lake Townsend Motel, 266-3461
  Canyon Ferry Mansion B&B, 266-3599.
Helena is just up the road, offering travelers all the amenities in one large package.

Fast Facts

Contact Info: MT Fish, Wildlife and Parks, Townsend, 266-3367.

Getting There: From U. S. Highway 287 on the west and Highway 284 on the east, Canyon Ferry WMA can be reached by several gravel roads. Also, from Townsend, one can follow U. S. Highway 12 east for a short distance, then turn north onto Harrison Road. Gravel roads heading off this road lead to the WMA.

Activities: Wildlife viewing, bird watching, hiking, hunting, boating, fishing.

Principle Mammals: White-tailed deer, beaver, raccoon, mink and red fox; river otters and moose are seen infrequently.

Mammals of Special Interest: River otter, shiras moose.

Principle Birdlife: Waterfowl, shorebirds, wading birds, songbirds, birds of prey.

Birds of Special Interest: Double-crested cormorants, American white pelicans, Caspian terns and ospreys.

Habitat Overview: Cottonwoods, willow, Russian olive thickets, river islands, shelter belts, wetlands and dry uplands, surrounded by croplands.

Flora of Special Interest: None.

Best Wildlife Viewing Ops: White-tailed deer abound year round in the thick cover (except for hunting season) early and late in day.

Best Birding Ops: Spring and fall migrations attract thousands of migrants.

Best Photo Ops: Migration is best for migrants; spring and summer are tops for resident songbirds.

Hunting Ops: Waterfowl, upland birds and white-tailed deer, shotgun, muzzleloader, archery and traditional handgun only; non-toxic shot is required for both waterfowl and upland bird hunting.

Fishing Ops: Canyon Ferry is a top walleye destination, rainbow trout and yellow perch are popular also.

Camping Ops: None on WMA, developed campsites surround Canyon Ferry Reservoir.

Boating Ops: Unlimited on Canyon Ferry Reservoir.

Hiking Trails: No developed trail within the WMA, hiking, however, is a popular activity.

Motor Trails: Driving is allowed only on designated access roads.

Canyon Ferry Birds

American avocet
American coot
American crow
American golden plover
American goldfinch
American kestrel
American pipit
American redstart
American robin
American tree sparrow
American white pelican
American wigeon
Baird's sandpiper
Baird's sparrow
Bald eagle
Bank swallow
Barn swallow
Barrow's goldeneye
Belted kingfisher
Black tern
Black-bellied plover
Black-billed magpie
Black-capped chickadee
Black-crowned night-heron
Black-headed grosbeak
Black-necked stilt
Blue-winged teal

Bobolink
Bohemian waxwing
Bonaparte's gull
Brewer's blackbird
Brewer's sparrow
Brown-headed cowbird
Bufflehead
Bullock's oriole
California gull
Canada goose
Canvasback
Caspian tern
Cedar waxwing
Chipping sparrow
Cinnamon teal
Clark's grebe
Clay-colored sparrow
Cliff swallow
Common goldeneye
Common grackle
Common loon
Common merganser
Common nighthawk
Common raven
Common redpoll
Common snipe
Common tern

Common yellowthroat
Cooper's hawk
Dark-eyed junco
Double-crested cormorant
Downy woodpecker
Dunlin
Dusky flycatcher
Eared grebe
Eastern kingbird
Eurasian wigeon
European starling
Ferruginous hawk
Forster's tern
Franklin's gull
Gadwall
Glaucous gull
Golden eagle
Golden-crowned kinglet
Gray catbird
Gray partridge
Great blue heron
Great egret
Great horned owl
Greater scaup
Greater yellowlegs
Green-winged teal
Gyrfalcon
Hairy woodpecker
Hammond's flycatcher
Harris' sparrow
Hermit thrush
Herring gull
Hooded merganser
Horned grebe
Horned lark
House finch
House sparrow
House wren
Killdeer
Lark sparrow
Lazuli bunting
Least flycatcher
Least sandpiper

Lesser scaup
Lesser yellowlegs
Lincoln's sparrow
Loggerhead shrike
Long-billed curlew
Long-billed dowitcher
Long-eared owl
Sandhill crane
Macgillivray's warbler
Mallard
Marbled godwit
Marsh wren
Mccown's longspur
Merlin
Mountain bluebird
Mountain chickadee
Mountain plover
Mourning dove
Northern flicker
Northern goshawk
Northern harrier
Northern pintail
Northern rough-winged swallow
Northern shoveler
Northern shrike
Northern waterthrush
Orange-crowned warbler
Osprey
Pectoral sandpiper
Peregrine falcon
Pied-billed grebe
Pine siskin
Prairie falcon
Red knot
Red-breasted merganser
Red-eyed vireo
Red-naped sapsucker
Red-necked grebe
Red-necked phalarope
Red-tailed hawk
Red-winged blackbird
Redhead
Ring-billed gull

Ring-necked duck
Ring-necked pheasant
Rock dove
Rock wren
Ross' goose
Rough-legged hawk
Ruby-crowned kinglet
Ruddy duck
Ruffed grouse
Sage thrasher
Sanderling
Savannah sparrow
Say's phoebe
Semipalmated plover
Semipalmated sandpiper
Sharp-shinned hawk
Sharp-tailed grouse
Short-eared owl
Snow goose
Snowy egret
Solitary sandpiper
Song sparrow
Sora
Spotted sandpiper
Spotted towhee
Stilt sandpiper
Surf scoter
Swainson's hawk
Swainson's thrush
Townsend's solitaire

Tree swallow
Trumpeter swan
Tundra swan
Turkey vulture
Veery
Vesper sparrow
Violet-green swallow
Warbling vireo
Western grebe
Western kingbird
Western meadowlark
Western sandpiper
Western tanager
Western wood pewee
White-crowned sparrow
White-faced ibis
White-throated sparrow
White-throated swift
White-winged scoter
Wild turkey
Willet
Williamson's sapsucker
Willow flycatcher
Wilson's phalarope
Wilson's warbler
Wood duck
Yellow warbler
Yellow-headed blackbird
Yellow-rumped warbler

Canyon Ferry Mammals

Richardson's ground squirrel
Striped skunk
Reptiles
Gopher snake or bullsnake
Western terrestrial garter snake
Painted turtle

Canyon Ferry Amphibians

Boreal toad
Columbian spotted frog
Long-toed salamander
Western chorus frog
Northern leopard frog

Humbug Spires
Wilderness Study Area

11,175 ACRES, 26 MILES SOUTH OF BUTTE
VIA I-15 AT MOOSE CREEK

In typical understated fashion, geologists explain the Humbug Spires (south of Butte along the western foothills of the Highland Mountains) as: "an uplifting of the Boulder Batholith, a large granitic intrusion pierces the earth with one of its most spectacular outcroppings of quartz monzonite".

Contrast that with one my own descriptions (which almost always tend to be a bit more braying): "Silently eroding beside Moose Creek is a collection of stunning rock towers, some jutting 300-600 feet above the surrounding forest. As a life long, card-carrying rock gawker the scene is a heady one, awesome to behold, one actual rock climbers must find irresistible indeed."

In other words if you like rocks, this is one you don't want to miss. To get to the spires, turn off I-15 at the Moose Creek exit between Melrose and Divide, follow the gravel northeast to the trailhead.

Our first time up Moose Creek we knew nothing of the spires and, I'm pretty certain neither of us expected to see a moose. I mean the tiny creek is, after all, named Moose Creek and everyone knows you don't see moose in a place called Moose Creek.

Wrong.

"Yep, that's a moose all right, and a rather large bull at that, in the parking lot no less." But not for long. As we rounded the bend he took one look our way and pounded off upstream. Amid loud crashing and cracking of crusted snow, ice and brush he soon vanished into the trees. However atypical the hasty exit (moose aren't usually flighty, shy or wary, especially once the chaos of hunting season ends), his headlong flight did bring to mind the proverbial bull in a china closet (subtle he was not). So engrossed by it all that not until the crashing subsided did we notice the real surprise — the awesome rocks.

By now, we are liking this Moose Creek (a.k.a. Humbug Spires) place — and although we didn't yet know it, we were hooked for life.

Wanting a better look, we donned snowshoes, slogged up the icy trail beside the creek, generally following in the footsteps of the now departed bull. In the places where the creek flowed strong enough not to freeze, trout scattered at our approach. We discovered later that those finning in the pools below a series of waterfalls upstream are a mix of brook, rainbow and cutthroat/rainbow hybrids (cuttbows). Those above the waterfalls are pure-strain westslope cutthroats — native jewels, if you will. That day, mule deer and moose tracks littered the game trails that crisscrossed the stream corridor and, though not to be seen this time around, evidence of hard-working beavers greeted us at every turn.

But the biggest surprise was yet to come. This being winter and a dark day at that, dusk came early. Not wanting to negotiate the treacherous icy trail in the dark we turned around and headed for the truck. Halfway down we came upon the unmistakable pug marks of what appeared to us a fair-sized mountain lion. The cat had come downhill to the trail, his tracks on top of ours, the cat had followed the trail for 25 yards or so, then crossed the creek and headed up the other side. Even though the cat clearly did not follow us up, being in low light and unarmed (not even carrying pepper spray), the sight spooked us and sent us packing. Not running mind you, but no dinking around either. It seemed we couldn't shake the idea of the lion waiting in ambush. Cree — py. And not unexpectedly, none showed.

The sequel happened the very next winter, in almost the exact same spot on the trail following a fresh snow. We came upon another set of cat tracks. Smaller by far, these certainly belonged to a marauding bobcat; not nearly as creepy but still a good story, don't you think?

One day we decided to enter the spires by the backdoor, so to speak. At dawn on a clear, frosty, September morning we climbed up to the top of Mount Humbug, on the north side of the spires. From up there, you get a whole different perspective than from down by Moose Creek. The view, as they say, is "high, wide and handsome". The rugged Highland Mountains to the east, the jagged peaks beyond Cherry Creek in the Pioneer Range to the south, rounded Mount Fleecer to the west, Mount Haggin and the eastern most peaks of the Pintlars to the northwest, even the outskirts of the Mining City (Butte) are visible. Immediately below lay the scattered individual spires. The spires are still jutting above the dark timber, but seen from above, lack the awe-inspiring aspect of looking straight up from below — what you see now resembles just a measly bunch of scattered rocks.

But, of course, anytime you perch yourself high above the surrounding Montana landscape, measly seldom cuts it, at least for long. There, silhouetted against the high, wispy cirrus-cloud backdrop, two golden eagles and a red-tailed hawk soar on uplifting thermals. Down below, at the edge of trees, a fork horn mule deer buck, still in velvet, grazes the yellow grass and a red-shafted flicker, apparently unaware (uncaring?) of us sitting just a few feet away, mines insects on a gray-as-limestone ancient Douglas fir snag.

Besides wanting to catch the view and gain a new perspective this morning, we've an ulterior motive. Spring and summer excursions revealed a burgeoning blue grouse population and with Kate the wirehair's expertise, we hope to bag a couple for the freezer. A tall order, it seems, now that we've discovered, painfully I might add, how tilted the landscape is up here. So the plan, somewhat flawed and suspect from the beginning, begins to unravel quickly. Oh, Katie does her part just fine, but the grouse she points are way down in the dark timber, at the same time the gimpy-kneed gunner is way up above. While blues aren't the spookiest grouse around, even they apparently have their limits, flushing wild way before I manage to hobble anywhere close to shooting range. How's the old saying go, "Some days you eat chicken, some days..."

The Humbug Spires Wilderness Study Area is the official handle. At slightly over 11,000 acres, the WSA is comprised of a series of rolling and steep hills, predominately Douglas fir (some stands are more than 250 years old) and lodgepole pine forest, punctuated by the aforementioned granite spires. Numbering over 50 in all, the spires lend a uniqueness and beauty to an otherwise ordinary Rocky Mountain theme. Mixed stands of younger trees dominate the periphery and give way to the more spectacular old growth toward the center. The bigger trees are especially prevalent on the steeper slopes, no doubt bypassed during logging due to the difficult terrain.

Intertwined among the trees and rocks are several drainages: Moose Creek and

Water Ouzel (dipper)

its tributaries — MacLean Creek, South Fork of Tucker Creek, Lime, Pine and Selway Gulches. Sagebrush and bunchgrasses characterize the higher, outer extremities while willows, dogwood, aspen and lush grass meadows, dotted with beaver dams, dominate the riparian corridors.

Under foot, the soils appear to be more coarsely ground rock than dirt. Geologists seem to agree, describing the soils as "mostly granitic in nature, coarse-grained, shallow, acidic, well-drained and highly erosive; others are formed from both alluvial and metamorphic materials; in contrast, these tend to be finer-grained, richer in nutrients, capable of holding more water and are less erosive." Ah-hah! Just as I thought.

The diverse habitat supports a wide variety of wildlife. Bighorn sheep, black bear, elk, moose, mule deer, mountain lion, coyote, red fox, bobcat, weasel, chipmunk, red squirrel, porcupine, cottontail rabbit, snowshoe hare and a host of smaller mammals either reside full-time or visit more or less on a regular basis. Birds include blue and ruffed grouse, many different raptors and a whole host of songbirds.

Please note: Being at least three decades beyond any inclination whatsoever to participate, anything you read here on rock climbing is all hearsay. That said, the Spires are well known in rock climbing circles and consist of rocks to challenge climbers of all levels. My neighbor, Steve Mock, an internationally known climber of all things climbable (ice to mountains to rocks) tells me, "The Wedge is most popular but some climbs are tougher." Rock climbers apparently rate individual rocks according to difficulty. Overall route ratings within the spires vary from 5.12 to 5.7 in difficulty, with the former being the toughest. Due to the smooth, nearly featureless rock surfaces with limited spots for hand and toe holds, roping in, etc., the majority of the climbs lean toward difficult. Vertical cracks, of course, make for the best climbing. Man, doesn't this sound like fun? It almost makes me wish I was 30 years younger, but not really. To each his own is my motto.

Off-trail activities, whether you are climbing, hiking, hunting or whatever, naturally require staying oriented and hydrated. A map, compass and drinking water (or a good filter) are basic requirements. To cover the entire WSA you will need the 7.5-minute Tucker Creek, Mount Humbug, Melrose and Wickiup USGS topographic maps.

Nearby Restaurants and Accommodations

Nearest eateries are in Melrose, the Hitchin' Post or the Melrose Bar and Restaurant. Both offer decent food, friendly service and reasonable prices. The Sportsman Motel, 835-2711, is clean, reasonable and popular; during height of fishing and hunting season might be a good idea to make reservations as early as possible. The Blue Moon Saloon in Divide was a popular watering hole, but burned down the summer of 2005; as of this writing nothing is being done to replace it. Primitive camping abounds within the WSA while okay semi-primitive camping can be had at the Moose Creek trailhead, Divide Bridge (MT 43 north toward Wise River) and the Salmon Fly Fishing Access in Melrose. All three are strictly do-it-yourself, no amenities save vault toilets.

Fast Facts

Contact Info: Bureau of Land Management, 106 North Parkmont, Butte, MT 59701 Phone: 406-538-7461.

Getting There: Get off I-15 at Moose Creek exit between Divide and Melrose; trailhead is three miles east via a narrow winding gravel road along the creek.

Activities: Rock climbing, hiking, fishing, hunting, XC skiing, snowshoeing, horseback riding, primitive camping, wildlife viewing.

Principle Mammals: Black bear, moose, elk, mule deer, bighorn sheep, mountain lion, coyote, fox, bobcat, weasel, chipmunk, red squirrel, porcupine, cottontail and snowshoe hare as well as miscellaneous small rodents.

Mammals of Special Interest: None.

Principle Birdlife: Variety of non-game birds, ruffed and blue grouse, several species of raptors, including eagles, hawks and owls.

Birds of Special Interest: None.

Habitat Overview: Douglas fir and lodgepole pine covered rolling hills, lush sagebrush and grass covered meadows, willow, dogwood, aspen and lush grass carpeted riparian areas accented by over 50 rock towers (spires) mostly found along and near Moose Creek — nine of which tower between 300 and 600 feet tall.

Flora of Special Interest: Old growth Douglas fir, some more than 250 years old, are particularly impressive.

Best Wildlife Viewing Ops: Mornings and evenings, year around except for fall hunting seasons when naturally wildlife is less approachable.

Best Birding Ops: Spring, summer and early fall.

Best Photo Ops: The spires themselves are a rock photographers dream.

Hunting Ops: A good place for foot hunters to dodge the growing ATV/pickup crowd; fair to good big game and blue grouse opportunities.

Fishing Ops: Moose Creek, a tributary of the Big Hole River, supports brook, cutthroat and rainbow trout mostly pan sized even in the lower reaches; pure-strain westslope cutthroat are found above a series of steep waterfalls that block movement upstream by the other non-native species.

Camping Ops: Primitive camping only within the WSA; limited space available at the trailhead but there are vault toilets. Offsite developed camping facilities are found at BLM's Divide Bridge Campground, two miles west of I-15 Divide Interchange on MT 43 beside the Big Hole River.

Hiking Trails: Most popular trail winds along Moose Creek; winter travelers should be prepared with snowshoes or cross-country skis; about 1.5 miles upstream the trail forks, the right fork being the more popular route since it leads to the Wedge, one the tallest spires. Game trails extend the possibilities for just about any length day hike and/or overnight excursion.

Motor Trails: None within the WSA itself although several gravel roads give access to the perimeter boundary; Moose Creek road is the primary access to the spires themselves and principle hiking trailhead.

Mount Haggin Wildlife Management Area

56,151 ACRES IN DEER LODGE & SILVER BOW COUNTIES, SOUTH OF ANACONDA

Montana is blessed with spectacular, scenic vistas, but the view that unravels just beyond the turn-off of MT 43 onto MT 274N gets our vote as one of the best. Especially stunning in the fall, the gilded aspens aflame interspersed among the black timber and bull elk-tan grass meadows running up to the treeless snow-splashed peaks of the eastern flank of the Pintlar Mountains (Mounts Haggin, Short, Evans, Howe, Tiny, Kurt and Goat). The scene gets even better when framed by the wide and, often as not, stark blue sky dotted by all those fluffy white clouds. The view sort of overwhelms and we never tire of gazing at it.

Two-thirds of the way up sits the crumbling remains of the Mule Ranch. The ranch sprung up following many years of environmental abuse by the infamous Anaconda Copper Company. Seems the 500-foot tall stack constantly spewed toxic fumes, poisoned livestock, crops and timberlands for miles around and the locals, at least those not employed by the company and able to speak their peace, were sick of it (some literally). To avoid hassle and costly lawsuits the company purchased much of the affected property including acreage that would become the Mule Ranch. The ranch was used to raise and rehab mules for work in the nearby mines.

Later the ranch was acquired and operated by veterinarian Dr. Henry Gardiner. Utilizing what were considered at the time ground-breaking techniques involving selective breeding, the ranch became home to one of the nation's largest herds of purebred Hampshire sheep. The operation was an important chapter in the development of Montana's livestock industry.

These days, Montana Fish, Wildlife, and Parks utilizes what remains of the infrastructure as a seasonal work center. A series of signs beside the highway depicts the past social and cultural history, current WMA management scheme,

Shiras moose (bull/cow)

species present, and has a particularly poignant quote from the late naturalist, John Burroughs.

"I am in love with this world. I have nestled lovingly in it, climbed its mountains, roamed its forests, felt the sting of its heats, the drench of its rains, the fury of its winds, and always have beauty and joy waited upon my goings and comings."

While Burroughs most likely uttered the refrain elsewhere it's easy to envision ranch hands thinking along those same lines. Damn, it must have been a hard place to concentrate on work and, without doubt, a good thing that I never had to try, since it's highly unlikely idle gawking would have been a part of the company's benefits package.

On a surprisingly cool day for the end of August of one the state's hotter, drier summers, we sit eating lunch in the shade of a small island of lodgepole pines, amid a sea of baked brown grass. Down below a band of pronghorn grazes the narrow green belt along willow-lined California Creek. Closer in, a small flock of mountain bluebirds creates apparent chaos amongst an army of grasshoppers, evident by the rise in intensity of the monotonous buzz and click as the birds press the attack. Keeping one eye on the carnage, the other on the scenic view, we munched peanut butter crackers and slurped chicken noodle soup, cooked, by the way, on an MSR propane stove we carry in the grub box. Alternately switching our gaze from the barren rock peaks, to the antelope, to the search and destroy operation unfolding in the grass. Then suddenly...a coyote!

He appears in the grass as if somehow dropped there by an invisible aircraft or something. What he is hunting we can only guess. Perhaps, like the bluebirds, the coyote is bent on feasting upon grasshoppers, though mice seem a more plausible answer. At any rate, apparently engrossed in the stalking, he fails to notice us, two humans and a dog, sitting in plain view not thirty-five yards away.

More surprising to us is that Katie, our German wirehaired pointer, fails to see the coyote...at first that is. Suddenly she comes to full alert. Obviously catching a whiff of coyote carried on an errant breeze she lets out a low, ominous growl. And just like that, the coyote is gone. One second right there almost in our laps, next flat out gone, vanished into the trees as ghost-like as he'd appeared in the first place. Katie, not really the ferocious watch dog she sometimes acts like when Mom and Dad are there to protect, half-heartedly gives chase, but then evidently thinks better of pressing the attack, and races back and the crisis is over. Though the big grin on her whiskered maw leaves little doubt how proud she is of the performance.

Evidence points to man's earliest arrival to the area at around 10,500 years ago. Artifacts like stone tools, projectile points, ancient hearths and even a stone quarry where flint was mined point to the region as a once popular hunting ground. The animals pursued by early hunters have long since disappeared — ancients such as camels and wild horses, behemoth bison and hairy mammoths — though the primary quarry, deer, elk, bison, mountain sheep, goat, moose and many other critters, except for the bison and sheep, still remain.

Settlement came with the discovery of gold on French Creek. Thousands of prospectors who swarmed the area calved the boomtown of Mountaineer City, a few miles to the south. The first placers were up and running by early 1864 and soon the 20 best claims were yielding as much as $300 per ten-hour run. The highest paying claims were located above the discovery, where pay dirt lay just seven to eight feet above bedrock. A year later Mountaineer City had grown to 20 to 30 homes, two or three shops, two blacksmiths and a shoemaker shop, with the usual array of saloons, banks and at least one hurdy-gurdy outfit. By 1868, the mines reportedly produced between one and five million dollars, depending on whose figures you choose to believe. Today not much remains as hard evidence of the miners' quest; scattered mounds of washed rock, collapsed mine shafts and crumbling remains of isolated prospector's cabins are about the only remnants of the boom and bust era.

During the last years of the 19th century, loggers stripped the forested slopes surrounding Mt. Haggin. Untold millions of board feet of lumber in the form of huge saw logs were floated to a trailhead near Anaconda via an elaborate—nearly 18 miles long—wooden flume for use in the Anaconda smelters and Butte mines. Remnants of the engineering masterpiece can still be seen here and there along the way.

Later, in the early 1900s, Haggin became the training center for the nation's first forest rangers in the employ of the newly minted US Forest Service. Gifford Pinchot, the Forest Service's first chief, visited during the design and development stage that would eventually lead to implementing the first harvest regulations for western forests.

After lunch, we continued exploring, hiking along Ten Mile Creek. Ever alert, Katie found and pointed a large covey of blue grouse. Never one to waste a training opportunity, I cautioned her to hold steady before moving in for the flush.

The flush, if you could call it that, revealed a mixed-aged group, obviously more than a single brood. Adults and the more mature juveniles buzzed away in fine grouse fashion. But the smallest, those barely feathered, had trouble getting off the ground. A flaw Katie recognized immediately and came within an eyelash of nabbing one as it scratched for enough lift to just make the top rung of a nearby jack-fence. Fortunately there was nothing between me and her but a few feet of open timber, and I was able to make the collar-grabbing save. Just in the nick of time because the wicked gleam in her eye left no doubt of her evil intentions. Meanwhile, the poor bird, obviously shocked by the hullabaloo, perched there on the rail, gawked as if to say, "What the hell..."

After handing the dog off to Gale, even though I had no telephoto lens mounted on the camera, I was able to creep close enough to snap a full-frame portrait. And yes, it would have been a major faux pas in bird-dog etiquette had Katie made the grab, to say nothing of illegal, since opening day of bird season was still a few days away. Of course I confided this to her and of course she sat there, cocked her head and grinned wickedly.

Shiras moose live here. In winter, with the bears all warm and snug in their beds, and with the deer, elk and pronghorn having migrated downhill and the goats uphill to the highest windswept peaks. And with the mountain lions having followed the deer, by default moose become the WMA's marquee mega fauna. The deep snow along the many willow-lined creeks allows the long-legged overwintering moose to get at browse otherwise unreachable in warmer seasons — some say a little too well.

Recent studies indicate the thriving winter moose population is negatively impacting willow regeneration. The fear is that moose will eventually eat the cupboard bare. Little wonder when you consider a single mature moose probably consumes 40-60 pounds of browse per day; and when you are talking browse over the course of winter that adds up to a pretty big pile of twigs.

Lewis and Clark recorded the first Shiras moose ever May 10, 1805 on the Milk River in Montana. Today they range across western Wyoming, western Montana, northern and central Idaho, southwestern Alberta, southeastern British Columbia, as well as isolated areas of Utah, Colorado and extreme northwestern Washington.

Moose are not herd animals. Unlike elk, for example, rutting bulls do not gather harems but rather tend one cow at a time. It's not unusual during rut to see several bulls following one cow. The largest in the bunch gets closest to the cow and the rest tag along more or less according to size and, I suppose, spunk. Moose, particularly bulls, come off as comic-characters, no doubt because of their goofy looks — gangly legs, apparent aloof attitude and dopey, don't-have-a-clue stares. Go ahead and laugh, that is, so long as the clown moose is not too close. Up close and personal, you best watch it. Rutting bulls have been known to take on logging trucks and train locomotives; cows with calf at close range can be even more frightening. I learned this first hand a few years ago.

While hunting blue grouse, right here on Mount Haggin by the way (this time with a gun, even), I stepped out of the timber into a small opening and fifteen yards out a cow moose stood up from the tall grass with a half-year-old calf right behind her. Immediately, the cow laid her ears flat and took two steps forward. Worse, Katie comes bouncing into the clearing. Spying the moose, she circles, makes her stand, you guessed it, about five yards in front of me; spot on between us and mamma moose. Hair bristling, she lets loose the infamous see-coyote-run low growl (perhaps thinking, "It worked on Mr. Coyote, why not on Mamma Moose?") Regardless, you didn't need to be a moose behaviorist to tell right away this turn of events didn't sit well with Mom Moose. I don't profess to know the signals a cow moose makes prior to stomping the crap out intruders, but somehow I just knew we were close. Really close. Ears flat, eyes bulging, rapidly licking her lips seemed to suggest she was not all happy, that I'd better get the damn dog under control.

No problem.

Inching forward, I got a grip on Kate's collar, and while muttering all the sweet-nothings I could think of, we backed slowly into the trees. Each step we took backwards, the cow took a step or two our way, all the while stomping her feet, licking jowls. And those damn ears, I mean they were flat out laid flat! Finally, 40 to 50 yards separated us, and the cow stopped. Taking no chance that she might change her mind, I hauled Kate up on her hind feet and hightailed it up the mountain. All bluff you say? Well, all I can say is you should have been there.

Shiras moose are the smallest subspecies of moose. Still, a big bull is an imposing sight whether or not he happens to be currently sparring trucks or trains. Weighing in at 1,200 to1,400 pounds, standing as high as seven feet at the shoulder and ten feet long, with wide palmate antlers sometimes spreading 50 inches (or more) and weighing 50 pounds, Mr. Bull is quite the beast. While moose often wander far from the mountains, surrounded by sage and grass, perhaps munching alfalfa beneath a center pivot, it's the mountains, the dark timber he usually calls home. Moose are particularly adapted to living in thick, blow-down-infested timber, swamps and deep snow. Moose swim like beavers; in fact, one was clocked at about six miles per hour kicking across a wide lake (just a little dip, by the way, which took about two hours). It seems fitting, don't you think, that where mules (from the Anaconda Copper Mule Ranch) once reigned, moose are now king.

Nearby Restaurants and Accommodations

Anaconda provides grocery and convenience stores, restaurants and motels; we've had good eats at Granny's Kitchen, 1500 E. Commercial, 563-2349; Daily Grind Deli and Mesquite Grill, 100 Main St., 563-2393; The Wise River Club is a fun spot to eat and wet your whistle. You can cop gas and limited groceries at the village convenience store. Primitive camping opportunities are abundant within the surrounding Beaverhead-Deerlodge National Forest, along the Big Hole River. There is a USFS campground a few miles west of the WMA at Lower Seymour Lake, by and large, a pretty decent fishin' hole.

Fast Facts

Contact Info: Montana FWP, Butte Area Resource Office, 1820 Meadowlark Lane, Butte, MT 59701; Phone: 406-494-1953 Fax: 406-494-2082
Getting There: From Anaconda (MT 1, Anaconda/Pintlar Scenic Byway) MT 274 south approximately ten miles; from Big Hole River valley, MT 43 to MT 274 north approximately six miles; gravel roads provide limited access to the interior.
Elevation: 6000 +
Principle Mammals: Moose, elk, mule and white-tail deer, pronghorn, black bear* mountain lion, goat, bobcat, coyote, marten, muskrat, mink, beaver.
*In fall 2005, a grizzly bear was killed by a poacher nearby, a fairly large one at that. Are there more? Stay alert, is all I can say.
Mammals of Special Interest: Moose, goat, mule deer and black bear.
Principle Birdlife: Blue, Franklin, ruffed and sage grouse, waterfowl and shorebirds especially during spring and fall migration, mountain bluebirds.
Birds of Special Interest: Four species of grouse and large variety of songbirds.

Habitat Overview: High mountain pine/spruce forest interspersed by numerous willow-choked riparian corridors, quaking aspen stands and numerous grassy meadows and sagebrush.

Flora of Special Interest: Quaking aspen and willow provide important winter browse for moose.

Best Wildlife Viewing Ops: Moose in winter; pronghorn and deer spring, summer and fall, mountain goats up high.

Best Birding Ops: The many brushy creek bottoms and wet areas provide abundant birding opportunities spring through fall.

Best Photo Ops: Moose in winter, general wildlife and scenic throughout the year.

Hunting Ops: Archery and rifle hunting for mule deer bucks by permit only (HD319); moose and cow elk by permit only; upland birds and predators (check regulations); limited waterfowl.

Fishing Ops: 28 streams in the area contain brook, cutthroat, rainbow and brown trout; mostly pan sized, although their beauty more than makes up for size.

Camping Ops: No campfires and no improved campgrounds.

Hiking Trails: Continental Divide Trail cuts across a portion; other than that unimproved roads and game trails are about it.

Motor Trails: Limited vehicle access on designated routes only east and west of MT 274.

Coyote

Missouri Headwaters State Park

535 ACRES; AT THREE FORKS, CONFLUENCE OF THE GALLATIN, JEFFERSON AND MADISON RIVERS

Prior to 1805, when Meriwether Lewis and William Clark named the Gallatin River after then treasury secretary Albert Gallatin, Indians called it the Cherry (or Berry) River (apparently for all the wild fruits found beside it), while the Madison was called the Straight River, as it appeared to flow straight from the mountains.

About 90 species of birds have been observed within the park, including: American goldfinch, American robin, belted kingfisher, black-billed magpie, black-capped chickadee, black-headed grosbeak, Brewer's blackbird, brown-headed cowbird, cedar waxwing, common grackle, common nighthawk, European starling, gray catbird, hairy woodpecker, least flycatcher, Lewis's woodpecker, mourning dove, northern flicker, red-winged blackbird, yellow-headed blackbird, ringneck pheasant, song sparrow, tree sparrow, violet green swallow, yellow warbler, bald eagle, osprey, red-tail hawk and a variety of other raptors. Mallard, common and Barrow's goldeneye, double-crested cormorant, cinnamon, blue-winged and green-winged teals, common merganser, red-breasted merganser, hooded merganser, Canada goose, snow goose, sandhill crane, great blue heron, great horned owl, long-eared owl, a variety of warblers and other neotropical migrants, raven and common crows. Mammals include beaver, muskrat, porcupine, raccoon, deer mouse, mink, river otter, least chipmunk, meadow vole, badger, coyote, red fox, Richardson's ground squirrel, white-tailed deer, striped skunk, yellow-bellied marmot, yellow pine chipmunk and mountain cottontail. Keep a wary eye for the occasional prairie rattlesnake; bull, racer and western terrestrial garter snakes inhabit the park as well. Wildflowers abound, especially in spring and early summer.

For one of the better birding/wildlife/scenic viewing drives in the area, keep on going past the park entrance to Trident (on the Missouri River), bear right and return to MT 205 at Logan, just a few miles east of the original turn off to the park.

Yellow-headed blackbird

It's difficult for me to visit a park such as this and not consider its natural, cultural and social histories. The Headwaters Region has attracted the hunter-gatherer since man first found his way here. There's a chert (used for making arrowheads and cutting tools) mine nearby with positive evidence of use dating back at least 11,000 years. Seven miles south is the Madison Buffalo Jump State Park, where Indians herded and harangued buffalo over a bluff to obtain meat, which dates back about 4,000 years. The Shoshone last used the jump in about 1700, or 100 years prior to Lewis and Clark's passing. To reach the Buffalo Jump get off I-90 at the Logan Exit (283) follow the signs south on Buffalo Jump Road.

Nearby, the renowned mountain man John Colter began his famous 300-mile naked run to freedom, pursued by a nasty band of Blackfeet warriors hell bent on finally lifting the hair of their longtime nemesis. Later the forks became the site of Gallatin City, first white settlement in the area, built as a supply depot to outfit prospectors bound for the goldfields springing up around southwest Montana. Gallatin City was first built on the west side (later moved to the park side) where it became the county seat and site of the first school, complete with fair grounds, racetrack and a gristmill. The old Gallatin Hotel still stands, the last monument left of what must have been a grand old town.

Common muskrat

Nearby Restaurants and Accommodations

Three Forks Café, 285-4843
Wheat Montana Farms and Bakery, off I-90 at Three Forks Exit, 285-3614
Headwaters Restaurant, Three Forks, 285-4511
Sacajawea Inn, Three Forks, 285-6515
Willow Creek Café and Saloon, Willow Creek, 285-3698
Broken Spur Motel, Three Forks, 285-3237
Fort Three Forks Motel and RV Park, Three Forks, 285-3233.

Fast Facts

Contact Info: Missouri Headwaters, 1400 S. 19th St. Bozeman, MT 59715; phone: 994-4042.
Getting There: Four miles northeast of Three Forks via MT 205, turn at sign onto MT 286.
Activities: Wildlife viewing, birding, camping, boating, bicycling, hiking, picnicking, fishing, hunting, interpretive programs.
Principle Mammals: White-tailed deer, beaver, muskrat, mountain cottontail.
Mammals of Special Interest: None.
Principle Birdlife: Waterfowl, songbirds, birds of prey, upland game birds.
Birds of Special Interest: Sandhill crane, ringneck pheasant, bald eagle, osprey.
Habitat Overview: Rivers, riparian bottomlands, native and domestic grasslands, willow and cottonwood forest, dense shrub and cattails.
Flora of Special Interest: None.
Best Wildlife Viewing Ops: White-tailed deer and furbearers, year round, early and late in day.
Best Birding Ops: Numbers peak during spring and fall migrations, spring and summer for nesting residents and seasonal migrants.
Best Photo Ops: Year around opportunities exist for wildlife, birds and scenic.
Hunting Ops: Open to hunting with restrictions, check game law first.
Fishing Ops: Excellent trout fishing in all three rivers, mountain whitefish and carp too.
Camping Ops: 20 campsites, picnic tables, fire rings, no hookups, pack out what you pack in; seasonal campground host.
Boating Ops: Boat launch; day use only.
Hiking Trails: Approximately four miles total, including the Gallatin River Trail, Pictograph Trail and Confluence Trail.
Motor Trails: None.

Red Rock Lakes
National Wildlife Refuge

APPROXIMATELY 25,000 ACRES; LOCATED IN EXTREME SOUTHWEST MONTANA EAST OF MONIDA AND WEST OF HENRY'S LAKE, IDAHO

"For a perfect conception of their beauty and elegance, you must observe them when they are not aware of your proximity, as they glide over the waters of some secluded inland pond. The neck, which at other times is held stiffly upright, moves in graceful curves, now bent forward, now inclined backwards over the body. The head, with an

extended scooping movement, dips beneath the water, then with a sudden effort it throws a flood over its back and wings, while the sparkling globules roll off like so many large pearls. The bird then shakes its wings, beats the water, and, as if giddy with delight, shoots away, gliding over and beneath the surface of the stream with surprising agility and grace. Imagine a flock of fifty swans thus sporting before you. I have more than once seen them. And you will feel, as I have felt, happier and freer of care than I can describe." — J. J. Audubon

Located in the Centennial Valley in extreme southwest Montana—elevations range from nearly 7,000 feet on the valley floor upward to 10,000 feet on the Continental Divide to the south—the peaks of the Centennial Range are spectacular. To the north the more rolling-hill-like Gravelly Range stands equally high. The valley and the refuge itself a diverse mix of grasslands, marshlands, wetlands, montane-forest, numerous, and ponds and the Red Rock River which runs through it, combined are among the handsomest and most remote in the state. Principle access to the refuge is by gravel road about midway (28 miles) between Henry's Lake, ID and Monida. Difficult when wet, the only way in winter is by snow machine, due to no winter maintenance whatsoever. The refuge ranges from high elevation prairie grasslands and sagebrush to the Red Rock Lakes, the namesake river and surrounding small streams, wetlands and marsh. Such diverse habitat affords a unique character and opportunity for wildlife few places can match. As we all know, diverse habitat equates to diverse wildlife.

Cool even in summer, about as harsh as harsh gets in winter in any Montana valley, typically even the valley receives heavy snows; which of course is necessary to replenish the vast wetlands, marsh, lakes and streams so vital to every living thing. The refuge ranks high among trumpeter swan breeding areas in North America; by far the largest breeding population anywhere in the contiguous lower 48 states.

A quick stop at the kiosk out front the refuge headquarters in Lakeview to pick up a brochure cancels any doubt just how important:

"Loud trumpeting signals new arrivals to 'come on down, join the crowd.'

Gregarious and loud, trumpeters' yodels and hisses sound clearly as hounds on a hot track as swans descend en masse to the last puddle of open water on Wigeon Pond. Soon another flock arrives, circles, finally chooses to set down on the open water of nearby Elk Springs Creek. The din is almost deafening as the two flocks continue to yell back and forth well into the night.

Both flocks appear mixed; snow white parents and sooty gray youngsters, or cygnets as young swans are called. As more late arrivals hove into view there is much loud talking and even more communication by body language, nodding and dipping heads, flapping wings and so forth.

Rescued from near extinction, trumpeters breeding in the Greater Yellowstone Ecosystem, including Red Rock Lakes, have grown in number from a low of only

Sandhill cranes

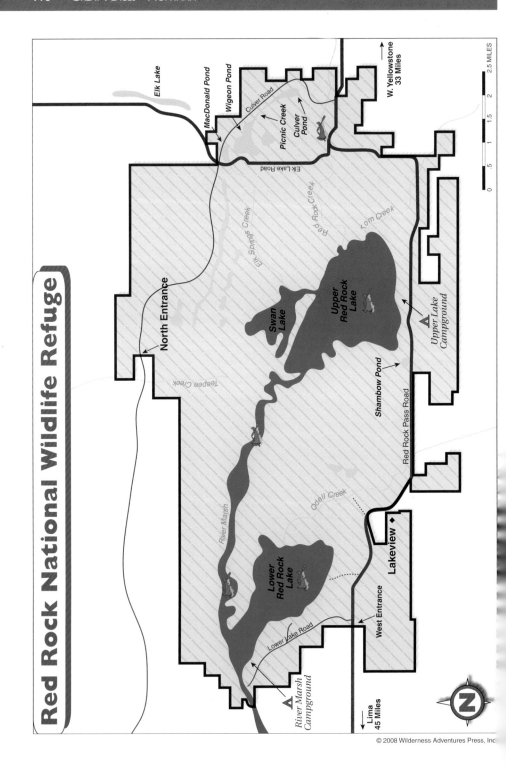

Red Rock National Wildlife Refuge

Elk Lake

MacDonald Pond

Wigeon Pond

Culver Road

Picnic Creek

Culver Pond

Elk Lake Road

W. Yellowstone
33 Miles

North Entrance

Elk Springs Creek

Red Rock Creek

Tom Creek

Swan Lake

Upper Red Rock Lake

Teepee Creek

Shambow Pond

Upper Lake Campground

Red Rock Pass Road

River Marsh

Odell Creek

Lower Red Rock Lake

Lakeview ♦

West Entrance

Lower Lake Road

River Marsh Campground

Lima
45 Miles

0   .5   1   1.5   2   2.5 MILES

© 2008 Wilderness Adventures Press, Inc

69 birds in 1932, to more than 500 in recent years. These birds are joined each winter by an additional 2000 trumpeters from Canada to form the Rocky Mountain population of trumpeter swans. A very shy bird by nature, the trumpeter swan is the subject of intense study in an attempt to learn how to ensure their survival.

The largest of all North American waterfowl, mature trumpeters reach lengths of four feet, weigh 20 to 30 pounds, and sport wingspans of up to eight feet. Their preferred diet, aquatic plants, includes waterweed, pondweed, water milfoil and duck potato. A mature swan consumes up to 20 pounds daily plus occasional side dishes, such as grain, seeds, freshwater invertebrates, snails and worms.

Trumpeters gather in large flocks over winter, but break up comes early. As soon as there is open water sub adults form loose flocks and head for the summer grounds, such as Canada and Red Rock Lakes. Paired adults return to take up traditional nesting territories. Generally speaking, lifelong partnerships are formed at 2 to 3 years old. Courtship is spectacular with much wooing and ritualized displays, synchronized swimming, bill-dipping, and blowing water.

Breeding soon follows and the pair teams up to build a nest, or in some case fix up an abandoned one. Muskrat houses amongst beds of marsh plants are favored locations; though a good view is most urgent. Nests often measure 6 to 7 feet in diameter and rise two feet or more above the waterline.

Despite all, it is not until 6 or 7 years of age trumpeters lay their first eggs. Early spring, the pen, or female swan, lays from three to nine pale white eggs. The huge eggs, four and a half inches long, weigh about 12 ounces are apparently cause for celebration. As the pen and cob (male) engage in considerable loud trumpeting and display. Incubation takes about five weeks and the pen does all the sitting; carefully concealing the eggs whenever she leaves the nest. Although both parents are protective of the nest, attempt to drive off all intruders, trumpeters are notorious for abandoning nest sites subject to repeated intrusions.

Cygnets hatch in June and are paddling after the parents within a day or two. The diet the first month consists solely of insects, crustaceans and aquatic beetles. Unlike most waterfowl swans return to the nest each night for about a month. Initial molt occurs between four and six weeks and aquatic plants dominate the daily diet. One of parents also molts during this time frame, rendering it flightless for about a month. The other molts later, insuring one adult is always capable of flight during brood rearing.

Fly lessons begin at about four months. Weighing now around 15 pounds cygnets struggle greatly getting airborne. As the clock ticks, winter and ice loom on the horizon, the parents engage in an all out, all day grind to attain flight. At about this time, the cygnets begin to trumpet. With parents and kids all yelling at once this is not the time to visit Red Rocks in search of peace and quiet.

Victory, however, is inevitable and soon the cygnets are flying almost as effortlessly and gracefully as the adults. Red Rocks' families join up with the northern migratory flocks and head to wintering areas in Idaho, Yellowstone Park and elsewhere where open water exists.

By their second year, young trumpeters have full adult plumage and coloring, with brown eyes, black legs and feet, and a black bill accented with a thin red streak.

The continued existence of trumpeter swans in the Yellowstone Region depends in a large part upon the willingness of people to forego development in important swan habitat. Trumpeter swans are extremely sensitive to many human activities and development in or near their habitats. Only a limited amount of suitable habitat exists in the region that is used regularly by trumpeters for breeding and wintering activities. When these areas are disturbed by inappropriate recreational activities, summer home development, or through improper logging or road building practices, the birds will abandon these habitats. Since most of the suitable swan habitat in the region is already occupied, the displaced birds have great difficulty finding new areas. Winter habitat is especially critical and limiting."

Due to the high elevation, spring comes late and winter comes early, roads are impassable in winter except by snow machine. No snow is plowed roughly from December to May or even later in years of unusually heavy snow pack. The main road is a mix of gravel and gumbo and can become extremely slippery when wet. About the only permanent residents in the entire valley are a handful of crusty ranchers, refuge staff and the family who operate the Elk Lake Resort; a rustic, nevertheless nifty restaurant/bar/rental cabin complex at nearby Elk Lake, which, at this writing, is open year around, phone 276-3282.

Visitors are advised to come prepared for cool, often downright chilly summer temperatures (frost generally occurs every month of the year) and don't be surprised to find snowstorms cropping up any season. The wetlands are hazardous, bogs and sinkholes are found throughout so it pays to tread carefully. To say mosquitoes are abundant is perhaps the understatement of all time; do not even think about coming here from early spring through late summer without a plentiful supply of deet. Like Wisdom (other end Beaverhead County) where locals will tell you, "We have eleven months of winter, one month of mosquitoes." The saying might very well have originated here, trouble is, there aren't enough year around residents to promote it.

One of the more remote spots in the lower 48 there are no services. The nearest gas is in Lima approximately 40 miles from refuge headquarters. The expansive and quite beautiful valley remains surprisingly free from any sort of development; even the large majority of 15 or so ranchers are content to graze cows here, live elsewhere. This is one spot where wildlife really does outnumber people big time.

"To date 232 species have been recorded within the refuge and surrounding area. Edge, where habitats collide, offers the best chance to view a variety of birds."

Our first visit we popped the where-best-to-observe-birds question to staff members at Lakeview headquarters and were surprised to be directed to Upper Red Rock Lake Campground. However, once we got there we realized why. Almost literally within the campground several habitats come together — open water, mudflats, willows, aspen, sagebrush, grass and evergreen trees — creating "the best bird watching spot in the valley."

Considering it was too early this trip for many migrants, especially waterfowl and shorebirds, we were further surprised to find what seemed to us an amazing array of birds: bald and golden eagles, blue grouse, raven, mallard, common goldeneye, rough-legged hawk, black-capped chickadee, white- and red-breasted nuthatch, snow bunting, hairy and downy woodpeckers, Stellar's jay, black-billed magpie, Clark's nutcracker, a great gray owl, pine grosbeak and pine siskin.

Apparently we missed a few; for later we ran into a local resident, obviously an avid birder she informed us the year-round or winter residents also include American dipper, belted kingfisher, northern goshawk, ruffed grouse, red crossbill, northern

Trumpeter swan

shrike, mountain chickadee, American tree sparrow, rosy finch and common redpoll. Mallard, Barrow's goldeneye, Canada goose, trumpeter swan, American wigeon, bufflehead, and hooded merganser are among the most common waterfowl, residents in all but the bitterest winter weather.

Since then, we've learned other popular bird watching places include the Lower Structure, Idlewild, Odell Creek to Sparrow Pond, between Shambo Pond and the Upper Lake Campground, along Elk Lake Road, and Pintail Ditch West.

Once spring arrives and the water opens up completely the marshy edges of the lakes and ponds and riparian zones teem with birdlife: Marsh and shorebirds such as sora, American avocet, killdeer, marbled godwit, willet, spotted sandpiper, Wilson's phalarope, marsh wren, yellow-headed blackbird and red-winged blackbird. Waterfowl of course abounds in spring and summer, but contrary to the norm Red Rock Lakes often draws more species in fall than spring. The reason for this is the harsh climate, where winter and ice often hangs on long past when most other places open up. In other words, spring migrants often take one look and keep on trucking.

Still some summer residents show up no matter what: mountain bluebird, European starling, western wood-pewee, olive-sided flycatcher, Townsend's solitaire, kinglets, warbling vireo, yellow-rumped warbler, western tanager, red crossbill, Cassin's finch, dark-eyed junco, chipping sparrow, white-crowned sparrow, spotted sandpiper, common snipe, willow flycatcher, house wren, yellow warbler, common yellowthroat, Wilson's warbler, Lincoln's sparrow, song sparrow, long-billed curlew, willet, sandhill crane, western meadowlark, horned lark, Savannah sparrow, vesper sparrow, sage grouse, sage thrasher, vesper sparrow, Brewer's sparrow, short-eared owl, red-tailed hawk, Swainson's hawk, American kestrel, prairie falcon, peregrine falcon, and northern harrier usually arrive early and stay late.

"Of the 232 bird species, 53 are considered rare or accidental; seen very infrequently and/or are outside their normal range: great egret, whooping crane, wood duck, turkey vulture, dunlin, northern mockingbird, northern parula, black-and-white warbler, northern oriole, rose-breasted grosbeak, grasshopper sparrow and rock dove are some of the more recent rare bird sightings."

At headquarters we also found an interesting brochure on the Peregrine Falcon:

"In the early 1950s, American peregrine falcon (Falco peregrinus anatum) numbers took a nose dive. Twenty-years later it hit the endangered species list, five years after than fewer than 20 percent remained. Dichlorodiphenyl trichloroethane (DDT), a chlorinated organic insecticide used in agriculture was the main culprit, caused eggshell thinning which led to poor reproductivity. Peregrines ingested DDT mainly from preying on migrant insectivorous birds.

In Montana, prior to 1975, 23 nesting territories were documented. By 1980, there were none. Zero.

In an effort to re-establish peregrines, young birds produced in captivity were released in Centennial Valley, deemed the ideal location because of its abundant cliffs and nearby bird populations.

The processes, known as hacking or hacking out, young were raised in captivity. Prior to fledging were placed at a hack site or hack tower in the valley. Attendants fed and watched over the young falcons until able to fly and fend for themselves. The process worked better than maybe any but the most optimistic imagined. Hacking produced birds and soon peregrines began to show up on the occasional check-off lists. In 1984, the first wild pair nested on a cliff in the valley. These were hacked out birds of several years earlier. The pair has produced young every year since. In 1986, a second pair returned to a hack tower in the valley. One of these was hacked out in Colorado. In 1987, a third pair returned to another hack tower, and in 1988, a fourth pair returned to the valley. By 1989, all hack sites were being used by wild pairs, in addition to one natural site. Efforts to hack-out captive-reared birds were discontinued. There are now four confirmed breeding pairs in the valley and peregrines are once more familiar sights."

Gale's favorite bird I believe is the sandhill crane and we often make the 200-mile round trip from our home in Dillon just to watch and listen to their wonderful wild ratcheting cries, which at times overwhelm all else. In the Centennial,

"the greater sandhill cranes, one of six subspecies of sandhills, is most common arriving in early spring and spending summer and early fall. Mature birds stand three feet, wear a red crown and range in color from light grey to a rusty brown. The rusty coloration is acquired from iron in the soil which gets on their bills and stains their feathers when they preen. On average about 400 sandhill cranes regularly summer in the Centennial Valley, many of them within the refuge. Hunting of sandhill cranes is not allowed on the refuge, although there is a special permit hunt in Beaverhead County.

Sandhill cranes mate for life. Courtship time is April and May. The ritual dance, features a series of complex moves, bows, leaps, pirouettes, often involving anywhere from two to a hundred participants. Sandhill cranes sport a unique ratcheting call, loud enough it can be heard well over a mile. Omnivorous, sandhill cranes use their dagger-like bills to kill rodents, frogs, snakes, insects, worms, even small birds and to glean grain. Young crane diets lean heavily toward insects.

Red Rock Lakes' cranes often winter at Bosque del Apache NWR in New Mexico."

Nearby Restaurants and Accommodations

Elk Lake Resort, Elk Lake just outside the refuge, open year round, features gourmet meals as well as sandwiches and finger food, 276-3282
Jan's Café and Cabins, Lima, 276-3484
Sports Bar and Grille, Lima, 276-3200
Camping is allowed on the refuge at two primitive campgrounds, Upper and Lower Red Rock Lakes; camping is also allowed outside the refuge on BLM and USFS lands.

Fast Facts

Contact Info: Red Rock Lakes NWR, 27820 Southside Centennial Rd., Lima, MT 59739; Phone: 276-3536 Fax: 276-3538; Email: redrocks@fws.gov

Getting There: I-15 south, turn east at Monida, follow gravel road 28 miles to Lakeview HQ; From MT 87 just north of Henry's Lake, Idaho, follow Red Rock Road south then west, approximately 28 miles to Lakeview. Both roads are impassable in winter.

Activities: Wildlife viewing, bird watching, hunting, fishing, boating, hiking, camping.

Principle Mammals: Elk, moose, pronghorn, mule and white-tailed deer, badger, coyote, red fox, yellow-bellied marmot, pika, snowshoe hare, white-tailed jackrabbit, pygmy rabbit, beaver, muskrat, porcupine, a variety of ground squirrels, mice and shrews.

Mammals of Special Interest: Moose, refuge numbers peak in summer.

Principle Birdlife: Bird list counts 232 species, 53 of which are considered rare; a cross section including waterfowl, upland game birds, shorebirds, wading birds, birds of prey, songbirds.

Birds of Special Interest: Peregrine falcon, trumpeter swan, sandhill cranes.

Habitat Overview: Large lakes, smaller ponds, streams, wetlands, uplands, aspen and evergreen forest, and grasslands.

Flora of Special Interest: Aspens, sagebrush-steppe grassland associates, willow thickets.

Best Wildlife Viewing Ops: Spring and summer are best moose viewing times; wildlife is most active early and late in day.

Best Birding Ops: Summer through fall for peregrines, trumpeters and sandhill cranes. Due to often harsh conditions in spring the fall waterfowl, shorebird migration is often more spectacular.

Best Photo Ops: Spring, summer and early fall, early and late in day provides best light. Commercial photographers must obtain a permit.

Hunting Ops: Excellent opportunities for waterfowl, upland birds and big game but special refuge regulations apply; check with Lakeview staff and request a Hunting Brochure for latest.

Fishing Ops: Excellent fishing opportunities for a variety of trout but special refuge regulations, seasons, etc. apply; special float tube and watercraft regulations also; for information check with Lakeview staff.

Camping Ops: Allowed at Upper Lake and River Marsh campgrounds only; maximum 14-day stay limit applies.

Boating Ops: Limited to canoes, kayaks, rowboats, rafts and other non-mechanized vessels in designated areas.

Hiking Trails: None, although hiking is allowed unless otherwise posted.

Motor Trails: Vehicles are restricted to maintained refuge roads and through roads as posted. No designated Auto Tour route.

Red Rock Lakes Bird List

A total of 232 species of birds have been recorded at Red Rock Lakes and the Centennial Valley. A small percentage of this total is year-round resident birds. Because of the short summer season, most birds migrate out of this area to winter. Spring migration is very slow, and many migrants pass over Red Rock Lakes without stopping due to the harsh conditions. Fall migration, however, is much more spectacular.

The following birds have been observed in the Centennial Valley and are considered rare or accidental. These birds are either observed very infrequently in highly restrictive habitat types or are out of their normal range:

Artic loon
Common tern
Clark's grebe
Caspian tern
Great egret
Band-tailed pigeon
Mute swan (feral)
Rock dove
Black swan (feral)
Yellow-billed cuckoo
Ross' goose
Black-billed cuckoo
Greater white-fronted goose
Western screech owl
Wood duck
Pileated woodpecker
Greater scaup
Red-headed woodpecker
Harlequin duck
Least flycatcher
Old squaw
Blue jay
White-winged scoter
Winter wren
Surf scoter
Nothern mockingbird
Turkey vulture
Red-eyed vireo
Gyrfalcon

Yellow-breasted chat
Sharp-tailed grouse
Common grackle
Ring-necked pheasant
Northern oriole
Whooping crane
Rose-breasted grosbeak
Yellow rail
House finch
Mountain plover
White-winged crossbill
Black-bellied plover
Rufous-sided towhee
Snowy plover
Grasshopper sparrow
Red-necked phalarope
Sage sparrow
American woodcock
Clay-colored sparrow
Pectoral sandpiper
Harris' sparrow
Dunlin
White-throated sparrow
Parasitic jaeger
Mccown's longspur
Herring gull
Chestnut-collared longspur
Bonaparte's gull

Robb-Ledford/Blacktail Creek Wildlife Management Area

Approximately 50,000 acres, southeast of Dillon

The Robb-Ledford WMA/Blacktail Creek WMA, located in the foothills of the Snowcrest Mountains generally southeast of Dillon, is a critical habitat for sage grouse, beaver, native trout, elk, moose, mule deer, antelope and a variety of other wildlife. It lies along the west side of the Snowcrest Range, and contains superb winter range for area wildlife. Unlike the dense, once unbroken forest (though now largely carved with clear cuts) of northwest Montana, here the forest occurs naturally in patches broken by huge grass and sagebrush parks. Largely due to the enormous edge effect, wildlife is both abundant and visible. For example, hundreds of elk spend the winter months here and even though the WMA itself is closed from Dec. 1 to May 15, visitors can easily spot the elk from various roads around the perimeter. Primary access is via Blacktail Creek Road south of Dillon or Upper Ruby River Road south of Alder.

Each spring, itching to get out into the backcountry, this WMA is one of our first objectives. Tramping the rolling terrain is perfect for burning off excess dunnage accumulated over winter. A bonus is finding an occasional shed elk, mule deer and moose antler. Once the snow melts and summertime temperatures start to soar, all three species tend to retreat to the cooler, timbered high country. But in spring, hikers can expect to spy numbers of all three as well as pronghorn and white-tailed deer. The East and West Forks of Blacktail Deer Creek provide decent small stream angling (don't expect big, just drop-dead pretty), especially during late spring and early summer.

Dominated by open country, the WMA consists of grass and sage interspersed by dark timber patches. Trees include lodgepole pine, Douglas fir, limber pine, juniper and curl leaf mountain mahogany, while the open areas are dominated by Idaho fescue, bluebunch wheatgrass and low sagebrush. Such diversity (the edge effect) makes for ideal living conditions for all sorts of wildlife including numerous small mammals, songbirds and upland game birds, such as Hungarian partridge, blue grouse and sage grouse. In spring especially, raptors and owls are particularly evident. Highlights are the many mama moose, elk, pronghorn and deer with youngsters in tow. A few years ago, I experienced an exhilarating encounter with an irate mama moose who obviously took exception to my photographing her newborn calf. I managed to escape unscathed, though barely. The way-too-up-close-and-personal encounter forever changed my modus operandi when it comes to photographing wildlife. Never, do I press the issue. Not ever (hint, hint).

The diverse habitat, high prairie sagebrush and grass to dark timber attract a large variety of songbirds, both neotropical migrants and year-round residents. Birds such as mountain bluebird, European starling, western wood-pewee, olive-sided flycatcher, Townsend's solitaire, ruby-crowned kinglet, warbling vireo, yellow-rumped warbler, western tanager, red crossbill, Cassin's finch, dark-eyed junco, chipping sparrow, white-crowned sparrow, common snipe, willow flycatcher, house wren, yellow warbler, common yellowthroat, Wilson's warbler, Lincoln's sparrow, song sparrow, long-billed curlew, willet, sandhill crane, western meadowlark, horned lark, Savannah sparrow, vesper sparrow, sage grouse, blue grouse, sage thrasher, vesper sparrow, Brewer's sparrow, great horned owl, long and short-eared owls, red-tailed hawk, Swainson's hawk, American kestrel, prairie falcon, peregrine falcon, and northern harrier show up frequently.

A nifty option to camping is to rent Notch Cabin, a Forest Service cabin at the end of the Robb Creek road. The cabin is located near Notch, a relatively low pass through the Snowcrest Range and provides easy access to hiking the Snowcrest Trail and is accessible by four-wheel drive. For information contact the Beaverhead-Deerlodge National Forest office in Dillon at 683-3900.

Beyond the WMAs, the peaks of the Ruby, Greenhorn, Tobacco Root and Snowcrest Mountain Ranges provide a drop-dead perfect "Montana" backdrop. The highest peaks soar beyond 10,000 feet, which is an especially pleasing view with sun setting on the snow-covered Snowcrest Range. The area is rich in history and the scenery hasn't changed all that much in the 200 years since Lewis and Clark first viewed it.

Following Lewis and Clark came the trappers, followed by miners, followed by cattle barons who settled the country. Miners tapped what is perhaps the "mother lode" of western-U.S. gold mining. Alder Gulch is the site of the largest placer gold strike in world history. In its first year of production, 1863, the fields produced $10 million worth of gold. Nearby Bannack, and later Virginia City, served as Montana's initial territorial capitals.

The infamous Vigilantes, Plumber's Gang and Robbers Roost, still haunt what's left of Virginia City, Lauren and Bannack. Within the popular "ghost towns", some 150 original buildings are preserved. Both WMAs were once incorporated within the sprawling one million-acre-plus Poindexter-Orr Cattle Co. ranch, whose square and compass brand became the first registered brand in Montana Territory. Since the early days, ranching has grown to dominate the economy in the region. More recently, due to trout-filled rivers, abundant and widespread wildlife, spectacular big sky vistas and friendly people, outdoor recreation has grown into an equally important industry. The trout streams in the region are legendary. The nearby Beaverhead, Big Hole, Jefferson and Ruby have become household names for visiting flyfishers. Dozens of lesser known creeks and high country lakes provide anglers an interesting and rewarding respite from the often-crowded big rivers.

Nearby, off Upper Ruby River Road, is the Cottonwood Creek Natural Area. Of interest to elk enthusiasts, the Gravelly Range supports one of largest and healthiest elk herds in Montana. Of special note is that one of the largest elk ever taken in Montana, a giant 7X7 scoring 429 Boone and Crockett points was taken in the Maverick Basin area north and east of Cottonwood Creek in 1956 by Fred Mercer. For many years this elk placed number two in the Boone and Crockett record book, exceeded only by a giant that scored 450 taken in Colorado in 1895. The magnificent trophy is on display at the Rocky Mountain Elk Foundation headquarters in Missoula. The Upper Ruby is a great place to camp and fish while exploring the WMAs just over the hill. Ledford Creek provides interesting summer flyfishing as well.

Sage Grouse

Another excellent side trip is the Gravelly Range Road, which extends along the crest of the mountains for about 30 miles, mostly between 8500 and 9500 feet elevation. The views are tremendous, the wildflower display and wildlife viewing can be unmatched. There are several roads that lead to the Gravelly Range Road from the Ruby River, but two of the better ones are the Warm Springs and Cottonwood roads — it's best to use a vehicle with reasonable ground clearance and four-wheel drive.

Indispensable for all visitors seeking to enjoy the WMAs or the surrounding backcountry is the Interagency Visitor Map for Southwest Montana, which is available at the Beaverhead-Deerlodge Forest Headquarters in Dillon.

Poindexter Slough WMA, just outside Dillon, is not only a popular flyfishing destination, but also a popular spot for birders and photographers. The mix of marsh, riparian zone and uplands, tall cottonwoods and dense willows provide wildlife a diverse a healthy habitat, despite the proximity to town and I-15. A large resident whitetail herd, ducks and geese galore, and songbirds of every color, size and description are the main attractions. But there are striped skunks, muskrats, red foxes, coyotes, Richardson's ground squirrels, bald eagles, numerous ospreys, great horned owls, the occasional river otter, and once in awhile, even a mountain goat sets up temporary residence on a nearby bluff. In other words, keep your eyes peeled. You never know what might show up. No camping allowed, no developed trails, no auto tour route. Toilet and parking facilities are about it. All in all, it's a delightful spot to poke around.

Nearby Restaurants and Accommodations

Dillon offers all the amenities, motels, commercial campgrounds and restaurants.
For starters check out the KOA, 683-2749
The Comfort Inn, 683-6831
Sparky's Garage restaurant, 683-2828
Sweetwater Coffee, 683-4141
Patagonia Outlet, 683-2580.
Sheridan, Alder and Virginia City also offer places to eat and stay the night. Public camping is allowed in the WMAs; however some access roads are primitive and probably not conducive to towing large trailers. The best place for large rigs is the campground at the entrance to East Fork WMA or the Upper Ruby Road. There are restrictions (consult Montana FWP).

Fast Facts

Contact Info: Beaverhead-Deerlodge National Forest, Dillon, 683-3900; Montana Fish, Wildlife and Parks, Dillon, 683-9310/9305.

Getting There: From Dillon, turn onto MT 91 south at Barrett Hospital, about a half mile out, take a left onto Blacktail Creek Road; 30 miles south, normally a teeth-rattling drive, to the WMA gate.

Activities: Closed December 1 to May 15, wildlife viewing, birding, upland bird and big game hunting in season, hiking, biking, camping, fishing and shed hunting (major elk and moose winter range).

Principle Mammals: Elk, moose, antelope, white-tailed and mule deer, coyote and beaver.

Mammals of Special Interest: Largest southwest Montana elk herd winters here.

Principle Birdlife: Sage and blue grouse and Hungarian partridge; riparian corridor and timbered ridges attract a variety of songbirds, including mountain bluebirds, warblers and meadow larks; raptors.

Birds of Special Interest: Sage grouse.

Habitat Overview: Sage brush steppe-grasslands, timbered ridges with many large parks; heavy willows surround much of Blacktail Creek.

Flora of Special Interest: Wildflowers, sagebrush, native grassland and quaking aspen.

Best Wildlife Viewing Ops: Wintering elk and moose are commonly seen from road; immediately following the May 15th opening, moose and white-tailed deer are common sights, especially in the willows beside the creek.

Best Birding Ops: May 15 through early fall; extremely popular hunting area, birders should consider wearing blaze orange during hunting seasons.

Best Photo Ops: Spring and summer; wildlife tends to scatter and be unapproachable once hunting seasons begin.

Hunting Ops: Most popular among western Montana elk hunters; excellent moose hunting (permit required) and white-tailed deer continue to increase in numbers. Limited sage grouse and Hungarian partridge hunting; blue grouse hunting can be excellent.

Fishing Ops: Willow-choked Blacktail Creek makes for challenging, though interesting trout fishing; mostly small to average size brook and rainbow trout, occasional westslope cutthroat and cuttbows, especially in upper reaches.

Camping Ops: Two primitive campgrounds, one at the gate, the other 12 miles in at the end of the road, some sites have picnic tables and fire rings and both campgrounds have vault toilets, no drinking water or garbage collection; camping is allowed most anywhere on the WMA but vehicles are restricted to designated routes.

Boating Ops: None.

Hiking Trails: No developed, but two tracks, horse and game trails abound. Nearby is the Snowcrest Trail.

Motor Trails: Numerous two-tracks in the open sage and grasslands; no off-road/designated trail driving allowed.

Fish, Wildlife, and Parks: Region 4

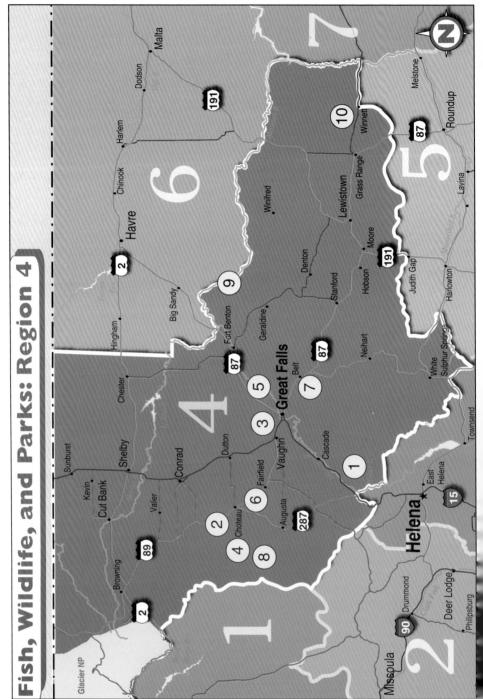

REGION 4

1. Beartooth Wildlife
   Management Area 135

2. Blackleaf Wildlife
   Management Area 141

3. Benton Lake National
   Wildlife Refuge 150

4. Ear Mountain Outstanding
   Natural Area 159

5. Giant Springs Heritage
   State Park 165

6. Freezeout Lake Wildlife
   Management Area 168

7. Sluice Boxes State Park 179

8. Sun River Wildlife
   Management Area 182

9. Upper Missouri Breaks
   National Monument. 186

10. War Horse National
    Wildlife Refuge 189

Beartooth
Wildlife Management Area

32,318 ACRES; LOCATED IN LEWIS AND CLARK AND CASCADE COUNTIES ABOUT 30 MILES NORTH OF HELENA AND 80 MILES SOUTH OF GREAT FALLS

Wildfires are seldom good news. For Wildlife Management Areas in general, wildfires usually spell disaster. But such is not the case here. On Nov. 13, 1990 two separate careless events caused a wildfire that burned nearly 80 percent of the 32,318 acres and essentially turned things around at the Beartooth WMA.

Prior to the fire, the WMA was in danger of death by overuse and abuse. Summertime was party time, as dozens of hard partying campers trashed and vandalized the WMA on an almost continuous basis. Come fall, too many hunters chased the elk (the primary reason for the WMA in the first place) off the property onto private lands. The resultant low harvest snuffed any hopes of managing the herd. Naturally, numbers skyrocketed, habitat declined, herd health suffered and area ranchers wailed. Some winters the Beartooth housed as many as 1,250 elk, most of which ended up summering on surrounding private ranch lands.

Following the fire, the managers took a long, hard, look and decided that a big change was in order. Extensive reseeding efforts helped the habitat to get off to a fast start on the road to recovery. Use restrictions, including a drastic change in the overall travel plan, made the area more wildlife friendly and a permit-only system during the general rifle season has helped to bring herd numbers into line, and above all, heal the age structure to a healthy mix of cows, calves, spikes and mature six point bulls. Mule deer are responding well to the new management scheme as well and reintroduced bighorn sheep are thriving in the regenerated habitat.

At one time or another during the year, every species of big game found in Montana visits the Beartooth. At any given moment, you might spot an elk, moose, black bear, mountain goat, bighorn sheep, mule deer, white-tailed deer or pronghorn.

Bull elk

Raptors such as bald and golden eagles, peregrine falcons, a variety of hawks and owls and ravens, are common sights soaring high above. Countless songbirds are attracted to the regenerating habitat — mountain bluebird, northern flicker, hairy and downy woodpecker, warblers such as yellow throat, yellow-rumped, Canada, and black and white sparrows such as song, white crowned, and savannah, gold and house finch, western meadowlark, mourning dove, black-billed magpie, robin, pinyon jay and flycatchers to name just a few. Upland birds, blue and ruffed grouse, Hungarian partridge also share space within the management area.

The Beartooth lies at the north end of the Little Belt Mountains. The name derives from Beartooth Mountain on the other side of Holter Lake. Elevation varies from water level, approximately 3,500 feet to 7,000 feet at Shellrock Ridge. Gates of the Mountains Wilderness, at 28,500 acres, abuts the south boundary.

The area is rich in history. Pictographs indicate that the area was used heavily by early hunters. Lewis and Clark passed by in July 1805. Lewis' journal entry of July 19...

"wh[en]ever we get a view of the lofty summits of the mountains the snow presents itself, altho' we are almost suffocated in this confined vally with heat. ... this evening we entered much the most remarkable clifts that we have yet seen. these clifts rise from the waters edge on either side perpendicularly to the hight of (about) 1200 feet. every object here wears a dark and gloomy aspect. the tow[er]ing and projecting rocks in many places seem ready to rumble on us. the river appears to have forced it's way through this immence body of solid rock for the distance of 5 3/4 Miles and where it makes it's exit below has th[r]own on either side vast collumns of rocks mountains high. ... from the singular appearance of this place I called it the gates of the rocky mounatains.

Capt. C. feell in with a gang of Elk of which he killed 2. and not being able to obtain as much wood as would make a fire substituded the dung of the buffaloe ... prickly pear of the leveler part of the rout much less painfull; they have now become so abundant in the open uplands that it is impossible to avoid them and their thors are so keen and stif that they pearce a double thickness of dressed deers skin with ease. Capt. C. informed me that he extracted 17 of these bryers from his feet this evening after he encamped by the light of the fire. I have guarded or reather fortigyed my feet against them by soaling my mockersons with the hide of the buffaloe in parchment..."

Settlement followed, and by the 1870s the Beartooth WMA and surrounding area were a patchwork of homesteads which, later consolidated, formed the base for huge cattle and sheep operations. With the railroad came a boom in commerce, and the interest fueled subsequent land swaps, which continued until finally, in 1957, the Beartooth itself came under the ownership of M. Pierce Milton. When he died, the Nature Conservancy bought the land and in 1970 sold it to MTFWP. Deed covenants dictate that, "The land be used only in accordance with sound game managemen practices and the mountainous portions of the preserve shall be held inviolate as far as intensive recreational developments are concerned."

With that in mind, even before the fire, a change in management strategy was being discussed by an organization known as the Devil's Kitchen (a local term for the area) Management Team — a consortium of sportsmen, landowners, outfitters and FWP personnel. The fire in effect sealed the deal.

First up came aerial seeding of 4,200 acres of the most severely burned timber stands. Sediment control was initiated in Elkhorn and Cottonwood drainages. New travel and camping restrictions soon followed: No camping, walk-in/horseback only in Cottonwood; non-motorized vehicles (mountain bikes) are allowed in Elkhorn; while motorized vehicles are allowed in Willow Creek drainage on established roads during the hunting season only. Beyond those and the permit-only hunting system, there is a three-pasture, rest rotation grazing system in place; whereby the 16,000-acre Sieben Ranch's cattle use about 5,000 acres along the eastern border where the two properties adjoin.

Today about 1,500 elk winter on the property and about 400 to 600 use the WMA year round. Combined with all the other wildlife, this makes for a popular summertime

Mountain bluebird

destination for wildlife viewers (WMA manager reports of several vehicles per week are not uncommon).

An interesting side trip is a boat ride through the "Gates of the Mountains" on the Missouri River. Hit it right and it can be a spectacular voyage. Not much has changed since Lewis made his observations (see above), as the steep rock walls still provide homes for eagles, osprey, and bighorn sheep. Last time, we observed ten adult ewes trailing five young lambs. In one area, petroglyphs are clearly visible on the rock face. Our check-off list includes red-necked grebes, a rare flowering plant, Kelseya uniflora, growing on the canyon walls and a new (to us) butterfly, Weidemeyer's Admiral, flitting about throughout the trip, almost as if he was tagging along for company. In a small bush clinging to the sheer rock wall, Gale spotted a yellow warbler, closer inspection revealed its tiny, frail-looking nest.

Nearby Restaurants and Accommodations

Developed campgrounds at Holter Lake
Primitive camping on the WMA with restrictions
Beartooth Ranch, 7955 Birdtail Rd, Wolf Creek, MT 59648-8602, Phone: 562-3552
Frenchman & Me, 260 Wolf Creek Main St, Wolf Creek, MT 59648, Phone: 235-9991
Frenchy's Motel & Trailer Ct, I-15, Wolf Creek, MT 59648 Phone: 235-4251
Oasis Bar & Café, Old Highway 91, Wolf Creek, MT 59648-8715 Phone: 235-9992

Fast Facts

Contact Info: MTFWP, Region 4 Headquarters, 4600 Giant Springs Road, Great Falls, MT 59405; Phone: 454-5840; Fax: 761-8477; e-mail: fwprg42@mt.gov

Getting There: I-15, Wolf Creek exit (south Great Falls, north Helena) to Wolf Creek Bridge, turn on Beartooth Rd. to WMA.

Activities: Wildlife viewing, bird watching, photography, hunting (elk, mule deer and antelope by permit only), fishing, hiking and limited camping (check regulations).

Principle Mammals: All of Montana's big game animals live on or visit the WMA at various times; furbearers and small mammals are common sights.

Mammals of Special Interest: Elk, mule deer, antelope, bighorn sheep.

Principle Birdlife: Songbirds, upland game birds and raptors.

Birds of Special Interest: Peregrine falcon, golden and bald eagles, osprey, a variety of neotropical migrants.

Habitat Overview: Recently (1990) burned, the WMA is a recovering mix of grasslands and regenerating timbers.

Flora of Special Interest: Classic example, "what happens after the fire?"

Best Wildlife Viewing Ops: WMA is closed to all visitation from the end of big game season to May 15. Viewing opportunities are excellent May 15 to start of archery hunting, September 1.

Best Birding Ops: Large raptors can be seen almost daily soaring above the WMA, spring and fall migrations bring dozens of songbird species, some just passing through many others permanent residents, numbers peak in summer after the eggs hatch.

Best Photo Ops: Elk, mule deer and bighorn sheep are common sights throughout spring and summer but tend to get scarce once hunting starts.

Hunting Ops: Elk, mule deer and antelope by permit only; limited upland bird hunting for mountain grouse, Huns and sharp-tailed grouse.

Fishing Ops: Cottonwood, Elkhorn and Willow Creek, tributaries of the Missouri River all contain trout; typical little cricks full of mostly little trout.

Camping Ops: No camping in Cottonwood Creek drainage; no potable water and no amenities available anywhere on WMA.

Boating Ops: Nearby on Holter Lake, Upper Holter Lake and Gates of Mountains stretch of the Missouri River.

Hiking Trails: No developed trail, nonetheless hiking is a popular summertime activity.

Motor Trails: Willow Creek drainage, motor vehicles are allowed on designated roads during hunting season only. Remainder of WMA is closed to motor vehicle traffic.

Bighorn sheep

Blackleaf Wildlife Management Area

11,107 ACRES LOCATED IN NORTHWESTERN TETON COUNTY, 15 MILES WEST OF BYNUM; 85 MILES NORTHWEST OF GREAT FALLS

All along the Rocky Mountain Front, spring and fall are transition times; As fall transcends to winter, bears, blacks and grizzlies, climb into the high country to hibernate in dens often covered under feet of snow. Meanwhile, ungulates — elk, mule and whitetail deer, and bighorn sheep — wander downhill to eventually spend the winter in the less snowy, more hospitable foothill habitat below — a large number of which end up grazing the long winter within the Blackleaf WMA.

Established in 1979, the WMA comprises over 11,000 acres of prime habitat where bears spend the warm months growing fat more or less as elk, deer and sheep fend off growing lean over winter.

As you might expect such a large and diverse area, managed exclusively for wildlife, acts like a magnet to a wide array of songbirds and waterfowl, as well as upland game birds — blue and ruffed grouse and Hungarian partridge find it especially appealing.

Considering the 21st century and all the relatively pristine and largely undeveloped Rocky Mountain Front, it seems almost too idyllic to be true. But thanks to public lands such as Blackleaf, Ear Mountain and Sun River WMAs, the BLM's Blind Horse and Ear Mountain Outstanding Natural Areas, the associated Lewis and Clark National Forest, the Theodore Roosevelt Memorial Ranch and a fair amount of State School Trust Lands, public access abounds all along the front and perhaps even more importantly puts in place the sort of protections to safeguard it so future generations can enjoy it as well. Assuming of course the powers that be continue their vigilance, do their part to keep the energy and development wolves at bay — alas, it's something they've not always measured up to in the past.

Mule deer

To reach Blackleaf WMA, turn west at Bynum (US 89 north of Choteau) and the Rocky Mountain Front so dominates the view that it takes a special effort to keep at least one eye on the road. Thank goodness for lonely, empty backcountry roads, since keeping both eyes on the road is impossible for me. One eye or the other continually wanders, seemingly of its own volition, between the mountains and the almost-constant parade of wildlife beside the gravel — often it seems a little like driving through a wildlife theme park.

Today our critter list is growing at a particularly rapid rate. In the first ten miles or so of gravel we have noted two Huns, a cock and hen, several pheasants, both roosters and hens, numerous whitetails and even more mule deer, mountain bluebirds in singles, pairs and bunches, several chorusing male meadow larks, a half dozen sharp-tailed grouse, several bunches of antelope, horned larks too numerous to count, a flock of dark-eyed juncos, two pileated woodpeckers, sundry ground squirrels, sandhill cranes at every turn, three great-horned owls, one (mature) sitting a nest and two, (both mature), perched on the same limb nearby (and what's that all about?). A short detour and surveillance of Bynum Reservoir (nearly dry, by the way) adds canvasbacks, Canada geese, mallards, common mergansers, pintails, northern shovelers, widgeon, tundra swans, several raptors, magpies galore, a jackrabbit, several red-shafted flickers and two cow elk to the check-off. All that and still a few miles to the end of the road, the canyon, and the WMA itself. It's just like driving through a petting zoo, but there are no high fences, the wildlife is all wild, and yes, to answer your obvious question. I am not making this up.

For us, the sandhill cranes hold a special appeal. Paired for breeding season, it seems the gangly birds are just waiting for an audience to show off. The show begins with loud calling and much strutting, flapping and spreading wings, a few high jumps, a little beak clacking and cursory bows. The high jinks often continue for as long as the audience (us) remains, although sometimes the show is cut short when one or the other simply walks off. Regardless, the performances always beg the questions: Are sandhills really mad? Do they really just stand around waiting for folks like us to come along and gawk? What is the deal? All I know is spring sure wouldn't be the same without sandhills for entertainment.

In fall, prior to migration, sandhills stage in great numbers at various locations throughout Montana. Along the Beaverhead River in mid-October marks the beginning of the staging period. The early arrivals are mostly singles, pairs and family groups, but later on, fairly large flocks arrive. What determines which hay meadow is more than I know. But over the past several years, the biggest concentration has varied from up near Glen to just outside Dillon, a distance of about 20 miles. Regardless where the staging takes place, it's like, one day just a few sandhills, the next, sandhills everywhere.

As the flock grows, their unique ratcheting calls grow in volume and each new arrival is greeted loudly by those already on the ground. At peak, the loud conversation goes on nonstop morning to night. As the departure date nears, the crescendo builds to fever pitch. And then, suddenly, liftoff; like a great invisible vortex at work, the birds

DRILLING AND DEVELOPMENT:
NOT IN MY WILDLIFE MANAGEMENT AREA

While environmental rants are perhaps beyond the scope of this book, forgive me please, but I must add my two cents to a longstanding firestorm of a debate: to allow energy extractors to despoil the front or not. Almost forever it seems energy extractors and other would-be developers have been wringing their hands, scheming every which way in one attempt after another to get a foothold. The good news is most attempts have been foiled, but there have been setbacks. And the developers are, if nothing else, relentless and not about to give up the quest anytime soon. Somewhat ironically, one setback actually came at the expense of the Blackleaf WMA. Briefly, a Colorado firm conspired to drill within the WMA promising state of the art environmental and wildlife sensitivity safeguards, small footprints and all the rest of mumbo jumbo the oil and gas exploration industry is so good at. Somewhat surprisingly, given their mandate to protect sportsman's interests at all costs, FWP Commissioners agreed to allow the drilling. The drillers then negotiated the required reclamation and mitigation plan, posted a small bond, and started drilling. The resulting well produced, but shortly thereafter the firm declared bankruptcy, abandoned ship and guess who was left with the cleanup? As usual the cleanup proved extensive and costly and the remains will be noticeable for quite sometime. So much for state of the art, reclamation and mitigation plans and promises of small footprints, eh?

That another company is, at this very moment, trying its damnedest to take over the lease should not come as a surprise to anyone. The good news is the current commission is, this time around, standing firm — so far, so good anyway, and we can only hope.

begin to fly off, circling higher and higher until just whirling specks against the blue sky. So high, to the unaided eye, the birds often disappear, their location noted only with the aid of binoculars or by the continued loud calling. Still spinning, the flocks begin to drift south, soon the cries diminish and the birds are gone for the winter. By nightfall, the day of the big liftoff, except for perhaps a straggler or two, the fields are empty.

That is, until sometime in March or early April when the first sandhills show up and ...

Upon entering the Blackleaf WMA, a prominent sign reminds us that while the county road remains open year round, the WMA itself is still closed to human intrusion until May 15 to protect the wintering elk and deer herd. As if on cue, just inside the boundary line, we spy several bands of grazing mule deer. This day, there are no elk to be seen but signs of their presence are everywhere, including tracks and even some shed elk hair on the leftover snow banks and debarked trees beside the road. Perhaps the early thaw and unusually warm last weeks of winter have pushed the big deer to higher ground.

Expect to see elk and deer from the county road during winter with binoculars or spotting scope. Bears are reclusive by nature and rarely easy to see even in spring and summer; the best chance is early and late in the day along streams or forest edges. During spring, summer and fall, when bears are most likely to be on the prowl, it pays to be "bear aware." Don't travel alone and avoid thickets and other places to prevent surprise encounters. Being sneaky is not the best idea, so anywhere grizzlies are a possibility, make noise. Keep an eye peeled for fresh sign, droppings, tracks, signs of bears feeding and do not under any circumstances investigate "dead smells." All bears are known to be extremely jealous when it comes to guarding food sources. Birds, coyotes, beavers, muskrats and other small fur-bearers are of course easier and much safer to observe.

The Front is a haven for plant diversity; rare flowering plants such as the corralroot orchid and several varieties of primrose are out there for the keen observer. So too are uncommon wildlife species such as the northern bog lemming.

In all more than 700 plant species, as well as 290 species of wildlife live on the front: 190 birds, 72 mammals, 13 fish, eight amphibians, and seven reptiles.

The front is home to the state's largest elk herd and more bighorn sheep, 600 to 700 head, than anywhere in the country.

Among the 190 bird species found on the front, there are at least 21 species of raptors, including nine species of owl and some of the densest concentrations of golden eagles anywhere.

Fourteen species of duck and six species of grebe are known to breed here. Sandhill cranes, "a living fossil," migrate along the front, as do trumpeter swans, curlews, white-faced ibis. The state's only white-tailed ptarmigan are found at highest elevations.

Among the bird species are many listed as vulnerable or threatened; species such as common loon, trumpeter swan, Harlequin duck, greater sage grouse, piping plover, mountain plover, least tern, flammulated owl, burrowing owl, black-backed woodpecker, olive-sided flycatcher, brown creeper, Sprague's pipit, Baird's sparrow, horned grebe, white-faced ibis, Barrow's goldeneye, hooded merganser, bald eagle, northern goshawk, ferruginous hawk, peregrine falcon, long-billed curlew, marbled godwit, Franklin's gull, Caspian tern, common tern, Forster's tern, black tern, black-billed cuckoo, yellow-billed cuckoo, black swift, Vaux's swift, calliope hummingbird, Lewis's woodpecker, red-headed woodpecker, red-naped sapsucker, Williamson's sapsucker, American three-toed woodpecker, pileated woodpecker, willow flycatcher, Hammond's flycatcher, cordilleran flycatcher, winter wren, veery, loggerhead shrike, red-eyed vireo, Lazuli bunting, Brewer's sparrow, lark bunting, grasshopper sparrow, McCown's longspur, chestnut-collared longspur, black rosy-finch, pinyon jay, and Cassin's finch.

Beyond the open grasslands, the landscape is dominated by stunted limber pine and quaking aspen thickets. Straight trees are scarce. The norm is twisted and bent, grotesquely sculpted by the near constant wind. The front is famous for its ferocious gales. How ferocious? Well, that one's a bit hard to fully grasp until you've actually been blasted. This is serious wind and it blows here more days than not. Wind capable of flattening your tent, upsetting your camper trailer, wind has been known to topple 18-wheelers, even train cars. Sorry, that's not a typo.

Volcano Reef

The road ends at the base of the front itself, the magnificent Sawtooth Range, at the mouth of a rugged canyon where sheer limestone rock walls soar skyward for several hundred feet. Actually the elevation jumps abruptly from around 4,700 to over 8,000 feet; even "awesome" understates the effect. The scene is unrivaled and unique even in a landscape as varied and spectacular as Montanans are used to.

Following a narrow trail into the canyon (good to go since the canyon itself is outside the WMA boundary) we are immediately struck by the force of water it must have taken to carve such a groove in solid rock. At the moment, Blackleaf Creek is a mere trickle, as snow in the high country is not even thinking of melting this early. Though it doesn't take much of an imagination to picture what the creek will look like once it does.

"What the hell sort of force does it take to roll rocks (the size of small houses) like those, or build such log jams?" I asked my wife, Gale.

"Pretty big I guess," she replied with a shrug, and continued up the trail.

The front is the last place where grizzlies still regularly move between the mountains and the high plains. The WMA and surrounding lands are critical to grizzly (and black) bear survival and well-being. Despite the rather healthy numbers of a slowly-but-surely increasing population, bears are shy and secretive, and sightings occur infrequently. Your best (or worst) shot occurs along the stream corridors and edges where grassland and trees collide. Sows with cubs are particularly dangerous and should never be approached for any reason.

Under the heading, "Do as I say, not as I once so foolishly did": Upon spying a sow with two small cubs from a great distance, I thought, why not get closer to snap a few photos. The bears were in a long open grassy park between two fingers of dark timber; the edge of one finger appeared perfect so I went for it.

Still quite a ways off from good photo range, the wind suddenly did a 180. Just like that the sow quit grazing and charged my way — her direct manner left no doubt she'd caught a whiff of the hated man-scent and was determined to do something about it.

Her obvious intent didn't register right away, as she was still 300 to 400 yards off. But when she just kept coming, at some point it dawned she might really be serious and I might really be in serious trouble.

So enlightened, I turned tail and beat my feet back into the trees, headed fast back to where I should have stayed in the beginning. Apparently I lucked out or maybe she was bluffing all along. Either way, when I broke out of the timber and looked, the bear family was nowhere to be seen. Needless to say, I have not stalked a grizzly, near or far, since.

Nearby Arod (Eyraud) Lakes WPA is an 800-acre unit located about 15 miles northeast of Choteau in Teton County. To get there head east out of Choteau on the Dutton Highway, MT 221, turn north on the paved Farmington Road, MT 220; turn east onto a gravel road at the first Fishing Access Sign. Then follow the signs at all the major turns as the country road winds eastward to the lake complex. The WPA is deemed a significant sight for monitoring water birds.

According to USFS archives, "The WPA was established in 1993 when the land was purchased from area farmers, the WPA encompasses three main lakes and several smaller ponds and canals, surrounding wetlands and uplands. The main lake is dubbed Arod (Eyraud) Lake while the other two larger bodies are Middle and Round Lakes.

"More than 500 acres have been seeded to a dense nesting cover of tall wheatgrass, intermediate wheatgrass, alfalfa and sweet clover. The primary management goal for the area is to provide breeding and migration habitat for migratory birds. Secondarily, the area is designed to provide year-round recreational opportunities for bird watching, game and bird hunting (non-toxic shot is required) and fishing. There are designated parking areas and dogs must be leashed except during the hunting season.

"Wildlife includes a wide variety of waterfowl, pheasants, Huns, and mule and white-tailed deer. The area also enjoys large concentrations of snow geese in the spring of the year and high numbers of ring-billed and California gulls. Double-crested cormorants, Canada geese, white pelicans and gulls nest each spring on several islands on the main lake."

Toilet facilities are available and information signs posted throughout the area explain access, road use, hunting and fishing regulations.

Arod Lake is popular among locals year around for northern pike fishing. Ice fishing is especially popular; anglers are allowed six unattended lines (setlines) with two hooks per line to be used to fish through the ice only. Spearing is allowed for northern pike and non-game fish through the ice only.

For more information, contact Benton Lake National Wildlife Refuge, 922 Bootlegger Trail, Great Falls, MT 59404; 727-7400.

Nearby Restaurants and Accommodations

In Choteau, we have enjoyed good food and friendly services at John Henry's (466-5642), the Log Cabin (466-2888) and the Outpost Deli (466-5330). The Stage Stop Inn (466-5900) is the town's newest motel; clean, friendly and reasonable (it works for us).

Camping is allowed on the WMA but there are no amenities; Bynum Reservoir provides individual sites with picnic table, fire ring and vault toilets. The BLM maintains a picnic ground at the Ear Mountain Outstanding Natural Area, just north of the Ear Mountain WMA and there are several campgrounds along the Teton River within the Lewis and Clark National Forest.

Fast Facts

Contact Info: MT FWP, Region 4, 4600 Giant Springs Rd., Great Falls, MT 59405; Phone: 454-5840; E-mail: fwprg42@state.mt.us

Getting There: US 89 north Choteau, turn off on Black Leaf Road at Bynum, WMA is 15 miles west on a pretty good gravel road.

Activities: Closed to visitation Dec. 1 to May 15; walk-in only to Antelope Reservoir, May 15-July 1; wildlife viewing, birding, hiking, biking, camping, hunting for big game (special permits required, check the regulations) and upland birds; limited waterfowl.

Principle Mammals: Elk, mule and white-tailed deer, black and grizzly bears, beaver, muskrat, coyote.

Mammals of Special Interest: Elk, mule deer and grizzly bear.

Principle Birdlife: Primo habitat lures a variety of raptors, shorebirds, songbirds and waterfowl, in addition to upland game birds such as Hungarian partridge, ruffed, blue and sharp-tailed grouse.

Birds of Special Interest: Broad-tailed hummingbird, dickcissel, black and white warbler.

Habitat Overview: Mix of open grasslands, wetlands and stunted pine and aspen thickets.

Flora of Special Interest: Wind-sculpted limber pine, aspen and willow stands.

Best Wildlife Viewing Ops: Winter, spring and summer, early and late in the day.

Best Birding Ops: Spring and summer, dawn and dusk.

Best Photo Ops: Winter, spring and summer for wildlife; year around scenic opportunities.

Hunting Ops: White-tailed deer, mule deer, elk, bear, upland game birds and waterfowl are open to licensed hunters during regular seasons. Permits apply, check regulations.

Fishing Ops: None within WMA, nearby Bynum Reservoir, however, is a popular spot.

Camping Ops: None developed, primitive camping allowed within the WMA.

Boating Ops: None within the WMA, nearby Bynum Reservoir allows boats with motors.

Hiking Trails: None developed; hiking opportunities abound on game trails, roads and two tracks.

Motor Trails: Vehicles allowed on designated roads and two-tracks, no off-road vehicle access.

Canada Goose

Benton Lake National Wildlife Refuge

12,383 ACRES; LOCATED APPROXIMATELY 10 MILES NORTH OF GREAT FALLS

Ice out, which usually occurs from mid-March to the beginning of April, signals the start of the waterfowl migration. Dabblers such as mallards, pintails, Canada geese and tundra swans are among the early birds. Soon after several, hundreds to many thousands of snow geese join in and the show begins. Depending on conditions, snow geese may hang around for several days to two weeks or more. Raptors, a variety of hawks, bald eagles, ospreys and peregrine falcons show up, and as the season advances, more and more bird species arrive — waterfowl, shorebirds and wading birds. Shorebirds are the last to arrive in early summer.

Canada geese broods come off in late April; duck broods by late May. Early spring is the best time to observe crowing pheasants and sharp-tailed grouse performing ritual courtship dances on traditional leks. For sharp-tail lovers, the refuge offers a free viewing blind (fondly nicknamed "The Grouse House") in April and May (reservations required). Richardson's ground squirrels, white-tailed jackrabbits and muskrats are commonly observed mammals.

Benton Lake is not really a lake, rather a 5,000-acre shallow wetland carved by a glacier 10,000 years ago. In 1885, the government looked upon Benton Lake as a valuable irrigation resource, and excluded the entire basin from homesteading. The plan proved somewhat flawed and was soon abandoned. Later, local businessmen again tried to exploit the basin, converting it to croplands. The plan called for a drainage ditch, 26 feet deep and over 1.5 miles long, but when that too failed the project was abandoned.

As settlement spread, sportsmen saw the wetlands as a valuable wildlife resource and urged then President Hoover to consider adding Benton Lake to the ever-expanding federal "refuge and breeding grounds" program. In 1929, he ordered it done and signed the papers. However, the ensuing years were more dry than wet, so in 1957, members of the Cascade County Wildlife Association took steps to transform the basin into the consistently wet marsh it is today. A pipeline and pump station brought water from Muddy Creek and a dike system installed was to allow for more sophisticated water regulation. Subsequent improvements allow refuge staff to maintain water levels within the various units at optimum levels for growing aquatic plants.

The uplands are intensively managed to provide optimum habitat for ground nesting birds and other wildlife. The ten-year rotation calls for a mix of haying, burning, grazing and reseeding as necessary.

Obviously, all this manipulation is working as spring and fall migrations typically attract 150,000 ducks, 50,000 shorebirds, 40,000 snow geese, 5,000 tundra swans, 2,500 Canada geese, and countless raptors and other migrants. About 20,000 ducks are produced each season and active Franklin's gull nests alone typically approach 10,000. Ninety of the 240 bird species listed are confirmed nesters, and there are 28 species of mammals known to use the refuge. Just a few reptiles and amphibians and only one species of small minnow call the refuge home.

Benton Lake is just one of many thousands of "potholes" created in the last ice age (about 10,000 years ago). Stretching east from here to the Dakotas, these potholes produce the vast majority of North American waterfowl.

In 1975, the Benton Lake Wetlands Management District (WMD) was established. Today, the WMD encompasses 25,000 square miles in ten counties, comprising the largest WMD in the country. Since the WMD's inception, 22 Waterfowl Production Areas (WPAs) varying in size from 80 to 3,700 acres or 16,000 acres total of productive waterfowl habitat have been protected for now, and to ensure that future generations can enjoy waterfowl and wildlife as we do today. In addition, more than 10,000 acres of wetlands and 41,000 acres of grasslands are protected through conservation easements. By the way, every dollar spent comes from the sale of Federal Duck Stamps purchased each year by hunters, collectors and concerned citizens.

Although wetlands (WPAs) are primarily for waterfowl, a surprising diversity of wildlife uses them. On the Blackfoot WPA, for example, sandhill cranes nest, as do bald eagles, beavers thrive and elk winter. Among other wildlife, Jarina WPA boasts mountain lions, grizzly bears and even the occasional gray wolf, and raptors abound at Kingsbury Lake WPA. And the beat, as they say, goes on: 7,300 acres native prairie, 3,000 acres former cropland converted back to native grassland or dense nesting cover, countless acres of wetlands restored, rejuvenated and replenished. The wildlife benefits, as do people.

Let me count the ways: Healthy wetlands store water, slow spring runoff, prevent flooding, purify water by absorbing excess nutrients, reducing sediments and serve as rendering plants for chemical and organic wastes. Stored water eventually ends up in the ground water system but also serves to replenish drought stricken livestock and croplands. Still, despite the fact that wetlands are a vital cog in the natural process, more than 56 percent of the nation's wetlands have been drained in the name of "progress." Hopefully, thanks to WMDs and WPAs, that trend is now a dead-end street. The present and future powers that be, will realize protection of remaining wetlands is hugely beneficial for everyone, not just for duck hunters and wildlife lovers. All WPAs within the district are open to wildlife observation and photography — all but Sands and H2O are open to hunting, trapping and fishing. Foot access only and no fires or camping, in accordance with Montana law. Some WPAs are closed seasonally to protect nesting birds.

Nearby Restaurants and Accommodations

Bert and Ernies Saloon and Grill, 453-0601
5th Street Diner, 727-1962; Daily Grind, 452-4529
Kickers Eatery and Grill, 453-5292
The Breaks, 453-5980
Blackfoot River Cabin, Great Falls, 453-4145
Great Falls Inn, 453-6000
Missouri RV, Great Falls, 761-7524.
Great Falls, Montana's third largest city, obviously the above listings are just a start.

Fast Facts

Contact Info: Benton Lake NWR, 922 Bootlegger Trail, Great Falls, MT 59404; Phone: 727-7400 Fax: 727-7432 e-mail:bentonlake@fws.gov

Getting There: US 87, one mile north of Great Falls turn north on Bootlegger Trail (MT 225) approximately nine miles to refuge headquarters.

Activities: Wildlife viewing, bird watching (sharp-tailed grouse viewing blind), Auto tour route, hiking, hunting waterfowl (handicap accessible blind) and upland birds in designated areas; no big game hunting; ice skating and cross-country skiing as conditions warrant.

Principle Mammals: Mountain cottontail, white-tailed jackrabbit, Richardson's ground squirrel, muskrat, coyote, white-tailed deer.

Mammals of Special Interest: None.

Principle Birdlife: 243 species, including waterfowl, wading birds, shorebirds, songbirds, upland game birds and birds of prey; nearly 70 of which are known to nest on the refuge.

Birds of Special Interest: Peregrine falcon, bald eagle.

Habitat Overview: Prairie wetlands surrounded by native shortgrass prairie surrounded yet again by croplands.

Flora of Special Interest: Associated native shortgrass prairie forbs, grasses and wildflowers.

Best Wildlife Viewing Ops: Year round, early and late in day.

Best Birding Ops: Tens of thousands waterfowl and other migrants descend upon the refuge in spring and fall.

Best Photo Ops: Spring and fall migration, beginning as early as mid March (ice out).

Hunting Ops: Excellent waterfowl, upland birds (pheasant, sharp-tailed grouse, Huns); waterfowl hunting closes Nov. 30, non-toxic shot only. Area restrictions apply, check in first.

Fishing Ops: None.

Camping Ops: None.

Boating Ops: None.

Hiking Trails: Marsh boardwalk.

Motor Trails: Prairie Marsh Wildlife Drive, nine miles with interpretive signs along the way.

Benton Lake Bird List

*Denotes birds known to nest on refuge

LOONS

Common loon

GREBES

Horned grebe
Pied-billed grebe*
Red-necked grebe
Eared grebe*
Western grebe*
Clark's grebe

PELICANS

American white pelican

CORMORANTS

Double-crested cormorant*

BITTERNS, HERONS, AND IBIS

American bittern*
Great blue heron

Snowy egret
Black-crowned night-heron*
White-faced ibis*

SWANS, GEESE, AND DUCKS

Tundra swan (whistling swan)
Trumpeter swan
Greater white-fronted goose
Snow goose
Ross' goose
Canada goose*
Wood duck
Green-winged teal*
American black duck
Mallard*
Northern pintail*
Blue-winged teal*
Cinnamon teal*
Northern shoveler*
Gadwall*
Eurasian wigeon
American wigeon*
Canvasback*
Redhead*
Ring-necked duck
Greater scaup
Lesser scaup*
Oldsquaw
White-winged scoter
Common goldeneye
Barrow's goldeneye
Bufflehead
Hooded merganser
Common merganser
Red-breasted merganser
Ruddy duck*

HAWKS, EAGLES, AND FALCONS

Osprey
Bald eagle
Northern harrier (marsh hawk)*
Sharp-shinned hawk
Cooper's hawk
Northern goshawk
Swainson's hawk*

Red-tailed hawk
Ferruginous hawk*
Rough-legged hawk
Golden eagle
American kestrel*
Merlin
Peregrine falcon
Gyrfalcon
Prairie falcon

GALLINACEOUS BIRDS

Gray partridge*
Ring-necked pheasant*
Sharp-tailed grouse*

RAILS AND COOTS

Virginia rail
Sora*
American coot*

CRANES

Sandhill crane

SHOREBIRDS

Black-bellied plover
American golden plover (lesser gol-pl.)
Semipalmated plover
Piping plover
Killdeer*
Black-necked stilt*
American avocet*
Greater yellowlegs
Lesser yellowlegs
Solitary sandpiper
Willet*
Spotted sandpiper*
Upland sandpiper*
Whimbrel
Long-billed curlew*
Hudsonian godwit
Marbled godwit*
Ruddy turnstone
Red knot
Sanderling
Semipalmated sandpiper

Western sandpiper
Least sandpiper
Baird's sandpiper
Pectoral sandpiper
Dunlin
Stilt sandpiper
Short-billed dowitcher
Long-billed dowitcher
Common snipe
Wilson's phalarope*
Red-necked phalarope

GULLS AND TERNS

Franklin's gull*
Bonaparte's gull
Ring-billed gull*
California gull*
Sabine's gull
Common tern*
Forster's tern
Black tern*

DOVES

Rock dove
Mourning dove*

CUCKOOS

Black-billed cuckoo

OWLS

Great horned owl
Snowy owl
Burrowing owl*
Long-eared owl
Short-eared owl*
Northern saw-whet owl

GOATSUCKERS

Common nighthawk

KINGFISHERS

Belted kingfisher

WOODPECKERS

Downy woodpecker*
Northern flicker (common flicker)

FLYCATCHERS

Say's phoebe*
Western kingbird*
Eastern kingbird*

LARKS

Horned lark*

SWALLOWS

Tree swallow
Violet-green swallow
Northern rough-winged swallow
Bank swallow
Cliff swallow*
Barn swallow*

MAGPIES AND CROWS

Black-billed magpie*
American crow*

CHICKADEES

Black-capped chickadee
Mountain chickadee

NUTHATCHES

Red-breasted nuthatch

WRENS

Rock wren*
House wren*
Marsh wren*

THRUSHES

Golden-crowned kinglet
Ruby-crowned kinglet
Mountain bluebird
Townsend's solitaire
Veery
American robin*
Varied thrush

MIMIC THRUSHES

Gray catbird
Northern mockingbird
Brown thrasher

PIPITS

American pipit (water pipit)
Sprague's pipit

WAXWINGS

Bohemian waxwing
Cedar waxwing

SHRIKES

Northern shrike
Loggerhead shrike

STARLINGS

European starling

WARBLERS

Orange-crowned warbler
Yellow warbler
Yellow-rumped warbler
American redstart
Macgillivray's warbler
Common yellowthroat*
Wilson's warbler

TANAGERS

Western tanager

SPARROWS

Rufous-sided towhee
American tree sparrow
Chipping sparrow
Clay-colored sparrow*
Brewer's sparrow
Vesper sparrow
Lark sparrow
Lark bunting*
Savannah sparrow*
Baird's sparrow*
Grasshopper sparrow*

Song sparrow
White-crowned sparrow
Harris' sparrow
Dark-eyed junco
Mccown's longspur*
Lapland longspur
Chestnut-collared longspur*
Snow bunting

BLACKBIRDS AND ORIOLES

Bobolink
Red-winged blackbird*
Western meadowlark*
Yellow-headed blackbird*
Rusty blackbird
Brewer's blackbird*
Common grackle
Brown-headed cowbird*
Northern oriole

FINCHES

Rosy finch
Red crossbill
Common redpoll
House finch
Pine siskin
American goldfinch

WEAVER FINCHES

House sparrow*

ACCIDENTALS

Mute swan
Black scoter
Surf scoter
Garganey
Green-backed heron
Great egret
Curlew sandpiper
Parasitic jaeger
Long-tailed jaeger
White-winged dove
American dipper
Cattle egret

Golden Eagle

Ear Mountain Outstanding Natural Area

3,047 ACRES IN WESTERN TETON COUNTY, 22 MILES WEST OF CHOTEAU, 75 MILES NORTHWEST OF GREAT FALLS

From Choteau turn east toward the Rocky Mountain Front and the first thing you see is Ear Mountain; prime candidate it would seem for Mega Hedron of Teton County, if it weren't for the many other prominent escarpments dotting the skyline of the front. A.B. Guthrie Jr. credits fur trappers of the early 1800s with naming the formation "Elephant's Ear." To me the ear comparison is more the product of a vivid imagination than real likeness, but I harbor little doubt travelers like us forever have used the "ear" as a point of reference. Indians supposedly went there to fast, and again Guthrie tells us it "appears in countless tales and writings of the fur trade, grizzly conflicts; life and death and isolation involved in surviving the often brutal front environment, told and retold around countless campfires and hearth stones within the area." Be that as it may, we, as do many others we know, find it indeed a nifty sight and an even niftier spot.

Apparently the BLM agrees wholeheartedly; and in 1986 set aside about 1,900 acres as an Outstanding Natural Area; in 1994, added a trailhead and kiosk, built a few picnic tables, added toilet facilities and a trail to help visitors interpret and further enjoy the area.

The trailhead, picnic area and kiosk are open year round. Access to the ONA itself is limited to July 2 and Dec. 14 each year. During that time you can hike, horseback or mountain bike the trail for three miles up the foothills and onto the plateau toward the "ear." In season the area is open to hunting.

Wildlife abounds, bighorn sheep, birds of prey, a variety of songbirds, elk, deer, black bears, even grizzlies, and other lesser critters are common. Lacking critters for entertainment, look down and enjoy the wild flowers or look up and take in the view,

Grizzly Bear

both are unsurpassed. The front holds the record for more golden eagle sightings in a single day than anywhere else in the country. The trail is closed from Dec. 15 through July 1 to protect raptors and other wildlife during critical periods in the life cycles.

In 1996, The Nature Conservancy set out to document the rich array of plant life on the front. Botanists studied a narrow area bounded by the Conservancy's Pine Butte Swamp Preserve (see below) and the 8,580-foot summit of Ear Mountain. The narrow transcept recorded an astonishing 682 plant species from 71 families — a third of all the plants known to exist in Montana. The diversity reflects the collision of landscapes found on the front. A transition zone sandwiched between mountains and plains features alpine highlands, limber pine and Douglas fir forests, grasslands and a unique groundwater-fed wetland habitat, known as a fen, at Pine Butte Swamp.

Any visit to the Rocky Mountain Front usually includes a variety of natural spectacles, not the least of which is wind. Wind is an almost constant companion, for many of us a troublesome nemesis. On the other hand, like a river in the sky, wind carries thousands of migrant birds, waterfowl, shorebirds, songbirds and raptors during migration. For example, hundreds of thousands of snow geese sail by during the peak migration in early spring. At the same time nearly everywhere you look are new, feathered arrivals. It is possible to count dozens upon dozens of raptors, hawks and owls of every species on any given day in May and June.

Spring rains transform the normally brown short-grass prairie into a svelt green and wildflowers bloom in numbers and colors to make even the most ardent domestic gardeners blush with envy. About the only thing missing from earlier times is the thunder of a million bison passing by ...

The ONA is more or less surrounded by wonderful places; the state owned and managed Ear Mountain WMA, the Nature Conservancy's Pine Butte Swamp Preserve and, just up the gravel road, the Conservancy owned Circle 8 ranch — a place of considerable history and a significant cog in the plan to preserve the front. The original homestead cabin on the Circle 8 was built in the 1920s. In the spring of 1930, newlyweds Alice and Kenneth Gleason arrived at the then abandoned homestead and set up housekeeping. The Great Depression looming on the horizon, the couple had way more grit than dollars in their pockets but were determined to turn the rat-infested cabin into a dude ranch. The rest, as they say, is history. In 1978, the Nature Conservancy took the reins, renamed it the Pine Butte Guest Ranch, where guests come to study nature, enjoy the scenery and solitude and just plain relax. Contact lbarhaugh@tnc.org.

Nearby Pine Butte Swamp Preserve, a unique wetland encompassing 18,000 acres along the front is also administered by the Nature Conservancy Preserve. Well over 150 species of birds, as well as bighorn sheep, elk, mule deer, moose, mountain lions and both black and grizzly bears, find forage and shelter within this rare wetland habitat.

Like a giant thumb, the preserve extends downward from Ear Mountain, taking in limber pine forests, foothills, prairie and swamp. Today, golden eagles prey on jackrabbits, awesome grizzlies pad amongst diminutive warblers flitting about dense underbrush surrounding beaver ponds. But the layered earth offers wildlife viewing of a far different ilk; a glimpse of long ago, ancient critters, times past.

Within the preserve lies Egg Mountain, where the Maiasaura dinosaur once nested. Fossil hunters discovered a series of small badlands hills that yielded the first known nests of baby dinosaurs, eggshell fragments and whole, fossilized eggs. Jack Horner and Bob Makela, of Museum of the Rockies fame, named the adult duck-billed dinosaur unearthed at that location Maiasaura peeblesorum. The first name coming from Greek and meaning 'Good mother lizard' and the second acknowledgment of the Peebles family, the local ranchers who owned the badlands up until 1987, when they sold that portion of their ranch to The Nature Conservancy. The badlands then became a part of the Conservancy's Pine Butte Swamp Preserve.

For a grand viewing vista, follow the signs to the information board, park and take a short hike up a marked trail overlooking Pine Butte. Hiking is limited in other parts of the preserve to protect bears. Contact the Nature Conservancy by phone: 443-0303. Pine Butte Swamp is located off Highway 89, west of Choteau. From Choteau, drive north on US Highway 89 for five miles. Turn west on Teton Canyon Road and follow for 17 miles. Turn south, cross the Teton River, and proceed straight for three and a half miles following signs to an information kiosk

Immature red-tailed hawk

Nearby Restaurants and Accommodations

In Choteau check out the good food and friendly services at John Henry's (466-5642), the Log Cabin (466-2888) and the Outpost Deli (466-5330). The Stage Stop Inn (466-5900), the town's newest motel, provides clean rooms, friendly service and reasonable rates. Primitive camping is allowed on the WMA but there are no amenities; Eureka Reservoir provides individual sites with picnic table, fire ring and vault toilets. The BLM maintains a picnic ground at the Ear Mountain Outstanding Natural Area, just north of the WMA and there are several campgrounds along the Teton River within the Lewis and Clark National Forest.

Fast Facts

Contact Info: MT FWP, Region 4, 4600 Giant Springs Rd., Great Falls, MT 59405; Phone: 454-5840; E-mail: fwprg42@state.mt.us

Getting There: MT 287, one half-mile south Choteau, turn west on Bellview Rd. (Pishkun Reservoir sign). Continue past turnoff to Pishkun (about five miles in) proceed about 17 miles to the WMA. No vehicle access within the WMA.

Activities: Closed to visitation Dec. 1 to May 15; wildlife viewing, birding, hiking, camping, hunting for big game — white-tailed and mule deer, elk, black bear and bighorn sheep (special permits for some species, check the regs) and upland birds.

Principle Mammals: Elk, black and grizzly bear, bighorn sheep, white-tailed and mule deer, furbearers such as beaver and muskrat, and coyotes.

Mammals of Special Interest: Mule deer, grizzly and black bears and bighorn sheep.

Principle Birdlife: Variety of songbirds, raptors and upland birds.

Birds of Special Interest: None.

Habitat Overview: Grasslands, aspen and pine forest, with several small, willow-lined stream corridors.

Flora of Special Interest: Native prairie grasses and wildflowers.

Best Wildlife Viewing Ops: Spring through summer, early and late in the day

Best Birding Ops: Spring through summer, early and late in the day

Best Photo Ops: Spring through summer, early and late in the day.

Hunting Ops: Archery and gun hunting for white-tailed and mule deer, elk, black bear and upland birds; special permits and regulations for elk and bighorn sheep.

Fishing Ops: None.

Camping Ops: Primitive camping allowed, no developed campgrounds

Boating Ops: None.

Hiking Trails: A nature trail links to the nearby BLM Outstanding Natural Area

Motor Trails: No vehicle access within the WMA.

Semipalmated sandpiper

Giant Springs Heritage State Park

3,000 ACRES; FOUR MILES FROM THE CITY CENTER OF GREAT FALLS

Sioux Indians called the Great Falls of the Missouri River Minni-Sose-Tanka-Kun-Ya. Lewis and Clark's Corps of Discovery reached the Great Falls of the Missouri on June 13, 1805. Finding water travel upstream blocked by a series of five cascades — Great Falls (the highest at about 80 feet), Colter Falls, Crooked Falls, Rainbow Falls and Black Eagle Falls — it was not until July 15 the expedition finally managed a way around to get underway once again. These days the natural falls are largely lost, replaced by concrete dams, but the area remains rich in both cultural and natural history.

The heart of the park itself is the giant spring. Clark, obviously impressed, noted, "the largest fountain or Spring I ever Saw, boils up from under the rocks near the edge of the river." One of the world's largest freshwater springs, flowing at a measured 156 million gallons per day, Giant Springs is an impressive site and sight, to say the least. The out flow is such that it is officially named North Fork Roe River; at 58 feet long, it is one of the two shortest rivers in the world. Imagine the delight of the founding fathers of Great Falls (1884) upon discovering such a bonanza, like they sure didn't have to fret about getting a drink of water.

Established as a Montana state park in the mid-1970s, Giant Springs encompasses some 3,000 acres, most of which is on the river's north bank. The remaining 400 acres or so, on the south shore where the springs are located, is the hub of the park and where most folks come to view wildlife, bird watch, sightsee, fish, picnic, or just hang out. Day use only, the park offers great opportunities to commune with nature, photograph and (don't spread it around but) the fishing isn't too shabby either. The Rivers Edge Trail leads the way to adventure. Then too, there is the spectacular Rainbow Falls overlook, the fish hatchery, visitor center and of course the recently completed Lewis and Clark Interpretive Center.

All of the water and riparian habitat attracts legions of birds. Bird watchers can expect to check off a large variety of species, including cliff swallow, western, eared

Canada goose

and red-necked grebes, Canada geese, numerous duck species, warblers, California gull, white pelican, western meadowlark, gray catbird, house wren and goldfinch to name just a few of the more common. The Christmas Bird Count, conducted by the Upper Missouri Breaks Chapter of the Audubon Society, tallied over 12,000 birds of nearly 50 species — two unusual finds were a herring gull and Townsend's solitaire. While certainly not all of the birds in the annual count are spotted at Giant Springs, many are.

Wildlife viewing of a different ilk is available at the Giant Springs Fish Hatchery. Built in 1922 to take advantage of the constant 54-degree spring water, the hatchery produces roughly 1.25 million trout annually (most rainbow trout, but chinook salmon also). The fish are stocked in lakes and reservoirs throughout the state, but as you might or might not suspect, a relative handful finds its way into the nearby river... just imagine.

The River's Edge Trail is one of many Rails To Trails springing up these days all around the state and the country. The RET is the result of a cooperative partnership effort involving, Great Falls, Cascade County, MTFWP, Montana Department of Transportation, PPL Montana (a power company), Recreational Trails, Inc. (a volunteer trail advocacy group) and the supportive community. The 25-mile trail wanders through the City of Great Falls, connecting parks and other points of interest along the Missouri River including Black Eagle Falls, Rainbow Falls, Crooked Falls and The Great Falls of the Missouri, just below Ryan Dam; 11 miles which are paved and wheelchair accessible; while 14 miles are gravel, both single and double track. The trail runs on both the north and south shores, accessed at 11 trailhead parking areas. The River's Edge Trail is free and open to non-motorized public recreation during daylight hours, year round.

Nearby Restaurants and Accommodations

Bert and Ernies Saloon and Grill, 453-0601
5th Street Diner, 727-1962
Daily Grind, 452-4529
Kickers Eatery and Grill, 453-5292
The Breaks, 453-5980
Montana's third largest city, the above listing is obviously but the tip of a large iceberg; ditto finding a bed to sleep, the possibilities are nearly endless.

Fast Facts

Contact Info: Giant Springs, 4600 Giant Springs Rd Great Falls, MT 59405; phone: 454-5840.
Getting There: From US 87 turn east on Giant Springs Road, 2 miles.
Activities: Wildlife viewing, bird watching, photography, hiking, boating, bicycling, picnicking.
Principle Mammals: Mule and white-tailed deer and a variety of small mammals including furbearers, muskrat, beaver, river otter.

Mammals of Special Interest: None.

Principle Birdlife: Waterfowl, shorebirds, wading birds, raptors, including osprey and bald eagle, a large variety of songbirds.

Birds of Special Interest: White-winged scoter in winter.

Habitat Overview: River bottom, riparian zone.

Flora of Special Interest: None.

Best Wildlife Viewing Ops: Year around opportunities.

Best Birding Ops: Numbers peak during spring and fall migrations, but the river attracts a large number of year-round residents.

Best Photo Ops: Year around opportunities, light is best early and late, especially dramatic on cold winter days.

Hunting Ops: None.

Fishing Ops: Excellent fishing opportunities for large rainbow trout and a variety of warmwater species.

Camping Ops: Day use only.

Boating Ops: Boat launch within the park.

Hiking Trails: River's Edge Trail runs for 25 miles along both shores of the Missouri River.

Motor Trails: None.

Common goldeneye

Freezeout Lake
Wildlife Management Area

11,239 ACRES IN TETON COUNTY 40 MILES WEST OF GREAT FALLS ALONG US HIGHWAY 89 BETWEEN FAIRFIELD AND CHOTEAU

Ice out. Late March. Freezeout Lake. If you have a hankering to view one of nature's finest spectacles, this is the time and place. With the ice gone, waterfowl numbering in the tens of thousands, to say nothing of the equally spectacular backdrop (the still, snow-clad peaks of the Rocky Mountain Front) makes for quite a scene. Snow geese are the headliners, but the supporting cast of legions of mallards, pintails, coots, northern shovelers, canvasbacks, tundra swans, goldeneyes, Canada geese, shorebirds and waders such as willets, marbled godwits and common snipe are particularly plentiful and vocal. I've never seen so many Wilson's phalaropes in one spot. Other highlights are yellow-headed blackbird, common yellowthroat, lark sparrow, willet, avocet, gadwall, blue-winged and cinnamon teal, savannah sparrow, black-crowned night heron (lots), horned lark, ruddy duck, bufflehead, widgeon, Forster's tern and black-necked stilt; killdeers are especially visible as are red-winged blackbirds, ringnecks (roosters crowing every direction), sharp-tailed grouse (dancing at a nearby lek) and across the road a pair of Huns settling into the still-brown grass. Meanwhile, meadow lark music adds a melodious touch to the raucous background din as flock after flock of inbound and outbound geese vie for elbow room on the increasingly crowded lake. To really get a feel for what is happening here, try camping nearby, but bring your earplugs. If you thought the daytime racket was something, wait till after dark.

Freezeout tops the list as Montana's primo, most popular birding destination. Almost any day in early spring, people come from all over to view the extravaganza. In a single day, we counted license plates from five different states and three Canadian provinces, as well as those from all over Montana.

For waterfowl, Freezeout has it all: Water, food in spades, the nearby Greenfield Bench is a huge, nearly continuous grain operation and assuming there is safety in numbers, at night huge flocks nearly cover the lake surface and, well, what more is there?

The routine is fairly straightforward, get up early, first hint of dawn signals lift off and almost as if choreographed, thousands of waterfowl take off for the nearby grain fields — by the way, barley is the favorite and wheat a distant second. After several hours of feeding, the flocks return to loaf and preen until about 4 p.m. Then its deja vu all over again: out to feed, back to the water for the night — often the return flight takes place well after dark.

Somewhat surprisingly to us amateurs, close inspection reveals Ross' geese intermingled amongst the snows. How do we know? Christopher Smith, Field Guide to Upland Birds and Waterfowl (Wilderness Adventures Press, 2000), writes, "Snows are bigger than the smaller Ross' goose, which have light pink feet and a shorter, stubbier bill with a warty base that lacks the typical grinning patch of the snow goose... Snows have scarlet feet and a longer bill with a characteristic black grinning patch." Even to our untrained eyes the Ross' wings beat faster and the book says snows are "most vocal of all waterfowl, gabbling a constant low-ow-ow-ow or high-pitched cry resembling barking dogs. Ross' geese make similar but higher pitched sounds." Somewhat tone deaf, I can honestly say this call business does little for me, although Gale says she can tell the difference. We later stopped at the headquarters and the biologist said the mix of Ross' and snow geese "had mostly to do with similar migration schedules, rather than anything like actual co-mingling for the greater good." Apparently hoping to further clarify the identification puzzle, he went on to say, "Canada geese fly in a fairly even V, while leaders change the change, is rather infrequent; whereas snows and Ross' fly in an undulating, wavy skein, frequently shifting, even sharing the lead. By the way, the Inuit call snows, 'wavys' and Ross', 'horned wavys.'"

At peak, usually toward end of March, we learned snows often top 350,000, while Ross' max out around 50,000. How long the flocks remain, several days or several weeks, depends. Occasionally the geese that depart Freezeout run into bad weather up north, thus they turn around and return. Eventually, they all find their way to nest on the increasingly ravaged (too many snows) tundra of the Arctic prairies.

Like Canada geese, snows pair for life, usually by the third year. Nesting takes place in the far north between Hudson's Bay and the Arctic Ocean, and sometimes the same nest or nest site is used over and over again by the same pair. Males are extremely aggressive around the nest, willing to take on all intruders. Females lay four or five eggs and in a brilliant ploy aimed at overwhelming predators with a flood of prey, all the eggs in a particular colony are laid, incubated and hatched within a couple hours of each other. Throughout the incubation process the gander stands guard day and night.

Without getting too far afield here: Imagine watching 400,000 white geese sitting on nests within a colony for three weeks, three days later...flat out gone. With no food left in the colony, here are these thousands and thousands of paired geese, trailing more thousands and thousands of little yellow fuzz balls, journeys often of 50 miles or more to find food.

Six weeks later, the goslings, or what's left of them, are fledged and begin the long migration trek south, a trip that involves several legs. One of the fall stops being Freezeout... maybe. Witnessing snows at Freezeout, or anywhere in Montana for that matter, in fall, is nowhere near the sure thing of seeing them in spring. In good years, usually around Halloween, snow geese peak at just over 150,000 birds. Some snows, it seems, punch non-stop, or nearly so, all the way from Arctic nesting grounds to wintering areas in south Texas and Louisiana.

Freezeout, actually more wetlands than lake, receives water from adjacent irrigated land as part of the Sun River Project. A 1986 reconnaissance study and subsequent 1990-to-1992 detailed study indicated selenium concentrations in water, bottom sediment and biota in wetlands higher than established criteria and standards, raise concerns about potential toxicity to aquatic organisms and water birds. In 1994 and 1995, a second detailed study attempted to determine the distribution, mobilization, and accumulation of selenium associated with irrigation drainage from land underlain by glacial-lake deposits within the WMA, particularly the southern portion.

The study revealed that precipitation and selenium-free irrigation water infiltrate the deposits and dissolve and mobilize selenium. Selenium-rich ground water then discharges into open irrigation drains. The irrigation drains discharge into wetlands of Freezeout Lake and Pond 5 on the WMA. In the wetlands, selenium is removed from water and accumulates in bottom sediment and biota.

Biota samples are typically higher in selenium concentrations than national-average background concentrations. Concentration increases from water and bottom sediment to biota, and from lower to higher trophic levels, indicate that selenium is bio-accumulating. In addition, most invertebrate and fish samples collected from irrigation drains that convey water from glacial-lake deposits, and from wetlands at the mouths of those drains, had selenium concentrations that exceeded the critical threshold concentration for waterfowl dietary ingestion of 5 micrograms per gram dry weight. However, the study revealed no indication of reproductive impairment in water birds nesting on the WMA. Embryo viability, as well as nest and hatching success rates, were within the expected range for healthy avian populations. Likewise, reproductive impairment was not evident in brook stickleback fish, based on abundance.

Although irrigation water is not the source of selenium, irrigation of seleniferous soils near Freezeout Lake has mobilized naturally-occurring selenium from glacial-lake deposits and made it biologically available, primarily in irrigation drains and in wetlands at the mouths of drains. Ongoing efforts to conserve irrigation water will reduce irrigation drainage and potentially could decrease biological exposure to selenium by reducing selenium loading to wetlands, but could concurrently increase selenium concentrations in irrigation drains.

At Freezeout Lake Wildlife Management Area (WMA), you'll see more camouflage jackets than blaze orange — a rarity in Montana, where big game hunting reigns supreme. The WMA was established in the early 1950s and covers almost 12,000 acres, nearly 10,000 of which are open to public shooting. In recent years, waterfowl numbers have steadily increased. Reservations are not required, and both marsh and lake hunting are available. Try ponds 1, 3, 5 and 6 in the center of the area for mallards, gadwalls and blue-winged teal. Around Halloween, snow goose populations peak at just over 150,000 birds. Set up for snows in the private fields (ask permission first) on the east side of the lake, where they feed, or pass-shoot on the WMA as they return to roost. Tundra swans can be hunted if you have a state-issued permit.

Be sure to bring your spotting scope and, if you are into photography, this is not the place to forget the big lens or skimp on film. Mule deer and antelope, while not prevalent within the WMA, abound within the area and are available for viewing along MT 287/200. This is mostly private land, and dirt roads are often impassable when wet, so heed the signs and respect private property.

Nearby Restaurants and Accommodations

John Henry's, Choteau, 466-5242
Log Cabin, Choteau, 466-2888

Outpost Deli, 466-5330
Cozy Corner Café, Fairfield, 467-2420
Pioneer Motel, Fairfield, 467-5656
Rimrock Lodge, Fairfield, 467-5885
Camp on the WMA or stay in Choteau
7 Lazy P, 466-2044
Choteau City Park, 466-2510
KOA, Choteau, 466-2615
Nature Conservancy, 466-5526
Big Sky Motel, 466-5318
Bella Vista Motel, 466-5711
Stage Stop Inn, 466-5900.

Fast Facts

Contact Info: Freezeout Lake WMA, 467-2646.
Getting There: From Helena, I-15 north to Wolf Creek, MT 287 to MT 200 to Simms, MT 500 to US 80. From Great Falls, US 89 north to just north of Fairfield.
Activities: Birding, photography, hunting, hiking.
Principle Mammals: Mule deer, pronghorn, coyote, red fox, striped skunk, muskrat.
Mammals of Special Interest: Muskrats are particularly numerous, mounds can be seen throughout.
Principle Birdlife: Snow geese, waterfowl, ringneck pheasant, Huns, shorebirds, raptors.
Birds of Special Interest: Snow geese, Franklin's gulls.
Habitat Overview: Wetlands, shallow ponds, cattail, bulrush marsh, surrounded by extensive grass and cereal grain farmlands.
Flora of Special Interest: Cattail/bulrush marsh, grasslands.
Best Wildlife Viewing Ops: Spring and fall, dawn and dusk.
Best Birding Ops: Spring and fall migration, generally mid-March to mid-April and again in October/November.
Best Photo Ops: Spring and fall migration, first and last two hours of daylight.
Hunting Ops: General public hunting for waterfowl and upland game birds. Tundra swan hunting by permit only. Muskrat trapping available for successful applicants.
Fishing Ops: None.
Camping Ops: Primitive camping on WMA at designated spots.
Boating Ops: None.
Hiking Trails: No developed trails, hiking on established auto routes and on WMA with seasonal restrictions.
Motor Trails: Auto tour route, and several auto trails open seasonally.

Freezeout Lake WMA Bird List

Loons and Grebes

Common Loon
Pied billed grebe
Horned grebe
Eared grebe
Western grebe
Clark's grebe

Pelicans

American white pelican

Cormorants

Double crested cormorant

Herons

American bittern
Great blue heron
Snowy egret
Cattle egret
Black-crowned night heron
White-faced ibis

Waterfowl

Tundra swan
Trumpeter swan
Greater white-front goose
Lesser white-front goose
Ross' goose
Canada goose
Wood duck
Green-winged teal
Mallard
Northern pintail
Blue-winged teal
Cinnamon teal
Northern shoveler
Gadwall
Eurasian wigeon
American wigeon
Canvasback
Redhead
Ring necked duck

Tufted duck
Lesser scaup
Oldsquaw
Surf scoter
White-winged scoter
Common goldeneye
Barrow's goldeneye
Bufflehead
Hooded merganser
Common merganser
Red-breasted merganser
Ruddy duck

Hawks

Osprey
Bald eagle
Northern harrier
Sharp-shinned hawk
Swainson's hawk
Red-tailed hawk
Ferruginous hawk
Rough-legged hawk
Golden eagle

Falcons

American kestrel
Merlin
Peregrine falcon
Gyrfalcon
Prairie falcon

Upland Game Birds

Gray partridge
Ringneck pheasant
Sharp-tailed grouse
Blue grouse
Ruffed grouse

Rails and Coots

Virginia rail
Sora
American coot

Cranes

Sandhill crane

Plovers

Black-bellied plover
American golden plover
Snowy plover
Semipalmated plover
Killdeer

Sandpipers

Black-necked stilt
American avocet
Greater yellowlegs
Lesser yellowlegs
Solitary sandpiper
Willet
Spotted sandpiper
Upland sandpiper
Whimbrel
Long-billed curlew
Hudsonian godwit
Marbled godwit
Ruddy turnstone
Red knot
Sanderling
Semipalmated sandpiper
Western sandpiper
Least sandpiper
Baird's sandpiper
Pectoral sandpiper
Dunlin
Stilt sandpiper
Long-billed dowitcher
Common snipe
Wilson's phalarope
Red-necked phalarope
Red phalarope

Gulls and Terns

Parasitic jaeger
Franklin's gull
Bonaparte's gull
Ring billed gull
California gull
Herring gull
Glaucous gull
Sabine's gull
Caspian tern
Common tern
Forster's tern
Black tern

Pigeons

Rock dove
Mourning dove

Owls

Great horned owl
Snowy owl
Burrowing owl
Long eared owl
Short eared owl

Goatsuckers

Common nighthawk

Woodpeckers

Hairy woodpecker
Northern flicker

Flycatchers

Western wood peewee
Least flycatcher
Say's phoebe
Western kingbird
Eastern kingbird

Larks

Horned lark

Swallows

Tree swallow
Violet-green swallow
Rough winged swallow
Bank swallow
Cliff swallow
Barn swallow

Crows

Black-billed magpie
American crow
Common raven

Tits, Nuthatches and Tree Creepers

Red-breasted nuthatch

Wrens

House wren
Marsh wren

Kinglets

Ruby crowned kinglet

Thrushes

Mountain bluebird
Townsend's solitaire
Swainson's thrush
American robin
Brown thrasher

Wagtails and Pipits

American pipit
Sprague's pipit

Waxwings

Bohemian waxwing
Cedar waxwing

Shrikes

Northern shrike
Loggerhead shrike

Starlings

European starling

Vireos

Warbling vireo
Red-eyed vireo

Warblers

Yellow warbler

Yellow-rumped warbler
American redstart
Common yellowthroat
Wilson's warbler

Sparrows and Finches

Chipping sparrow
Tree sparrow
Clay-colored sparrow
Vesper sparrow
Lark sparrow
Lark bunting
Savannah sparrow
Baird's sparrow
Grasshopper sparrow
Song sparrow
Lincoln's sparrow
White-throated sparrow
White-crowned sparrow
Harris sparrow
Dark-eyed junco
McCown's longspur
Lapland longspur
Chestnut-collared longspur
Snow bunting
Gray-crowned rosy finch
House finch
Common redpoll
Pine siskin
American goldfinch

New World Blackbirds

Bobolink
Red-winged blackbird
Yellow-headed blackbird
Brewer's blackbird
Bullock's oriole

Old World Weavers

House sparrow

Yellow-bellied marmot

Sluice Boxes State Park

1,454 ACRES; 15 MILES SOUTH OF BELT IN THE LITTLE BELT MOUNTAINS

Montana's mining history is a series of boom and bust towns; connected by railroads of similar fate, good as long as the ore held out. Such was the story of the mining towns of Monarch, Neihart, Hughesville and Albright, in the Little Belt Mountains south of Great Falls and the rails that once connected them. Today, Monarch and Neihart remain, though just barely, Hughesville and Albright are ghost towns and the only train whistles are in your dreams.

On Belt Creek, the silver boom was short lived, just a couple of years, but various mining operations continued until1943; the railroad dissolved soon after. While the trains are long gone, these days the railroad bed provides walking access to Sluice Boxes State Park. Established in 1970, the park consists of the upper most eight miles of rugged Belt Creek Canyon, features towering, vertical rock cliffs and ledges, dense coniferous forest, with impassable tangled willow, cottonwood, chokecherry, wild rose and assorted brambles. To make foot travel worse, the bridges, like the rails, are all gone and to negotiate the trail requires fording the creek several times — in other words, hiking is pretty much cancelled during high water. Runoff can run into July and because the water is always cold, it's a good idea to come prepared during any season. Beware, too, of the quickly changing weather due to the elevation. For the adventurous, the rewards are spectacular scenery, abundant wildlife and, if trout are your bag, decent trout fishing. Although, aquatic habitat conditions are somewhat unstable in Belt Creek due to land-use and abuse activities, such as mining, railroad and road building, logging and so forth. There are no facilities beyond the Riceville Bridge trailhead (bottom end).

Interesting to note, the basic geology is limestone. Limestone is characterized by sinks and faults. As Belt Creek flows downhill much of the flow is lost underground and a lot of that eventually spills out at Giant Springs (Great Falls). Some of it, however, ends up in Manitoba.

Hairy woodpecker

Along the creek, look for black-capped and mountain chickadee, red-breasted nuthatch, winter wren, a variety of warblers, including common yellowthroat and yellow-rumped and MacGillivray's warblers, red crossbill, calliope hummingbird, red-naped sapsucker, dusky flycatcher, gray catbird, ovenbird, ruby-crowned kinglet, dipper, a variety of birds of prey including eagles and osprey and the rarely seen (in these parts) great gray owl and blue grouse to name just a few of the many possibilities.

Nearby Restaurants and Accommodations

Belt Creek Café, 277-3361
Harvest Moon Brew Pub, Belt, 277-3188
There are no motels closer than Great Falls, check out the Blackfoot River Cabin, Great Falls, 453-4145
Great Falls Inn, 453-6000
Showdown Ski Area, 727-5553
Missouri RV, Great Falls, 761-7524
Camping is allowed in the Park backcountry and the surrounding Lewis and Clark National Forest.

Peregrine falcon

Fast Facts

Contact Info: Sluice Boxes State Park, MTFWP, 4600 Giant Springs Rd., Great Falls, MT. 59405; phone: 454-5840.

Getting There: US 89; 15 miles south of Belt (southeast from Great Falls); turn west at the sign a half mile up and take Evans -Riceville Road to trailhead. To reach the top end (Logging Creek Bridge), continue on Evans-Riceville Road to Lick Creek Road to Meade Ranger Station, and turn east (left) on Logging Creek Rd.

Activities: Wildlife viewing, birding, photography, hiking, fishing, picnicking, camping, kayaking, mountain biking, and rock climbing.

Principle Mammals: Mule and white-tailed deer, beaver, muskrat, bobcat, black bear, elk, moose, a variety of bats frequent the area's many limestone caves.

Mammals of Special Interest: None.

Principle Birdlife: Bald and golden eagle, osprey, a variety of owls and raptors, forest dwelling songbirds, dipper and waterfowl, mainly puddle ducks, such as mallard and teal.

Birds of Special Interest: None.

Habitat Overview: Rugged limestone canyon, vertical cliffs, dense coniferous forest; willow, cottonwood, chokecherry, and wild roses grow along it in scattered spots in the canyon and in a continuous band up to a quarter mile wide.

Flora of Special Interest: None.

Best Wildlife Viewing Ops: Opportunities year around, beside the creek and the surrounding uplands.

Best Birding Ops: Opportunities year around, neotropical migrants in spring and fall during migration.

Best Photo Ops: Year around, early and late in day affords best light.

Hunting Ops: Hunting according to Montana game law; somewhat restricted by the rugged landscape.

Fishing Ops: Brook, brown and rainbow trout; mountain whitefish. Open year around from Riceville Bridge downstream.

Camping Ops: Primitive camping allowed in backcountry only; stay length 7 days.

Boating Ops: Popular kayaking spot.

Hiking Trails: Trail begins at Riceville Bridge and ends at Logging Creek Bridge, length 7.5 miles.

Motor Trails: None.

Sun River Wildlife Management Area

20,199 ACRES; IN LEWIS AND CLARK COUNTY,
APPROXIMATELY NINE MILES NORTHWEST OF AUGUSTA

Established in 1913, the Sun River Preserve was Montana's first attempt at providing a safe haven for wildlife, mainly elk and other big game. In 1947, the name was changed to Sun River Game Range, and the purpose was changed to primarily provide winter range for migrating elk and other big game species from the high country of the Bob Marshall Wilderness. Today, it is still called Sun River Game Range but its official designation is Sun River Wildlife Management Area. MTFWP completed the first of

nine land purchases in 1948, with the last in 1974. The goal of the WMA is to maintain and improve habitat diversity and quality for elk and other wildlife, both game and non-game species and to provide hunting and wildlife-viewing opportunities.

While the WMA is closed to human visitation Dec. 1 to May 15, wildlife can be viewed from the county road; including many of the several hundred elk that winter here. The rest of the year, look for a variety of big game, smaller mammals, furbearers and countless bird species — waterfowl, raptors, owls, songbirds and upland game birds. You name it, odds are good it's around somewhere.

Excellent fishing can be enjoyed on the Sun River, on several smaller creeks and lakes and on nearby Willow Creek Reservoir (a popular spot among locals). Hiking on the WMA during summer and early fall is also a popular activity as is mountain biking on designated roads and trails. Primitive camping is allowed on the WMA, though no off-road vehicle travel is allowed anytime.

Nearby Restaurants and Accommodations

Sun Canyon Lodge and Restaurant, 562-3654
Bunkhouse Inn, Augusta, 562-3654
Log Cabin Family Restaurant, Choteau, 466-2888
Buckhorn, Augusta, 562-3344
Ford Creek Resort, 562-3670.

Fast Facts

Contact Info: Montana Fish, Wildlife and Parks, 4600 Giant Springs Road, Great Falls, MT 59405; phone: 454-5840.

Getting There: From Augusta, take the Gibson Reservoir/Sun Canyon Road northwest approximately 3.5 miles. Where the road forks, take the left fork and proceed west 5 miles to the WMA. Vehicles may enter at the southeast corner of the WMA or 2.5 miles farther west at Swayze Lake. The WMA can also be accessed (walk-in only) at several turnoffs along the Gibson Reservoir Road. Closed to all visitation Dec. 1 to May 15.

Activities: Wildlife viewing, birding, hunting, hiking, camping, fishing.

Principle Mammals: Elk, mule and white-tailed deer, black bear, coyote, badger.

Mammals of Special Interest: One of the largest elk herds in Montana winters on the WMA.

Principle Birdlife: Mountain grouse and a variety of songbirds and waterfowl.

Birds of Special Interest: None.

Habitat Overview: A mix of rolling grasslands and coniferous timber.

Flora of Special Interest: None.

Best Wildlife Viewing Ops: A variety of game and non-game species may be viewed from May 15 to December 1. Large numbers of elk can usually be observed from the county road during the winter months.

Best Birding Ops: Peak times for birding include spring and fall migrations.

Best Photo Ops: From May 15-Dec. 1, early and late in day.

Hunting Ops: Elk hunting during the archery season. Antlerless elk and antelope hunting by permit only. Mule deer, white-tailed deer, black bear, and grouse hunting during archery and general seasons outside the Dec. 1 - May 15 closure. Limited waterfowl hunting for both ducks and Canada geese.

Fishing Ops: Swayze Creek, Barr and Dickens Lake afford angling opportunities within the WMA, the Sun River forms the northern boundary and nearby is Willow Creek Reservoir, a popular spot among locals.

Camping Ops: Allowed except for closed season, Dec. 1-May 15.

Boating Ops: Small craft can be used on the two lakes, Barr and Dickens, no motors.

Hiking Trails: None developed; otherwise hiking is pretty much unlimited except for the closed season.

Motor Trails: Vehicles may enter at the southeast corner of the WMA or 2.5 miles farther west at Swayze Lake; no off road driving allowed.

Elk herd

Sun River Specialty Bird List

There about 190 species of birds found along the Rocky Mountain Front, including 21 species of raptors, nine species of owl and some of the densest concentrations of golden eagles anywhere. Fourteen species of duck and six species of grebe are known to breed here. Sandhill cranes migrate along the front as do trumpeter swans, curlews and white-faced ibis; the state's only white-tailed ptarmigan are found at highest elevations. The following list contains some of the less common species you are likely to encounter at Sun River WMA.

Common loon
Trumpeter swan
Harlequin duck
Piping plover
Mountain plover
Least tern
Flammulated owl
Burrowing owl
Black-backed woodpecker
Olive-sided flycatcher
Brown creeper
Sprague's pipit
Baird's sparrow
Horned grebe
White-faced ibis
Barrow's goldeneye
Hooded merganser
Bald eagle
Northern goshawk
Ferruginous hawk
Peregrine falcon
Long-billed curlew
Marbled godwit
Franklin's gull
Caspian tern
Common tern
Forster's tern
Black tern

Black-billed cuckoo
Yellow-billed cuckoo
Black swift
Vaux's swift
Calliope hummingbird
Lewis' woodpecker
Red-headed woodpecker
Red-naped sapsucker
Williamson's sapsucker
American three-toed woodpecker
Pileated woodpecker
Willow flycatcher
Hammond's flycatcher
Cordilleran flycatcher
Winter wren
Veery
Loggerhead shrike
Red-eyed vireo
Lazuli bunting
Brewer's sparrow
Lark bunting
Grasshopper sparrow
McCown's longspur
Chestnut-collared longspur
Black rosy-finch
Pinyon jay
Sprague's pipit
Cassin's Finch

Upper Missouri Breaks National Monument

377,346 ACRES IN CENTRAL MONTANA LOCATED NORTH AND SOUTH OF THE WILD AND SCENIC MISSOURI RIVER GENERALLY DOWNSTREAM OF THE CONFLUENCE OF EAGLE CREEK (APPROXIMATELY 20 MILES SOUTH OF BIG SANDY) TO THE WESTERN BOUNDARY OF THE CHARLES M. RUSSELL NATIONAL WILDLIFE REFUGE (JUST WEST OF THE FRED ROBINSON BRIDGE (US 191)).

Established in 2001 the monument is a vast landscape, much of which lies virtually unchanged since Lewis and Clark's monumental 1805 Voyage of Discovery. Like the CMR NWR, this is a rugged land; at times and in places it reminds one more of a moonscape than anything resembling what I would imagine most of us picture in our minds as 21st Century America. Largely unpopulated and with just a handful of all-weather roads like the CMR the monument is home to some 260 birds and 60 mammals — except for bison, grizzly bears and gray wolves, essentially everything Lewis and Clark laid eyes on is still a possibility today. Any birder and/or wildlife viewer with a bit of adventure in the soul is likely to think he died and went to heaven. Those I know call it "paradise; truly, the last best place."

Administered by the BLM, the mix of river bottoms and upland breaks provide birds and other wildlife ideal, intact habitat to go about their lives largely undisturbed, by humans except for perhaps hunting season. Within its boundaries are six Wilderness Study Areas (WSAs) which, depending how the Congressional winds blow, might someday add even more luster to its wild, remote and beautiful facade.

While most consider the monument one of those all-too-rare (it seems these days) "giant steps for mankind," the signing on the dotted line did not pencil out all the threats. Boundary hassles and adjustments are ongoing and some not likely to be settled anytime soon. The oil and gas industry continues to lobby to explore within the boundaries. This despite the fact the largest area with oil and gas potential was intentionally excluded, and that the Monument Proclamation language specifically recognized the right to explore for oil and gas on the 60,000 acres already under valid lease. Ranchers within the monument worry (and rightly so) what will happen to long established grazing allotments should the managers decide, as one irate landowner bluntly put it, "to kick out my cows to grow their elk to sell more hunting licenses to fuel their goddamn new shiny pickups."

And the beat goes on.

Within the monument you can float the river, fish, hike, hunt, camp, drive for pleasure, find a little solitude, enjoy a sense of exploration, or simply marvel at the variety of resources, birds and wildlife around you. To get into the monument one way — and one that comes highly recommended by those I know who have done it — is to float the river. The Wild and Scenic section runs for 149 miles, much of it through the monument. You can put in at Fort Benton, Lippard, Coal Banks Landing, Fort Clagget (mouth Judith River) or McClelland Ferry. There are several river outfitters who will gladly arrange and take care of any or all the fine details — for a fee of course. Google "Upper Missouri River Outfitters" for a more or less complete listing.

The other way in is via the relative handful of roads. U.S. Highway 87 accesses the western portion of the monument at Fort Benton. On the eastern edge, U.S. Highway 191 crosses the monument (and the Missouri River) at the Fred Robinson Bridge (CMR's James Kipp Recreation Area). Montana Highway 236 provides access north from Winifred and south from Big Candy. Beyond the three routes, lies a vast network of mostly unimproved, unmaintained roads. Except for a handful of all-weather gravel most are not suitable for low clearance vehicles and many are just two tracks in gumbo-type soils that become absolutely impassable when wet. Much of the monument is not accessible by any road, inviting visitors to explore on foot. Off-road driving (cross-country travel) is not allowed in the monument.

For those who can't float the Upper Missouri or otherwise visit the backcountry, you'll still be able to experience the cultural and natural history of the monument at the Missouri Breaks Interpretive Center at 701 7th Street in Fort Benton. Winter hours are 8 a.m. to 5 p.m. Monday through Friday except for federal holidays. Summer hours (the Saturday of Memorial Day weekend through September 30) are 8 a.m. to 5 p.m. seven days a week.

War Horse National Wildlife Refuge

3,232 ACRES; WAR HORSE AND WILD HORSE UNITS NORTHWEST WINNETT; YELLOW WATER SOUTHWEST OF WINNETT.

Established in 1937, the refuge consists of three units — War Horse Lake, Wild Horse Lake and Yellow Water — intended as sanctuaries and breeding grounds for waterfowl and wildlife. All are open for wildlife viewing and hunting. Yellow Water also offers boating and angling opportunities. The refuge is administered by CMR NWR staff, headquartered in Lewistown.

The three units support waterfowl and other migratory birds, especially shorebirds and neotropical migrant songbirds. Spring and fall afford visitors the best opportunities.

Wild Horse Lake is a natural depression. Although rarely wet, it attracts legions waterfowl and shorebirds when there is water. The surrounding uplands, primarily sagebrush, are primo for sage grouse and pronghorn, especially critical for the former over winter. Prairie dogs, mule deer and rattlesnakes are common.

Its twin sister to the south is War Horse Lake: A rarely wet natural depression, similarly productive but only during wet years. Local farmers and ranchers tried using it for irrigation but soon gave it up as a bad idea, as it is way more dry than wet. The uplands are a unique mix of sagebrush steppe grassland with ponderosa pine lands to the south, and are part of the acid-shale pine forest unique to a few scattered areas of central Montana. In addition to sage grouse, prairie dogs, pronghorn, mule deer and rattlesnakes, the pines attract a different mix of songbirds and raptors than usually associated with central Montana.

Yellow Water includes a portion of the state-owned reservoir, managed by DNRC for irrigation. Thus, visitors can expect wildly fluctuating water levels even in wet years. As such both wildlife and fish suffer. Like the two above, the surrounding uplands are critical for sage grouse, both for nesting and wintering. Other common

Mule deer

residents are pronghorn, mule deer and rattlesnakes. There is a large prairie dog town west of the reservoir.

The reservoir usually contains rainbow trout, which, in all fairness, depend upon...you guessed it, water (and a rather loose tooth FWP stocking schedule.

Fast Facts

Contact: War Horse NWR, P.O. Box 110, Lewistown, MT, 59457, Phone: 538-8706, E-mail: r6rw_cmr@fws.govS

Getting There: War Horse Lake: take Cemetery Road, northwest out of Winnett, approximately 12 miles; Wild Horse Lake: from Winnett drive north on Dovetail-Atkinson Rd. 12 miles, turn west on Welter Divide Rd., nine miles; or take Blakeslee Rd. north from Tiegen, six miles to War Horse, 5 more miles to Wild Horse; Yellow Water Reservoir: From Winnett, seven miles south on MT 244, turn west, seven miles.

Activities: Hunting, wildlife viewing, walking, photographing (all three units); fishing and boating on Yellow Water.

Principle Mammals: Pronghorn, mule deer, badger, coyote.

Mammals of Special Interest: Pronghorn.

Principle Birdlife: Waterfowl, shorebirds, raptors, sage grouse and songbirds.

Birds of Special Interest: Sage grouse.

Habitat Overview: War Horse and Wild Horse are rarely wet natural depressions; Yellow Water is a man-made reservoir managed primarily for irrigation. The uplands are a mix of sagebrush and grass, with a unique pine forest in the War Horse area.

Flora of Special Interest: Sagebrush and ponderosa pines.

Best Wildlife Viewing Ops: Pronghorn are visible throughout the day and year, best early and late in day.

Best Birding Ops: Spring during migration, the wetter the better.

Best Photo Ops: Spring, early and late in day.

Hunting Ops: Pronghorn, mule deer and sage grouse in the uplands, waterfowl when there is ample water.

Fishing Ops: Rainbow trout in Yellow Water Reservoir, the more water the better.

Camping Ops: No developed campgrounds.

Boating Ops: Yellow Water Reservoir only.

Merriam's turkey gobbler

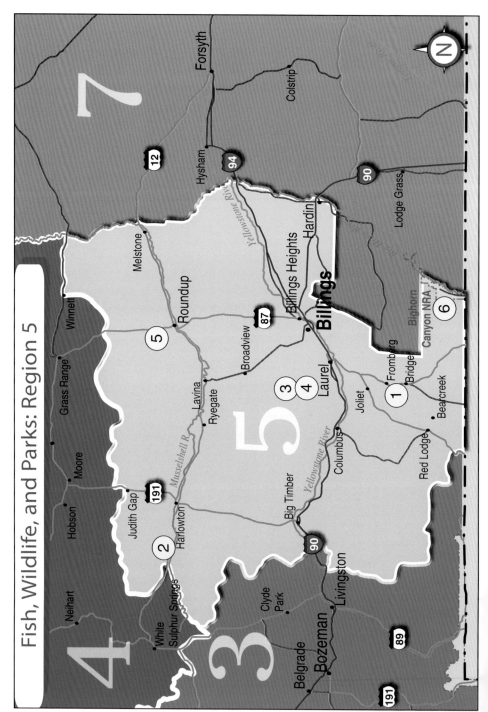

Fish, Wildlife, and Parks: Region 5

REGION 5

1. Bridger Waterfowl
   Production Area 195
2. Haymaker Wilderness
   Management Area 200
3. Hailstone National Wildlife
   Refuge 203

4. Halfbreed National Wildlife
   Refuge 207
5. Lake Mason National Wildlife
   Refuge 211
6. Pryor Mountains Wild
   Horse Range 215

Long-eared owls

Bridger Waterfowl Production Area

The Bridger WPA is the most recent addition to the CMR NWR complex. A 66-acre wetland, surrounded by excellent nesting and brood-rearing habitat, it's managed in cooperation with MTFWP and Ducks Unlimited. A variety of wildlife can be observed year round and seasonally, including waterfowl, upland game birds (sharp-tailed grouse and pheasants), white-tailed deer, numerous non-game species such as songbirds, other migrants and furbearers.

Activities allowed are wildlife viewing, birding, hiking, hunting and fishing. To access the area, turn east approximately a half mile north of Bridger, go a half mile, then north another half mile. Park in designated parking area, access by foot only.

Central Plains and Island Mountain Ranges Bird List

Obviously, all species listed below do not occur everywhere or in all seasons, but there is a good chance most will show up within the region, the above listed sites and elsewhere, sometime during any given year...

SWANS, GEESE

Tundra swan
Trumpeter swan
Canada goose
Whitefronted goose
Snow goose
Ross goose
Mallard
American black duck
Northern pintail
Gadwall
American wigeon
Eurasian wigeon
Northern shoveler
Blue-winged teal
Cinnamon teal
Green-winged teal

DUCKS, MERGANSERS

Wood duck
Redhead duck
Canvasback duck
Ring-necked duck
Greater scaup

Lesser scaup
Common goldeneye
Barrow's goldeneye
Bufflehead
Oldsquaw
Black scoter
White-winged scoter
Hooded merganser
Red-breasted merganser
Common merganser
Ruddy duck

LOONS GREBES PELICANS CORMORANTS

Common loon
Red-throated loon
Western grebe
Clark's grebe
Red-necked grebe
Horned grebe
Eared grebe
Pied bill grebe
White pelican
Double-crested cormorant

PLOVERS, SANDPIPERS

American avocet
Black-necked stilt
Lesser golden plover
Mountain plover
Black-bellied plover
Piping plover
Semipalmated plover
Killdeer
Long-billed curlew
Whimbrel
Marbled godwit
Hudsonian godwit
Upland sandpiper
Buff-breasted sandpiper
Solitary sandpiper
Spotted sandpiper

Willet
Greater yellowlegs
Lesser yellowlegs
Stilt sandpiper
Short-billed dowitcher
Long-billed dowitcher
Wilson's phalarope
Rednecked phalarope
Common snipe
Ruddy turnstone
Pectoral sandpiper
Dunlin
Sanderling
White-rumped sandpiper
American woodcock
Red knot
Baird's sandpiper
Least sandpiper
Semipalmated sandpiper
Western sandpiper

VULTURES, HAWKS, FALCONS

Turkey vulture
Northern goshawk
Coopers hawk
Sharp-shinned hawk
Northern harrier
Rough-legged hawk
Ferruginous hawk
Red-tailed hawk
Swainson's hawk
Broad-winged hawk
Golden eagl
Bald eagle
Osprey
Gyrfalcon
Prairie falcon
Peregrine falcon
Merlin
American kestrel

TURKEY, GROUSE, PHEASANT, PARTRIDGE

Turkey
Blue grouse
Spruce grouse
Ruffed grouse
Sharp-tailed grouse
Sage grouse
Chukar
Ringnecked pheasant
Gray partridge

EGRETS, HERONS, CRANES, RAILS

Great egret
Snowy egret
Cattle egret
Great blue heron
Black-crowned night heron
American bittern
White-faced ibis
Whooping crane
Sandhill crane
Virginia rail
Sora rail
Yellow rail
American coot

GULLS, TERNS

Glaucous gull
Herring gull
California gull
Ringbilled gull
Franklin's gull
Bonaparte's gull
Common tern
Forster's tern
Caspian tern
Black tern

PIGEONS, DOVES, CUCKOOS

Rock dove
Mourning dove
Yellow-billed cuckoo

Black-billed cuckoo

OWLS

Western screech owl
Eastern screech owl
Great horned owl
Long-eared owl
Short-eared owl
Barn owl
Snowy owl
Barred owl
Burrowing owl
Boreal owl
Northern saw-whet owl
Northern hawk owl

GOATSUCKERS, SWIFTS

Common poorwill
Common nighthawk
Chimney swift
White-throated swift

HUMMINGBIRDS, KINGFISHERS, WOODPECKERS

Ruby-throated hummingbird
Calliope hummingbird
Broadtailed hummingbird
Rufous hummingbird
Belted kingfisher
Common flicker
Redheaded woodpecker
Lewis woodpecker
Red-naped sapsucker
Yellow-bellied sapsucker
William's sapsucker
Hairy woodpecker
Downy woodpecker
Three-toed woodpecker
Black-backed woodpecker

FLYCATCHERS

Eastern kingbird
Western kingbird

Cassin's kingbird
Say's phoebe
Willow flycatcher
Alder flycatcher
Least flycatcher
Gray flycatcher
Eastern wood pewee
Western wood pewee
Olivesided flycatcher

LARKS, SWALLOWS, JAYS, MAGPIES, CROWS

Horned lark
Barn swallow
Violet-green swallow
Cliff swallow
Tree swallow
Bank swallow
Rough-winged swallow
Purple martin
Gray jay
Stellar jay
Blue jay
Pinyon jay
Black-billed magpie
Clark's nutcracker
Northern raven
American crow

CHICKADEES, NUTHATCHES, CREEPERS WRENS

Black-capped chickadee
Dipper
White-breasted nuthatch
Red-breasted nuthatch
Pygmy nuthatch
Brown creeper
House wren
Winter wren
Marsh wren
Sedge wren
Rock wren
Canyon wren

MOCKINGBIRDS, THRASHERS

Gray catbird
Brown thrasher
Sage thrasher

THRUSHES, BLUEBIRDS

American robin
Varied thrush
Townsend's solitaire
Wood thrush
Hermit thrush
Swainson's thrush
Gray-cheeked thrush
Veery
Eastern bluebird
Mountain bluebird
Western bluebird

KINGLETS, PIPITS, WAXWINGS

Golden-crowned kinglet
Ruby-crowned kinglet
American pipit
Sprague's pipit
Bohemian waxwing
Cedar waxwing

VIREOS, WARBLERS

Solitary vireo
Bell's vireo
Redeyed vireo
Philadelphia vireo
Warbling vireo
Black-and-white warbler
Tennessee warbler
Connecticut warbler
Orange-crowned warbler
Nashville warbler
Yellow warbler
Magnolia warbler
Cape May warbler
Yellowrumped warbler
Blackburnian warbler
Chestnut-sided warbler

Bay-breasted warbler
Blackpoll warbler
Pine warbler
Palm warbler
Ovenbird
Northern waterthrush
Common yellowthroat
Yellow-breasted chat
Macgillivray's warbler
Wilson's warbler
American redstart

SHRIKES, STARLINGS

Northern shrike
Loggerhead shrike
European starling

WEAVER, FINCHES, BLACKBIRDS ORIOLES TANAGERS

House sparrow
Bobolink
Eastern meadowlark
Western meadowlark
Yellow-headed blackbird
Red-winged blackbird
Rusty blackbird
Brewer's blackbird
Common grackle
Brown-headed cowbird
Orchard oriole
Northern oriole
Western tanager

GROSBEAKS, BUNTINGS, FINCHES, REDPOLLS

Rose-breasted grosbeak
House finch
Cassin's finch
Black-headed grosbeak
Evening grosbeak
Blue grosbeak
Indigo bunting

Lazuli bunting
Purple finch
Pine grosbeak
Rosy finch
Common redpoll

SISKINS, GOLDFINCHES, CROSSBILLS, TOWHEES

Lesser goldfinch
Pine siskin
American goldfinch
Red crossbill
White-winged crossbill
Dickcissel
Rufous-sided towhee
Green-tailed towhee
Sparrows
Savannah sparrow
Grasshoppper sparrow
Baird's sparrow
Lark bunting
Vesper sparrow
Lark sparrow
Darkeyed junco
Tree sparrow
Chipping sparrow
Claycolored sparrow
Brewer's sparrow
Field sparrow
Harris sparrow
White-crowned sparrow
White-throated sparrow
Fox sparrow
Lincoln's sparrow
Swamp sparrow
Song sparrow
Sage sparrow

LONGSPURS, SNOW BUNTINGS

Snow bunting

Haymaker
Wilderness Management Area

1,321 ACRES ON THE SOUTH SIDE THE OF LITTLE BELT MOUNTAINS IN WHEATLAND COUNTY APPROXIMATELY 16 MILES NORTH OF TWO DOT

The WMA was established in 1957. The management goal is to provide winter range for elk and mule deer, thereby helping to alleviate depredation on area ranch lands; to provide archery and rifle hunting opportunities for elk, mule deer, antelope and black bear and upland bird hunting — primarily for blue grouse; and to provide wildlife viewing opportunities for both game and non-game species, including a variety of raptors and songbirds. The last four miles or so are rough going for anything but high clearance vehicles and four-wheel drive is highly recommended especially when wet or snow covered. The WMA is closed to visitation from the end of big game season to May 15 to protect wintering big game.

Fast Facts:

Contact Info: Jay Newell 1425 2nd St W Roundup, MT 59072; phone: 323-3170; e-mail: jaynewell@mt.gov

Getting There: Turn north off US 12 at Two Dot (west of Harlowton) on Haymaker Rd. about seven miles in, turn left, follow the Morrisy Coulee Rd. to WMA.

Activities: Birding, wildlife viewing, hiking, upland bird — blue grouse — and big game hunting — elk, mule and whitetail deer, black bear; there are no developed facilities.

Principle Mammals: Mule and whitetail deer, elk, black bear, American badger, coyote, mountain cottontail rabbit, Richardson's ground squirrel, a variety of shrews, voles and mice.

Mammals of Special Interest: Elk and mule deer winter range.

Principle Birdlife: American kestrel, northern harrier, golden eagle, red-tail hawk, American crow, nighthawk, raven, American robin, black-billed magpie, savannah and vesper sparrows, yellow warbler, upland sandpiper, Wilson's jacksnipe to name just a few.

Birds of Special Interest: None.

Habitat Overview: Upland prairie grasslands, scattered coniferous forest foothills running up to the more heavily timbered Little Belts of the Lewis and Clark National Forest.

Flora of Special Interest: None.

Best Wildlife Viewing Ops: Early and late in the day; more difficult to see during hunting season which runs from September to December.

Best Birding Ops: Spring through fall, early and late in the day.

Best Photo Ops: Early and late in the day provide the most dramatic lighting.

Hunting Ops: Elk and mule deer; limited blue grouse and spring bear hunting are popular, mostly among locals.

Fishing Ops: None.

Camping Ops: No developed campsites, primitive camping allowed but there is no drinking water or other facilities.

Boating Ops: None.

Hiking Trails: None developed; unlimited otherwise.

Motor Trails: No off road driving anytime.

Wintering Elk

Hailstone National Wildlife Refuge

2,700 ACRES; LOCATED FIVE MILES NORTHEAST OF RAPELJE

Hailstone NWR is part of the Big Lake Complex, a drainage area with Hailstone Lake to the north, Halfbreed Lake in the middle, and Big Lake to the south. When there is water, Hailstone, along with the entire Big Lake Complex, is an important and productive breeding, nesting and brood-rearing site. For bird watchers and photographers, Hailstone is a great spot to greet familiar faces and grow the life list. But water is the key. No water, no birds.

Established in the mid-1930s as nesting and brood-rearing grounds for migratory birds and other wildlife. It was a non-hunting refuge until 1980, when the Waterfowl Production Area was acquired. Its complex ownership and cooperative administrative program includes 160 acres of fee title refuge, 760 acres of refuge easement and 1,828 acres of Waterfowl Production Area (WPA). Historically short-grass prairie, the surrounding area has long been plowed and converted to wheat. Consequently, for waterfowl and shorebirds, the primary habitat ingredient these days is the 300-acre reservoir itself, which is a large alkaline lake surrounded by wide-open short-grass prairie with a mix of rocky outcroppings and small hills and coulees, mostly made up of grass sagebrush and greasewood.

A satellite refuge, administered by Charles M. Russell National Wildlife Refuge staff headquartered in Lewistown, Hailstone's bird population peaks in spring. Summer and fall usage fluctuates greatly between dry and wet years. The refuge is noted primarily for its waterfowl (typically several thousand during migration) and shorebirds, including mallards, gadwalls, teals, redheads, canvasbacks, American avocets, phalaropes, American white pelicans, grebes, and gulls. During migration, shorebirds abound, while most of the duck species common in Montana visit. A good place to view water birds is a small hill that overlooks the lake. At times, the lakeshore warms with a large variety of shorebirds; the mudflats are a good spot. Transients, such as the laughing gulls, pomarine jaegers and long-tailed jaegers we spotted last

Black-tailed prairie dog

spring, also stop by during migration. Sharp-tailed grouse, Baird's sparrow, golden eagles, a variety of raptors such as northern harrier, short-eared owls and long-eared owls, frequent the uplands. Peregrine falcons are occasionally sighted, and pronghorns and badgers are common. There is a black-tailed prairie dog town on the east side of the lake where burrowing owls and hawks prey on the dogs. Especially in spring, large numbers of songbirds use the area, although so far as I know, there are no bird lists specific to the refuge. Rattlesnakes are frequently observed with several dens known to exist, so watch your step.

Hailstone Basin was the location of a gun battle between Piegen and Crow warriors who enlisted the help of local ranchers from Park City on February 16, 1885. The Piegens had stolen numerous horses from both parties and fled to this site where two ranchers and one Piegen warrior were killed in the ensuing battle.

No recreation facilities are available; however, the refuge is open to hunting, hiking, wildlife viewing and bird watching. In addition to compliance with all applicable state hunting regulations, non-toxic shot must be used to harvest waterfowl and upland game birds.

Nearby Restaurants and Accommodations

Buffalo Trail Café, Ryegate, MT, 568-2377
Stockman Café, Rapelje, MT, 663-2231
Country Skillet Columbus, MT, 322-0108
Mountain Range RV, 30 Mountain Range Rd, Columbus, MT, 322-1140
Riverside Cabins, 44 W Pike Ave, Columbus, MT, 322-5066.

Fast Facts

Contact: Hailstone NWR, P.O. Box 110, Lewistown, MT, 59457, Phone: 538-8706, E-mail: r6rw_cmr@fws.gov

Getting There: The refuge is located five miles northeast of Rapelje, Montana, MT (306 north from Columbus, MT 300 south Ryegate). Expect rather dicey travel conditions when wet.

Activities: Wildlife viewing, hiking, hunting in season.

Principle Mammals: Pronghorn, prairie dog, muskrat, badger, coyote, skunk.

Mammals of Special Interest: Pronghorn, black-tailed prairie dog.

Principle Birdlife: Waterfowl, shorebirds, raptors, eagles, sharp-tailed grouse.

Birds of Special Interest: horned grebe, great blue heron, American avocet, ring-billed gull.

Habitat Overview: Principle waterfowl habitat is the lake itself.

Flora of Special Interest: Upland areas of sagebrush, greasewood and native grasses.

Best Wildlife Viewing Ops: Early and late in day.

Best Birding Ops: Spring migration.

Best Photo Ops: Spring during migration, early and late in day.
Hunting Ops: Waterfowl and upland birds according to state seasons and bag
limits, non-toxic shot required; big game according to state regulations and
seasons.
Boating Ops: Boating is allowed as posted (no motors).

Common coot

Halfbreed National Wildlife Refuge

4,286 ACRES, SIX MILES EAST OF RAPALJE, (NORTH OF COLUMBUS, SOUTH OF RYEGATE)

Halfbreed NWR is another potential hotspot for wildlife viewing but, like Hailstone, how hot depends on water. Generally, given water, Halfbreed attracts more migrants than its sisters, Hailstone and Lake Mason. Within the Big Lake Complex, Halfbreed Lake occupies the middle ground.

The refuge was initially managed as a flowage and non-hunting refuge easement. In 1907, 3,240 acres were purchased in fee title, which included most of the original easement. The refuge now includes 3,246 acres in fee title and 640 acres of state land; an additional 400 acres, private lands and grazing lease, are administered by USFWS. When wet, the refuge provides productive breeding and staging habitat for waterfowl and shorebirds. Hunting is not allowed. Public use is limited to wildlife viewing, bird watching and hiking, as it is intended as a sanctuary for all wildlife, free from disturbance by human activities. Walk-in access is through the north boundary.

The wetlands attract a variety of waterfowl and shorebirds. We have spied grebes (western, eared, pied-billed, horned), white pelicans, teals (blue- and green wing, cinnamon), pintails, shovelers, widgeon, gadwalls, lesser scaup (bluebills), redheads, mallards, ring-necks, canvasbacks, buffleheads, golden eyes, several species geese, tundra swans, loons, mergansers (common, hooded, red-breasted) and ruddy ducks, as well as a multitude of shorebirds, including American bittern, white-faced ibis and several herons, plovers, stilts, avocets, sandpipers, phalaropes, yellow legs and more. At times there are raptors galore and songbirds including phoebes, kingbirds, shrikes, vireos, wrens, pipits, warblers and a bunch more. Naturally peak sightings occur during migration. Birds of special interest include sharp-tailed grouse, solitary sandpiper, Baird's sparrow, and a variety of raptors. Check-off wise, you are on your own as there is no bird list specific to the refuge, at least none I'm aware. Keep your eyes peeled for a variety of snakes, both harmless and the not-so-harmless western rattlesnake. There is one active and four inactive oil or gas wells on the refuge. Like

Sharp-tailed grouse

Hailstone, Halfbreed appears on Montana's threatened waters list. Agriculture, saline seeps and, of course, drought, are the major players.

The Spidel WPA is 1,250 acres, nearly 700 of which are wetlands. When there is adequate water, the wetlands support large numbers of nesting waterfowl and shorebirds; summer brood-rearing conditions are iffy during dry spells. USFWS is currently working to retain water through the season. Botulism die-offs have been a problem though better water retention and management should remedy both situations.

Western grebe

The WPA is open to wildlife viewing, birding, hiking and hunting according to state law for waterfowl and upland game birds (non-toxic shot only and big game). To access the WPA turn east at Broadview, go one mile, then north two miles. Access is by foot only.

The Tew WPA is 538 acres, comprising several natural, depressional wetland basins, and is surrounded by uplands seeded to dense nesting cover. When wet, the area provides excellent nesting and brood-rearing habitat for waterfowl and other game and non-game species of wildlife.

The area is open to hunting, wildlife viewing, birding and hiking. To access, drive 12.5 miles east of Broadview, then north four miles.

Nearby Restaurants and Accommodations

Buffalo Trail Café, Ryegate, MT, 568-2377
Stockman Café, Rapelje, MT, 663-2231
Country Skillet Columbus, MT, 322-0108
Mountain Range RV, 30 Mountain Range Rd, Columbus, MT, 322-1140
Riverside Cabins, 44 W Pike Ave, Columbus, MT, 322-5066.
Columbus offers most services of interest to travelers.

Fast Facts

Contact: Halfbreed NWR, Airport Road Lewistown, MT 59457; phone 538-8706; E-mail: cmr@fws.gov

Getting There: Six miles east of Rapelje, MT., approximately 22 miles south Ryegate, MT (US 12 between Harlowtown and Roundup); or, 25 miles north Columbus, MT, on MT 306.

Activities: Wildlife viewing, bird watching, photography and hiking.

Principle Mammals: Pronghorn, muskrat, badger, coyote, skunk.

Mammals of Special Interest: Pronghorn.

Principle Birdlife: Waterfowl, shorebirds, raptors, eagles, sharp-tailed grouse.

Birds of Special Interest: Sharp-tailed grouse, solitary sandpiper, Baird's sparrow, peregrine falcon, short-eared owl, long-eared owl.

Habitat Overview: Marsh, two shallow lakes and surrounding uplands, mostly sagebrush, grass and greasewood with rocky outcroppings.

Flora of Special Interest: Cattail, bullrush and associated marsh vegetation.

Best Wildlife Viewing Ops: Early and late in day.

Best Birding Ops: Spring migration.

Best Photo Ops: Spring during migration, early and late in day.

Hunting Ops: None.

Fishing Ops: None.

Camping Ops: None.

Boating Ops: None.

Hiking Trails: No developed trails, walk-in access from north boundary.

Motor Trails: None.

Lake Mason National Wildlife Refuge

8,700 ACRES; 10 MILES NW OF ROUNDUP

Comprised of three units: North (5,323 acres), Willow Creek (2,160 acres) and Lake Mason (1,300 acres), the refuge was established in 1941 to provide breeding, nesting and brood-rearing habitat for waterfowl and shorebirds. Originally administered by the BLM, it wasn't until 1959 that USFWS took control of then 11,740 scattered acres. Bankhead-Jones lands (covered under the Bankhead-Jones Farm Tenant Act, which is a program of land conservation and utilization developed in order to correct maladjustments in land use and thus assist in such things as control of soil erosion, reforestation, preservation of natural resources and protection of fish and wildlife) that were once homesteaded, but failing to prove up were ceded back to the government. Following acquisition, USFWS found the widely scattered parcels impossible to manage for wildlife. Subsequent land swaps resulted in the above three contiguous units. Like Hailstone and Halfbreed NWRs, Lake Mason is a satellite refuge administered by CMR staff, headquartered in Lewistown.

The North Unit comprises a mix of rolling grasslands and sagebrush and grass bottoms. Several small, intermittent ponds along Jones Creek provide water (in adequate snowpack years). Long-billed curlews, upland sand pipers, sage grouse, a variety of raptors and pronghorn are common sights. Elk are occasional visitors, moving to or from the Little Snowy Mountains. Livestock are allowed to graze the unit on a rotational basis to enhance the grasslands for wildlife.

Willow Creek Unit consists primarily of native shortgrass prairie managed for mountain plovers, a species of concern, that relies on early successional grassland communities for survival. A mix of prescribed burning and livestock grazing are the primary management tools within the unit. In addition to the above mentioned residents, look for black-tailed prairie dogs and a variety of neotropical migrants (birds summer and nest in North America, winter in the tropics) adapted to shortgrass prairie environments. Examples are Baird's and grasshopper sparrows, mountain plover, burrowing owl, long-billed curlew, upland sandpiper and bobolink.

Pronghorn (buck)

Other neotropical migrants (warblers, vireos, thrushes and so forth) are common during migration, but their numbers (144 classified species in Montana) are in general decline due to habitat loss. Native short-grass prairie, grasses such as buffalo, blue gramma and wheatgrass, are in sharp decline due to the usual culprits: conversion to cropland, invasive weeds and domestic grasses, and development. Drought resistant and historically shaped by fire and intermittent grazing by wildlife, native grasses prevented the habitat from growing into a shrub- and/or forb-dominated landscape. Thus, within the refuge, prescribed fire has replaced periodic natural wild fire and grazing and domestic livestock replaced native bison, supplemented somewhat by the continuing presence of native prairie dogs and pronghorn.

Consequently, what remains of the short-grass prairie is largely confined to the refuge-dependent bird fauna. While short grass certainly occurs on rangeland managed exclusively for cows, missing is the diversity of site characteristics once common on naturally grazed or burned grassland (grazing and burning ranged from light to severe). Bird fauna evolved to select from the variety of different site characteristics created within the overall grasslands. While livestock grazing per se isn't all bad, current range management practices strive for uniformity. Lost in the bargain are the specific habitat requirements of individual species. For example, mountain plovers require heavily grazed or burned sites for breeding, but lark buntings prefer somewhat denser vegetation. On the other hand, insufficient grazing and preclusion of fire invites invasive shrubs and forbs, again the bottom line is lost habitat. With bison gone and prairie dogs occupying about 2 percent of their native range, the future of the remnant short-grass prairie and indigenous bird species is solely dependent on the continuing sound management of public lands, both at the federal and state levels.

Lake Mason itself constitutes the refuge's third unit, expect for prolonged wet periods because the lake really isn't a lake, rather a large natural marsh. Obviously, the same rules apply: No water, no birds. When there is water the lake unit teams with wildlife. Like Hailstone, Halfbreed and the above two units, thousands of migrants show up. Some stay, some move on. Pronghorn, badgers, long-billed curlews, mountain plovers and burrowing owls are common sites in the surrounding uplands.

Nearby Restaurants and Accommodations

Busy Bee Café, Roundup, 323-2204
Pioneer Cafe, Roundup, 323-2622
The Keg, Roundup, 323-1414
The Morning Grind, Roundup, 323-1579
Best Value Inn, Roundup, 323-1000
Big Sky Motel, Roundup, 323-3203
Broken Wheel Ranch, Roundup, 323-1742.

Fast Facts

Contact: Lake Mason NWR, Airport Road Lewistown, MT 59457; Phone 538-8706; E-mail: cmr@fws.gov

Getting There: In Roundup turn off on Golf Course Rd.; follow Wildlife Viewing signs, approximately 10 miles.

Principle Mammals: Pronghorn, badger, coyote.

Mammals of Special Interest: Pronghorn.

Principle Birdlife: Waterfowl, shorebirds, raptors, songbirds.

Birds of Special Interest: Mountain plover, upland sandpiper, burrowing owl.

Habitat Overview: Consists of three units: North, rolling grasslands, with sagebrush bottoms; Willow Creek, native short-grass prairie; Lake Mason itself, which is more natural marsh than actual lake.

Flora of Special Interest: Native short-grass prairie, associated marsh vegetation.

Best Wildlife Viewing Ops: Spring, early and late in day.

Best Birding Ops: Spring, early and late in day; water is key. No water, no birds.

Best Photo Ops: Spring and early summer, early and late in day.

Red-tailed hawk

Pryor Mountains Wild Horse Range

31,000 ACRES; EXTREME SOUTH CENTRAL MONTANA AND WYOMING, SOUTHEAST OF PRYOR, MONTANA AND NORTHWEST OF LOVELL, WYOMING

Pryor Mountain wild-horse country is a landscape largely unchanged by time. Early on, people came to take advantage of the low-snow winters and perennial sunshine of the foothills.

The Bureau of Land Management's Pryor Mountain Wild Horse Range, established in 1968, is located on the south slope of East Pryor Mountain in a wild corner of Montana, overlooking the Bighorn Basin of Wyoming. In addition to Pryor mustangs, as the wild (actually feral is more accurate) horses are known, the rugged and mysterious Pryor Mountain country is home to a variety of wildlife and bird life including what is essentially Montana's only chukar partridge population. For wildlife lovers in search of isolation and solitude to spice up adventures, look no further. Isolation is one thing the Pryors have in spades.

About 140 to 200 wild horses typically range across the high meadows and rugged juniper-covered foothills to the colorful desert-like badlands that border the green fields of Crooked Creek Valley. This rugged terrain, carved by ridges, canyons and coulees, provides lots of room for horses to roam, and offers no guarantees of even catching a fleeting glimpse.

The herd produces about 30 to 40 foals each year. Because the wild horses have few enemies, (primarily mountain lions and black bears occasionally preying on foals) the herd is kept in check through periodic roundups and subsequent sales to the highest bidder. In an attempt to assuage the opposition, recently, the concept of injecting mares with contraceptives has been tested. So far the results have been positive — lower birth rates and older mares are giving birth to healthier, more vigorous foals.

In early 2008, the BLM recommended reducing the herd from 143 (not counting several dozen foals) to 92 because overgrazing by the herd, coupled with longterm

Feral horses

drought, was degrading the land. Public adoptions of the horses have been used to reduce the herd in the past.

Unlike the rest of the places in this book, access to the Wild Horse Range is via one of three roads, only one of which is in Montana (the other two are in Wyoming). None are a piece of cake and all eventually lead to the same junction: whereupon Tillet Ridge and Sykes Ridge Roads lead off in opposite directions thru the range itself. Beware, these roads are often challenging for the faint of heart and NOT for low clearance vehicles, and in wet weather, for...get...it. Do not go alone, and two vehicles are a much better idea than one.

To reach the junction mentioned above: From Bridger, Montana (south of Laurel) follow US 310 south to Warren, turn east and follow the main road, stay right (on the main road) and eventually you will cross the Wyoming Line and come to a "T". Turn left and continue for about three and a half miles, turn left onto the cottonwood-lined gravel road that crosses Crooked Creek and joins County Road 16. At this junction a sign points left to Tillet/Burnt Timber Ridge and right to Sykes Ridge (to continue, see below).

In Cowley, Wyoming turn north from Main Street (Highway 310) onto Division Street which is the road to the airport. Division Street is bordered by a park and a water tower. Drive north on Division Street (Airport Rd.). In about 9.1 miles you will come to a junction that features a BLM sign, which reads "Crooked Creek Left". DO NOT TURN LEFT! Continue about three and a half miles and turn left onto the gravel road that crosses Crooked Creek and meets County Road 16. At this intersection, a sign points left to Tillet/Burnt Timber Ridge and right to Sykes Ridge.

From Lovell, Wyoming take US 14A for 2.4 miles east of town. Then turn north onto State Highway 37 and drive nine miles to the Crooked Creek Road turnoff. The turnoff is less than one mile south of the Bighorn Recreation Area boundary. Turn from the state highway and go 1.7 miles west. Turn right on the cottonwood-lined lined gravel road that crosses Crooked Creek and joins County Road 16. At this junction a sign points left to Tillet/Burnt Timber Ridge and right to Sykes Ridge.

You can also reach the Wild Horse Range from Warren, Montana but the road is long with plenty of wrong turn opportunities and other hazards.

Back to Sykes Ridge Road. The first three miles are usually dry year round and passable, though not maintained regularly. At the red bluffs, a short hike uphill affords a view of Turkey Flats, where up to 30 wild horses sometimes hangout in winter. Small bands roam the juniper foothills year round, but in winter and early spring, February through May, horses strongly prefer this area. Beyond the red bluffs the road drops into Sykes Coulee and driving becomes an adventure; don't even think about it unless armed with four-wheel drive, high clearance and heavy-duty tires. Three miles past red bluffs is a good stopping point, a good spot to hike around and view the breath-taking view to the south. Keep an eye out for horses but mule deer are especially fond of the mountain mahogany (low, grayish green shrubs) for winter browse.

Eventually (about six to eight miles) the road climbs onto the open, rocky, South Ridge of East Pryor Mountain; which offers more outstanding landscape and a good spot for mustangs, mule deer and even bighorn sheep. The sheer cliffs to the east are

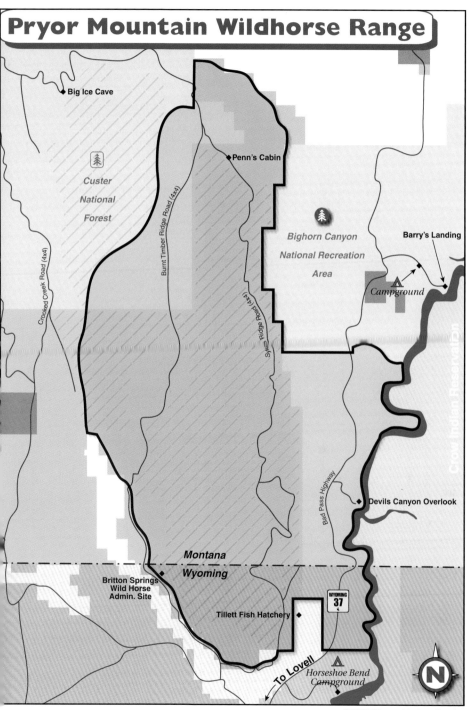

Pryor Mountain Wildhorse Range

◆ Big Ice Cave

Custer
National
Forest

◆ Penn's Cabin

Burnt Timber Ridge Road (4x4)

Crooked Creek Road (4x4)

Bighorn Canyon
National Recreation
Area

Barry's Landing

△ Campground

Sykes Ridge Road (4x4)

Crow Indian Reservation

Bad Pass Highway

◆ Devils Canyon Overlook

Montana
Wyoming

◆ Britton Springs
Wild Horse
Admin. Site

◆ Tillett Fish Hatchery

WYOMING
37

To Lovell

△ Horseshoe Bend
Campground

N

the Bighorn and Devil's Canyons, while the unfolding diorama includes Bighorn, Beartooth, Absarokee, and Wind River mountain ranges. Travel beyond South Ridge to the Dryhead Vista Road is usually not possible until July because of snowdrifts.

When passable the road continues to climb through forest, a mix of Douglas fir and limber pine and eventually tops out in a grassy park, Wild Horse Park. Rustic and charming Penn's cabin is open for free public use on a first-come first-served basis. The cabin contains wood-board bunks (bring your own sleeping bag) and a wood stove. Mustangs are common, grazing on the grassy slopes nearby. For the more adventurous, check out the trails leading up to several higher parks commonly used by horses. Layout Ridge, northeast of the cabin is primo. Even if you don't spy a mustang the sweeping vistas are worth the hike; bring a picnic lunch and a warm jacket (a must-have in any season as high country weather is notoriously fickle) and enjoy the view, it doesn't get much better, or wilder for that matter.

Tillet Ridge Road is passable to high clearance two-wheel drive vehicles as far as the mines (from there it's four-wheel drive, high clearance and heavy duty tires). The road passes BLM's Britton Springs Corrals, the scene of the famous wild horse roundup usually held in March. Mustangs are commonly sighted from the mines to the USFS boundary. Above the mines, to the west is Demijohn Flat, a centuries-old campsite on a grassy flat, waterless mesa. The nearest water is a long way down a rough and crooked trail to Crooked Creek. Why the high and dry campsite remains a mystery. Sacred ground? Vision quest? No one yet has come up with a defining answer.

While the above descriptions are offered as starting points, the wild horse herd roams far and wide, in bands from two to three, up to 15 or more. Bands commonly consist of a dominant stallion and his harem, mares and their colts; other bands comprise young, bachelor stallions. A good rule of thumb: As the snowline rises mustangs tend to follow, the new grass of the high mountain parks is particularly relished; come early summer as many as half the herd are drawn to the high peaks. As winter deepens the horses tend to leave the high country, band up in the foothills and lowlands. Mares usually drop foals in May. Soon afterward, stallions engage in often-spectacular battles for the right to gather harems and breed. Photographic opportunities tend to peak also.

The Pryor herd is of Spanish descent, still exhibiting features attributed to horses of European lineage—small (on average about 14 hands), narrow, deep chest and short, strong back; colors vary—bay, black, blue roan, brown, dun and gray. Many sport unusual markings, zebra stripes on the legs, black dorsal stripes down the spine line. As a rule the horses are hardy, survive hot summers and cold winters and extreme dry easily. Brought as domesticated wild stock from Spain to North America around five centuries ago by the conquistadors the horses were eventually turned loose, later rounded up, redomesticated and divvied up amongst the various Indian tribes as well as white settlers. Many escaped confinement and by the mid-1800s as many as two million roamed freely all across the West. The Pryor Mountain herd is believed to have originated from Crow/Shoshone stock and has been a fixture since the late 1800s.

Not everyone is endeared to the idea of wild horses competing with native wildlife. Most wildlife biologists don't consider wild horses wildlife but rather feral livestock that competes with natives, such as mule deer and bighorn sheep for too often scarce grocery items, grasses and forbs. Wild horse lovers counter the animals are naturalized citizens and merit the same respect given to other alien wildlife such as ring-necked pheasant, chukar partridge and even fish, such as brook, brown and rainbow trout none of which are Montana natives.

In addition to mustangs, the Wild Horse Range supports a diverse wildlife and bird population: elk, mule deer, bighorn sheep, black bears, over 200 species of birds have been identified, including chukar partridge, blue grouse, peregrine falcons and golden eagles. In the coniferous forest areas look for cordilleran flycatchers, hermit thrushes, warblers, nuthatches, chickadees and a variety of other forest dwelling birds.

Several species of bats inhabit numerous limestone caves and cutthroat trout dwell in Crooked Creek; the area boasts a flourishing rattlesnake populace, i.e. watch your step and keep eyes and ears tuned in warm weather.

Petroglyphs

While poking around the Pryors in search of wild mustangs, Petroglyph Canyon provides an interesting diversion — if you can find it. To get there: South of Bridger the road, MT 310, rises for almost 20 miles then levels off—the Pryors dominate the view to your left. Turn at Warren, where the paved road splits and hook a right. Head southeast and be sure to keep on the main road (not always obvious). About eight miles from Warren is a cattle guard marked by large tractor tires, take the narrow two-track to the right. Assuming you are on the right track a large juniper-spotted butte should be dead ahead. On the right side of the butte you should find the obvious parking spot. If not you have made a miss somewhere, go back and start over. Do not try this in a low-slung, two-wheel drive vehicle.

There are no signs to get you here, but assuming you made it, take the trail into the canyon. The trail is marked, not to the petroglyphs, which are about a mile down, but in lizard, snake, mouse, cottontail and small bird tracks that litter the way. The further you drop into the canyon the more mysterious and difficult the trail becomes and, if warm, do watch your step—this is major rattlesnake country.

The petroglyphs themselves date back to between 750 and 1500 A.D. Reputedly there are three times as many human stick figures as animal caricatures, (bison, bear, sheep and thunderbirds). Real or make believe, all were spiritual creatures to the ancients. If you go, please take only pictures, tread lightly and, above all, NO rock carving, there is way too much of that already.

On the way to the petroglyphs be sure to check out Bear Canyon. In the rain shadow of the Beartooths, it is one of the driest places in the state, averaging less than six inches of precipitation a year. This is the only place in Montana to see black-throated gray warblers, blue-gray gnatcatchers; other common sightings include common poorwills, Cooper's hawks, canyon wrens, dusky flycatchers, green-tailed towhees, loggerhead shrikes (butcher birds), mountain plovers, pinyon jays, Say's phoebes, white-throated swifts and yellow-breasted chats.

Nearby Restaurants and Accommodations

Best pack a lunch; better still toss in the camp outfit. Nearest amenities are a long way down a bumpy, dusty trail, especially when tired and hungry following an exhilarating day gazing at wild horses. Oh, and be sure to top off the gas tank.
Ain't no petrol either. Nearest towns are Bridger, Montana and Lovell, Wyoming
In Bridger, check out the
Buckeye Bar and Grill, 662-3230
Bridger Motel, 662-3212
In Lovell, try
Langes Kitchen, (307) 548-9370
Cattlemen Motel, (307) 548-2296

Fast Facts

Contact Info: BLM, Billings Field Office, PO Box 36800, 5001 Southgate Dr., Billings, MT 59107; phone: 896-5013.

Getting There: See above.

Activities: Wildlife viewing, bird watching, hunting, hiking, camping, fishing, you name it. No off road driving, however.

Principle Mammals: Wild horses, elk, mule deer, bighorn sheep, black bears.

Mammals of Special Interest: Wild horses, bighorn sheep.

Principle Birdlife: Over 200 species, blue grouse, peregrine falcon, chukar partridge, golden eagle.

Birds of Special Interest: Peregrine falcon, chukar partridge, golden eagle.

Habitat Overview: High mountains, grassy parks, mountain mahogany, juniper, limber pine and Douglas fir.

Flora of Special Interest: Mountain mahogany

Best Wildlife Viewing Ops: See text above.

Best Birding Ops: Along Crooked Creek and the edge surrounding grassy parks.

Best Photo Ops: After foals drop in May, stallions engage in dramatic battles for mare favors.

Hunting Ops: Mule deer, upland birds, black bear and elk according to state regulations and permits.

Fishing Ops: Excellent small stream cutthroat fishing in Crooked Creek, watch for rattlesnakes.

Camping Ops: Penn's cabin (see above), several primitive campgrounds and pretty much unlimited camping on BLM and USFS.

Boating Ops: None

Hiking Trails: Several primitive trails in the Penn's Cabin area, numerous game trails afford hikers almost unlimited opportunities.

Motor Trails: See descriptions above. Travel is restricted to designated roads and trails.

Pryor Mountain/Bighorn Canyon Bird List

SWANS, GEESE, DUCKS, MERGANSERS

Tundra swan	Gadwall
Trumpeter swan	American wigeon
Canada goose	Eurasian wigeon
Greater white-fronted goose	Northern shoveler
Snow goose	Blue-winged teal
Ross goose	Cinnamon teal
Mallard	Green-winged teal
American black duck	Wood duck
Northern pintail	Redhead duck

Canvasback duck
Ring-necked duck
Greater scaup
Lesser scaup
Common goldeneye
Barrow's goldeneye
Bufflehead
Oldsquaw
Black scoter
White-winged scoter
Hooded merganser
Red-breasted merganser
Common merganser
Ruddy duck

LOONS, GREBES, PELICANS

Common loon
Red-throated loon
Western grebe
Clark's grebe
Red-necked grebe
Horned grebe
Eared grebe
Pied-billed grebe
White pelican

CORMORANTS

Double-crested cormorant

PLOVERS, SANDPIPERS

American avocet
Black-necked stilt
Lesser golden plover
Mountain plover
Black-bellied plover
Piping plover
Semipalmated plover
Killdeer
Long-billed curlew
Whimbrel
Marbled godwit
Hudsonian godwit
Upland sandpiper

Buff-breasted sandpiper
Solitary sandpiper
Spotted sandpiper
Willet
Greater yellowlegs
Lesser yellowlegs
Stilt sandpiper
Short-billed dowitcher
Long-billed dowitcher
Wilson's phalarope
Red-necked phalarope
Common snipe
Ruddy turnstone
Pectoral sandpiper
Dunlin
Sanderling
White-rumped sandpiper
American woodcock
Red knot
Baird's sandpiper
Least sandpiper
Semipalmated sandpiper
Western sandpiper

VULTURES HAWKS FALCONS

Turkey vulture
Northern goshawk
Coopers hawk
Sharp-shinned hawk
Northern harrier
Rough-legged hawk
Ferruginous hawk
Red-tailed hawk
Swainson's hawk
Broad-winged hawk
Golden eagle
Bald eagle
Osprey
Gyrfalcon
Prairie falcon
Peregrine falcon
Merlin
American kestrel

TURKEY

Turkey

GROUSE

Blue grouse
Spruce grouse
Ruffed grouse
Sharp-tailed grouse
Sage grouse

PHEASANT, PARTRIDGE

Chukar
Ring-necked pheasant
Gray partridge

EGRETS HERONS CRANES RAILS

Great egret
Snowy egret
Cattle egret
Great blue heron
Black-crowned night heron
American bittern
White-faced ibis
Whooping crane
Sandhill crane
Virginia rail
Sora rail
Yellow rail
American coot

GULLS, TERNS

Glaucous gull
Herring gull
California gull
Ring-billed gull
Franklin's gull
Bonaparte's gull
Common tern
Forster's tern
Caspian tern
Black tern

PIGEONS DOVES CUCKOOS

Rock dove
Mourning dove
Yellow-billed cuckoo
Black-billed cuckoo

OWLS

Western screech owl
Eastern screech owl
Great horned owl
Long-eared owl
Short-eared owl
Barn owl
Snowy owl
Barred owl
Burrowing owl
Boreal owl
Northern sawwhet owl
Northern hawk owl

GOATSUCKERS SWIFTS

Common poorwill
Common nighthawk
Chimney swift
White-throated swift

HUMMINGBIRDS, KINGFISHERS

Ruby-throated hummingbird
Calliope hummingbird
Broad-tailed hummingbird
Rufous hummingbird
Belted kingfisher

WOODPECKERS

Common flicker
Red-headed woodpecker
Lewis woodpecker
Red-naped sapsucker
Yellow-bellied sapsucker
William's sapsucker
Hairy woodpecker
Downy woodpecker
Three-toed woodpecker
Black-backed woodpecker

FLYCATCHERS

Eastern kingbird
Western kingbird
Cassin's kingbird
Say's phoebe
Willow flycatcher
Alder flycatcher
Least flycatcher
Gray flycatcher
Eastern wood pewee
Western wood pewee
Olive-sided flycatcher

LARKS, SWALLOWS

Horned lark
Barn swallow
Violet-green swallow
Cliff swallow
Tree swallow
Bank swallow
Rough-winged swallow
Purple martin

JAYS, MAGPIES, CROWS

Gray jay
Stellar jay
Blue jay
Pinyon jay
Black-billed magpie
Clark's nutcracker
Northern raven
American crow

CHICKADEES, NUTHATCHES

Black-capped chickadee
Dipper
White-breasted nuthatch
Red-breasted nuthatch
Pygmy nuthatch

CREEPER, WRENS

Brown creeper
House wren
Winter wren

Marsh wren
Sedge wren
Rock wren
Canyon wren

MOCKINGBIRDS, THRASHERS

Gray catbird
Brown thrasher
Sage thrasher

THRUSHES, BLUEBIRDS

American robin
Varied thrush
Townsend's solitaire
Wood thrush
Hermit thrush
Swainson's thrush
Gray-cheeked thrush
Veery
Eastern bluebird
Mountain bluebird
Western bluebird

KINGLETS, PIPITS, WAXWINGS

Golden-crowned kinglet
Ruby-crowned kinglet
American pipit
Sprague's pipit
Bohemian waxwing
Cedar waxwing

VIREOS, WARBLERS

Solitary vireo
Bell's vireo
Red-eyed vireo
Philadelphia vireo
Warbling vireo
Black-and-white warbler
Tennessee warbler
Connecticut warbler
Orange-crowned warbler
Nashville warbler
Yellow warbler
Magnolia warbler
Cape May warbler

Yellow-rumped warbler
Blackburnian warbler
Chestnut-sided warbler
Bay-breasted warbler
Blackpoll warbler
Pine warbler
Palm warbler
Ovenbird
Northern waterthrush
Common yellowthroat
Yellow-breasted chat
Macgillivray's warbler
Wilson's warbler
American redstart

SHRIKES STARLINGS

Northern shrike
Loggerhead shrike
European starling

WEAVER FINCHES BLACKBIRDS ORIOLES TANAGERS

House sparrow
Bobolink
Eastern meadowlark
Western meadowlark
Yellow-headed blackbird
Red-winged blackbird
Rusty blackbird
Brewer's blackbird
Common grackle
Brown-headed cowbird
Orchard oriole
Northern oriole
Western tanager

GROSBEAKS, BUNTINGS

Rosebreasted grosbeak
House finch
Cassin's finch
Black-headed grosbeak
Evening grosbeak
Blue grosbeak
Indigo bunting
Lazuli bunting

FINCHES, REDPOLLS

Purple finch
Pine grosbeak
Rosy finch
Common redpoll

SISKINS, GOLDFINCHES, CROSSBILLS, TOWHEES

Lesser goldfinch
Pine siskin
American goldfinch
Red crossbill
White-winged crossbill
Dickcissel
Rufous-sided towhee
Green-tailed towhee

SPARROWS

Savannah sparrow
Grasshoppper sparrow
Baird's sparrow
Lark bunting
Vesper sparrow
Lark sparrow
Dark-eyed junco
Tree Sparrow
Chipping Sparrow
Clay-colored Sparrow
Brewer's Sparrow
Field Sparrow
Harris Sparrow
White-crowned Sparrow
White-throated Sparrow
Fox Sparrow
Lincoln's Sparrow
Swamp Sparrow
Song Sparrow
Sage Sparrow

BUNTINGS

Snow Bunting

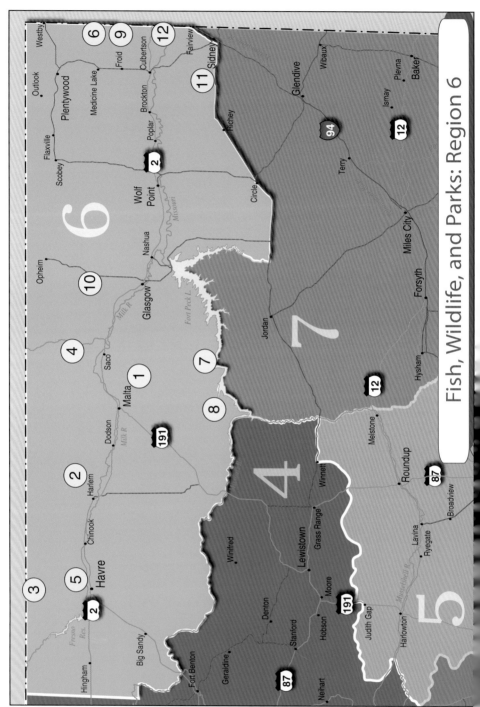

Fish, Wildlife, and Parks: Region 6

© 2008 Wilderness Adventures Press, Inc

REGION 6

1. Bowdoin National
   Wildlife Refuge 229
2. Black Coulee National
   Wildlife Refuge 239
3. Creedman Coulee National
   Wildlife Refuge 241
4. Hewitt Lake National
   Wildlife Refuge 243
5. Lake Thibadeau National
   Wildlife Refuge 246
6. Brush Lake State Park 249

7. Charles M. Russell National
   Wildlife Refuge 253
8. UL Bend National
   Wildlife Refuge 269
9. Medicine Lake National
   Wildlife Refuge 273
10. Bitter Creek Wilderness
    Study Area 282
11. Fox Lake Wildlife
    Management Area 284
12. Fort Union Trading Post 286

Bowdoin National Wildlife Refuge

6,616 ACRES (WETLANDS) AND 8,935 ACRES (UPLANDS), SEVEN MILES EAST OF MALTA OFF OLD HIGHWAY 2

Bowdoin's mission statement is "to preserve and enhance resting, feeding and breeding habitat for migratory birds and other wildlife." Judging by the thousands of migrating waterfowl that show up each spring, many of which hang out, build nests and propagate — to say nothing of the legions that move on only to return in the fall, many with youngsters in tow — the refuge is right on track to fulfill its mission. Ideal habitat, both in the wetlands and the contiguous uplands, provides nesting and brood rearing cover for countless ducks, geese and colonial nesting water birds such as American white pelicans, California gulls, ring-billed gulls, double-crested cormorants, and great blue herons. The refuge is home to the largest breeding population of white pelicans in the state.

Looking back, the refuge has come a long way since 1936. For instance, the year prior (1935), just seven breeding pairs of Canada geese were observed; compared to over 100 broods counted in a recent spring. Typically, the fall migration attracts as many as 100,000 ducks and geese, and spring counts are not much different.

Numerous shorebirds — willets, marbled godwits, Wilson's phalaropes, American avocets, black-necked stilts, killdeer, upland sandpipers and long-billed curlews (too name just a few)—nest here. As do countless grassland nesting songbirds such as the threatened Baird's sparrow, Sprague's pipit and the more common such as the grasshopper sparrow, savannah sparrow and chestnut-collared longspur, to name just three. Unless you are tone deaf like me, it's difficult to miss the melodious warbling of our state bird, the western meadowlark. Introduced pheasants at times seem numerous enough to be taking over. While native sharp-tailed grouse are fairly common, and even native sage grouse (not a lot of sagebrush, so not ideal habitat) are seen occasionally as are introduced Hungarian (gray) partridge. Hunting upland game birds and waterfowl is allowed but there are restrictions, so check first.

White pelicans

The refuge also supports healthy resident and migrant wildlife populations, including raptors, whitetail and mule deer, pronghorn, coyotes, muskrats, whitetail jackrabbits, mountain cottontails, Richardson's ground squirrels, least and long-tailed weasels, masked shrews, mink, a variety of mice, prairie and meadow voles, porcupines, bats, beaver, raccoons, badgers, and striped skunks. Franklin's gulls, white-faced ibis, black-crowned night herons, American coots, eared grebes, sora rails and American bitterns thrive in the marshy environs. You can build a pretty impressive life list based exclusively on sightings here alone.

Information gleaned from refuge headquarters reveals, "Bowdoin was named for the railroad siding town originally located just south of the Dry Lake Unit; Crumbling cement foundations and the grain elevator are all that remain. Nearby is the bustling town of Malta.

"The heart and soul of the wetlands is Lake Bowdoin. In the beginning there were no dikes to hold back the spring runoff and the lake often went dry in summer. No (or low) water severely curtailed waterfowl and shorebird production, further hampered by all too common botulism outbreaks. The lack of water led to building a system of dikes and ditches for water delivery and enabled the refuge staff to at last formulate a sound management program. These days the combination spring runoff and water purchased from the Bureau of Reclamation's Milk River System are usually sufficient to insure decent nesting success and prevent serious disease outbreaks.

"Located in the Milk River Valley of Phillips County the refuge landscape underwent extensive glaciations some 15,000 years ago. But unlike the true-glaciated prairie further east the retreating ice cap failed to leave the area pocked with an abundance of semi- and permanent wetlands. But the glaciers did leave their mark and what remains today is far different than before. For example, Lake Bowdoin was once an oxbow of the pre-glacial Missouri River, which now flows 70 miles south. Refuge water these days is derived from rain, snowmelt, spring flooding of Beaver Creek, irrigation returns and the main source, Milk River, via the canal system.

"The refuge, 15,551 acres, consists of 6,616 acres of wetlands and 8,935 acres of uplands; a mix of shortgrass prairie interspersed with impoundments, bordered by extensive bullrush and cattail marsh and numerous shelterbelts. Somewhat unique the refuge includes both saline and freshwater wetlands. Overall the refuge is a productive mix of dense nesting and brood rearing habitat. A variety of species includes 263 species of birds, 26 of mammals as well as several reptiles, amphibians and fish. Remarkable, especially considering the region gets less than 12 inches precipitation in most years.

" Once sculpted by migrating bison and wildfires, today's refuge staff relies on prescribed (controlled) burning, haying, mowing, controlled livestock grazing, and other modern land management practices to maintain a healthy vegetative state for wildlife."

In the 1990s, Bowdoin served as a black-footed ferret breeding and pre-conditioning facility. At times the facility housed up to 16 adult females and eight adult males of the endangered ferrets. Kits were reared and released to black-tailed prairie dog towns mostly to nearby CMR and UL Bend NWRs but to other suitable sites around the state and throughout the Intermountain West as well. The refuge provides nesting opportunities for the threatened piping plover which nests on open, sandy or gravel beaches. The refuge also provides ideal nesting habitat for other species of concern such as the bald eagle and peregrine falcon.

A handicap accessible blind located at the Pearce Waterfowl Production Area on the northeast boundary of the refuge is available for bird watching, wildlife photography, and waterfowl hunting. The pier adjacent to the main boat ramp on Lake Bowdoin affords visitors both a convenient photography platform and at times offers an up close and personal view of waterfowl, waterbirds and other wildlife. Adjacent to the main parking lot, a short, handicap accessible loop trail encircles a small wetland. Visitors are welcome to explore the refuge on foot. Driving is allowed only on designated routes, including the AutoTour Route. Boating is prohibited on the refuge, except during the waterfowl hunting season. Due the high alkalinity of Lake Bowdoin no fish are present. Public hunting of waterfowl and upland game birds is allowed (check in for current dates and regulations) but big game hunting is prohibited anytime.

Waterfowl viewing peaks in spring and fall migration. In spring when the eggs hatch brood sightings are commonplace enough to at times become sort of ho-hum. Peak viewing times are early and late in the day as usual. The first broods of Canada geese come off in early May, while other waterfowl broods generally appear a few weeks later. Young pronghorns are born about the third week of May. Whitetail deer fawns are born in late May or early June. Shorebird populations peak later, in July and early August. The refuge has been designated a Globally Important Bird Area by the American Bird Conservancy and is a Western Hemisphere Shorebird Reserve Network site.

Managed primarily for ducks and geese, the refuge is a haven for colonial nesters. Franklin's gulls, black-crowned night-herons, eared grebes and white-faced ibises, set up housekeeping in the bulrush marshes of Lake Bowdoin. While other colonials — American white pelicans, double-crested cormorants, great blue herons and California and ring-billed gulls — tend to prefer the lake's several islands. Coots and eared grebes are especially numerous. In the uplands look for Sprague's pipit, Baird's sparrow and chestnut-collared longspur among many other songbirds, as well as native sharptail and sage grouse and non-natives ringneck pheasant and the occasional Hungarian partridge.

Refuge personnel also administer the The Bowdoin Wetland Management District WMD) which consists of four satellite NWRs — Black Coulee, Creedman Coulee, Hewitt Lake, and Lake Thibadeau — encompassing nearly 10,000 acres and seven Waterfowl Production Areas (WPAs) — Holm, Webb, Dyrdahl, Korsbeck, Pearce, McNeil Slough, and Beaver Creek — nearly 9,000 acres total. All WPAs are open to the public and all but Holm allow public hunting and trapping. Access to the various satellite refuges, WPAs and so forth can be difficult due to their remoteness and the need to sometimes gain landowner permission to cross private land. The best way is to contact refuge headquarters and go from there.

The Bowdoin staff also monitors over 8,300 acres of wetland easements and several thousand acres of grassland easements in Phillips, Blaine, Hill, and Valley Counties.

Armed with Auto Tour Guide and Refuge Bird List (available at headquarters), binoculars, spotting scope and camera gear ready, we set off on a late spring tour. Barely started, Gale spied the first of several gaudy cock pheasants. At the first bend in the road, an anxious hen pheasant urged her brood of newly hatched chicks along. From there on, the check offs came fast and furious: pied-billed grebe, white pelican, double-crested cormorant, great blue heron, black-crowned night heron, white-face ibis, Canada geese, a single greater white-fronted goose (our first), wood duck, gadwall, wigeon, blue-winged, cinnamon and green-winged teals, pintail, shoveler, canvasback, redhead, blue-bill, bufflehead, Barrow's and common goldeneye, hooded and common merganser, marsh hawk, sparrow hawk, peregrine falcon (murdered a Franklin's gull in spectacular fashion as we watched), killdeer, coot, a pair of sandhill cranes, black tern, snipe, Wilson's phalarope and common flicker. Songbirds of every color and size seemed to flit about in all directions. Other wildlife sighted on our brief tour included mountain cottontail rabbits, whitetail jackrabbits, whitetail deer, pronghorn, muskrat, Richardson's ground squirrel and a single giant striped skunk added spice to the already delicious stew. Due to a heavy travel schedule, we did the tour in less than four hours, but you could easily spend all day and not run out of subjects.

Nearby Restaurants and Accommodations

Malta is nearby, and although small, it offers several choices for motels and restaurants. For breakfast check out the Hitchin' Post Café, 654-1882; for dinner the Great Northern Hotel, 654-2100; sleep over at the Maltana Motel 654-2100; RV camping is available at the Edgewater Inn and Campground, 654-2100 and at nearby Nelson's Reservoir. No camping or fires allowed on the refuge.

Fast Facts

Contact: Bowdoin NWR, HC 65, Box 5700, Malta, MT 59538; phone: 654-2863; E-mail, Bowdoin@fws.gov.

Getting There: Seven miles east of Malta off Old Highway 2, follow signs from town

Activities: Photography, hiking, bicycling, cross-country skiing, wildlife observation, and bird hunting.

Principle Mammals: Muskrats, white-tailed deer and pronghorn.

Mammals of Special Interest: Black-footed ferret.

Principle Birdlife: Canada geese, variety of ducks, shorebirds, songbirds and colony nesters such as pelicans, cormorants and great blue herons.

Birds of Special Interest: Endangered piping plover, bald eagle and peregrine falcon

Habitat Overview: A mix of wetlands, shelterbelts and uplands dominated by extensive cattail and bulrush marshes surrounding Lake Bowdoin.

Flora of Special Interest: Native prairie grasslands, cattail and bulrushes.

Best Wildlife Viewing Ops: Late spring and early fall, early and late in the day.

Best Birding Ops: Late spring and early fall for waterfowl, peak shorebird migration is July.

Best Photo Ops: Year around, early and late in the day provides the best light.

Hunting Ops: Waterfowl and ring-necked pheasant hunting (check in first for current dates and regulations).

Fishing Ops: None.

Camping Ops: None.

Boating Ops: None.

Hiking Trails: Hiking on the refuge is permitted (with seasonal restrictions). There is a loop trail near HQ (handicap accessible). Handicap accessible boardwalk and viewing blind at nearby Pearce WPA.

Motor Trails: 15-mile Auto Tour route and on designated routes only.

Bowdoin Bird List

Loons and Grebes

Common Loon
Pied-billed grebe
Horned grebe
Red-necked grebe
Eared grebe
Western grebe
Clark's grebe

Pelicans

American white pelican

Cormorants

Double-crested cormorant

Herons

American bittern
Great blue heron
Great egret
Snowy egret
Cattle egret
Green heron
Black-crowned night-heron
White-faced ibis

Waterfowl

White-fronted goose
Snow goose
Ross' goose
Canada goose
Tundra swan
Wood duck
Gadwall
Eurasian wigeon
American wigeon
Black duck
Mallard
Blue-winged teal
Cinnamon teal
Northern shoveler
Northern pintail
Garganey
Green-winged teal
Canvasback
Redhead
Ring-necked duck
Greater scaup
Lesser scaup
Harlequin duck

Surf scoter
White-winged scoter
Oldsquaw
Bufflehead
Common goldeneye
Barrow's goldeneye
Hooded merganser
Common merganser
Red-breasted merganser
Ruddy duck

Hawks

Osprey
Bald eagle
Northern harrier
Sharp-shinned hawk
Cooper's hawk
Northern goshawk
Broad-winged hawk
Swainson's hawk
Red-tailed hawk
Ferruginous hawk
Rough-legged hawk
Golden eagle

Falcons

American kestrel
Merlin
Gyrfalcon
Peregrine falcon
Prairie falcon

Upland Birds

Hungarian partridge
Ring-necked pheasant
Sage grouse
Sharp-tailed grouse
Wild turkey

Rails and Coots

Yellow rail
Virginia rail
Sora

American coot

Cranes

Sandhill crane

Plovers

Black-bellied plover
American golden plover
Snow plover
Semipalmated plover
Piping plover
Killdeer
Mountain plover

Sandpipers

Black-necked stilt
American avocet
Greater yellowlegs
Lesser yellowlegs
Solitary sandpiper
Willet
Spotted sandpiper
Upland sandpiper
Whimbrel
Long-billed curlew
Hudsonian godwit
Marbled godwit
Ruddy turnstone
Red knot
Sanderling
Semipalmated sandpiper
Western sandpiper
Least sandpiper
White-rumped sandpiper
Baird's sandpiper
Pectoral sandpiper
Dunlin
Stilt sandpiper
Buff-breasted sandpiper
Short-billed dowitcher
Long-billed dowitcher
Common snipe
Wilson's phalarope

Red-necked phalarope
Red phalarope

Gulls and Terns

Franklin's gull
Bonaparte's gull
Ring-billed gull
California gull
Herring gull
Sabine's gull
Caspian tern
Common tern
Arctic tern
Forster's tern
Black tern

Pigeons

Rock dove
Mourning dove
Black-billed cuckoo
Yellow-billed cuckoo

Owls

Eastern screech owl
Great-horned owl
Snowy owl
Burrowing owl
Long-eared owl
Short-eared p owl
Northern saw-whet owl

Nighthawks

Common nighthawk

Hummingbirds

Ruby-throated hummingbird

Kingfishers

Belted kingfisher

Woodpeckers

Red-headed woodpecker
Yellow-bellied sapsucker

Downy woodpecker
Hairy woodpecker
Northern flicker

Flycatchers

Western wood-peewee
Alder flycatcher
Willow flycatcher
Least flycatcher
Say's phoebe
Western kingbird
Eastern kingbird
Scissor-tailed flycatcher

Shrikes

Logger-headed shrike
Northern shrike

Vireos

Warbling vireo
Red-eyed vireo

Jays

Blue jay

Crows

Black-billed magpie
American crow

Larks

Horned-lark

Swallows

Tree swallow
Rough-winged swallow
Bank swallow
Cliff swallow
Barn swallow

Tits, nuthatches and creepers

Black-capped chickadee
Mountain chickadee
Red-breasted nuthatch
Brown creeper

Wrens

Rock wren
House wren
Winter wren
Sedge wren
Marsh wren

Kinglets

Golden-crowned kinglet
Ruby-crowned kinglet

Thrushes

Mountain bluebird
Townsend's solitaire
Veery
Gray-cheeked thrush
Swainson's thrush
Hermit thrush
American robin
Varied thrush
Gray catbird
Northern mockingbird
Brown thrasher

Starlings

European starling

Pipits

American water pipit
Sprague's pipit

Waxwings

Bohemian waxwing
Cedar waxwing

Warblers

Tennessee warbler
Orange-crowned warbler
Yellow warbler
Cape May warbler
Yellow-rumped, Myrtle and Audubon's
    warbler
Townsend's warbler

Blackburnian warbler
Palm warbler
Blackpoll warbler
American redstart
Ovenbird
Northern waterthrush
Mourning warbler
MacGillivray's warbler
Common yellowthroat
Wilson's warbler
Yellow-breasted chat

Tanagers

Scarlet tanager
Western tanager
Spotted towhee

Sparrows

American tree sparrow
Chipping sparrow
Clay-colored sparrow
Brewer's sparrow
Vesper sparrow
Lark sparrow
Lark bunting
Savannah sparrow
Grasshopper sparrow
Baird's sparrow
LeConte's sparrow
Lincoln's sparrow
White-throated sparrow
Harris sparrow
White-crowned sparrow
Golden-crowned sparrow
Dark-eyed junco
McCown's longspur
Lapland longspur
Smith's longspur
Chestnut- collared longspur

Buntings

Snow bunting
Lazuli bunting

Grosbeaks

Rose-breasted grosbeak
Black-headed grosbeak
Blue grosbeak
Pine grosbeak

Blackbirds

Bobolink
Red-winged blackbird
Western meadowlark
Yellow-headed blackbird
Rusty blackbird
Brewer's blackbird
Common grackle
Great-tailed grackle
Brown-headed cowbird

Orchard oriole
Baltimore oriole
Bullock's oriole

Finches

Cassin's finch
House finch
Red crossbill
Common redpoll
Hoary redpoll
Pine siskin
American goldfinch
Evening goldfinch

Old World Weavers

House sparrow

Pheasant

The following four refuges, Black Coulee, Creedman Coulee, Hewitt Lake, and Lake Thibadeau National Wildlife Refuges, are administered by Bowdoin NWR staff. Important to waterfowl and other wildlife species visitation is sometimes difficult and in some cases you will need private landowner permission. As a general reference use the Bowdoin Bird List. Other wildlife possibilities are mule and white-tailed deer, pronghorn and a variety of lesser mammals, including furbearers.

Black Coulee National Wildlife Refuge

1,494 ACRES; LOCATED NORTHEAST OF HARLEM, SOUTH OF TURNER IN NORTHEASTERN BLAINE COUNTY

The mission statement reads in part, "managed primarily as a resting and nesting place for migratory birds and other wildlife species." Missing, it seems to us, is the caveat, "when there is water." In several visits, we have yet to see a single duck, and water, it seems, is more fantasy than reality. Though we have seen numerous pronghorns, a variety of raptors, a large covey of Huns, sharp-tailed grouse and evidence of a healthy badger population, although we've yet to actually spy an artful digger. Lack of water, of course, is something none of us can do much about; one of those cross all digits and pray for rain deals.

Waterfowl use, or lack thereof, centers around a large retention reservoir. The surrounding uplands are mostly low-quality native rangeland. Substantial wheat operations dominate the adjacent private holdings and in years of heavy snow runoff, silt has drastically reduced the reservoir's holding capacity. It is also no doubt the reason, in large part, for no water come fall, when we usually visit.

Technically the refuge is part NWR, part WPA and part easement only. Thus, management issues are derived more or less by committee (USFWS, MTFWP and the landowner). Despite the complex management scheme and the fact that the refuge is remote and unstaffed, cooperation is evident in recent improvements to the water control apparatus and concrete spillway.

Fences are maintained and gates are locked to exclude trespass grazing. Resource values are maintained by natural processes. The refuge is monitored to ensure that these values have not been compromised. No other upland management occurs.

Pronghorn antelope does

Fast Facts

Contact Info: Administered by staff at Bowdoin NWR, HC 65 Box 5700, Malta, MT 59538; 654-2863

Getting There: MT 241 north from Harlem, at sign six miles south of Turner (Hutterite Colony) turn east, then south on gravel road. The refuge is about five miles south. The road is all but impassable when wet, with a dangerous hill to negotiate about halfway.

Activities: Wildlife viewing, waterfowl and upland game bird hunting is allowed on that portion east of the road, walk-in access only. In high-water years it is possible to drag or carry a small boat to the water.

Principle Mammals: Pronghorn, badger, coyote.

Mammals of Special Interest: None.

Principle Birdlife: Waterfowl, shorebirds, wading birds, how many depends on water.

Birds of Special Interest: None.

Habitat Overview: A single large retention reservoir surrounded by low, quality native uplands.

Flora of Special Interest: None.

Best Wildlife Viewing Ops: Pronghorns can be seen year round, fawns are dropped in May.

Best Birding Ops: Wet springs through early summer.

Best Photo Ops: Spring migration but the reservoir is some distance from the road so bring a big lens or a portable blind.

Hunting Ops: Waterfowl hunting can be excellent when there is water; upland bird hunting too, but the birds aren't always on the open area.

Fishing Ops: None.

Camping Ops: None.

Boating Ops: Suitable for shallow draft vessels, canoe, duck boat, etc.

Hiking Trails: None.

Motor Trails: None.

Creedman Coulee
National Wildlife Refuge

2728 ACRES; 30 MILES NORTH OF
HAVRE IN HILL COUNTY

Creedman is a large retention reservoir with surrounding uplands, primarily sage-brush-steppe grasslands and croplands. The good news is that the reservoir catches runoff from a rather large area so there is usually water; the bad news is that the water is encumbered by private water rights. It took a court case to determine and

Sandhill cranes

reserve the critical water level necessary to maintain healthy waterfowl nesting and rearing habitat. The refuge was established as a resting and breeding ground for migratory waterfowl, shorebirds, wading birds and other wildlife. During spring and fall migration, large numbers of a wide variety of species use the refuge, which would seem to make for a duck hunter's paradise. Such, however, is not the case, as private acreage far outstrips public; the USFWS owns just 80 acres. The large imbalance rules out most recreational activities, as well as wreaking havoc with any sort of management plan; in fact, 97 percent is private easement held by USFWS. Thus, USFWS is legally responsible for managing the water and maintaining the water control structure, but beyond that, the workings of the refuge are left largely to Ma Nature. Bowdoin NWR staff does monitor to ensure nothing is compromised.

FYI, Creedman Coulee is about as far north in Montana as you can get, like look up the road, lo and behold you'll see the Port of Willow Creek (border crossing) buildings clearly visible, and not just on a clear day either. Barring some unforeseen turnaround in ownership/access, Creedman remains an important cog in the overall refuge system, but one most of us will never get the chance to share.

Fast Facts

Contact Info: Administered by staff at Bowdoin NWR, HC 65 Box 5700, Malta, MT 59538; 654-2863

Getting There: From Havre, take MT 232/233 north; 2.5 miles out the road forks, take the right fork, proceed approximately 27 miles north to refuge. Note: Just 80 acres are public, landowner permission is required for trespass.

Activities: Limited bird watching, wildlife viewing, hunting with landowner permission.

Principle Mammals: Pronghorn, white-tailed and mule deer, coyote, small furbearers.

Mammals of Special Interest: Pronghorn.

Principle Birdlife: Migratory waterfowl and shorebirds, sandhill cranes, Hungarian partridge, sharp-tailed grouse and a variety of songbirds.

Birds of Special Interest: Hungarian partridge.

Habitat Overview: Large retention reservoir, surrounded by grasslands, croplands

Flora of Special Interest: None.

Best Wildlife Viewing Ops: Largely limited to what you can see from roads.

Best Birding Ops: Spring and fall migration, early summer brood sightings.

Best Photo Ops: Limited, bring a big lens.

Hunting Ops: Very good waterfowl and upland bird hunting for Huns and sharp-tailed grouse, if you can get landowner permission.

Fishing Ops: None.

Camping Ops: None.

Boating Ops: None.

Hiking Trails: None.

Motor Trails: None.

Hewitt Lake National Wildlife Refuge

1,680 ACRES; WEST OF NELSON RESERVOIR, IN PHILLIPS COUNTY NORTHEAST OF MALTA

This is another Bowdoin satellite refuge that suffers greatly from lack of water in dry years. The lake is surrounded by a large natural basin which, in wet years, becomes more or less continuous wetland habitat for migratory waterfowl, shorebirds, wading birds and numerous songbirds. The uplands are home to pronghorns, prairie dogs, white-tailed jackrabbits and mountain cottontails, to name just the most common animals. Threatened mountain plovers are seen occasionally, but more common

Mallard ducks

sights are beaver, mink, great blue herons, sandhill cranes, cormorants and white pelicans. Our personal Hewitt Lake check list includes wood duck, green-winged, blue-winged and cinnamon teals, northern shovelers, widgeon, gadwall, black duck, mallard, pintail, canvasback, ringnecked duck, blue bills (lesser scaup), common goldeneye, Barrow's goldeneye, hooded, red-breasted, and common mergansers, white-winged scoters, Canada geese and ruddy ducks. Our check list also includes such uncommon/rarities as yellow-billed cuckoo, Forster's tern, common nighthawk, piping plover and all the fly catchers known to visit the area except the extremely rare alder and scissor-tailed flycatchers, western wood peewee, willow and least flycatchers, Say's phoebe, western and eastern kingbirds. Summer skies swarm with cliff, barn and tree swallows.

Resource values are maintained through natural processes. Bowdoin staff monitors Hewitt to ensure these natural processes are not compromised. Management is limited to maintaining reservoir and fencing to exclude trespass livestock grazing.

Hewitt is within the BLM's Area of Critical Environmental Concern for the Big Bend of the Milk River. Encampment sites and bison kill areas surround the refuge.

The USFWS-owned portion of the lake is open to waterfowl hunting. Permission from the private landowner is needed to hunt the easement portion. All other hunting is closed. Like many, Hewitt Lake suffers that old bugaboo, "when there is water." In other words, before striking out to view wildlife, hunt, whatever, check in at Bowdoin headquarters for the latest.

Fast Facts

Contact Info: Administered by staff at Bowdoin NWR, HC 65 Box 5700, Malta, MT 59538; 654-2863

Getting There: Access via a graveled county road which crosses the dam of Nelson reservoir, and then proceeds west for two miles to Hewitt Lake. Nelson Reservoir is about 17 miles northeast of Malta, off US 2.

Activities: Birding, wildlife viewing, hunting.

Principle Mammals: Muskrat, mink, mountain cottontail, white-tailed jackrabbit, badger, coyote; pronghorn, mule and white-tailed deer are common throughout the area.

Mammals of Special Interest: None.

Principle Birdlife: Waterfowl, shorebirds, wading birds assuming there is water; numerous songbirds and raptors.

Birds of Special Interest: Occasional and rare species are best seen during migration; the surest bet is spring since water is more likely than fall.

Habitat Overview: Hewitt Lake, surrounded by intermittent wetlands, the Milk River riparian corridor and low, quality upland range.

Flora of Special Interest: None.

Best Wildlife Viewing Ops: Winter, spring and summer, hunting hampers fall viewing opportunities.

Best Birding Ops: Wet springs; birds are most active early and late in day.

Best Photo Ops: Spring migration, later when broods hatch, early and late provides the best opportunities and the best light.
Hunting Ops: Waterfowl, ducks and geese, (when there is water).
Fishing Ops: Excellent in nearby Milk River, Nelson Reservoir.
Camping Ops: None.
Boating Ops: None within refuge; excellent opportunities at nearby Nelson Reservoir.
Hiking Trails: None.
Motor Trails: None.

Turkey vulture

Lake Thibadeau
National Wildlife Refuge

LOCATED 12 MILES NORTH OF HAVRE, IN HILL COUNTY, ACCESS IS PRIVATE TREATY ONLY WITH LANDOWNER

The refuge consists of Lake Thibadeau, a diversion dam, along with Grassy and Dry Lakes (which are both actually intermittent wetlands, rather than lakes per se) and associated uplands, most of which are cultivated. The refuge serves as a resting and breeding ground for migratory birds and other wildlife. A variety of raptors and Hungarian (gray) partridge are common, as are pronghorns and coyotes. There is no legal public access, although refuge rules allow waterfowl hunting, permission to hunt is at the discretion of the landowner.

By and large, USFWS management is restricted to maintaining the water control structures both on Lake Thibadeau and the diversion dam. Resource values are left to natural processes and Bowdoin staff monitors to insure these are not compromised.

To reach the refuge, drive north of Havre on MT 233 (the right fork two and a half miles out), approximately 12 miles; a large private grain elevator complex marks the refuge area. To discuss access protocol, contact Bowdoin NWR, 654-2863.

Fast Facts

Contact Info: Administered by staff at Bowdoin NWR, HC 65 Box 5700, Malta, MT 59538; 654-2863.

Getting There: There is no legal access to the refuge; access is at the discretion of the landowner. To discuss access protocol, contact Bowdoin NWR. North of Havre on MT 233 (the right fork two and a half miles out), approximately 12 miles; a large private grain elevator complex marks the refuge area.

Activities: Assuming access is granted, birding, wildlife viewing, limited hunting.

Principle Mammals: A variety of migratory birds and waterfowl, various raptors and Hungarian (gray) partridge are common, as are pronghorns and coyotes.

Principle Birdlife: Waterfowl, shorebirds, wading birds assuming there is water; numerous songbirds and raptors.

Birds of Special Interest: Occasional and rare species are best seen during migration; the surest bet is spring since water is more likely than fall.

Habitat Overview: Lake Thibadeau and surrounding intermittent wetlands, low, quality upland range and associated agricultural lands.

Best Wildlife Viewing Ops: Spring, when water is most likely.

Best Birding Ops: Wet springs; birds are most active early and late in day.

Best Photo Ops: Spring migration, later when broods hatch, early and late in the day provides the best opportunities and the best light.

Hunting Ops: Waterfowl and other hunting is at the discretion of the landowner, contact Bowdoin NWR.

Whitetail jackrabbit

Brush Lake State Park

450 ACRES, SOUTHEAST PLENTYWOOD, NEAR DAGMAR

Montana's newest state park, Brush Lake features cool, clear water, sandy beaches, picnic facilities and some of the best birding anywhere. In the bird world, this is the place where east and west clash; the premier spot in all of Montana to check off eastern bird species. What's with that? Well, it all has to do with migration routes. It seems in Canada many eastern species nest well west of their normal range. Come fall migration time, the birds swing south along the North Dakota-Montana line to about Brush Lake, then swerve southeast toward their winter homes (many head for the Gulf Coast, some as far as Central and South America). In spring, of course, the route is reversed.

Surrounded by a monotony of yellow wheat stubble and tan/gray grasslands, it's hard to imagine a blue-water lake looking more out of place than Brush Lake. More than 60 feet deep and fed by springs, the lake remains cool and clear despite air temperatures that often peg out in triple digits. Unlike the typical pothole, the lake is relatively algae-free, lacks the sulfur (soda) odor, and does not stagnate. Typical of potholes, it's location in a depression on an otherwise table flat prairie serves as an effective wind break. Birds take advantage and flock to the surrounding chokecherry and buffalo berry thickets for both shelter and the tasty fruits. At nearly 300 acres, it dwarfs the many shallow, alkaline prairie potholes that dot the surrounding countryside; even more incongruous are the lake's white sand beaches. It begs the questions: who hauled it all in and where, pray tell, from?

Montana's 50th, Brush Lake is the only state park in Region 6. It was sold to the state agency by a private trust that owned the lake for years and still retains a one-third interest — the state park only encompasses the northern two-thirds of the lake. Birds and birding aside, locals will tell you Brush Lake is "Flat out, Montana's best swimming hole east of the mountains."

The huge spring and no inlet or outlet, means evaporation and seepage are the mechanisms that maintain the water level. Evaporation concentrates minerals in the water, creates the mineral salts (calcium carbonate, manganese and sodium sulfate)

carlet tanager

often found in hot springs. High concentrations prove inhospitable to fish, which suffocate from calcium deposits on the gills. In other words, bring the binocs and spotting scope, leave the rod to home.

Thousands of years ago, the Missouri River flowed through here, eventually spilling its waters in Hudson Bay. Glaciers forever changed its course, shoving its way south in the bargain. As the glaciers receded, huge ice chunks scoured the depressions that are now prairie potholes, including Brush Lake. Core samples of the lake bottom indicate the region was once covered in montane forest — modern day northern and high altitude species spruce and fir.

At present, there are no amenities or developments in the park; swimming, picnicking, wildlife viewing, birding, camping and such are strictly do-it-yourself. In the fall, more and more bird hunters show up to camp, taking advantage of the rare opportunity to camp on public land in a region dominated in large part by private lands. Listed among the top birding spots in the state, it is not at all surprising to find many of the campers are birders, an especially popular late-summer and early-fall activity as many species of birds normally associated with the eastern U.S. migrate through here from Canada. Just up the road is the tiny town of Westby on the North Dakota border and another birding mecca. This is a good spot to check off hard-to-find breeders that barely get into Montana like the Sedge wren, LeConte's sparrow, Nelson's sharp-tailed sparrow and yellow rail. You can also expect piping plover, Sprague's pipit and Baird's sparrow. With luck, wading birds such as white-rumped and stilt sandpipers will be observed.

Starting in 2006, FWP plans to begin developing the park further to eventually include rental cottages, a bathhouse, and a shower facility. First on the agenda though, is upgrading the existing road, picnic tables, a gravel parking area, installing toilet facilities, a boat ramp and dock. Beyond physical improvements, the plans call for restoring the uplands to native prairie. An interpretive nature trail detailing geology, social, cultural and natural history, prairie birds and plants is also planned.

Nearby Restaurants and Accommodations

Four Winds Café, Plentywood, 765-1060
The Prairie Kitchen Café, Westby, 765-1060
Plains Motel, Plentywood, 765-1240
Sherwood Inn, Plentywood, 765-2810
Lions RV Park, Plentywood.

Fast Facts

Contact Info: Woody Baxter, Region 6 Parks Supervisor; phone: 228-3707.
Getting There: Turn east onto MT 258, off MT 16 south of Plentywood, at Reserve, follow highway to Brush Lake Rd. to the park.
Activities: Birding, swimming, picnicking, camping, hiking, boating (no motors), waterfowl and upland bird hunting.

Principle Mammals: Pronghorn, mule deer.
Mammals of Special Interest: None.
Principle Birdlife: Songbirds, waterfowl, upland game birds, shore birds, wading birds, birds of prey.
Birds of Special Interest: Eastern species rarely seen in most parts of Montana.
Habitat Overview: 280 acre, spring fed lake, uplands a mix of native grasslands and croplands.
Flora of Special Interest: Native grasslands.
Best Wildlife Viewing Ops: Year around opportunities.
Best Birding Ops: Bird numbers peak during spring and fall migrations; late summer and early fall is primo.
Best Photo Ops: Good chance to capture birds rarely seen in most of Montana.
Hunting Ops: Waterfowl, upland game birds.
Fishing Ops: None.
Camping Ops: Primitive camping allowed; should be toilet facilities available soon.
Boating Ops: No motors.
Hiking Trails: None developed.
Motor Trails: None.

Sharp-tailed grouse

Charles M. Russell
National Wildlife Refuge

APPROXIMATELY 1,100,000 ACRES IN NORTH-CENTRAL MONTANA, EXTENDING 135 AIRLINE MILES UP THE MISSOURI RIVER FROM FORT PECK DAM (ACREAGE INCLUDES 245,000-ACRE RESERVOIR)

Lewis and Clark's epic journey to the Pacific Ocean must have been full of surprises. But perhaps none that would compare to that first glimpse of the Missouri Breaks; the piece of wild, wild west, we now know as the Charles M. Russell (CMR) National Wildlife Refuge. On May 23, 1805, encamped beside the Mighty Mo (probably now beneath the sprawling waters of Fort Peck Reservoir) Lewis entered in his journal, "The musquetoes troublesome this evening, a circumstance I did not expect from the temperature of the morning. The Gees begin to lose the feathers of their wings and are unable to fly. Capt. Clark walked on shore and killed 4 deer and an Elk. We killed a large fat brown bear which took to water after being wounded and was carried under some driftwood where he sunk and we were unable to get him; buffalow is scarce today, but the elk, dear and antelopes are very numerous. We saw five bear."

Surprisingly, Lewis made no mention of the rugged badlands spreading west before him. For beyond acquiring meat and staying safe from bears, reaching the objective hinged on finding a way. A way through who knows how many miles of badlands must have appeared, at times, all but impenetrable. Sculpted by eons of wind and water, actually more moon-like than earth-like, at least anything Lewis was used to. "Thank God for the river" surely must have come up in more than one campfire discussion.

Today, the CMR is one of the largest intact chunks of the Northern Short Grasslands left. According to USFWS personnel, "The NSG is the largest grassland eco-region in North America; including parts of southeastern Alberta and southwestern Saskatchewan, much of the area east of the Rocky Mountains, central

Bighorn sheep (ram)

and eastern Montana, western North and South Dakota, and northeastern Wyoming. Of course, in many places, it's no longer easily recognized, having been long since chopped and plowed nearly to oblivion.

"Four major features distinguish it from other grasslands: the harsh winter climate, with much of the precipitation falling as snow; short growing season; periodic, severe, droughts; and vegetation. Two environmental gradients determine species composition in mixed and short grass prairies: increasing temperatures from north to south and increasing rainfall from west to east. With increasing latitude, the short grass prairies become more mixed-grass prairie, dominated by cool season grasses, such as in this eco-region, where many cool-season species predominate. Typical yearly swings in temperature are huge, triple digits in summer to well below zero in winter. Droughts lasting several months to several years are common; overall the region is semi-arid, as some say, 'just one thunderstorm removed from true desert.'

Before settlement, drought, fire, and grazing were probably the major disturbance factors, with fire playing less of a role than in other grassland regions. Today, virtually all of the eco-region is either converted to wheat farms or rangelands, which makes the CMR not only unique within the region, but valuable in terms of preserving (reestablishing) native species, not only flora but fauna. Recent attempts at reestablishing native black-footed ferret populations are examples.

Within the CMR itself, grass communities are quite varied. Included are grammas, needle grass and wheatgrass as well as wheatgrass-needle grass; to a lesser extent, June grass and dry land sedge also occur. Of the variety of shrubs and herbs sagebrush is most abundant, and on drier sites yucca, yellow cactus and prickly pear. On coulee slopes Ponderosa pine and juniper dominate while the river terrace itself, are scrubby aspen, willows, cottonwoods and box-elder. Saline areas support alkali grass, wild barley, greasewood, red samphire and sea blite.

Prior to 1850, what is today the CMR, provided bison some of the most extensive habitat remaining. Bison herds drastically impacted both the species structure and composition. Black-footed ferrets were also once common here, and reintroductions should eventually capitalize the abundant prairie dog populations. The CMR is surprisingly rich in mammals for a region so far north. Elk, bighorn sheep, mule and whitetail deer, bobcat, coyote and cougar are common large mammals. Short-horned lizard, bull snake and prairie rattlesnake occur as well. Much of the bird-life is composed of species typically associated with the prairie potholes; burrowing owl, ferruginous hawk and Swainson's hawk, golden eagle, sharp-tailed and sage grouse, mountain plover and clay-colored sparrow, to name just a few of the 240 species known to use the refuge."

In the lower 48 states, the CMR, as far as being remote and inhospitable, rival just about anywhere. Except for US 191, a handful of macadam roads in the dam area, and a few gravel all-weather roads, most roads and two tracks are gumbo. To the uninitiated, gumbo is a form of bentonite clay, a wonderful substance with such an affinity for moisture, even the hint of rain turns it to grease — the likes of which wi confound you. At its best, vehicles are instantly rendered useless; even four-wheel drive and chains all around don't always work. Walking, just staying upright is sometimes impossible, and even standing still can be a chore given any sort of incline. I once met an older gent in Lewistown who grew up in the breaks before automobiles were the norm.

"A couple times a year we would pack up our outfit, hitch up a wagon or two and head for town (Lewistown) for supplies," he told me. "Our place was quite a ways out from Roy so imagine you are talking 50, 60 miles one way. Well, heaven help us should it rain. One time we got about halfway to Roy and could see real gully washer comin'. We quick set up camp and...did it rain! All night and part of the next mornin'. We set there for five days afore the gumbo let us get on to town. Sonny, when it rains out there, you, don't, go. Per-i-od."

In case you wondered, we met when he noticed our rig covered every inch in gumbo, a little skirmish we happened to win, though just barely. Before heading into the CMR backcountry it is a good idea to check first with refuge staff.

While there aren't many full-time residents left, signs of their passing are well preserved in the semi-arid climate in the form of crumbling, now long abandoned buildings. Proof how empty this place really is comes at night when often the only lights visible are the zillion stars and the moon in the wide, inky-black sky. In daylight, the mix of chiseled coulees and mesas, atop which offer visitors mostly empty imposing vistas, horizon to horizon. I think it's safe to say that the wildlife far outnumbers permanent human residents. There are scattered private inholdings within the CMR, though relatively speaking, not many.

And perhaps its biggest commodity is the emptiness itself. There are few places left anywhere within the lower 48 states that can match the feeling of "enormity of space" the CMR and surrounding landscape provides. Technically speaking, this is semi-arid country as opposed to true desert. In reality, about one thunderstorm removed from true desert though. Years of ample snow and/or bountiful spring rains green things up for awhile, but you just know the look is temporary. Somehow, even at its greenest, the tan, dry look just never disappears completely. In normal and dry years, the tan look overwhelms the senses. The life force driving it all is the mighty Missouri, nowadays mostly massive Fort Peck Reservoir. In times of extended drought, such as the one ongoing, life for inhabitants is tough, to put it mildly. At its harshest, only the hardiest survive but even the toughest of the hardy must find life tenable at best.

Once Lewis and Clark showed the way, settlers followed, and it wasn't long until the Missouri served as the main travel route for heading west. Riverboats ferried passengers and freight from St. Louis to Fort Benton, a distance of 2,200 miles. Downriver cargo first included such wilderness commodities as beaver and buffalo hides and later gold and other precious metals mined in central Montana. As riverboat traffic increased, wild and sometimes lawless settlements grew along the river. Desperadoes, cattle rustlers and bank robbers thrived at the expense of river travelers and found hiding out from the then short arm of the law, easy amongst the remote breaks. Not until vigilantes, such as "Stuart's Stranglers," took it upon themselves to introduce justice did travel along the river finally become relatively safe.

The remoteness and vastness of the CMR catches many a visitor by surprise. Experiencing the CMR in its entirety might be possible in a single lifetime, but rest assured that doing so would certainly rank right up there as a most daunting task. Just exploring Fort Peck alone, at 245,000 acres and hundreds of miles of shoreline, is beyond the grasp of most. More inland sea than mere reservoir, it was created in 1939. At the time it was the most massive construction project ever for the U.S. Army Corps of Engineers, an outfit who knows something about massive construction projects. According to The World Almanac, it's "the largest embankment dam in the United States and the reservoir ranks as the fifth largest in the world, boasting some 1,500 miles of shoreline.

The CMR's remoteness and geography, in combination with a wildlife-first management scheme, makes it well suited to wildlife diversity. Toss in minimum development and that there are only 12 public access points that permit recreation like boating, fishing, exploring and seasonal hunting, and it's little wonder wildlife and habitat remain healthy and intact. That wildlife far outnumbers permanent human residents should not surprise.

Over the eons, the Pleistocene glaciers spread over northern Montana, literally shoved the Missouri River from its former course (now the Milk River, 60 miles north) southward. Eventually the glaciers began a snail-like melt and retreat, runoff formed streams that coursed across the soil, and began sculpting the narrow coulees, or breaks; the resulting river cut its present-day channel at the base of these breaks.

In looks, the breaks or "badlands" of the Missouri differ little from those in other drainages, but the scale and enormity is far different. Deep, heavily eroded coulees, many rugged beyond description, extend like convoluted fingers upward from the river, some for several miles. To this day natural forces, wind and water, continually conspire to sculpt the landscape. These days the primary soil type (if you can call it that) is Bearpaw shale. Brown/gray in color and extremely unstable, it periodically collapses; the resultant landslides contribute to a wild land, one always in flux, minute by minute, hour by hour, and so on.

U.S. Fish and Wildlife Service, headquartered in Lewistown, administers the CMR. There are five additional outpost stations staffed by refuge personnel. Part of their job is to coordinate with other agencies and help administer certain public uses, such as fishing, hunting, educational programs and others. Visitors tallies average between 100,000 to 150,000 per year — a relatively small number for a refuge of such magnitude (the second largest in the entire NWR system). Most are sportsmen who have enjoyed fishing and hunting the CMR for years. Big game hunting for elk, antelope and deer rivals the best anywhere. The reservoir is world class for smallmouth bass, walleye, northern pike and catfish. In total there are some fifty species of game fish swimming in Fort Peck. Nature photographers, birders, wildlife viewers, backpackers, campers, boaters and sightseers make up the rest.

While managing people is important, the bulk of the staff's duties concerns preserving wildlife habitat. This involves complex issues ranging from securing water rights and obtaining easements to complying with federal endangered species regulations and conducting scientific studies of wildlife populations.

American badger

Beyond people and wildlife one of the big issues is cattle grazing within the refuge. Unchecked grazing imparts a detrimental impact on native wildlife. Thus, grazing reductions are becoming more wide-spread. The refuge manager, explains,

"In certain instances, cattle grazing can be a useful management tool," the refuge manager explained. "But left unchecked, over-grazing destroys critical habitat used by birds and fish."

As throughout the West, the 19th and 20th centuries were not always kind to the land, or the natives who peopled it. The Missouri River offered the Crow, Blackfeet, Sioux and Cree tribes choice hunting grounds, which included some of the largest herds of the 60 million bison most experts agree once roamed the continent. With the bison long gone, and much of the big game devastated through over-hunting and habitat loss due to various land abuses following settlement, President Franklin D. Roosevelt signed an order establishing the Fort Peck Game Range in 1936. His farsighted aim was to halt the decline, reconstruct habitat 'to sustain the 400,000 sharp-tailed grouse, 1,500 antelope and other wildlife species before it's too late.' With almost no enforcement you can imagine how popular a hunting spot the range was for the 11,000 workers at the Fort Peck Dam site. It was only after construction was completed and the workers moved on that the boomtown dwindled to about 300 year-round residents, that the president's proclamation was able to have a lasting positive affect on the region's wildlife. Still, the move was a giant step in the right direction.

In 1963, the name was changed to Charles M. Russell National Wildlife Range and in 1976, the "range" became a "refuge" named after this country's most venerable cowboy artist. Charlie Russell provided easterners, and the world for that matter, a glimpse of Wild West life in Montana. In his later years, it is said that Russell grew weary of the unbridled progress, that what he saw would eventually change the character of his beloved Montana for the worse. Many believe the namesake refuge embodies the qualities that Charlie loved most about the Old West.

No visit in September or early October is complete without an evening stop at the Slippery Ann Elk Viewing Area. To reach Slippery Ann, turn on the Auto Tour Route just north of Fred Robinson Bridge (signs point the way, but most September evenings all you need to do is follow the crowd). The lure is a chance to watch bugling bull elk interact with each other and harems of cows and calves gathered by the dominant bulls in the herd. It's quite a spectacle and one you don't want to miss. Elk are quite the success story within the refuge — 4,000 to 5,000 now call the CMR home. Considering that by the early 1900s, elk were eliminated from the region because of over-hunting, it was an impressive turn around. The current herd sprung from a joint effort in 1951 by USFWS and Montana Fish, Wildlife and Parks, and private individuals to reintroduce the big ungulates using stock from Yellowstone National Park. Obviously the Yellowstone elk found CMR to their liking; white-tailed and mule deer, antelope, sage and sharp-tailed grouse inhabit the area and opportunities for viewing them are quite good.

Roberta Donovan wrote a story in the Great Falls Tribune highlighting the story of a former CMR employee named Harold Jones. The following information was taken from her article:

For 27 years Harold "Casey" Jones (now retired) was foreman and work leader at the Slippery Ann Station. For the first six years, he was the only employee there.

"I started it from nothing," he recalled, "and when I left there was nothing left."

Jones was referring to the fact that the buildings have since been removed to a new location on US 191. The old station was on the north side of the river, about nine miles east of the highway, what is now the Elk Viewing Area.

When Jones took over at the station in 1954, jurisdiction had just been turned over to USFWS from the Army Corps of Engineers. Jones' task, to eventually establish a wildlife refuge, started with efforts to establish a captive Canada geese flock; one that would hopefully grow into a viable wild population. Geese were native to the area, but at the time none nested anywhere nearby. Hoping to lure migrating geese to stay, Jones built ponds and, like someone once said, if you build it they will come, and sure enough... As with the ponds to lure the geese, Jones planted cereal crops to provide wild turkeys incentive to stay and propagate.

The Auto Tour Route (mentioned above) begins just north of Fred Robinson Bridge and loops around to US 191 several miles north. Driving time is about two hours, depending of course, on how long and how often you stop. There are no facilities along the route other than primitive campsites and toilets. The road is one of the few graveled roads in the area and is passable when wet. Best times to view wildlife are early and late in the day.

There are 13 stops along the route, each with its interpretive signage. The stops give visitors an overview of the cultural, societal and natural history of the CMR. At stop 10, for example, it reads, "The area east of the road is a traditional sharp-tailed grouse dancing ground. From late March to mid-May males gather here at daybreak. With a hooting or cooing sound and short rapid stamping steps, they attempt to attract females. Sometimes two males pair off in battle. With wings spread and tails erect, they rush each other, stop short beak-to-beak. This display is repeated again and again."

Sharptails are important game birds throughout the plains of the central U.S. These birds are closely associated with grasslands and are dependant on good grass cover. They need eight to ten inches of plant cover for nesting; during the winter they utilize shrubs for food and cover.

Eastern Montana is in the Central Flyway. During spring and fall, migrations of thousands of migratory species, waterfowl and shorebirds drop in to Fort Peck and the river itself. In the spring many stay and nest, while others move on as the season progresses. During the height of migration, birders can add many species to their life lists. Since record keeping began in 1936, some 240 feathered species have been identified.

This section of the Missouri River is a stronghold for paddlefish. As such, about 25 miles of river between the Fred Robinson Bridge and the head of Fort Peck Reservoir draws quite a crowd of fishermen each spring hoping to snag one the primitive denizens. Most fishermen try snagging paddlefish from the bank, but snagging from the boat also is popular since more locations can be fished. Best fishing generally occurs in April, May and early June, particularly when the river is rising. Males are the first to run, followed later by the larger females. Other game fish such as sauger, walleye, channel catfish and northern pike and rough fish, such as goldeye and suckers are also popular targets.

Nearby Restaurants and Accommodations

Barring cook-it-yourself, CMR dinner spots are non-existent. Though widely scattered, such is not the case, however, in the surrounding towns. One of the more unique-looking eateries is the Kalamity Kafe in Zortman (673-3883) but in this case don't be fooled by the facade; the food inside is pretty tasty. Three spots for great steaks are The Mint, Lewistown, 538-9925, Sam's Supper Club in Glasgow (228-4614) and the Stockman Bar and Steakhouse in Malta (654-1919); all three feature full bar service and a menu includes many delicious entrées besides beef.

Motels are plentiful in the few bigger towns, such as Lewistown and Glasgow, and most whistle stops sport at least one. There are eleven developed campgrounds within the refuge. Eleven developed campgrounds for over a million acres doesn't sound like much, but except for peak big game hunting season finding the empty site is not a problem. Camping is also allowed just about anywhere within the refuge; for example, unless posted otherwise, you can camp along any designated road provided you don't drive more than 100 yards off-road to do so.

Fast Facts

Contact Info: Charles M. Russell NWR, P.O. Box 110, Airport Rd., Lewistown, MT 59457; Phone: 538-8706 Email: cmr@fws.gov; for adjacent lands information contact BLM, Lewistown District Office, PO Box 1160, Lewistown, MT 59547; phone: 538-7461

Getting There: Using MT 200 between Lewistown and a point east of Jordan, roads heading north generally dead end within the CMR; from the north use US 2 (Highline) between Malta and Glasgow, access roads run generally south. A word of caution, it is a long ways between gas stations and all but the main access roads are impassable when wet — gumbo is for real, not something to be taken lightly (see the above narrative).

Activities: Wildlife viewing, birding, hunting, fishing, horseback riding, hiking, biking, auto tour route, boating, fishing, hunting, camping, picnicking, berry picking and just about any other outdoor pursuit.

Principle Mammals: Elk, mule and white-tailed deer, bighorn sheep, pronghorn, beaver

Mammals of Special Interest: Black-footed ferret, mountain lion.

Principle Birdlife: Sage and sharp-tailed grouse, Hungarian (gray) partridge, pheasant, wild turkey (Merriam's).

Birds of Special Interest: Least tern, piping plover, mountain plover, double-crested cormorant, common loon, western grebe, marbled godwits, long-billed curlews, upland sandpipers, prairie and peregrine falcons, bald and golden eagles, burrowing and snowy owls (later occur only in the worst winters) and osprey.

Habitat Overview: A diverse mix of native prairies, forested coulees, riparian bottomlands, wetlands and badlands.

Flora of Special Interest: Native shortgrass prairie species, cottonwood.

Best Wildlife Viewing Ops: Spring, summer and fall, winter is tough; early and late in day.

Best Birding Ops: Spring and fall migration, highest diversity in the riparian zones.

Best Photo Ops: Spring, summer and fall, Slippery Ann EVA in September; early and late in the day.

Hunting Ops: Known for larger than average bull elk, a "breaks tag" is a much coveted item among Montana hunters; mossy-horned mule deer bucks and bighorn rams are also part of the hunting mystique; decent to excellent upland bird hunting, depending on conditions. The refuge encompasses parts of three FWP Regions, 4, 6 & 7 and their respective districts.

Fishing Ops: Fort Peck has become a "destination hotspot" for a growing army of western walleye fans; lake trout, chinook salmon, sauger, perch, bullhead, and smallmouth bass also have large followings and in spring, upstream, especially around the Fred Robinson Bridge, anglers come from all over in hope of snagging a prehistoric paddlefish. A remnant and closely monitored population of pallid sturgeon (listed as endangered) also live in the river above Fort Peck; no fishing allowed, incidental catches must be released immediately; no picture taking even.

Camping Ops: Camping is allowed anywhere. Vehicle access is allowed within 100 yards of "marked" roads and waterways; backcountry camps are by foot or horseback only—no off road motorized or bike travel allowed. Developed campsites: James Kipp Recreation Area, Rock Creek boat ramp, Crooked Creek, Devils Creek, Forchette Bay, Hell Creek (SP), The Pines, Nelson Creek, McGuire Creek, Bear Creek and Fort Peck Recreation areas. Facilities vary, request refuge guide map. Campfires are permitted; bring your own water, potable water is scarce to non-existent.

Boating Ops: Fort Peck Reservoir and the Missouri River offer nearly unlimited boating opportunities although access to both is limited.

Hiking Trails: None developed but mile upon mile of game trails, two-tracks and roads offer the adventurous hiker untold numbers of options.

Motor Trails: Gravel Auto Tour route begins just north of the Fred Robinson Bridge, follow the signs.

Charles M. Russell National Wildlife Refuge

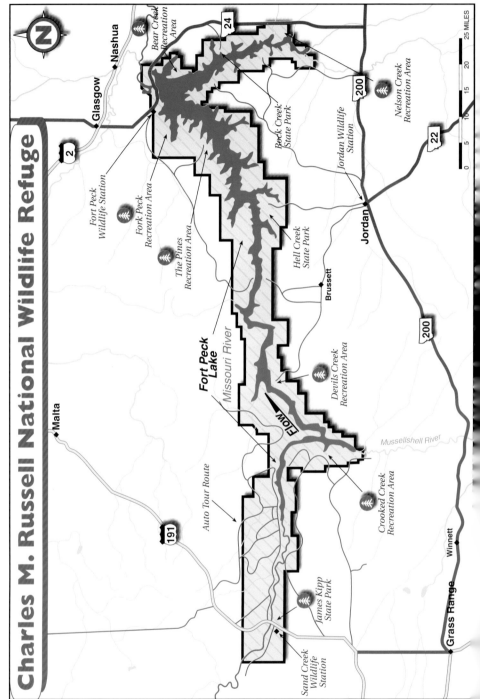

N

Glasgow

Nashua

Bear Creek Recreation Area

24

200

Nelson Creek Recreation Area

Peck Creek State Park

Jordan Wildlife Station

22

2

Fort Peck Wildlife Station

Fork Peck Recreation Area

The Pines Recreation Area

Hell Creek State Park

Jordan

Brussett

Fort Peck Lake

Missouri River

Devils Creek Recreation Area

200

Malta

FLOW

Mussellshell River

Auto Tour Route

Crooked Creek Recreation Area

191

Winnett

James Kipp State Park

Grass Range

Sand Creek Wildlife Station

25 MILES

20

15

10

5

0

© 2008 Wilderness Adventures Press, Inc

THE CHARLES M. RUSSELL NATIONAL WILDLIFE REFUGE: A BRIEF HISTORY

The following is courtesy of CMRNWR and the Montana Historical Society.

The Missouri River is a great slash across northern Montana. It collects melt water from the western mountains and delivers it through the dry plains of eastern Montana. The rushing waters of the Missouri carved the landscape and shaped the history of Montana.

In early times, the Missouri divided the hunting grounds of Indian tribes. Lewis and Clark followed the Missouri on their famous expedition. In May of 1805 they traversed the section of the Missouri River now surrounded by the Charles M. Russell National Wildlife Refuge and set up camps at several locations along the shores. The Missouri soon became the main route of travel into Montana and remained so until the arrival of the railroads in the 1880s. Traders labored against the current with loads of trade goods, then drifted downstream with loads of furs. Miners and buffalo hunters followed and outlaws were not far behind. The growing commerce along the river required protection and policing. Military posts were established at Ft. Carroll and at Ft. Musselshell. Homesteaders were very dependent upon river travel. The permanent settlement of the land was underway.

Steamboats were the major method of travel on the river for nearly 30 years. The standard route spanned the area from St. Louis to Fort Benton, a total of 2,200 river miles. The first steamboat arrived at Fort Benton in 1859. The last freight was unloaded there in 1888. Four hundred passengers and 8,000 tons of freight moved in and out of Fort Benton in 1867. Roughly 80 percent of all the precious metals mined in central Montana before 1875 was transported downriver by riverboats. The richest cargo ever to travel down the Missouri River was on the "Luella" in 1866 — $1 million in gold dust. The steamboat pilothouses were armored with boiler iron to protect them from the bullets of would-be robbers.

The fast current and numerous sandbars demanded the full attention of river captains. Scores of boats and cargos were destroyed by the treacherous river.

As the river traffic increased, wood hawkers established camps along the river and supplied firewood to the steamboats. Several riverside settlements soon sprang up. The town of Carroll was a steamboat landing which enjoyed brief prosperity during the low-water years of 1874 and 1875. This prosperity ended when the return of high water allowed the steamboats to continue upriver to Fort Benton.

The Great Northern and Northern Pacific railroads were built across Montana Territory in the 1880s and the Missouri River quickly lost its importance as a transportation route.

Some of the historic sites are located on what is now the western half of the Charles M. Russell National Wildlife Refuge. Rocky Point was a tough frontier town from the 1860s until the turn of the century. Fights, killings, and hangings were frequent. Rocky Point served legitimate ranchers and businessmen as well as thieves and outlaws. It became the rendezvous and center of trade for woodchoppers, trappers, miners, cowboys, whisky traders and all manner of outlaws, including the infamous Kid Curry and his gang. Many of the outlaws resided in the river bottoms and masqueraded as woodchoppers, Indian traders, and buffalo hunters. Rocky Point also served as a steamboat landing, with infantry companies occasionally stationed there to guard government freight.

The UL Bend has also been called the Great Bend of the Missouri River. Riverboat captains often allowed passengers to leave the boats and walk the two miles across the narrow peninsula for relief from the month-long journey from St. Louis. The steamboats loaded wood and then steamed the 13 miles around the tip of the bend.

The confluence of the Musselshell River with the Missouri River was a significant area. It was a major crossing point of the Missouri for the vast buffalo herds on their annual migrations. Since the site was a major fording point for the Indians of eastern Montana, battles and skirmishes occurred there between Indians and whites. A succession of fur trading posts, wood yards, military camps, ranches, and homesteads occupied the area.

The Musselshell confluence also was a hangout for horse rustlers and other outlaws. Large-scale organized horse stealing rings tormented the ranchers in the Missouri Breaks region in the early 1880s. The gangs raided ranches in Montana, Wyoming, the Dakotas and southern Canada. They drove the livestock to remote areas of the Breaks, "worked" the brands, then drove them to Canada for sale. They would then repeat the process with stolen Canadian livestock. The gangs of outlaws kept guards out day and night watching for law officers and vigilantes.

One of the most famous incidents of "vigilante justice" occurred at the Musselshell confluence in 1884. Granville Stuart, operator of the DHS ranch near Fort Maginnis, led a group of stockmen to the Musselshell to clean out a large horse-rustling ring. Two outlaws were hanged there and two more were hanged at Rocky Point. A few days later the stockmen, who later became known as "Stuart's Stranglers", apprehended more horse thieves at an abandoned wood yard at Bates Point, 15 miles below the mouth of Musselshell. Five outlaws were killed in the ensuing gun battle. Seven men managed to escape but five of these later were captured by soldiers in eastern Montana. These five were returned to the vigilantes and were hanged from cotton woods that grew in the broad flat bottoms of the Musselshell. The vigilantes' actions received considerable condemnation, but the organized horse rustling business ended in the Missouri Breaks. Granville Stuart was soon named first president of the Montana Stockgrowers Association.

At the far eastern end of the refuge was Old Fort Peck, located about one mile south of the current site of Fort Peck Dam. This was never a military fort, but a stockade built in 1867 by the firm of Durfee and Peck. This company operated several trading posts along the Missouri River. In 1871, the Milk River Indian Agency was moved to Fort Peck from its initial location on the Milk River. This agency served the Assinboine, Brule, Teton, Hunkpapa, and Yanktonai Sioux Tribes. The stockade remained a riverboat landing, trading post, and Indian agency until 1879 when the agency was moved to Poplar Creek and the trading post was abandoned. The main reason for abandonment was the action of the Missouri River which gradually washed away the bluff upon which the fort was built.

Some of the historic sites of the refuge include the Hess homestead, built of planking from a river barge. The Kendall, Bell, and Mauland ranch sites represent the evolution from homesteads to working ranches. They have not been moved, rebuilt, or extensively remodeled.

The Long-X Ranch, one of the first cattle operations in the Breaks, was in business from the late 1800s until about 1950. The Wiederrick homestead was built in the 1870s. Among others that homesteaded along the river were the McNulty, Knox, Caster, Anderson, Legg, and Doney families. There are also numerous marked and unmarked graves, tipi rings, and bison kill sites throughout the refuge.

The Cowboy Artist, Charles M. Russell, visited these lands in the 1880s. His painting and sculpture capture for all time the beauty and drama of the land, the wild animals, and the cowboy life of Montana. The Refuge is named for him.

In 1933, Congress authorized the U.S. Army Corps of Engineers and the Public Works Administration to begin construction of Fort Peck Dam and work was completed in 1939. During peak employment, over 10,000 people worked on the dam. The main purposes of the dam were flood control and improvement of navigation. Fort Peck Dam is the world's largest hydraulically earth filled dam.

Fort Peck Game Range was established in 1936 and converted to Charles M. Russell National Wildlife Refuge in 1976. After a century of exploration and development, the Refuge was created to restore and preserve some of the original natural beauty of Montana and its wildlife. Refuge managers now preserve on the land the same values that the Cowboy Artist preserved on canvas.

It is unlawful to search for, disturb or remove artifacts or fossils on Refuge lands.

UL Bend National Wildlife Refuge

200,000 ACRES PLUS, LOCATED WITHIN THE CMR AT UL BEND ON THE MISSOURI RIVER

UL Bend NWR, the "refuge-within-a-refuge," lies within Charles M. Russell NWR and contains 20,000 acres of federally designated wilderness (an additional 160,000 acres are pending). Adjoined on three sides by the CMR; to the north is a mix of public and private lands. Fort Peck Reservoir surrounds the southern reaches. The lake provides an effective ecological barrier for associated wildlife.

Administered as it is by staff at the Charles M. Russell NWR Complex, UL Bend's mission statement is to promote biological diversity and maintain the natural abundance of native flora and fauna. To that end, refuge staff continues to implement and act upon a multitude of management policies and programs. For instance, like at CMR, there is an active grazing program in place to manage and promote native grassland. Big game populations are managed by hunting. Biological, chemical, and mechanical control measures are targeted at eliminating noxious weed infestations. A reintroduction program for the endangered pallid sturgeon is ongoing, as is an active fire-management program.

The refuge provides nesting, resting, and feeding habitat for waterfowl and other migratory birds. The black-footed ferret is making a comeback within UL Bend, preying on countless black-tailed prairie dogs that find this largest and least disturbed short-grass prairie remaining anywhere so much to their liking. Ferrets raised at the Bowdoin NWR facility were released here in 1993. While their numbers remain low, there remains cautious optimism that the program will eventually be a success.

Mule deer are common in the uplands, while whitetails flourish in the river bottoms. Bighorn sheep, reestablished years ago to replace extinct Audubon sheep, along with elk and pronghorn. While sheep are less common than the ubiquitous deer are, all three are well-rooted residents. Like the neighboring CMR, some 240 species of birds use UL Bend, some year round, others part-timers, still others just passing through.

Bighorn sheep (ewes/lambs)

The black-tailed prairie dog plays an important role in the ecosystem. Thirty species of wildlife are thought to depend on dogs for at least a portion of their diet and habitat needs. Eagles, hawks, owls, coyote, badger prey on them; rattlesnakes and bull snakes eat them as well as occupy burrows during hibernation. Mountain plovers often nest near and raise young in and around dog towns. Black-footed ferrets almost solely depend on dogs for sustenance and living quarters; like sage and sage grouse the two are joined at the hip, as prairie dogs go, so go black-footed ferrets.

Recreational opportunities include boating, hunting, fishing, wildlife viewing, and archaeological/historic sites, as well as access to the wilderness region.

The art of wildlife watching has been redefined at UL Bend, one of the remotest areas in the state, where elk still occupy native prairie year round, and mule and white-tailed deer, pronghorn antelope, birds, prairie dogs, and bighorn sheep also frequent the refuge. The CMR NWR surrounds the UL Bend refuge; to get there requires a long drive on rough roads. Like most roads in the area these are impassable when wet, be advised to consult weather and road conditions beforehand.

Fort Peck Reservoir surrounds the southern half of the area. These impounded waters of the Missouri River provide an ecological barrier for wildlife associated with land. Although the water level fluctuates seasonally, the elevation at full pool is 2,250 feet above sea level. The refuge provides nesting, resting, feeding habitat for ducks, geese, swans, and other migratory birds. Recreational opportunities include boating hunting, fishing, wildlife viewing, and archaeological/historic sites, as well as access to the Missouri Breaks wilderness region.

Fast Facts

Contact: UL Bend NWR, Airport Rd. Lewistown, MT 59457 E-mail: cmr@fws.gov Phone: 538-8706.

Getting There: Perhaps the easiest way, if you can call it that, is by water. By road, follow signs to Fourchette Bay and good luck.

Activities: Boating, hunting, fishing, birding, viewing wildlife and archaeological/historic sites, as well as access to the wilderness region.

Principle Mammals: Elk, mule deer, pronghorn, bighorn sheep.

Principle Birdlife: 240 species of bird use the refuge, full-time, part-time or just passing through.

Birds of Special Interest: Sage and sharp-tailed grouse, bald eagle.

Habitat Overview: Native shortgrass prairie, forested coulees, river bottoms, and "breaks" badlands.

Flora of Special Interest: Grasses and plants associated with shortgrass prairie ecosystem (see CMR chapter for details).

Best Wildlife Viewing Ops: Spring, summer and fall, winter can be tough.

Best Birding Ops: Spring and fall migration.

Best Photo Ops: Spring, summer, fall before big game rifle season mid-October; early and late in day.

Hunting Ops: Excellent mule deer; elk, bighorn sheep and pronghorn but you nee the proper permits. Check the regulations; both state and refuge regulations apply. Good numbers of sharp-tailed and sage grouse in the appropriate habitats.

Fishing Ops: Fishing is permitted on the Missouri River and Fort Peck Reservoir. Walleye, sauger, smallmouth bass, paddlefish, and northern pike are the most targeted species but there are others. A state license is required, and state limits and seasons apply.

Camping Ops: No developed campgrounds within UL Bend, primitive camping is allowed almost anywhere.

Boating Ops: Numerous boat ramps and several marinas are located in the area; there are upstream boating restrictions in some areas during certain periods so be sure to check the boating regulations.

Hiking Trails: No developed trails but you can hike just about anywhere.

Sage grouse fighting

Medicine Lake
National Wildlife Refuge

31,660 ACRES; EXTREME NORTHEAST MONTANA ON THE HEAVILY GLACIATED PLAINS BETWEEN THE MISSOURI RIVER AND CANADA

"Like other refuges within the National Wildlife Refuge system, our mission is to provide nesting, rearing and resting habitat for migratory birds — waterfowl and shore birds. But here, in addition to water we also manage lor mixed grass, both native short prairie grasses and tame grasses. As such, we provide ideal habitat for not only migrants and year-round residents, such as pheasant and sharp-tailed grouse, but for several species of birds depend on healthy grasslands for survival. The Baird's sparrow, for one, endangered just about everywhere else, here it is common. So common, in fact, birders from around the world show up here in spring just to get a look at Baird's. The piping plover, a rare and endangered shorebird, while not as common, also nests on the refuge." — Ted Gutzke, Medicine Lake National Wildlife Refuge Manager

Established in 1935, refuge staff administers two primary, though non-contiguous parcels — North Tract (28,000 acres) and Homestead Tract (1,280 acre-lake plus adjacent uplands), in addition to the Northeastern Montana Wetlands Management District. Comprised over 40 separate waterfowl production areas (WPAs) totaling in excess of 10,000 acres the NMWMD sprawls across three counties, Richland, Roosevelt and Sheridan. Refuge staff also administers the Lamesteer National Wildlife Refuge, a relatively obscure, rather small satellite refuge south of Wibaux.

The main refuge, or North Tract, contains the 8,700-acre Medicine Lake and several smaller lakes. The Homestead Tract (or Unit) comprises Homestead Lake and adjacent uplands. Within the North Tract, 11,360 acres are considered wilderness. Officially labeled the Medicine Lake Wilderness Area, it was established by Congress in 1976. Like wilderness areas everywhere this one lives by the no-motorized vehicles or

Sandhill crane

equipment allowed rule, including outboard- and electric motor-powered watercraft, power ice augers and so forth. Prime example, ice fishers may bring icehouses, but must be wrestled onto and off the ice thru muscle power alone. The many islands within the complex are off limits to human visitors for any reason.

Also included within the North Tract is the unique 2,320-acre Sandhills Unit, a section of rolling hills that are actually sand dunes covered in native grass, brushy draws consisting of buck brush, buffaloberry, chokecherry and lots of prickly pear cactus. Warning to bird hunters: We're talking serious cactus here, not the usual scattered patches dogs easily avoid, but rather solid mats impossible to dodge. Before entering the sand dunes boot up the dog.

Medicine Lake is located within the ancestral Missouri River channel, which once ran north to Hudson Bay before the last ice sheet pushed it south, some 25 or 30 miles. The receding ice sheet carved the blanket of glacial till into a series of rocky hills, interspersed by hundreds of potholes. All that water and grass created a sort of mecca for migrating bison and waterfowl. Nomadic plains Indians took full advantage, shadowing the moveable feast throughout the year. Proof positive this was indeed a happy hunting ground are the many teepee rings scattered about the surrounding landscape.

The refuge, by almost any modern standard, is off the beaten path; a remote corner in a huge and still largely un-peopled state (Montana ranks fourth in land mass and a population of less than one million, most of which live in the west). Thus, visitor numbers are quite low, (just 15,000 to 16,000 annually, ranking ML NWR as the least visited of all refuges in the system). As in the past, the refuge's biggest draw are hunters; not surprisingly most of those are non-locals and non-residents, as there just aren't that many locals. Fishermen rank second, followed closely by birders and other non-consumptive wildlife viewers. But no matter what the season, one thing you won't find is a crowd.

Annually, over 40,000 waterfowl — the majority blue-winged teal, gadwall, shoveler, lesser scaup and mallard with lesser numbers of pintail, American widgeon, redhead and canvasback — are produced on the refuge. Waterfowl numbers peak during spring and fall migration when, in wet years, in excess of 100,000 birds stage there before continuing long journeys.

The refuge hosts the fourth largest white pelican rookery in the world — over 10,000 birds produce 3,000 to 5,000 young each spring. Pelicans are magnificent birds, huge actually, with adults often sporting nine-foot wingspans. Spring through fall, the refuge swarms with the big white birds. In every direction it seems, flocks, varying in size from just a few to several dozen, can be seen soaring high above or winging low and gracefully over the water. Pelicans in flight are especially stunning when illuminated by a low-sun highlighting black-tipped wings and white feathers against the dark water or wide-blue-sky backdrop — a truly spectacular sight.

They're so common here that it's easy to lose sight of the fact that white pelicans, in general, are in decline throughout their range. Once again, the culprits are habitat loss due to wide spread draining of wetlands and increased pesticide use. For birders and wildlife lovers, the decline is no doubt a hard pill to swallow. On the other hand, don't expect sympathy from teary-eyed fishermen. For you see, white pelicans dine exclusively on fish, and like any predator are quite good at what they do. Pelicans gang up, herd the prey to the surface, then employ massive pouch-laden bills to scoop their victims — draining off the water, of course, before swallowing. This, by the way, is a far different method than employed by their brown-feathered cousins. Brown pelicans soar about hunting potential individual victims, then plunge head-long below the surface to chase down victims via swift underwater swimming.

Other species commonly nest on the refuge include colonial nesters such as double-crested cormorants, California and ring-billed gulls and great blue herons. Look for the colonies on the many islands within the big lake. You may look, but don't encroach. The islands are off limits year round, for any reason. Grebes and many other marsh and shore bird's nests can be found secreted in the vegetation of the lakes' shorelines. In late October thousands of sandhill cranes stop by.

Recently during hunting season, a single, rare and endangered whooping crane showed up amongst the sandhills. Closely guarded by refuge staff during the stopover, lest some unaware hunter mistakenly pull the trigger on the "albino sandhill." Eventually the crisis ended when the whooper moved on. By the way, such mistaken identity would become a very expensive prize, so if in doubt, pass.

The whooping crane is the tallest North American bird. Males approach five feet when standing erect and average 16 pounds. Females stand nearly as tall and average 14 pounds. Wing spans can reach eight feet. Adult whoopers can be quickly separated from the common sandhills by their snowy white with black wingtips (visible only when the wings are extended). The neck is long. The bill is long, dark and rapier-like. Legs are long, thin and black. There is a distinctive patch of reddish-black bristly feathers on the top and back of the head. Black feathers on the side of the head below the yellow eye resemble a long, dark moustache. Whoopers are the only large white birds with black wingtips that fly with necks extended forward and legs trailing far behind. It also is the only one that walks or stands on long thin legs and does not swim. Juvenile whooping cranes exhibit a rusty or cinnamon brown color. At about four months of age, white feathers begin to appear on the neck and back. By the fall migration head and necks are brown with a mixture of brown and white body feathers. Come spring the young are predominantly white. No one should mistake a whooper for a sandhill or vice versa.

Whooping cranes are perhaps the best known of America's endangered species. A symbol of our effort to protect and restore endangered wildlife, so endeared are whoopers to wildlife lovers that nearly every move the big birds make is newsworthy, potential headline stuff. Little wonder, what with the grim details of their hanging-on-by-a-thread existence for now over a century and a half — 1,400 in the mid-1800s dwindled to just 16 in 1942. Today whoopers number about 180, a precarious number still, especially when you consider a single hurricane wiped out seven of 13 birds in a Louisiana flock. The catastrophe had wildlife managers scrambling to capture the rest and put them into protective custody. The current breeding population of wild

Yellow-headed blackbird

whoopers is restricted to a small area in the northern part of Wood Buffalo National Park near Fort Smith, Northwest Territories. The population is migratory and winters in and around the Aransas National Wildlife Refuge on the gulf coast of Texas. There are no breeding pairs in Montana.

And speaking of rare birds, the refuge houses up to 30 pairs of threatened piping plovers each spring. Common at the start the 19th Century, by 1900 the species was nearly extinct. At fault were the familiar culprits of the era: unregulated sport hunting and the high demand for fancy feathers for use in women's hats. On the fast track toward oblivion, the upland plover was saved at the brink by the Migratory Bird Treaty Act of 1918. With hunting and the feather trade banned, the population once again began to build and peaked in the 1940s. Unfortunately numbers have been falling ever since. Rampant development and increased recreational use of beaches resulting in drastic losses of suitable breeding habitat are the main deterrents. Coupled with the recent boom in plover predators — gulls, skunks, raccoons, foxes and coyotes — has further imperiled the survivors.

Piping plovers depend on camouflage as a primary defense mechanism. A motionless adult plover flat out disappears when guarding eggs and/or chicks amid sand, weed and rock strewn beaches. Bearing head and back the color of dried sand, contrasted by a white rump and partially black tail, a black band above a white forehead and the single, black "belt" or breast band (also referred to as a collar or neckband) breaking up the white breast and abdomen; when it comes to camouflage piping plovers are one of Ma Nature's best ideas.

Piping plover resemble the common killdeer (also a plover by the way) though are much smaller (about the size of a bluebird). Like killdeers, adult plovers are masters at the "broken wing game." Threatened, hatchlings instantly vanish as if by magic. Meanwhile, the adult(s) tease the potential murderer into thinking it's an easy meal. Then, a safe distance off, the pretenders simply fly away. It's an age-old ploy, though one sure to have left more than one predator scratching. Still, despite the effectiveness of the fancy evasive footwork, large numbers of chicks and eggs fall prey to untimely cold, wet weather and the flooding of nests.

The cumulative result, of course, is a threatened species. For instance, the Atlantic Coast population was thought to have dropped to an estimated 790 pairs by 1986 and was placed on the Federal Endangered Species List. Today, thanks to conservation efforts aimed at protecting and enhancing nesting and wintering habitat, as well as strict regulations prohibiting the destruction and/or abuse of critical habitat, the piping plover is still hanging in there, if only by a thread. It's good (and not at all surprising) to learn Medicine Lake ranks high among the bright spots, fledging about 80 percent of Montana's annual crop.

Overall, the most productive refuge nesting activity (for all species) takes place on the many islands and on peninsulas where an ingenious electric-fencing scheme effectively mimics the islands. Between the natural water barrier and the fence, predation from raccoons, foxes, coyotes, skunks and badgers has been cut way down.

Water, of course, is critical and the main attractant for waterfowl as well as other bird species. Both, however, depend on and are fond of the healthy grasslands surrounding the water. In light of this, refuge staff actively and aggressively manage about 18,000 acres of native prairie grass and 4,000 acres of the tame grass — alfalfa, clover and tall fescue.

The native grasses are primarily managed through prescribed grazing and burning. Periodically, local cattle are allowed in, which mimics the bison grazing of the past. Parcels are electrically fenced and grazed for periods lasting three days to three weeks, then rested for various lengths of time in between. On a similar, though much longer rotation (five or six years usually), each parcel is also burned. Prescribed burns are designed to mimic the occurrence of wildfires, historically a large cog in the propagation of native grasses.

Tame grasses, on the other hand, are managed much the same as any progressive rancher would. In this case, sharecroppers produce tame grasses and sow many acres of small grains. A portion of each is left unharvested for wildlife consumption. Leftovers, relished by just about every bird species present, including non-fish-eating waterfowl, wading and song birds as well as upland birds (pheasant, sharp-tailed grouse and Hungarian partridge). White-tailed deer, which thrive on the refuge, also enjoy the free lunch.

The prairie grasslands provide summer residence for a multitude of prairie birds — burrowing and short-eared owls, lark bunting, Baird's, LeConte's and grasshopper sparrows, chestnut-collared and McCown's longspurs and Sprague's pipit to name just a few. Two imports, the Hungarian partridge (a.k.a. gray partridge) and ringneck pheasant, share space with the natives. In the best years, pheasant numbers are remarkable enough that it's difficult to stand in any one spot for very long and not spy a colorful rooster or two, or perhaps a hen trailing a brood.

Another upland bird, the native sharp-tailed grouse finds the extensive grasslands much to its liking. Sharpies are among our favorite upland birds to hunt, but we actually like to watch the spring courtship displays even better. Like sage grouse, sharpies are arena birds. Males gather on breeding grounds, or leks, to perform an annual ritualistic dance designed to attract female suitors.

The best way to witness the action is from a blind and, for that, the refuge has you covered; just make reservations and you are all set. The blind is available seven days a week, mid-April through the end of May. Reservations and directions are available through refuge headquarters (406-789-2305).

The blind comfortably houses two to four people and campstools are provided. Dancing is most intense during the morning hours, but evenings can also yield some action. Morning visitors should plan to arrive at the blind about one hour before sunrise and stay until the birds are done displaying for the day (usually one to two hours after sunrise). The blind is approximately a two-and-a-quarter mile drive east from the refuge headquarters and requires a hike of about 100 yards south of the road.

Cocks vie for hen approval by performing a well-orchestrated dance with rival suitors. Wings outstretched, looking every bit like miniature F-18 fighter jets on the runway prepared for take-off, vivid pinkish purple neck air sacs bugling, cocks often face off, but actual fights are rare. Going beak to beak, eyeball to eyeball, the sparing cocks perform pirouettes and fancy foot stomping, usually capped by stare-downs sometimes lasting several minutes, before each goes his separate way to confront the next challenger. How this all works is beyond me but somehow it does. That is, one cock ends up on top — literally and figuratively. I admit, having watched and photographed dozens of face-offs, the rules of engagement still leave me baffled.

Hunters take note: Refuge seasons and regulations don't always jive with the state seasons and regulations, so be sure to check with headquarters first for any last minute changes. As a general rule, for hunting purposes the refuge is divided into three zones. Zone 2 is open to public hunting for upland game birds, mourning doves, waterfowl, coots, jackrabbits and deer in accordance with Montana seasons and bag limits. Zones 1 and 3 are open for hunting Nov. 15, the idea being the lake is normally frozen by that date and most of the waterfowl will have moved on. These two zones remain open for public hunting through the close of the various Montana hunting seasons. Normally, deer season closes the last weekend in November. Pheasant, Huns and sharp-tailed grouse now run to Jan. 1. Predator hunting is by permit only through the refuge headquarters.

Fishing wise, Medicine Lake is managed exclusively for northern pike; the only species believed to be native. However, Muddy Creek serves as an umbilical cord to the Missouri River and, especially during floods and other high water events, a variety of species migrate back and forth. Thus the lake contains more than just northern pike, notably walleye and catfish.

All activities within the refuge are governed by refuge regulations, available at the headquarters. Normally the lake is open to fishing from Nov. 15 to Sept. 15, in other words, no fishing from mid-September to mid-November. Because the lake itself falls within the wilderness boundary, no motors (including electric) are allowed. Also be aware of the year-round trespass ban on the islands. Bank fishing is allowed, but there are exceptions posted. Spearing pike is a popular winter activity. Ice houses are allowed, though because of the wilderness designation must be hauled on and off the ice via muscle power alone. Other lakes and impoundments may or may not be open to fishing, so be sure to check with headquarters.

A good rule of thumb is to check in first, not only to keep abreast of any changes, but refuge staff can point you in the right directions to best implement your game plans.

We arrive early (per staff instructions) on a Wednesday morning toward the end of April, with reservations to sit in the blind and photograph dancing sharpies. Setting up the tripods and cameras, we could hear geese calling from the nearby lake; a cock pheasant crowed somewhere close by and another far off in the distance. Even though still pitch black, we could hear sharpies chattering in the grass beyond, the cuk-a-cuk-a-cuk sound familiar and unmistakable. As the dawn light rises, heretofore unmoving grouse-shaped shadows now begin to dance and jive, as two males square off. Wings outspread, pointed tail erect, heads parallel to the ground, the cocks' posture reminds me very much of F-18 fighter jets on the runway about to take off.

In this case, the two perform a ritualistic dance, rhythmically stamping feet, as if to a tune only they can hear, beak to beak, eye ball to eye ball, spinning to and fro... suddenly stopping, mid-dance-step, to stare. The stare down goes on for what seems like several minutes but probably lasts more like 30 seconds. Suddenly both drop feathers, turn in opposite directions, and slowly disappear into the still inky dawn. And so it goes, cocks dancing, hens strolling about, what looks like utter chaos to us obviously works, judging the many broods the dog usually finds come fall.

Later, after the grouse have gone off to spend the day doing whatever it is sharpies do when not performing their crazy, dawn lek dancing, we take to the Auto Tour Route. Every piece of open water (there are still patches of ice on the main lake) is covered with waterfowl. Hundreds of ducks (pintails, widgeons, teals, mallards, bluebills, ring-necked ducks, a huge raft of redheads and canvasbacks, to name just the more obvious) are present, along with double-crested cormorants, grebes, coots and several great blue herons. Canada Geese are everywhere — in the water, in the air, in the grass, on the ice. Out near the dunes, Gale spots a cottontail in the grass and snoozing on a mound of dirt not ten feet away, a mangy looking red fox. Before I can train the big lens on the pair, the cottontail zips off, leaving me to focus on a very bad looking red fox. Continuing on, in addition to long-range views of soaring hawks, are northern harriers, a rare (for here) osprey, kestrels, and at least two Swainson's. Flapping along a line of trees is a pair of smallish owls, probably short-eared but the distance is long and we can't be sure. Shorebirds such as avocets, willets, spotted sandpipers, marbled godwits are common here but peak migration is still awhile off and today in short supply. Franklin's gulls, common and Forster's terns, however, are not. Neither are meadowlarks, crows, robins, redwing blackbirds or horned larks. We spy scads of little brown birds flitting about the grass, which are sparrows (that much we know). But our birding skills are lacking so, it is impossible to honestly check-off the coveted Baird's we'd earlier set our sights on. Oh well, maybe next time one will pose just long enough...

Nearby Restaurants and Accommodations

The Laketonian Café on Main St. serves up a full menu, breakfast, lunch and dinner—of tasty dishes. All served with a smile and as much friendly conversation as you so choose. Nothing fancy, but my judging system doesn't count fancy for much anyway. So judging solely on clean, reasonable, friendly and tasty the LC deserves two thumbs up. The Eight Ball Inn serves up terrific steak dinners. While the Club Bar and Hotel is the place to go for pizza and a cold brew.

Normally, liquor stores don't make the cut in a book like this, but Hutslar's Antique and Liquor Store isn't your run-of-the-mill booze outlet. HALS is worth a stop even if you don't drink.

There is limited sleeping space for rent at the Club Bar and Hotel and Lilac Lane (next door Hutslar's). Fee camping is available at Roger Krumwiede, 406-789-2546 and Wayne Stringer, 406-789-2244 in Medicine Lake. In nearby

Froid, there is Jan Peters, 406-766-9955, amenities include water, electricity, community showers and toilets and dump station. If you are looking for free, try the Froid City Park, which features restrooms and electricity. Sparks, 406-963-2248, is a nifty B&B in Froid, complete with dog kennels. The nearest full-fledged motels are in Plentywood, 20 miles north, Medicine Lake. Try the Sherwood Inn, 1st Ave., 406-765-2810, allows pets or in Culbertson, 20 miles south, try the Diamond Willow Inn, 406-787-6218, or the King's Inn, 406-787-6277.

Fast Facts

Contact Info: Medicine Lake NWR, 223 North Shore Rd., Medicine Lake, MT, 59247-9600, Phone: 406-789-2305, E-mail: r6rw_mdl@fws.gov

Getting There: I-94 to Glendive; north on MT 16 or US 2 to Culbertson; north on MT 16 to Medicine Lake. No matter which it is a long way from all major population centers.

Activities: Hunting, fishing, birding, wildlife viewing, photography.

Principle Mammals: White-tailed deer, jackrabbit, coyote, badger, red fox, skunk, raccoon, muskrat and other small mammals.

Mammals of Special Interest: White tailed deer.

Principle Birdlife: 224 species have been identified since its inception in 1935; about 104 of which nest on the refuge; a handful of those are year around residents.

Birds of Special Interest: White pelican, piping plover, pheasant, sharp-tailed grouse and a variety of waterfowl.

Habitat Overview: Transition zone between the tall and short grass prairie; diverse mix of open water, marsh, native and tame grasslands — invasive trees are actively discouraged.

Flora of Special Interest: Native grassland species are aggressively managed.

Best Wildlife Viewing Ops: Spring though fall, dawn and dusk.

Best Birding Ops: Mid-April through mid-May, sharp-tailed grouse on leks, waterfowl migration is in full swing; huge numbers of sandhill cranes often show up in late October.

Best Photo Ops: Spring through fall, mornings and evenings; sharp-tailed grouse can be photographed from the refuge blind by making reservations.

Hunting Ops: Excellent waterfowl (although some areas are difficult to access), sandhill crane and upland birds; good white-tailed deer hunting.

Fishing Ops: Northern pike fishing can be excellent although numbers can be affected by extended drought; spearing is a popular winter activity.

Camping Ops: None on refuge.

Boating Ops: Limited; no motors of any kind.

Hiking Trails: No developed trails.

Motor Trails: Several refuge roads some closed seasonally; an auto tour route that is also periodically closed due to road conditions.

Bitter Creek Wilderness Study Area (WSA)

59,660 ACRES IN NORTH CENTRAL MONTANA, 20 MILES NORTHEAST OF HINSDALE, NORTH OF GLASGOW IN VALLEY COUNTY

In anticipation of Congress removing the BCWSA from full wilderness protection, the BLM re-designated it as an Area of Critical Environmental Concern. The ACEC designation imposes restrictions now and in the future to protect its unique habitat and landscape qualities and to afford protection to the threatened mountain plovers known to nest within its boundaries. The new designation dictates parameters for specified land use such as grazing and oil and gas development not allowed in wilderness areas. It should be noted, although grazing is ongoing, there are no oil and gas leases within the area at this time. And unless things change no roads or other improvements are in the works.

One of the best native mixed-grass prairie ecosystems in Montana and the United States, it is home to the threatened mountain plover, as well as a variety of interesting grassland bird species of concern such as Sprague's pipit and Baird's sparrow; common also are burrowing owls, hawks, golden eagles, mule deer, bobcat, sage and sharp-tailed grouse. In a nutshell designating the Area of Critical Environmental Concern ensures any future development, i.e. oil and gas, will adhere to strict parameters to ensure propagation of birds and wildlife. For instance, April 1 to July 1, no driving or other human disturbance is allowed within a quarter mile of a nesting plover.

A recent joint study of the Montana Natural Heritage Program and the BLM's Glasgow Field Office noted: "Grasslands throughout the Great Plains have been converted to agricultural production. Thus the tall-grass prairie has been reduced to mere fragments. While more intact significant losses within the mid- and short-grass prairie have placed some grassland-obligate species in jeopardy. In recent decades grassland nesting birds have shown dramatic population declines over a wide geographic area. Within the Bitter Creek (including nearby Frenchman/Dry Fork creek areas) portion of Montana's Northwestern Glaciated Plains Section, large intact prairie communities can still be found. It is the largest remaining intact grassland north of the Hi-Line in Montana and stands out as one the most extensive naturally functioning glaciated plains grasslands in North America."

No less than seven different landscape types, in addition to its diverse wildlife and plant species, make this a naturalist's dream (albeit one relatively few even know exists let alone know firsthand). Off the beaten path roads into the area are few and those you do find are rough and tough to negotiate — four-wheel drive and high clearance vehicles only — and don't even think about going there when wet. Most of the area is BLM or state but there are private inholdings where landowner permission is required to proceed. In warm weather, especially in the badlands areas, keep an eye peeled for western rattlesnakes, which are not at all uncommon.

The area is semi-arid, on average 10 to 14 inches annual precipitation, and like much of Montana temperatures tend to yo-yo, warm to downright hot in summer, cold to downright frigid in winter; summer hail and winter blizzards, while not everyday occurrences, are worth mentioning.

More than 25 native grass and plant species have been identified in addition to the following (all, by the way species of concern, potential concern or under review): Ferruginous hawk, greater sage grouse, long-billed curlew, burrowing owl, loggerhead shrike, Sprague's pipit, Brewer's sparrow, lark bunting, grasshopper sparrow, Baird's sparrow, McCowan's longspur, chest-collared longspur, black-tailed prairie dog, swift fox; the plains spadefoot and great plains toads, the northern leopard frog, the short-horned lizard and the western hognose snake; flathead chub, western silvery and plains minnow.

Fast Facts

Contact Info: Administered by staff at BLM, Glasgow Field Station, 605 2nd Ave. South, PO Box 871, Glasgow, MT 59230 (228-3750

Getting There: To access Bitter Creek ACEC drive 20 miles north Hinsdale on Rock Creek Rd., the ACEC lies generally east of the main road.

Activities: Birding, wildlife viewing, hiking, camping, mountain biking, horseback riding, upland bird and big game hunting, solitude.

Principle Mammals: mule deer, black-tailed prairie dog, swift fox, bobcat, badger, coyote.

Mammals of Special Interest: Swift fox, black-tailed prairie dog, bobcat.

Principle Birdlife: A variety grassland bird species including Sprague's pipit, Brewer's sparrow, lark bunting, grasshopper sparrow, Baird's sparrow, McCowan's longspur, chest-collared longspur; also golden eagle, variety hawks including furruginous, burrowing owl, sage and sharp-tailed grouse.

Birds of Special Interest: Mountain plover, Sprague's pipit, Baird's sparrow, sage grouse.

Habitat Overview: The healthy mix grassland, shrubland, woodland, badland, makes more a unique and diverse area.

Flora of Special Interest: A variety of native grass and shrub species.

Best Wildlife Viewing Ops: Early and late in the day; more difficult to see during hunting season which runs from September to January.

Best Birding Ops: Spring through early summer and again in fall during migration.

Best Photo Ops: Sage and sharp-tailed grouse leks in early spring; mule deer bucks in early fall before rifle season starts in late October. Regardless season early and late in the day provide the best opportunities and the best light.

Hunting Ops: Mule deer, upland birds and predator hunting are popular, mostly among locals.

Camping Ops: Allowed within 300 feet designated roads; access limited to least obtrusive possible.

Boating Ops: None.

Hiking Trails: None developed; unlimited otherwise.

Motor Trails: Driving is allowed on designated routes only; no off-road vehicle travel.

Fox Lake Wildlife Management Area

1,546 ACRES IN RICHLAND COUNTY IN EASTERN MONTANA, 23 MILES WEST OF SIDNEY AT THE TOWN OF LAMBERT

Management goal is to provide waterfowl habitat, hunting and wildlife viewing opportunities. In wet years, the WMA plays host to a wide variety of waterfowl and shorebirds; dry years the activity wanes. But given enough snowmelt to at least partially fill the reservoir water birds show up, often in large numbers and visitors then enjoy some of the best viewing opportunities in the area. Pretty far removed from anything like a major population center this is one spot you should always call first before embarking on a long drive.

The WMA is open for visitation year around and to hunting during the appropriate open seasons. Due to its intermittent nature there is no fishing even with the reservoir brim full. There is no bird check-off list specific to the WMA but the Medicine Lake NWR list gives a good idea what to expect.

Fast Facts

Contact Info: Scott Thompson, PO Box 558, Culbertson, MT 59218; phone 787-5303; e-mail: sthompson@mt.gov

Getting There: Located in Richland County in eastern Montana, 23 miles west of Sidney. One mile south of Highway 200 near the town of Lambert. Access by county roads north and south of WMA.

Activities: Birding, wildlife viewing, hiking, upland bird and limited big game hunting; there are no developed facilities.

Principle Mammals: Whitetail and mule deer, common raccoon, deer mouse, house mouse, long-tailed weasel, masked shrew, meadow jumping mouse, meadow mole northern pocket gopher, red fox, thirteen-lined ground squirrel, western harvest mouse, badger, coyote.

Principle Birdlife: Waterfowl, a variety of song birds and numerous shorebirds including mallard, wigeon, blue-winged teal, Canada goose, savannah sparrow, grasshopper sparrow, meadow lark, lark bunting, brown-headed cowbird, barn swallow, brown thrasher, logger-headed shrike, northern harrier, kestrel, eastern kingbird, American avocet, American coot, willet, marbled godwit, Wilson's phalarope, various sandpipers, eared grebe, ringneck pheasant, Hungarian partridge, sharp-tailed grouse.

Habitat Overview: When there is water, the healthy mix grassland, marshland and open water makes Fox Lake one of the more productive, unique and diverse habitats in the area; lacking water, it reverts back to just another grassy spot on the prairie.

Flora of Special Interest: A variety of upland and marsh grasses.

Best Wildlife Viewing Ops: Early and late in the day; more difficult to see during hunting season which runs from September to January.

Best Birding Ops: Spring through early summer and during wet years again in fall during migration.

Best Photo Ops: Early and late in the day provide the most dramatic lighting.

Hunting Ops: Mule deer, upland birds and predator hunting are popular, mostly among locals.

Camping Ops: No developed campsites, primitive camping allowed but there is no drinking water or other facilities.

Boating Ops: Seasonal restrictions; no gasoline motors allowed anytime.

Hiking Trails: None developed; unlimited otherwise.

Motor Trails: Driving is allowed on designated routes only; no off-road vehicle travel.

Fort Union Trading Post

NATIONAL HISTORIC SITE, LOCATED ON THE NORTH OF THE DAKOTA-MONTANA LINE, 25 MILES SOUTHWEST WILLISTON, N.D., 24 MILES NORTHEAST OF SIDNEY JUST OFF ND 1804

Contrary to many of the forts scattered across the Great Plains frontier, Fort Union was privately owned. Established by the American Fur Company in 1828, the post did a booming business almost right up to its closure in 1867. And as forts and trading posts go, Fort Union lasted longer than most. During the nearly four decade run, Fort Union hosted most, if not all, of the legendary fur trappers and many other dignitaries on their way to the Shining Mountains and points further west.

At one time or another, representatives of most of the Great Plains Indian tribes — Assiniboin, Crow, Blackfeet, Cree, Chippewa, Mandan, Hidatsa, to name several — showed up to barter and sometimes just to socialize and mingle among the many whites passing through at the time.

On the banks of the Missouri River at relatively low elevation (1,900 feet) the site sits at the southern edge of glaciation; within the so-called Badlands Vegetation Zone. The present landscape is a mix of prairie grasslands, riparian and badlands-style coulees and breaks.

Each spring and fall during migration, birders can expect to see a wide array of waterfowl, raptors and songbirds, many of which are not your everyday check-offs. Especially in the fall, due to a peculiar east-to-west curve in the normal north-south migration flight pattern, birds show up here on their way south which are not normally seen this far west. The dichotomy is more prevalent a bit further north, but don't be surprised to find yourself gazing at, say, a flock of scarlet tanagers perusing the tall cottonwoods or, as we did one day, a solitary bright male perched atop the flagpole.

Fast Facts

Contact Info: Fort Union Trading Post, National Historic Site, 15550 Highway 1804, Williston, ND 58801; phone 701-572-9083

Getting There: From Culbertson follow US 2 East to Bainville. Turn right onto a scenic 15 mile gravel road into North Dakota, turn right onto County Road 5 just past Milepost 2; from Sidney go east on MT 200 through Fairview into North Dakota, turn left onto ND 58, proceed 10 miles to ND 1804 then left a mile and a half to the site.

Activities: Birding, wildlife viewing, hiking.

Principle Mammals: Whitetail deer, coyote, fox, raccoon, cottontail rabbit, ground squirrel, beaver, muskrat, porcupine and prairie vole.

Mammals of Special Interest: Beaver working the Missouri River.

Principle Birdlife: Waterfowl, raptors and songbirds; in fall the migration often includes species not normally seen this far west.

Birds of Special Interest: Golden and bald eagles and the chance to check-off visiting songbirds rare to the area.

Habitat Overview: A mix of prairie grasslands, riparian and badlands coulees.

Flora of Special Interest: Native grasses include needle and thread, western wheat grass and blue grama; trees include tall cottonwoods, ash and dogwood, and shrubs such as willows, buffalo berry and chokecherry.

Best Wildlife Viewing Ops: Year round, early and late in the day.

Best Birding Ops: Spring and fall during migration; fall is especially interesting for sighting songbirds rare to the area.

Best Photo Ops: Early and late in the day provide the most spectacular lighting and the best chance of finding wildlife.

Hunting Ops: No hunting within the park boundaries.

Fishing Ops: The Missouri River is home to a wide variety of warm water gamefish.

Camping Ops: None.

Boating Ops: None on site, however the river is unrestricted.

Hiking Trails: Bodmer Overlook, about a mile out and back.

Motor Trails: None.

Fort Union Trading Post

Fish, Wildlife, and Parks: Region 7

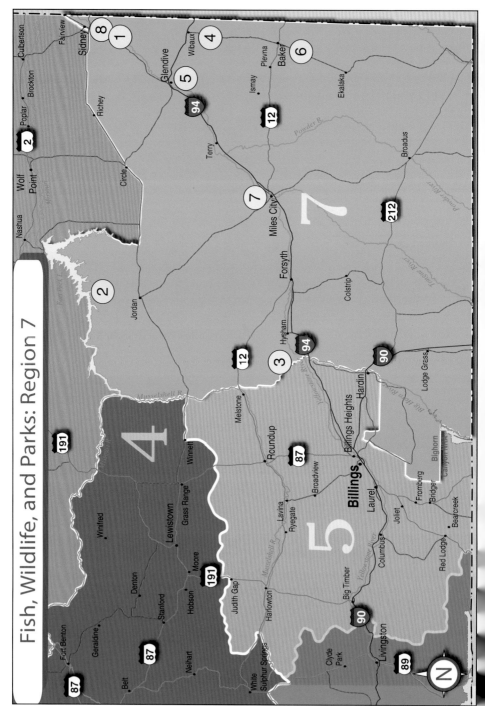

© 2008 Wilderness Adventures Press, Inc.

REGION 7

1. Elk Island Wildlife
   Management Area 291
2. Hell Creek State Park 297
3. Isaac Homestead Wildlife
   Management Area 309
4. Lamesteer National
   Wildlife Refuge 317
5. Makoshika State Park 327
6. Medicine Rocks State Park 333
7. Pirogue Island State Park 337
8. Seven Sisters Wildlife
   Management Area 341

Elk Island Wildlife Management Area

1046 ACRES; RICHLAND COUNTY APPROXIMATELY TWO MILES SOUTHEAST OF SAVAGE

Whitetails and pheasants, pheasants and whitetails. The more I hang out at the lower Yellowstone River bottoms the more it seems the two really are somehow joined at the hip. Elk Island WMA is typical. It's like no matter when, no matter where you look one or the other or both are in constant sight — hunting season, of course, would be the lone exception. The WMA also attracts legions of waterfowl spring and fall, and supports a healthy flock of wild turkeys, a variety of furbearers, assorted small mammals and songbirds galore. Still, the real dog and pony show is the pheasants and whitetails.

The ring-necked pheasant goes by many aliases: pheasant, ringneck, rooster, longtail, chicken and China chicken are common handles for this wily alien who has virtually stolen the hearts of American bird hunters; these days he is far and away the most popular game bird in America. To the vast majority of Montana bird hunters, "bird" translates directly to pheasant, period.

Pheasants were first let loose on American soil in the early 1800s. But the birds really didn't take hold until 1882, when 26 were let go in Oregon's Willamette Valley. Perhaps the work of the same importer who gave us the Hungarian partridge, perhaps not. It's one of those mysterious, though no less societal-altering, events to which we will never know the answer. Anyway, whoever masterminded the 1882 operation apparently knew his stuff, because those 26 chickens a decade later produced a harvest in excess of 50,000 birds. Obviously these aliens found the new digs to their liking.

With that first resounding success firmly established, the ringneck's odyssey in America was, as they say, off and running. Over the next several decades pheasants were introduced into every conceivable type habitat. As you might expect, some it found way more to its liking than others. In the early 1900s, Montana jumped on the pheasant introduction band wagon in a big way. And for a time, nearly border to

White-tailed deer

border, released pheasants became almost as common as magpies. Eventually, the bird sets its roots deepest in the river and creek bottoms of central and northeastern Montana.

Ringnecks are, for the most part, tied inexorably to agriculture, especially in areas rife with irrigated hay meadows and cereal grain fields bordering tight, gnarly cover for protection. It is rare to find appreciable numbers of birds in areas lacking large cropland acreages. Overall, Montana's ringnecks are in general decline, having peaked during the 40s, 50s, and 60s (as they did countrywide). However, the passage of the Farm Aid Bill in 1985 and the resultant huge acreage placed in Crop Reduction Program (CRP) has been a boon to pheasant wellness. Simply stated, CRP pays farmers and ranchers to plant cover crops on erodible acreage, which are then removed from harvest and livestock grazing. The result is a dramatic upturn in pheasant futures. Though it is unlikely numbers will ever again mimic those of the mid-20th century. Still, so long as CRP remains, the future looks pretty rosy, especially compared to the grim outlook at the start of the 1980s.

Visit Elk Island in the spring and cockbird music (crowing) resonates every direction, dawn to dusk. Roosters, dressed in their most colorful best, vie for breeding rights to female suitors, establish crowing territories and defend against all comers. Fierce battles are common. The fights though brief are often bloody, rarely fatal. The winner consummates the victory through loud crowing topped off by rapid wing beats — as distinctive a sound as there is in the wild — while the loser slinks away. For the most part, only temporarily defeated, he will likely soon be challenging another.

Hens establish nests in heavy cover, weeds or grass, alfalfa hay fields are a favorite At the rate of about one per day hens lay from one to twenty buff-olive eggs (average about 11). Incubation is 23 days. Precocious, the chicks hatch and, as soon as they are dry, the hen leads them away from the nest site, never to return. Foraging by day, the chicks spend the first few nights beneath the hen's outstretched wings. By the end of the first week the chicks have enough feathers to enable short flights. Mortality among chicks is high, estimates run the gamut and there are a lot of variables — predators, weather, highways, etc. — but on average about 35 percent perish over summer (first six to ten weeks) and the annual turnover rate (adults and young) is about 70 percent on average. Hens will re-nest should a nest be destroyed or a brood lost early on. I have seen young pheasants, barely feathered, barely able to fly, as late as mid-October.

Unlike pheasants, and contrary to what some might say, whitetail deer are Montana natives. For centuries mule deer held sway within the state; if a Montanan spoke of deer, he meant mule deer in almost every case. Whitetails were rare Confined to a few isolated pockets, mostly scattered river bottoms, some called them Cottonwood Deer. However, changing land use practices, particularly widespread logging and increased conversion to crop lands, created ideal habitat and it wasn't long until whitetails became as common as mule deer. Today, nearly statewide, the ranges overlap. In many areas, particularly along the major rivers, whitetails have literally taken over. Elk Island, along with much of the lower Yellowstone River valley is such a place. In some cases, whitetail bucks, being by far the more aggressive, have taken over to the point of actually breeding mule deer does. Biologically speaking, the resultant hybrids are of course a dead end.

Cattail-lined sloughs and irrigation ditches and dense, next to impenetrable, Russian olive thickets, dot the area and the big river cuts a wide swath down the center. This creates a lush and productive habitat for not only pheasants and whitetails but for all wildlife. Waterfowl, wading birds and shorebirds abound as do various furbearers, especially raccoons and mink, and at the moment at least, it seems as if every cottonwood has a resident fox squirrel or two. Songbirds of every size, color and description flit about the thickets; off the cuff we've seen everything from crows to ovenbirds. One afternoon Gale checked off magpie, robin, brown thrasher, blue jay, catbird, downy and hairy woodpecker, northern flicker, yellowthroat, mallard, cinnamon teal, cowbird, redwing blackbird, least flycatcher and house wren.

Bring a boat if you want to access the river and the islands themselves. There is a public boat ramp.

In spring, following ice breakup, the banks of the Yellowstone River become a hunting ground of a different sort. Rock hounds come from far and wide to hunt for moss agates. Elk Island is a particularly popular spot as is the Intake Diversion Dam just up river. Moss agates are treasured not only for their collective beauty, but for the uniqueness within individual stones. Moss agates are used in a variety of jewelry, ranging from rings to belt buckles; actually I just like to look at the polished stones.

New to the area, you might consider a guided boat tour on the Yellowstone River designed especially for agate hunters. Information on the tours is available through the Glendive Area Chamber of Commerce and Agriculture (406-377-5601). Or begin your hunt at the Agate Stop-Montana Agate Museum, 124 4th Ave. N., in Savage (406-776-2373) where you can get a first hand look at "God's Paintings in Stone." In addition to hand-crafted gold and silver jewelry featuring stunning examples of moss agate, one of the largest Yellowstone River agates (27 pounds) is on display along with many natural, or carved and sculpted stones, as well as, local art depicting the stories of Captain Clark's journey down the Yellowstone.

Ask for the abbreviated version of Agate 101 and you will learn as we did: "In the raw, agates are rough-textured, gray, tan, or brownish-colored rocks, often potato-shaped. For gathering no fancy equipment is needed; simply bring along a rock hammer for digging, a bucket or bag for carrying and a comfortable pair of walking shoes — waterproof unless you don't mind wet feet. Look for a translucent spot in the stone which hopefully means there are wonderful scenes in black, red, yellow, brown, green or blue inside. Perhaps above all remember to ask permission of the land owners before hunting for agates on private property."

Agate hunting aside, spring is a busy time up and down the lower Yellowstone and Elk Island is no exception. Wildlife is the main attraction. But others come to stalk wild asparagus, or simply to catch the sight of a sturgeon rolling in the muddy water, while anglers haunt the banks hoping to snag a prehistoric paddlefish.

Paddlefish, by the way, are fascinating creatures. The first thing you notice is the very large mouth and that lo-o-o n g, paddle-shaped snout (called a rostrum) typically comprises about one third the body length. The appendage, once believed to be used to dig or to dislodge food items is now considered little more than a cosmetic adornment (otherwise healthy paddlefish have been observed with rostrums completely missing; in other words, accidentally broken off). Since paddlefish are filter feeders, straining zooplankton out of the water column, the gill arches (open the big maw and they are readily apparent) are the preeminent feeding mechanisms. Swimming mouth agape, the gill arches have filaments on them called gill rakers that sieve the zooplankton organisms from the water — no digging or rooting required thank you.

Among the oldest fishes, fossil records date their first appearance 300 to 400 million years ago (at least 50 million years prior to the first dinosaurs). Incidentally, paddlefish are not related to sharks although the two do share some common traits, including a skeleton primarily composed of cartilage, and a deeply forked, abbreviated heterocercal tail fin (the top fin lobe is slightly larger than the lower fin lobe). Large as fresh water fish go, paddlefish commonly reach 5 feet in length and 60 pounds (the Montana record is 6 feet, 5 inches and 142.5 pounds); some live more the 50 years. And they are great river travelers, with some individuals moving as far as 2,000 miles in a single season.

One late March evening we stopped here hoping to photograph wood ducks and decided to set up camp and stay the night. Next morning, in the pre-dawn darkness, I set out, big lens on the camera, tripod slung over my shoulder, to hide amongst the cattails perhaps shoot a few wood ducks at first light. Already the early birds were in full chorus, other than the chatter it was pretty quiet. Suddenly a tom turkey chimed in, the raucous gobble so overwhelming, I ducked instinctively. Then another gobbled and another; and soon the entire river bottom filled with the wild yodeling sounds of the hot-to-trot toms. I would like to go on and tell you how the mob flew down and all the great shots I got of magnificent strutting toms but... First one tom flapped his great wings and sailed across the river, then a second and a third and...well, I was soon left sitting, camera ready, but not a single strutting tom in sight. Oh well, it was wood ducks drakes I'd come for anyway.

Nearby Restaurants and Accommodations

You can camp on the WMA and at most fishing accesses along the lower river, beyond that public lands and public campsites are scarce. Camping on the WMA is strictly primitive, so come prepared. There is a semi-developed campground at Intake (MT 16, milepost 16) open all year. Most sites have a picnic table, others just a bare spot to set camp. There are two private campgrounds in Sidney, The Place, behind McDonalds, and the Pizza Hut, 488-7169 or 489-0755 and Four Seasons, 501 N. Central, 482-2141. Should you rather stay in a motel in nearby Sidney try the clean, comfortable and reasonable Sunrise Motel, 2300 S. Central, 482-3826 or the Richland Motor Inn, 1200 S. Central, 433-6400; both are very reasonable, allow pets, offer visiting hunters even better rates. Sidney offers dining opportunities to suit just about any pocketbook and taste; café's and fast food restaurants featuring eggs and hash browns, burgers and fries, to table-cloth restaurants featuring great steaks and other delicious entrees. For what it's worth our pick of the litter is the Cattle-Ac, 119 N. Central, 433-7174.

Fast Facts

Contact Info: Montana FWP, Region 7, PO Box 1630, Miles City, MT 59301. Phone: 232-0900; Fax: 232-4368; E-mail: fwprg72@state.mt.us

Getting There: MT 16 between Glendive and Sidney, near Savage, follow signs.

Activities: Hunting, fishing, birding, wildlife viewing, agate hunting, asparagus and berry picking, trapping, boating.

Principle Mammals: Whitetail deer, raccoons, fox squirrels and various furbearers.

Mammals of Special Interest: Whitetail deer.

Principle Birdlife: Upland game birds, large variety songbirds, waterfowl, raptors (especially ospreys and bald eagles) and shorebirds.

Birds of Special Interest: Pheasants, sharp-tailed grouse, Canada geese, mallards, wood ducks, a large variety of songbirds, ospreys and bald eagles.

Habitat Overview: Lush riparian corridor, cottonwood over story, Russian olive, choke cherry, crab apple and other shrubs mid-story and dense grass and weed under story,

Flora of Special Interest: Huge cottonwoods and wild asparagus.

Best Wildlife Viewing Ops: Year around; dawn and dusk are best.

Best Birding Ops: Strutting Tom turkeys and crowing roosters in spring; spring and fall are best for migrants.

Best Photo Ops: Year around; although hunting season tends to make wildlife less approachable.

Hunting Ops: Turkey, pheasant, whitetail and waterfowl as seasons permit; some decent dove shooting can be had early in September.

Fishing Ops: Yellowstone River provides good opportunities for sauger, walleye and smallmouth bass. Spring paddlefish snagging is probably the most popular.

Camping Ops: Primitive; no facilities.

Boating Ops: Public boat ramp provides access to river and islands.

Hiking Trails: No developed trails; limited opportunities on two-tracks and access road.

Motor Trails: Access road winds through a portion of the WMA.

Hell Creek State Park

392 ACRES; 26 MILES NORTH OF JORDAN ON FORT PECK RESERVOIR

Interesting to note: Hell Creek is not named for its likeness to that bottomless pit we all so often refer, but rather from what geologists call the Hell Creek rock formation deposited at the very end of the age of dinosaurs, 65 to 67 million years ago. The formation is found in Montana, North Dakota and South Dakota and, according to fossil records, if you think Hell Creek, Montana is a wild place now...well, as the man might once have said, you hada been here... Some 40 species of mammals, although the largest was a badger-sized creature, known as a metatherian, 60 species of reptile, amphibian and fish, including sharks, rays, sturgeons, paddlefishes, bowfins, garfishes, salamanders, frogs, turtles, even turtle eaters, to say nothing of 30 or so dinosaurs representing no less than eight different families, munching some 200 plant species, everything from algae to small trees.

These days, despite the Hell Creek State Park area being amongst the richest wildlife landscapes in the lower 48, are rather tame by comparison. Still, elk, bighorn sheep, mule and whitetail deer, bobcat, coyote and cougar are common; short-horned lizard, bull snake and prairie rattlesnake are also common, although not always easily seen. While pterodactyls are in short supply, burrowing owls, ferruginous and Swainson's hawks, golden eagles, sharp-tailed and sage grouse, mountain plovers and clay-colored sparrows, to name just a few of the 240 indigenous species, are not. And Fort Peck still harbors such ancients as sturgeon and paddlefish, along with about four dozen other species. Overall, I'd say, wildlife lovers could do far worse than set up camp at Hell Creek State Park.

Until a few years ago, getting to Hell Creek was one thing, and getting back out quite another (should it rain, that is). As a long time Jordanite put it, "Our family used to go often, but woe be it, should it rain while we were in there. Then the road would turn to a gumbo quagmire and you just flat out stayed until it dried out. One weekend trip turned into nearly two weeks and I'm sure that ain't no record. Not to worry now, the road is gravel, so-called all weather, although I'd still be a bit cautious when wet, especially on the steeps."

Nearby Restaurants and Accommodations

The park offers developed campsites and you can camp anywhere on the CMR; you can drive to campsites within 100 yards of a designated road. Jordan has limited facilities, gas station, bar/café, motels. Hell Creek Bar, 557-2302; Rancher's Bar and Café, 557-2468; Fellman's Motel, 557-2209; Garfield Hotel/Motel, 557-6215.

Fast Facts:

Contact Info: Hell Creek, P.O. Box 1630, Miles City, MT 59301; phone: 234-0900.

Getting There: From Jordan take Hell Creek Road north, 26 miles; more or less all weather gravel, still caution is advised when wet.

Activities: Wildlife viewing, bird watching, photography, picnicking, camping, swimming, hiking, bicycling, boating, fishing.

Principle Mammals: Mule and whitetail deer, elk, bighorn sheep, pronghorn, mountain lion, coyote, bobcat and many lesser mammals, including furbearers, muskrat, beaver, mink.

Mammals of Special Interest: None.

Principle Birdlife: A large variety of waterfowl, shorebirds, songbirds, wading birds, upland game birds, birds of prey.

Birds of Special Interest: Sage and sharp-tailed grouse, neotropical migrants, bald and golden eagles, osprey and a variety of raptors.

Habitat Overview: Lake, rugged breaks, willow bottoms, sagebrush-steppe grasslands and open coniferous forest.

Flora of Special Interest: Native grasses, forbs and shrubs.

Best Wildlife Viewing Ops: Elk, mule deer and coyote are most common.

Best Birding Ops: Numbers peak in spring and fall during migration but year around opportunities exist, especially during mild open winters.

Best Photo Ops: Year around opportunities, early and late in the day offers best, most dramatic lighting.

Hunting Ops: No hunting in park, excellent opportunities in surrounding Missouri Breaks.

Fishing Ops: Excellent opportunities exist on sprawling Fort Peck, about 50 species exist in the lake.

Camping Ops: Developed sites, with hook ups, campground host, food concession, etc.

Boating Ops: Marina and boat launch facilities to Fort Peck Reservoir.

Hiking Trails: None developed but hiking is pretty much limited only by your imagination and endurance.

Motor Trails: None developed.

Isaac Homestead Wildlife Management Area

1,275 ACRES; IN TREASURE COUNTY, APPROXIMATELY SEVEN MILES WEST OF HYSHAM

Where the two track meets the Yellowstone River, rigs bearing empty boat trailers backed up to the river's edge belie a favorite activity. To my inquiry, "What's bitin'?", a friendly fisherman about to launch replies, "Sauger, walleye, a few smallies, I got a big channel cat last night."

Interesting.

We knew of Issac Homestead for its healthy pheasant and whitetail deer population, and we realized mallards, wood ducks, Canada geese and mourning doves, as well as dozens of songbird species nested there. We'd seen raccoon, mink, muskrat, beaver and a single, giant, striped skunk on previous visits. Somehow the idea of fishing Issac's escaped us. Consequently nary a fishin' pole. Pretty dumb, actually. We have fished the Yellowstone upstream on countless occasions and know how good the fishing, heck who doesn't. Yet another senior moment, who knows?

In the evening we pull on jackets to ward off the chill, pull up chairs outside the pickup camper, ready for the nightly whitetail show in the nearby alfalfa field. Alfalfa (corn too) is thanks to a crop sharing program between FWP and a local farmer. A deal whereby the farmer gets part and a part is left standing for wildlife. Along with the natural lushness of a healthy riparian corridor the added crops make for a mosaic of continuous wildlife habitat. Aside from the wildlife already mentioned, at least 16 other waterfowl species and several shorebirds show up, most during spring and fall migrations and over 100 species of songbirds.

As the light falls, deer begin drifting into the alfalfa and soon there are 30 or more, mostly whitetails, at least three mule deer, all does and fawns. Since October is just around the corner, only two fawns still wear spots, the rest are dressed in the traditional gray/brown winter coats of the parents. Just before dark, a group of four whitetail bucks emerge from the brush and begin to feed along the edge. All sport multi-pointed racks but one stands out. A real dandy, high, wide and heavy, looks to have five points on a side; assuming brow tines a 6x6 no less. Curious, there doesn't seem to be any archers around...this is September, right?

White-tailed deer (buck)

In the morning, we unleash the dog and take a practice run through the alfalfa. I say practice run because while upland bird season is open, it is not yet pheasant season (which starts in mid-October). And, since we expect to find only pheasants, I've left the gun in the truck. Midway down the field, Katie's hind end gets fidgety and pretty soon she locks down. As I walk past the frozen dog, birds erupt en masse. Hens and cocks fill the air. How many? Who can count? I zero in on a cock flying low right, point a finger, say "Bang your dead." I finger shoot two more and declare, "a limit." Hey, what can I say, I'm still just a kid at heart. Anyway, I wish I'd a brought the fishin' pole.

Another night we are serenaded by a bawling pack of coonhounds, something we don't hear too often around Dillon. So for this old Pennsylvania coon hunter listening to the excited bawls is heady stuff, indeed. Wanting to get a better listen, I step outside the camper, just in time to hear the intermittent bawling of the moving hounds cadence change to the steady chop indicates a treed coon; turns out the tree is not fifty yards away. Soon the hunters arrive, sweeping the big cottonwoods with their powerful hand lanterns. The hunters end it, not with the shots you might expect, but rather by leashing up the still wildly agitated hounds, handing out atta boys, atta girls all around and disappearing into the night. With fur prices down, coons are hardly worth skinning. Thus, it's all about the thrill of the chase and, of course, bragging rights should your hound be the first to bark treed (bark up as we used to say).

All in all, the scene stirs fond memories of a time long ago in a faraway place. Hound music is hound music. As I stood there listening it was easy to imagine my Boomer — or was it Banjo—barking up first.The long chases, short nights; some nights we didn't quit until the blush of dawn slapped us in the face. Yes fools, today is indeed another working day! Ah, to be young again...

That wildlife responds to Issac's well-managed and diverse habitat is obvious, signs of their passing are everywhere. While hunting is the big-ticket item, as pointed out, lots of fisher folks use the WMA to access about five miles of Yellowstone River. Bird and wildlife viewing probably ranks second to hunting and fishing in popularity. Others come simply to hike or bike or camp, or just to get away for awhile. Issac's is handy to a lot of people: Just an hour to Billings (Montana's largest city), still we've never found it crowded. Our first time, we inquired in a Hysham convenience store if we were close to Isaac Homestead. The clerk shrugged and said, "Never heard of it." Several others hanging out returned similar blank looks. Finally one guy, dressed in orange, obviously a hunter, sent us on our way with pretty clear and easy to follow directions... that led us...not to Issac's... but to the Howery Island Nature Trail and Myer's Bridge Fishing Access. Okay, maybe the good folks of Hysham were just trying to keep it to themselves.

These days there are signs, but the signage doesn't start in Hysham, rather several miles down the road. Perhaps the moral is: First you get yourself a good map.

Anyway, Howery Island turned out to be a nice surprise. Officially labeled Howery Island Nature Trail, it's a one-and-a-third-mile interpretive nature trail. Just follow the path and signs along the way provide a glimpse of some of the region's indigenous wildlife. The trail begins beside an abandoned man-made irrigation ditch. Wonderful habitat for a variety of waterfowl, shorebirds, wading birds, songbirds, birds of prey and mammals as well. We've noted blue-winged teal, mallards, wood ducks, lesser yellowlegs, spotted sandpipers, great blue herons and belted kingfishers, striped skunk, raccoon and red fox along the old canal. The vegetation is lush to the point of being nearly impenetrable, huge cottonwoods tower above introduced and somewhat out-of-control Russian olive thickets all interspersed by a jungle of wild rose, snowberry and various native and introduced grasses. Songbirds love it.

In late spring, standing in one spot we check off cowbirds, red-winged blackbirds, mourning doves, robins, tree swallows, a hairy woodpecker, killdeer, song sparrows, yellowthroats, gold finches, a northern oriole, several warblers (sorry they're moving too fast for us amateurs to identify), a bald eagle and a red-shafted flicker; and somewhere nearby, a cock ringneck pheasant crows. Moving further along the trail we come to the main river channel. Canada geese, mallards, common goldeneye are just three of several species of waterfowl within sight. Apparently our intrusion irritates the geese resting on the gravel of the island across the channel and a great ruckus erupts until we once again disappear around the bend.

Back at the truck, while I put the camera gear away, Gale reads aloud the last paragraph in the trail guide, "Riparian areas are the 'green belts' of trees, shrubs and grasses that occur along streams, rivers and lakes. These areas comprise only about one percent of lands in the West but are the most productive and valuable of all lands. They contain the greatest diversity of plants and animals of all vegetative communities. More than 75 percent of all wildlife species use or depend on riparian habitats."

Despite that a few residents could use a better look around the neighborhood to see what's out there, Hysham is a friendly and clean-looking place. And as with most small rural Montana towns, it comes complete with its own brand of colorful and local history. The town takes its name from Charlie J. Hysham, who was associated with an immense early cattle operation, known as the Flying E Ranch. The Flying E ran thousands of cattle in an area between the Bighorn River on the west to Reservation Creek on the east and from the Yellowstone River to the Wyoming line. During the early days of settlement the Northern Pacific railroad tracks passed by a busy branding site on the Flying E and supplies for Hysham were simply thrown out there from the speeding train.

Earlier, numerous forts sprang up as fur trappers and settlers discovered the lower Yellowstone country. Manuel Lisa built the first near the mouth of the Bighorn River in 1807. Fort Cass, built by the competing American Fur Co. soon followed three miles downstream. And later, in 1875, Fort Pease was constructed and served settlers as a safe-haven from raiding Sioux Indians and served as the region's primary trading center.

Today Hysham is home to Treasure County's Historical Museum and the historic Yucca Theater. With its sculpted white buffalo and statues of Lewis and Clark and Sacagawea out front, the distinctive stucco building with its Santa Fe art deco style of architecture stands out — it seems so oddly out place for a Montana farm community.

The building is a real headturner. Constructed in 1931 by David Manning, a local contractor, the theater was the focal point of entertainment in the area for more than 50 years. The first film shown there was the 1914 classic, A Room With A View. The last film to grace its screen in 1986 was Tillie's Punctured Romance — can't say I recall that either.

Manning later went on to become one of Montana's most prominent legislators, serving in the Montana House of Representatives continuously for 52 years until his retirement in 1985. In 1990, the Manning family donated the theater to the museum across the street. It seemed fitting as most of the museum contains the memorabilia and inventions of Senator Manning.

Nearby Restaurants and Accommodations

Limited primitive camping is available at the Howery Island Fishing Access and on the WMA itself, no improvements either site. In Hysham you'll find just one motel, the Hysham, 5th and Orchard, 342-5469, and we were able to locate just two B&Bs nearby, Sarpy Creek Guest House, 342-5668, and Cat Coulee Beds 'N' Birds, off Sumatra Road, N. of Hysham, 749-0095 or 342-5411.

Restaurants are sort of scarce in the area but, Patrick's Café, on the main drag, 342-5766, serves breakfast, lunch and dinner; nothing fancy just good down home cooking and, of course, friendly service.

Hen pheasant

Fast Facts

Contact Info: Montana FWP, Region 7, PO Box 1630, Miles City, MT 59301. Phone: 406- 232-0900; Fax: 406-232-4368; E-mail: fwprg72@state.mt.us

Getting There: I-94 to Hysham Exit; MT 311 west approximately seven miles, follow signs (which, by the way, first appear not in Hysham but several miles out on MT 311).

Activities: Hunting, fishing, birding, wildlife viewing, hiking, photography.

Principle Mammals: Whitetail deer, furbearers, numerous small mammals (fox squirrel especially), occasionally mule deer and pronghorn.

Mammals of Special Interest: Whitetail deer.

Principle Birdlife: Upland game birds, waterfowl, shorebirds, raptors, and about 100 species of songbirds.

Birds of Special Interest: Pheasants, sharp-tailed grouse, mourning doves, Canada geese, mallards, wood ducks and songbirds nest within the WMA.

Habitat Overview: Typical large western river riparian corridor, huge cottonwood over story, dense, lush mid-story (predominantly introduced Russian olive) with heavy under story, winterberry, various grasses, etc. with interspersed farm crops, alfalfa, wheat and corn.

Flora of Special Interest: Giant standing and dead cottonwoods

Best Wildlife Viewing Ops: Mornings and evenings prior to start of hunting season.

Best Birding Ops: Year around; dawn and dusk are primo; late spring/early summer best for viewing not yet fledged broods; during hunting season be sure to wear blaze orange.

Best Photo Ops: Year around; dawn and dusk and overcast days provide optimum light; during hunting season be sure to wear blaze orange.

Hunting Ops: Whitetail deer, waterfowl and upland bird hunting; especially early season.

Fishing Ops: Five miles of Yellowstone River frontage provide good access for sauger, walleye and smallmouth bass; during fall hunting seasons be sure to wear blaze orange.

Camping Ops: Primitive camping with no facilities available throughout; fire restrictions may apply.

Boating Ops: No developed boat ramp but small craft can be launched from several spots.

Hiking Trails: No developed trails, but nice day-hikes can be had by following various access road and two-tracks.

Motor Trails: Gravel access road and two-track wind throughout.

Issac's Homestead WMA/Howery Island Area Bird List

White pelican
Double-crested cormorant
Great blue heron
Canada goose
Mallard
Gadwall
Wigeon
Pintail
Blue-winged teal
Wood duck
Common goldeneye
Common merganser
Killdeer
Greater yellowlegs
Lesser yellowlegs
Spotted sandpiper
Bald eagle
Cooper's hawk
Red-tailed hawk
American kestrel
Ringneck pheasant
Mourning dove
Great horned owl
Belted kingfisher

Northern flicker
Downy woodpecker
Hairy woodpecker
Tree swallow
Barn swallow
Blue jay
Black-capped chickadee
White-breasted nuthatch
House wren
Robin
Brown thrasher
European starling
Warbling vireo
Yellow-rumped warbler
Common yellowthroat
Yellow-breasted chat
Rufous-sided towhee
Song sparrow
Western meadowlark
Red-winged blackbird
Brown-headed cowbird
Common grackle
Northern oriole
American goldfinch

Mule deer buck

Lamesteer National Wildlife Refuge

110 ACRES; APPROXIMATELY 20 MILES SOUTHEAST OF WIBAUX

Unlike Medicine Lake NWR (some 160 miles north), whose staff administers Lamesteer, this small wetland lies in a region unaffected by the last glacial period of 10,000 years ago. The region is known as the Missouri Slope, with a topography of gentle, rolling hills with very few natural lakes and wetlands. The surrounding soils are relatively poor compared to the rich, glacial till of areas further north, and what there is of the native shortgrass prairie consists of low native grasses, forbs and prickly pear cactus. Most years, water is precious, creating a typical western high plains semi-arid climate, with warm to blistering hot and dry summers, cold to brutal winters and widely variable seasonal precipitation. And unlike its mother refuge, the USFWS has no control over the surrounding uplands, only the water rights are included in the easement; as such, private landowners control access and is generally off limits to the public.

Still the impoundment serves an important link in the wellness of the region's waterfowl population. Being the only permanent water for miles around it provides critical nesting habitat and a much-needed water source for migrating birds and resident wildlife. Only during years of surplus water is pumping allowed for irrigation purposes.

No active management takes place and the resource is maintained solely through natural processes; although USFWS does monitor the impoundment closely to make certain the resource is not compromised.

Nearby Restaurants and Accommodations

Wibaux (pronounced wee-bo), eight miles from the North Dakota border on I-94 is the closest town. Rooms are available at Beaver Creek Inn and Suites (796-2666); Nunberg's N Heart Ranch B&B (796-2345); W-V Motel (796-2446); The Palace Café boasts homecooked meals and fresh daily baked goods with breakfast served all day except Sunday. Hot Tip: Worth the long drive no matter how skimpy the Lamesteer fare.

Fast Facts

Contact Info: Medicine Lake NWR, 223 North Shore Rd., Medicine Lake, MT, 59247-9600, Phone: 406-789-2305, E-mail: r6rw_mdl@fws.gov
Getting There: For all intensive purposes the refuge is closed to the public.
Activities: None
Principle Mammals: Mule and white-tailed deer, pronghorn and various small mammals including badger and coyote.
Mammals of Special Interest: None
Principle Birdlife: Waterfowl and a variety of shorebirds.
Birds of Special Interest: Nesting and migrating waterfowl.
Habitat Overview: Small (110) acre impoundment.
Flora of Special Interest: None.
Hunting Ops: Big game, waterfowl (surrounding uplands) None and upland birds by private landowner permission.

Medicine Lake NWR Bird List

LOONS

Common loon

GREBES

Pied-billed grebe
Horned grebe
Red-necked
Eared greb
Western grebe
Clark's grebe

PELICANS

American white pelican

CORMORANTS

Double-crested cormorant

BITTERNS, HERONS, AND EGRETS

American bittern
Great blue heron
Great egret
Snowy egret
Black-crowned night-heron

IBISES AND SPOONBILLS

White-faced ibis

NEW WORLD VULTURES

Turkey vulture

SWANS, GEESE, AND DUCKS

Greater white-fronted goose
Snow goose
Ross' goose
Canada goose
Trumpeter swan
Tundra swan
Wood duck
Gadwall
American wigeon
American black duck
Mallard
Blue-winged teal
Cinnamon teal
Northern shoveler
Northern pintail
Green-winged teal
Canvasback

Redhead
Ring-necked duck
Greater scaup
Lesser scaup
White-winged scoter
Long-tailed duck
Bufflehead
Common goldeneye
Barrow's goldeneye
Hooded merganser
Common merganser
Red-breasted merganser
Ruddy duck

OSPREY, KITES, HAWKS, EAGLES

Osprey
Bald eagle
Northern harrier
Sharp-shinned hawk
Cooper's hawk
Northern goshawk
Broad-winged hawk
Swainson's hawk
Red-tailed hawk
Ferruginous hawk
Rough-legged hawk
Golden eagle

FALCONS AND CARACARAS

American kestrel
Merlin falco
Gyrfalcon falco
Peregrine falcon
Prairie falcon

GALLINACEOUS BIRDS

Gray partridge
Ringnecked pheasant
Sage grouse
Sharp-tailed grouse
Greater prairie chicken

Rails

Yellow rail
Virginia rail
Sora
American coot

CRANES

Sandhill crane
Whooping crane

PLOVERS

Black-bellied plover
American golden plover
Semipalmated plover
Piping plover
Killdeer

STILTS AND AVOCETS

Black-necked stilt
American avocet

SANDPIPERS AND PHALAROPES

Greater yellowlegs
Lesser yellowlegs
Solitary sandpiper
Spotted sandpiper
Willet
Upland sandpiper
Eskimo curlew
Whimbrel
Long-billed curlew
Hudsonian godwit
Marbled godwit
Ruddy turnstone
Red knot
Sanderling
Semipalmated sandpiper
Western sandpiper
Least sandpiper
White-rumped sandpiper
Baird's sandpiper
Pectoral sandpiper
Dunlin

Stilt sandpiper
Ruff
Short-billed dowitcher
Long-billed dowitcher
Common snipe
Wilson's phalarope
Red-necked phalarope

SKUAS, JAEGERS, GULLS, AND TERNS

Franklin's gull
Bonaparte's gull
Ring-billed gull
California gull
Thayer's gull
Glaucous gull
Caspian tern
Common tern
Forster's tern
Least tern
Black tern

PIGEONS AND DOVES

Rock dove
Mourning dove
Passenger pigeon

CUCKOOS AND ANIS

Black-billed cuckoo
Yellow-billed cuckoo

TYPICAL OWLS

Eastern screech-owl
Great horned owl
Snowy owl
Northern hawk-owl
Burrowing owl
Long-eared owl
Short-eared owl

NIGHTJARS

Common nighthawk

SWIFTS

Chimney swift

HUMMINGBIRDS

Ruby-throated hummingbird

KINGFISHERS

Belted kingfisher

WOODPECKERS

Red-headed woodpecker
Yellow-bellied sapsucker
Downy woodpecker
Hairy woodpecker
Northern flicker

TYRANT FLYCATCHERS

Western wood-pewee
Eastern wood-pewee
Yellow-bellied flycatcher
Alder flycatcher
Willow flycatcher
Least flycatcher
Eastern phoebe
Say's phoebe
Great crested flycatcher
Western kingbird
Eastern kingbird

SHRIKES

Loggerhead shrike
Northern shrike

VIREOS

Plumbeous vireo
Blue-headed vireo
Warbling vireo
Philadelphia vireo
Red-eyed vireo

CROWS, JAYS, AND MAGPIES

Blue jay
Black-billed magpie

American crow
Common raven

LARKS

Horned lark

SWALLOWS

Purple martin
Tree swallow
Northern rough-winged swallow
Bank swallow
Cliff swallow
Barn swallow

TITMICE AND CHICKADEES

Black-capped chickadee

NUTHATCHES

Red-breasted nuthatch
White-breasted nuthatch

CREEPERS

Brown creeper

WRENS

House wren
Sedge wren
Marsh wren

KINGLETS

Golden-crowned kinglet
Ruby-crowned kinglet

THRUSHES

Eastern bluebird
Western bluebird
Mountain bluebird
Townsend's solitaire
Veery
Gray-cheeked thrush
Swainson's thrush
Hermit thrush
American robin

MIMIC THRUSHES

Gray catbird
Brown thrasher

STARLINGS

European starling

WAGTAILS AND PIPITS

American (Water)
Sprague's pipit

WAXWINGS

Bohemian waxwing
Cedar waxwing

WOOD WARBLERS

Tennessee warbler
Orange-crowned warbler
Nashville warbler
Yellow warbler
Chestnut-sided warbler
Magnolia warbler
Cape May warbler
Black-throated blue warbler
Yellow-rumped warbler
Black-throated green warbler
Townsend's warbler
Blackburnian warbler
Pine warbler
Prairie warbler
Palm warbler
Bay-breasted warbler
Blackpoll warbler
Black-and-white warbler
American redstart
Ovenbird
Northern waterthrush
Kentucky warbler
Connecticut warbler
Mourning warbler
Macgillivray's warbler
Common yellowthroat
Wilson's warbler

Canada warbler
Yellow-breasted chat

TANAGERS

Scarlet tanager

SPARROWS AND TOWHEES

Spotted towhee
American tree sparrow
Chipping sparrow
Clay-colored sparrow
Brewer's sparrow
Field sparrow
Vesper sparrow
Lark sparrow
Lark bunting
Savannah sparrow
Grasshopper sparrow
Baird's sparrow
Le conte's sparrow
Nelson's sharp-tailed sparrow
Fox sparrow
Song sparrow
Lincoln's sparrow
White-throated sparrow
Harris' sparrow
White-crowned sparrow
Dark-eyed junco
Mccown's longspur
Lapland longspur
Chestnut-collared longspur
Snow bunting

CARDINALS, GROSBEAKS, ALLIES

Rose-breasted grosbeak
Black-headed grosbeak
Lazuli bunting
Dickcissel

BLACKBIRDS AND ORIOLES

Bobolink
Red-winged blackbird
Western meadowlark
Yellow-headed blackbird
Rusty blackbird
Brewer's blackbird
Common grackle
Brown-headed cowbird
Orchard oriole
Baltimore oriole
Bullock's oriole

FINCHES

Pine grosbeak
Purple finch
House finch
Common redpoll
Hoary Redpoll
Pine Siskin
American Goldfinch

OLD WORLD SPARROWS

House sparrow

Medicine Lake NWR Mammal List

All mammals listed have been ovserved on the refuge. Some of these mammals are no longer found at Medicine Lake.

Insectivores

SHREWS

Arctic shrew
Baird's shrew
Cinereus or masked shrew
Pygmy shrew
Merriam's shrew
Northern short-tailed shrew

BATS

Long-eared myotis
Keen's myotis
Little brown myotis
Northern myotis
Small-footed myotis
Western red bat
Eastern red bat
Hoary bat
Silver-haired bat
Big brown bat

HARES AND RABBITS

Mountain cottontail
Snowshoe hare
White-tailed jackrabbit

SQUIRRELS

Least chipmunk
Woodchuck
Franklin's ground squirrel
Richardson's ground squirrel
Thirteen-lined ground squirrel
Black-tailed prairie-dog

POCKET GOPHERS

Northern Pocket gopher
Plains Pocket gopher

HETEROMYIDS

Olive-backed pocket mouse
Plains pocket mouse
Ord's kangaroo rat

BEAVERS

American beaver

MICE, RATS, AND VOLES

Western harvest mouse
Plains harvest mouse
White-footed mouse
Deer mouse
Northern grasshopper mouse
Bushy-tailed woodrat
Norway rat
House mouse
Boreal red-backed vole
Prairie vole
Meadow vole
Sagebrush vole
Common muskrat

JUMPING MICE

Meadow jumping mouse
Western jumping mouse

NEW WORLD PORCUPINES

Common porcupine

Carnivores

CANIDS

Coyote
Gray wolf
Swift fox
Red fox

BEARS

Black bear
Grizzly or brown bear

PROCYONIDS

Common raccoon

MUSTELIDS

Long-tailed weasel
Black-footed ferret
Least weasel
American mink
Wolverine
American badger
Northern river otter

MEPHITIDS

Striped skunk

CATS

Feral cat
Bobcat

CERVIDS

Wapiti or elk
Mule or black-tailed deer
White-tailed deer
Moose
Caribou

PRONGHORN

Pronghorn

BOVIDS

American bison
Domestic cattle

Antelope bucks

Makoshika State Park

11,000 ACRES, EAST OF I-94 AT GLENDIVE

"Makoshika," (Ma-ko'-shi-ka) a Lakota Sioux word, means "bad earth" or "bad lands." Apt description for Montana's largest state park, it is truly an otherworldly place; hoodoos, camels, goblins and who knows what else, of every size and description can be seen in every direction. Hoodoos, in geologic speak, are tall, isolated rock formations found in dry regions of sedimentary rock. The most common are mushroom shaped. In fact, other shapes, such as camels and goblins, are not proper hoodoos but rather hoodoo rocks. The defining feature of either is that its shape is bizarre or fantastic. Trust me; there is no shortage of either here.

Here the evolution of our planet, its plant and animal life over the past 80 million years, is laid bare. The wind-carved and eroded rock and soil formations contain an evolving fossilized record of plants and animals dating back to the age of reptiles, the first mammals, and the last great ice age. Cultural evidence belies the primitive tribes of long ago.

Badlands indeed, though at first glance, moonscape isn't too far off the mark either. But the more one looks the more doubt is cast that even the moon rivals the eerie, mysterious eroded folds of gray, hardened sand and rock. On the other hand, close inspection turns up an amazing variety of plant life—nothing moon-like there. Off-hand, there are at least two varieties sagebrush, salt brush, juniper and the occasional ponderosa pine, some sort of elm, snowberry, green ash, wild plum and a chokecherry thicket. Grasses include, blue gramma, needle and thread, wheat, prairie june varieties and a few others of which I'm not familiar. Intermingled amongst the grasses are wild onion and a trio of wilted wildflowers. As a wild guess, the trio is phlox, evening primrose and yellow pea, but don't bet the farm. And of course scattered about are the familiar and ever-present western arid-lands' plants—yucca and prickly pear cactus.

I'm pretty proud of that little piece of botanizing until a sign in the Visitor's Center pokes, large hole in my inflated ego. Turns out my short list is but the tip of the iceberg, so to speak. There are actually "over 200 species of wildflowers, grasses, trees, and shrubs" growing in the park. Other signage depicts the wildlife: whitetail deer, pronghorn, bull snake and prairie rattlesnake, bobcat and coyote; none of which we have spied personally over the course of several visits. Though we have spied sagebrush lizard, chipmunk, porcupine, mule deer and mountain cottontail. Admittedly both Gale and I are rather sorry birders. Still our personal Makoshika list includes a surprising number: magpie, golden eagle, goldfinch, prairie falcon, turkey vulture, horned lark, Brewer's and lark sparrow and mountain bluebird.

Present fauna and flora aside, the view still speaks to the idea of an ancient, pre-historic time when giant lizards, huge dinosaurs, saber-toothed tigers and hairy mammoths ruled. While at the same time warns that perhaps something very wrong happened here — like what the world might look like a day after the apocalypse. And the more you learn the more it seems an idea not all that much of a stretch.

Geologists theorize that "dramatic erosion followed an ancient grass fire charred the plain, exposed sand and clay and rock to the weathering effects of rain and wind." Park manager, Dale Carlson, calls it, "The most geologically spectacular badlands in the entire region." Normally, with me, most and best anything are contentious points but in this case what's to argue?

The constant erosion has created more than just unusual rock and soil formations. The area has attracted visitors for thousands of years. Local Indian legend contains scores of references of finding large bones (probably dinosaur) eroding from hillsides. Imagine the surprise of these ancient hunters, intimate as they must have been with anatomy having butchered countless animals, to have discovered these mysterious giant bones unlike anything any of them or their ancestors had ever seen.

These days a virtual smorgasbord awaits fossil hunters and paleontologists. Although digging, removing, even touching fossil finds is a no-no, many amateurs (pros too) still go there just to hunt and report. Incidentally, most finds are later officially removed for display in the Museum of the Rockies in Bozeman.

Dating back to December 15, 1963, when Robert "Doc" Hiatt, a Glendive optician who, over the years became so involved with park development, locals dubbed him "the parkologist", unearthed a series of large fossilized remains there have been many discoveries. Two stand out: In 1991 a triceratops skull and frill were excavated; and in 1996 the only complete skeleton of a rare dinosaur, thescelosaurus, ever found anywhere, was unearthed.

Since Doc Hiatt's revealing discoveries scientists have "found" the park. Among others, Jack Horner, the renowned paleontologist at the Museum of the Rockies, has conducted a long-term project aimed at "trying to figure out what life was like and what the ecosystem was like sixty-five million years ago". The project, ongoing both in the park and elsewhere in Montana, involves gathering, listing and evaluation of fossilized plants, invertebrates, herbivores and meat eaters with the hope of constructing a model of the ecosystem at the time of the mass die off of dinosaurs and other long extinct species.

Recent discoveries aside, mysteries still abound at Makoshika. One the most fascinating begs the question why, given today's northern climate, sparsely vegetated arid badlands continue to yield the bones of Mesozoic fish, alligators, crocodiles, a tyrannosaurus rex and fossilized remains of leaves from subtropical trees and plants? The answer lies in the fact that during the period between 210 million and 65 million years ago, during the Mesozoic time period, the climate of eastern Montana was in fact sub-tropical in nature, the lands covered with a lush savannah bordering a shallow inland bay of the Gulf of Mexico.

Badlands, wherever they exist, appear timeless, as if the evolving landscape suddenly stopped in mid-stride, though, of course, nothing could be further from the truth. Gone is what were — dinosaurs, Audubon sheep, bison and myriad plant species to name just a few. And, although the eroding landscape changes happen ever so slowly the place is forever changed and continues changing with each sweep of the second hand.

Apparently ancient peoples (like many moderns) found in badlands, not the usual notion of worthless wasteland, but a sort of spiritual altar—a place to go to heal the spirit, cleanse the soul, if you will. Others, such as us, simply enjoy the unique look and empty feel such a chunk of largely overlooked and forgotten land affords. Overlooked and forgotten, valueless to the masses simply because it's too poor to graze, no water to speak of and no riches to be found — no gold and silver, no coal deposits, no gas and oil, at least none discovered yet. Of course to those of us perhaps considered a bit off center therein lies its appeal.

And of course in America the ideas of worthless, overlooked and forgotten seldom go unchallenged, at least not for long.

In light of the fact the park's foundation clays and sandstones were set down 100 to 200 million years ago when an inland sea overspread the area from Texas to Canada, there has long been speculation oil just might lie beneath. Especially considering as the sea receded vegetation grew and flourished until as recent as two thousand years ago when an intense fire ravished the vegetation and sterilized the soil — hindering plant growth for centuries. It was during this period when erosion, both wind and water, created the earthen structures and rock towers that form not only the park's modern day signature but that of much of the region. One, the so-called Cedar Creek "anticline" (actually a long arch), extends into South Dakota. Uplifted by the push of natural forces far beneath the surface as long ago as 50 million years, the Cedar Creek arch is no longer visible since erosion has long since removed its top layers. But the fold in the landscape created a natural trap deep within, that actually holds the region's most productive oil reserves.

With this in mind in the 1970s the oil industry asked federal and state officials to grant drilling rights within the park itself. And of course whenever the oil barons come begging you can bet the farm there are politicians more than willing to stand in line to help out. The coup resulted in one "dry hole" being drilled somehow, perhaps by the grace of God, not in the park proper but just outside the boundary.

Still the option remained on the books until 1999 when public sentiment pushed the state legislature to pen a bill that would forever protect the park from further drilling. As you might expect, this caused a furor among oil industry lobbyists. What you may not know (and I find it a little hard to believe), is that the bill was furiously opposed by none other than the Montana Department of State Lands. But for once insanity lost out to clear thinking and the bill, though first stalled in committee, was later resurrected and finally passed. Though as written, oil drilling can still go on "under" the park so long as the drilling rigs are parked "outside" the boundary — in other words angled drilling is okay.

Ah, the power of the scent of money when wafted through the Halls of Congress.

Makoshika may be "badlands" but don't mistake that idea with nothing much to do other than gaze at eroding sand and rock. Within the Center itself are several illuminating exhibits including the well-preserved triceratops skull and the Seaway Exhibit renders clearly what the park was like submerged beneath the ocean, while the exhibits A Moment of Dinosaurs, Ages of Erosion and Makoshika Today show how the park evolved once the ocean receded. Outside are two developed hiking trails, the first being Cap Rock Nature Trail. It is a half-mile loop featuring close-up views of soil stratus, cap rocks and an awesome natural rock bridge. The trailhead is three miles in off the main access road. A mile further is the Kinney Coulee Trail, another half-mile hike drops 300 feet or so to the coulee floor then winds through the pines and eroded landscape giving hikers a real feel for what the park is all about.

Bicyclists can pedal through the park on the access road and on recently constructed bike trails. Shooters can test out their marksmanship on the rifle and pistol range, while archers will want to try out the archery range. In addition there is a frisbee-golf course, a campground with 22 sites, and picnic areas including a group site complete with modern pavilion, and an outdoor amphitheater which features a full line-up of programs during the summer months. Scattered throughout are interpretive displays, drinking water, picnic tables with fire rings, trash cans and both vault and flush toilets. In Glendive there is a regular golf course.

One of the park's summer highlights is the annual Buzzard Day celebration of the return of the turkey vultures (buzzards as they are known locally). Generally held around mid-June, the day's events include a pancake breakfast, buzzard runs (yes it's true, three actually, 10K, 5K and one mile), kite flying, nature walks, a compass/orienteering hike and an 18-hole golf tournament (frisbee, not traditional). It's a fun and lively affair and one every true-blue Montana son or daughter should attend at least once. Of course being a Montanan, native or otherwise, is not a prerequisite.

Makoshika. Just the name alone stirs the imagination and fuels fires of speculation. It's one thing to read of the remarkable conversion from lush tropical swampland to arid, near-sub-Arctic badland. It's another to see the makeover first-hand, up close and personal and quite another to believe...but it sure ain't hard to just sit back and enjoy the view.

Nearby Restaurants and Accommodations

For dining out try the Kings Inn, 1903 N. Merrill Ave., 365-5636, good steaks, better pasta and well-stocked full service bar; prime rib lovers should head for Doc and Eddie's, 1515 W. Bell, 365-6782; the Glendive breakfast hotspot is the Best

Western Jordan Inn, 223 N. Merrill, 377-5555; rumor has it the dinner entrées aren't bad either but we've never eaten dinner there, so...

Glendive offers a full complement of motels. The Best Western is downtown and very popular but we have personal experience only with the Days Inn, 2000 Merrill Ave., 365-6011.

Park campground features 22-sites — 14 trailer/RV, eight tent only — with picnic tables and fire rings, drinking water (May-October) and toilets. Actually the main reason for our lack of personal Glendive motel experience is that one of our favorite campgrounds in eastern Montana, Intake Fishing Access, on the Yellowstone River is just a few miles out on MT 16 north, so... Nothing particularly special or fancy, we just like sleeping to the babble of the big ol' river...

Fast Facts

Contact Info: Makoshika State Park, Box 1242, Glendive, MT 59330. Phone: 377-6256

Getting There: I-94, Glendive, MT, follow signs (Snyder Avenue); the park lays just at the edge of town.

Activities: Badlands gawking, wildlife viewing, photography, hiking, camping, rifle, pistol and archery shooting, picnicking, interpretive displays, etc.

Principle Mammals: mule deer, pronghorn, porcupine, cottontail rabbit.

Mammals of Special Interest: None.

Principle Birdlife: Magpie, golden eagle, goldfinch, prairie falcon, turkey vulture, horned lark, Brewer's and lark sparrow and mountain bluebird.

Birds of Special Interest: Turkey vulture (locally called buzzard).

Habitat Overview: Arid badlands, although there are over 200 species of plants.

Flora of Special Interest: Sagebrush, salt brush, juniper, ponderosa pine, elm, snowberry, green ash, wild plum chokecherry, blue gramma, needle and thread, wheatgrass, prairie junegrass, wild onion, phlox, evening primrose, yellow pea, yucca and prickly pear cactus.

Best Wildlife Viewing Ops: Weekdays, dusk and dawn, spring, fall and winter.

Best Birding Ops: Weekdays, dusk and dawn, spring, fall and winter; in mid-June with the return of the turkey vultures.

Best Photo Ops: Scenic are best shot in low, spectacular light; wildlife are most likely to pose dawn and dusk, weekdays when the crowds are thinnest, spring, fall and winter; mid-June when the turkey vultures return.

Camping Ops: Campground has 22 sites, 14 trailer/RV and eight tent only; picnic tables, fire rings, toilets, drinking water May-October, no hookups.

Hiking Trails: Two developed; each approximately one-half mile in length. Also bicycle trails.

Motor Trails: Main access road through park; part of the road has a trailer restriction.

Medicine Rocks State Park

Indians knew this area as a place of big medicine, where hunting parties mingled with magical spirits, garnered courage and asked for good luck. Today we go there mostly to soothe worn souls, listen to wind songs, relax amongst the weird rocks and ponderosa pines, commune with nature, and consider how it might have been eons ago.

Geologists speculate millions of years ago a sinuous river carved a path from Miles City southeast; eventually spilling its waters into an estuary of an ancient sea in the vicinity of what is now Camp Crook, in northwestern South Dakota. Wide and shallow, much like the Missouri River only much larger, the river's ever-changing sandbars grew into immense underwater sand dunes, perhaps 50 feet or more in thickness. Pressured by their own weight the dunes turned to stone. Sea levels rose, inundating the rock with salt water, evidenced by the top crusty layer filled with bore holes of various marine creatures. Later the sea receded leaving the stone high and dry to be sculpted over eons by wind and rain into the bizarre rock formations we see today.

Dating indicates this all occurred in the Torrejonian Age, some 61 million years ago.

Indian tribes — Arikara, Assiniboine, Cheyenne, Gros Ventre, Mandan, and Sioux—considered Medicine Rocks "holy, spiritual, sacred ground," for vision quests as well as spotting game and, no doubt, enemies. The Sioux called it, Inyan-oka-la-ka, or rock with a hole in it. Evidence of their camps remains in the many old teepee rings, bone and stone artifacts and clay cookware found throughout.

In the Carter County Museum in Ekalaka, old photos clearly show Indians were not the only ones intrigued by the cheesecake-like sandstone formations. The photos show wagons, buggies, Model Ts, folks all decked out in their Sunday best. Apparently Medicine Rocks was an even more popular picnic spot back then than now.

On the practical side, constant, year-round flowing springs provided travelers, Indian and white settlers alike, the ideal site to bivouac — locals still come to fill water jugs, coveted for its medicinal qualities. Other attractions might have been to gather medicinal roots and plants, or perhaps just pick up a souvenir, perhaps an ancient fossil or seashell, maybe an arrowhead or two. These days, of course, gathering is a no-no punishable by fines or worse — what you find there leave there.

Early travelers also left their marks in the form of pictographs, carved initials and such. Today of course it is illegal to further deface or otherwise disturb the original writings.

One of the first outsiders to become enamored with the rock formations was Teddy Roosevelt. In Hunting Trips of a Ranch Man, he wrote, "Altogether it was fantastically beautiful as any place I have ever seen; it seemed impossible that the hand of man should not have had something to do with its formation."

A sign outside Ekalaka tells the story of the first white settler in the region, Claude Carter. In 1884, hauling logs, his wagon broke down near Russell Creek. Story goes he unloaded the logs, declared the spot "as good as any to build a saloon." And the rest as they say is history. Ekalaka today is largely forgotten except during spring and fall hunting seasons, when turkey and deer hunters descend from all over — a sort of semi-annual boom-and-bust cycle. Though evidently enough, Ekalaka is one those places that just keeps on ticking no matter what.

Like most, Medicine Rocks was once privately owned. Private ownership fell into public coffers when the owners failed on back taxes in the Dust Bowl years of the 1930s. In 1957, Carter County sold 320 acres to the state of Montana. Originally managed by MTDOT, the highway department spread a little gravel and built picnic tables; in 1965, MTFWP took over and Medicine Rocks SP was born.

Strapped for funds to maintain such off the beaten path parks, in 1991 the state declared a $3-entrance fee in an attempt to recoup at least part of the roughly $20,000 annual maintenance bill. "No way," said the citizens of Ekalaka and Carter County and to aid the cause, Ekalaka Eagle editor, Lois Lambert, fired off an article to the Billings Gazette. In gist, the article said, "We gave it to the state and now they are charging us to use it." Not all acceptable, in protest the Carter County Museum moved its annual bash to Ekalaka rather than the park — the first time in over 40 years the picnic was held elsewhere. In this instance the protests did not fall on deaf ears and in 1993 the Montana Legislature declared 15 primitive parks within the system user free. And of course today, anyone in a vehicle bearing a Montana License plate gets in free to any state park.

In addition to the weird shapes there are stone arches, overhangs and caves reminiscent in a small way to the slick rock formations found in Utah and other sections of the southwest. The rocks are popular among boulderists and others who just like to explore and climb rocks.

Beyond rocks the area is rich in wildlife heritage as well. And today wildlife abounds, Merriam's wild turkey, sharp-tailed grouse, a variety of songbirds associated with grasslands, mule deer, pronghorn, turkey vulture, golden eagle, coyote, ground squirrel and a variety of raptors are common sights.

Nearby Restaurants and Accommodations

Guest House, 775-6337
Midway Motel, 775-6337
Rose Ranch, 775-6204
Deb's Coffee Shop, 775-8718
Old Stand Bar & Grill, 775-666
Wagon Wheel Café, 775-6639 (recommended).
Camping abounds in the nearby Custer National Forest.

Fast Facts

Contact Info: Medicine Rocks, P.O. Box 1630, Miles City, MT 59301; phone: 234-0900.
Getting There: Montana 7, 25 miles south of Baker mile post 10, then 1 mile west on county road.
Activities: Wildlife viewing, bird watching, camping, picnicking, bicycling, hiking. No metal detectors, digging, collecting or removal of artifacts.
Principle Mammals: Mule deer, pronghorn, coyote.
Mammals of Special Interest: None.
Principle Birdlife: Merriam's wild turkey, sharp-tailed grouse, grassland-associated songbirds, variety raptors, including golden eagle.
Birds of Special Interest: None.
Habitat Overview: Grassland, ponderosa pine over story, sandstone rock formations.
Flora of Special Interest: None.
Best Wildlife Viewing Ops: Merriam's turkey, golden eagle, pronghorn and mule deer, year around.
Best Birding Ops: Songbird numbers peak during spring and fall migration, gobbling, strutting tom turkeys and sharp-tailed grouse on nearby leks in spring.
Best Photo Ops: Year around opportunities abound for photographing wildlife and rock formations. Woodhouse's toad is known to frequent the area.
Hunting Ops: Limited hunting outside the developed use area and on surrounding private lands with permission.
Fishing Ops: None.
Camping Ops: 14-day limit, tent and RV sites.
Boating Ops: None
Hiking Trails: Three quarters of a mile developed, unlimited off trail opportunities.
Motor Trails: Gravel entrance road winds through a portion of the park.

Pirogue Island State Park

210-ACRE ISLAND OF YELLOWSTONE RIVER, TWO MILES NORTHEAST OF MILES CITY

Captain Clark and crew camped on Pirogue Island, July 29, 1806 on their return trip from the Pacific coast. The expedition had attempted to camp below the mouth of the Tongue River, but its muddy discharge "colored the water gave it a bad taste." At the time, the mouth of the Tongue was downstream of its present location — it was relocated by the railroad in the late 1800s. Subsequently, camp was moved downstream to Pirogue Island on the opposite side of river, to dodge the nasty water.

Four days prior to their encampment on Pirogue Island, Clark's party passed by a large rock formation on the bank of the river. Clark climbed the rock and inscribed his name and the date in its surface. He named it Pompey's Tower (or Pompey's Pillar) in honor of Sacagawea and Charbonneau's son. Visitors to the pillar can still see Clark's signature, the only physical evidence remaining of the expedition's passing. In a relatively flat river plain, Pompey's Pillar offers a grand, spectacular view of the Yellowstone River and surrounding landscape.

In the days following the encampment on Pirogue Island, the party entered into a desolate area of eastern Montana, near present-day Terry. Clark noted, "by far the worst place which I have seen on this river ... entirely bare of timber ... great quantities of Coal." Soon after, on Aug. 2nd, Clark wrote, "the troublsome muskeeteers return, and A Grizzly of the large vicious Species...plunged in the water and Swam towards us." The men fired at the bear and wounded it. Another grizzly swam downstream towards them, which Clark proceeded to shoot and skin it, noting it was "much the largest female bear I ever Saw."

Pirogue Island became part of the state park system in 1982 and visitors can hike its dense cottonwood forest, a haven for wildlife, like mule deer, white-tailed deer, and birds, go rock hounding for moss agates, or perhaps just to envision the Corps of Discovery's travel along the river. Some of the more common birds found here are kestrel, magpie, chickadee, belted kingfisher, mallard, Canada goose, goldeneye,

Common snipe

double crested cormorant, great blue heron, wigeon, teal, mourning dove, bald eagle, osprey, catbird, killdeer, northern flicker, turkey vulture, western meadowlark, a variety of warblers and other neotropical migrants, especially during the spring and fall migrations. In addition to deer, raccoon, striped skunk, muskrat, the occasional beaver and mink, a host of lesser mammals, mice and voles are known to inhabit the island.

The island is always accessible by floating, and during low water visitors can access via a narrow, wadeable channel that separates the island from the mainland.

Nearby Restaurants and Accommodations

Gallagher's, Miles City, 232-0099
Cellar Casino, Miles City, 232-5611
Hole in the Wall, Miles City, 232-9887
Boardwalk, Miles City, 232-0195
Cattle Ac, Miles City, 232-6987
Free camping on BLM is available at Strawberry Hill Recreation Area, 7 miles east of Miles City on US12
Fee camping is available at Miles City KOA; phone: 232-3991
Several chain motels are available in Miles City.

Fast Facts

Contact Info: Pirogue Island, P.O. Box 1630, Miles City, MT 59301; phone: 234-0900.

Getting There: One mile north of Miles City on MT 59, then two miles east on Kinsey Road, then two miles south on county road; follow signs.

Activities: Wildlife viewing, birding, photography, fishing, picnicking, hiking, biking, and floating.

Principle Mammals: Mule and white-tailed deer, raccoon, striped skunk, a variety of furbearers and small mammals.

Mammals of Special Interest: None.

Principle Birdlife: Waterfowl, song birds, shorebirds, wading birds, birds of prey.

Birds of Special Interest: None.

Habitat Overview: Island, cottonwood forest.

Flora of Special Interest: Old growth cottonwoods.

Best Wildlife Viewing Ops: Year around opportunities.

Best Birding Ops: Year around opportunities, numbers peak during spring and fall migration.

Best Photo Ops: Year around opportunities.

Hunting Ops: According to Montana game laws; check current regulations.

Fishing Ops: Excellent opportunities for smallmouth bass, channel catfish and other indigenous warm water species.

Camping Ops: No overnight camping allowed.

Boating Ops: No formal launch.

Hiking Trails: No developed trails but hiking is a popular activity.

Motor Trails: No motor vehicle access.

Pirogue Island Bird List

White pelican
Double-crested cormorant
Great blue heron
Canada goose
Mallard
Gadwall
Wigeon
Pintail
Blue-winged teal
Wood duck
Common goldeneye
Common merganser
Killdeer
Greater yellowlegs
Lesser yellowlegs
Spotted sandpiper
Bald eagle
Cooper's hawk
Red-tailed hawk
American kestrel
Ringneck pheasant
Mourning dove
Great horned owl
Belted kingfisher

Northern flicker
Downy woodpecker
Hairy woodpecker
Tree swallow
Barn swallow
Blue jay
Black-capped chickadee
White-breasted nuthatch
House wren
Robin
Brown thrasher
European starling
Warbling vireo
Yellow-rumped warbler
Common yellowthroat
Yellow-breasted chat
Rufous -sided towhee
Song sparrow
Western meadowlark
Red-winged blackbird
Brown-headed cowbird
Common grackle
Northern oriole
American goldfinch

Seven Sisters
Wildlife Management Area

1,761 ACRES; ONE MILE EAST OF CRANE ON COUNTY ROAD, BESIDE THE YELLOWSTONE RIVER

Seven Sisters WMA, located on the Yellowstone River at river mile 39, is one of 50 FWP managed sites on the Yellowstone. The Yellowstone River originates in Wyoming and flows through Yellowstone National Park before entering Montana at Gardiner. From the park boundary to Livingston, the river flows north through Paradise Valley, flanked by the Absarokee Mountains on the east and the Gallatin Range on the west. It continues in a northeasterly direction from Livingston and meets up with the Missouri River just across the North Dakota border. The Yellowstone is one of the last large, free-flowing rivers in the continental United States; about 550 miles of which flows within Montana's borders. Lack of main stem impoundments allows the river to operate within a natural rhythm — peak flows in spring, low flows in fall and winter — the result is a unique ecosystem and a valuable resource. From a fisheries standpoint, anglers get the entire package: coldwater native cutthroat trout upstream, warmwater catfish and smallmouth bass downstream. The fish species count is perhaps even more impressive than the wildlife: bigmouth buffalo, black bullhead, blue sucker, brassy minnow, brook trout, brown trout, burbot, channel catfish, chinook salmon, cisco, common carp, creek chub, cutthroat trout, emerald shiner, fathead minnow, flathead chub, freshwater drum, golden shiner, goldeye, green sunfish, lake chub, largemouth bass, longnose dace, longnose sucker, minnow, mottled sculpin, mountain sucker, mountain whitefish, northern pike, paddlefish, plains minnow, rainbow trout, river carpsucker, sailfin molly, sauger, saugeye, shorthead redhorse, shortnose gar, shovelnose sturgeon, sicklefin chub, smallmouth bass, smallmouth buffalo, spottail shiner, stonecat, sturgeon, sturgeon chub, sucker, walleye, western silvery minnow, western silvery/plains minnow, white sucker, yellowstone cutthroat trout, cuttbow hybrids and brook stickleback. The adjacent riparian zone is a mix

Marsh wren

of cottonwood-willow bottomlands and converted croplands, no longer pristine nonetheless still impressive. The river was a major factor in the settlement of Montana and continues in its role of cultural and historical significance.

In Greek mythology, the Pleiades were seven sisters: Alcyone, Asterope, Celaeno, Electra, Maia, Merope, and Taygete. Atlas, the Titan who held up the sky, and Pleione, the protectress of sailing, were the parents. Following a chance meeting with Orion the hunter, the Pleiades and Pleione became the object of his desire; apparently enamored with the young women he pursued them relentlessly. Zeus took pity and changed Pleione and the Seven Sisters to a flock of doves, which he set in the heavens. Thus to Atlas' original punishment — that of forever holding up the sky — was added the further penalty of eternal absence from wife and family.

Actually, just six of the seven stars are visible to the naked eye. The ancient Greeks, of course, had various explanations for the missing star: one held that the Pleiades were companions to the gods, except for Merope, who deserted her sisters, shamed by having a mortal husband; another said the "lost star" was none other than Electra, ancestress of the royal house of Troy, and following Troy's destruction, the grief-stricken Electra transformed into a comet. And of course, we could go on with this.

Back to the WMA.

In late spring, Seven Sisters comes alive: rooster pheasants crow, wild turkey gobbles greet the dawn, several pairs of Canada geese well on their way to fledging a bunch of goslings, ospreys and bald eagles fish the muddy waters and a white-tailed doe secrets her newborn twins to daytime beds in a cattail thicket beside the overgrown irrigation ditch.

Wild asparagus grows along the river and beside the ditch banks. A member of the lily family, it is not native to eastern Montana, probably having first escaped from a 19th century homesteader's garden. It has no fat, no cholesterol and is low in sodium. It is rich in both rutin and folic acid. Asparagus can grow over five inches in twenty-four hours. It first starts popping up at the end of April, and can be harvested until about the middle of June. Its flavor rivals the best garden varieties but when it comes to adventure the wild version wins hands down.

Red and diamond willows, green ash, chokecherry, box elder, and Russian olive tend a healthy mix of grasses and weeds beneath tall cottonwoods, along with several fields planted in alfalfa and corn, to form the foundation for this excellent piece of river bottom habitat. This is the sort of property that screams wildlife, I thought, just as a trio of large white-tailed bucks adorned with heavy, bulbous-looking velvet-covered antlers break from cover and trot across the newly planted corn. Sort of confirms the idea that it just doesn't get much better.

On a recent bird hunting expedition we camped beside the slough and for the next couple days, we chased pheasants and wood ducks in the ditch banks and thickets, shot doves in the corn, stalked geese in the slough, and although that didn't quite work out, it was still fun and made the long trip getting here more than worthwhile. Meantime our one and only neighbor, a bow and bird hunter hung a big

5x5 white-tailed buck beside his trailer one evening and limited out on roosters next morning.

"Me and old Rex here (a black Lab) are havin' us a helluva hunt and an even better time," he said.

Like other spots along the lower Yellowstone, agate hunting is a popular early spring post-ice-break-up activity. For agate lovers, Harmon's Agate and Silver Shop in Crane is a must stop, (406-482-2538).

Nearby Restaurants and Accommodations

You can camp on the WMA and at most fishing accesses along the lower river, beyond that public lands are scarce. Camping on the WMA is strictly primitive, so come prepared to do so strictly on your own. There is a developed campground at Intake (MT 16, milepost 16) open all year. Most sites have a picnic table, others just a bare spot to set camp. There are two private campgrounds in Sidney: The Place, behind McDonalds and the Pizza Hut, 488-7169 and Four Seasons, 501 N. Central, 482-2141.

If motels better suit your fancy, in nearby Sidney try the clean, comfortable and reasonable Sunrise Motel, 2300 S. Central, 482-3826 or the Richland Motor Inn, 1200 S. Central, 433-6400; both are very reasonable, allow pets, offer visiting hunters even better rates.

Sidney offers dining opportunities to suit just about any pocketbook and taste; café's and fast food restaurants featuring eggs and hash browns, burgers and fries, to tablecloth restaurants featuring great steaks and other delicious entrees. For what it's worth, our pick of the litter is hands down the Cattle-Ac, 119 N. Central, 433-7174.

Fast Facts

Contact Info: Pirogue Island, P.O. Box 1630, Miles City, MT 59301; phone: 234-0900

Getting There: MT 16, approximately 10 miles south Sidney, at Crane turn east on county road, one mile.

Activities: Hunting, fishing, trapping (permit required), boating, birding, wildlife viewing, photography, agate hunting, wild asparagus and berry gathering.

Principle Mammals: White-tailed deer, furbearers, small mammals (fox squirrels).

Mammals of Special Interest: White-tailed deer, river otters, raccoons and fox squirrels.

Principle Birdlife: Upland game birds, large variety songbirds, waterfowl, raptors (especially ospreys and bald eagles) and shorebirds.

Birds of Special Interest: Pheasants, various songbirds, Canada geese, wood ducks, mallards, ospreys and bald eagles, variety of shorebirds.

Habitat Overview: Lush riparian corridor enhanced further by farm fields.

Flora of Special Interest: Large cottonwood trees, Russian olive thickets, wild asparagus.

Best Wildlife Viewing Ops: Year around; hunting season would be the exception when increased human activity tends to make everything warier.

Best Birding Ops: Spring and early summer, dawn and dusk.

Best Photo Ops: Evening light is best; dawn a close second. Good opportunities year around except hunting season.

Hunting Ops: Good pheasant, waterfowl and deer hunting; fair spring turkey hunting. Raccoon hunting with hounds can be excellent, especially in early fall.

Fishing Ops: Paddlefish in spring; excellent fall fishing for sauger, walleye and smallmouth bass.

Camping Ops: Primitive; no facilities.

Boating Ops: Access is limited but available.

Hiking Trails: No developed trails; limited to access road and two-tracks.

Motor Trails: Good gravel access road.

Seven Sisters WMA Wildlife List (most common)

Amphibians

Northern Leopard frog
Woodhouse's toad

Birds

American crow
American goldfinch
American redstart
American robin
Baltimore oriole
Bank swallow
Barn swallow
Black-billed magpie
Black-headed grosbeak
Blue jay
Brown-headed cowbird
Canada goose
Cedar waxwing
Common nighthawk
Common snipe
Common yellowthroat
Downy woodpecker
Eastern kingbird
Gray catbird
Great horned owl
Western screech owl
Osprey
Bald Eagle
Harrier
Kestrel
Red-tailed hawk
Hairy woodpecker
House wren
Lark sparrow
Least flycatcher
Mourning dove
Northern flicker
Red-eyed vireo

Red-necked phalarope
Song sparrow
Warbling vireo
Wild turkey
Ringnecked pheasant
Hungarian partridge
Yellow warbler
Yellow-breasted chat
Mallard
Wood duck
Cinnamon teal
Blue-winged teal
Green-winged teal
Goldeneye

Mammals

American beaver
Common raccoon
Deer mouse
Meadow vole
Mink
Western harvest mouse
White-tailed deer mouse
Muskrat
Porcupine
Striped skunk
Mountain cottontail

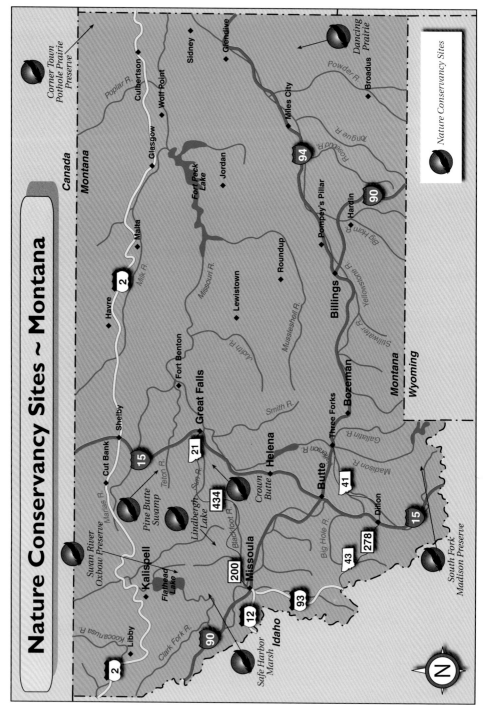

Nature Conservancy Sites ~ Montana

Nature Conservancy Sites

Nature Conservancy Sites

The Nature Conservancy is the world's leading private conservation group. Its aim is to conserve and enhance private lands to insure and preserve our natural heritage for future generations. Working within three broad landscapes — the 10-million acre Crown of the Continent ecosystem, the 27-million acre Greater Yellowstone Ecosystem and the Northern Prairies of Montana (Philips County) — about a half-million acres is currently enrolled. Through conservation easements with private landowners, the Conservancy works to create workable conservation plans for the good of all concerned — wildlife, the land itself, insuring the landowner's bottom line and the local economy. In addition, the Conservancy owns several preserves deemed unique and outstanding natural places.

Northern Prairies of Montana

While much has been lost to crop conversion and other development, much remains of the native grasslands that once ruled most of eastern Montana; in fact more remains here than anywhere else on the Great Plains. South of Malta (Philips County), the once heavily glaciated native grasslands are home to a wide array of native wildlife: pronghorn, mule deer, black-tailed prairie dog, swift fox, American badger, coyote and other mammals including Montana's rarest: the black-footed ferret, as well as a large number of grassland birds species — mountain plovers, burrowing owls, ferruginous hawks, Sprague's pipits, chestnut-collared and McCown's longspurs and long-billed curlews to name just a few. Of significance, this is one of just a few spots left where such a mix of native grasslands and native species still occurs. Most involved, I think would agree that, so goes the native prairie, so go the wildlife. The biggest threats are conversion of native grasslands to croplands and reduced natural grazing due to drastic prairie dog declines and increased unnatural livestock grazing.

In an effort to turn the skid around, a plan has evolved whereby 13 ranchers graze cattle on the Conservancy's 60,000-acre Matador Ranch and in exchange for lower grazing fees, agree to specific conservation measures on their home ranches; essentially an exchange of forage for conservation practices or, grass-banking, if you will.

Purchased in 2000, the hope is the Matador will demonstrate how conservation and ranching can work together. Originally partnered, the Tranel family sold its half of the Matador back to the Conservancy in 2002. Between the Matador and the 13 ranches, about a quarter-million acres are now under the blanket conservation management schemes — with about 300,000 acres under intensive noxious weed management and no native grasslands to be plowed for any reason.

Lindbergh Lake Pines - Swan Valley

Lindbergh Lake Pines is located in Swan Valley. Only 40-acres, it consists of a stand of old-growth ponderosa pine, Douglas fir and western larch; one of the few remaining anywhere in Montana outside wilderness. Especially poignant since the ponderosa is our state tree and very few true old-growth individuals remain. Located along the eastern shore of Lindbergh Lake the stand receives a surprising number of visitors. There is a well-maintained trail and signs warn visitors to keep one eye peeled for this is prime grizzly bear habitat. To reach Lindbergh Lake turn west off MT 83, onto Lindbergh Lake Road, south of Condon.

Dancing Prairie Preserve

Amid the Tobacco Plains, north of Eureka, a mix of grasslands surrounded by coniferous forest is a remnant (about 680 acres) of the short grass prairie known as Dancing Prairie Preserve. Following the last ice age, about 12,000 years ago the receding ice cap left in its wake a complex mosaic of native prairie grasses and gravely soils, ringed by mounds geologists call drumlin. The natural amphitheater is last known dancing ground (lek) in Montana of the Columbian sharp-tailed grouse. Equally significant, but far-less spectacular or well known, is the presence of the world's largest known population of a rare flowering plant, Spalding's catchfly. A perennial that stands about a foot tall, it bears a white flower in July and August, and has lime green foliage that is sticky to the touch.

Established in 1987, even then the Columbian sharpie was all but history in Montana and just three dances showed up that first spring; none in recent years and most I think would agree while the effort was good intentioned it came just a little too late.

On the Tobacco Plains and elsewhere the gathering of Columbian sharp-tailed grouse from mid-March to mid-May once ushered in spring as surely as bugling bull elk harbingers fall. Like other arena birds such sage grouse, male sharpies gather before dawn to perform ritual displays in hopes of attracting a mate. While hens nod approval cocks twirl and hop about, stamp feet, charge each other only to suddenly stop and stare down one another; sometimes these stare downs last several minutes, rarely two cocks engage in actual toe-to-toe physical combat. To me, how this all works is a bit puzzling, but obviously it does work and there's no denying it's quite a spectacle.

These days, Columbian sharptails are in sharp decline throughout. In the Tobacco Plains the decline is thought to be due to a combination of factors, including the loss of winter habitat along the nearby Kootenai River, where development and logging have decimated the deciduous trees and shrubs so vital for winter survival. And like all prairie grouse require extensive healthy grasslands for nesting and brood rearing areas, every acre of native grass loss is just another nail in the coffin.

The flip side: The Spalding catchfly continues to flourish, thanks in large part to the diligence of Conservancy volunteers. Not so elsewhere, as the catchfly is endangered throughout its historic range — the so-called Palouse Prairie — due mostly to habitat loss through conversion of prairie grass to cropland. To wit, the entire states of Idaho, Oregon and Washington are thought to contain but a few hundred plants, while the Dancing Prairie Preserve grows a minimum of 10,000 annually — at least 90 percent of what's left.

To reach Dancing Prairie Preserve, from Eureka take US 93 north one mile to the junction MT 37; turn west about one mile to Airport Road. Go north on Airport Road two miles; the preserve, parking area and kiosk, are on your right. It should go without saying, tread lightly, take only photographs, and leave only footprints.

Black bear

Safe Harbor Marsh
Preserve - Flathead Basin

Safe Harbor Marsh Preserve (Bird-Pinkney Marsh) is a low-elevation freshwater marsh, a leftover of the glaciers of 12,000 years ago. Similar in geology to the pothole region's remarkable array of ponds, sloughs, marshes, bogs, fens and lakes, SHMP is actually a small bay connected by a narrow channel to Flathead Lake, the largest natural freshwater lake west of the Mississippi.

Recognized as exceptional bird habitat, the SHMP is a 132-acre wetland comprised of a variety of plant communities amid rocky bluffs overlooking the lake. The marsh lies solely within the Flathead Indian Reservation, established by the Hellgate Treaty of 1855 as a permanent homeland for the Salish, Kootenai and Pend d'Oreille Tribes.

The marsh and surrounding uplands support a diverse mix of plants, animals and birds. On the south side is a man-made meadow early settlers planted with exotic pasture grasses. The marsh itself is surrounded by dense forest, Douglas fir in the cool, damp areas and ponderosa pine on the drier uplands. A large variety of shrubs, forbs and grasses comprise interstices between trees and overlaying the bluffs. In the marsh proper, cattail and bulrush dominate along with various sedges and rushes. Grass-leafed pondweed is common throughout the areas of standing water.

The diverse and complex plant communities attract a wide array of birds. Yellow-headed and red-winged blackbirds, marsh wrens, great blue herons; waterfowl, such as redheads, mallards, ring-necked ducks and common goldeneye and mergansers abound. Look for Canada geese, which frequent and nest on the two small islands. In the dead standing timber, cavity nesters such as wood ducks, screech owls, and a variety of woodpeckers are common. Song sparrows, yellow-throats, red-breasted nuthatches, western wood peewee, chickadees, assorted fly catchers, hummingbirds, thrushes and warblers are just a few of the more common songbirds. Birds of prey, such as bald eagles, osprey and prairie falcon frequent and nest on the preserve.

In all, 134 species have been recorded on the preserve, including a large number of neotropical migrants (birds that nest in the north but winter as far south as Mexico, Central and South America). During the 1993 breeding season, 81 neotropicals were identified during the Breeding Bird Survey, Point Counts and the Monitoring Avian Production and Survivorship project sponsored by the Confederated Salish and Kootenai Tribes; thanks to exceptional and diverse habitat and abundant nesting sites.

But there is more here than birds; black bears, beavers, coyotes, muskrats, mink and even marten are not uncommon; as you might expect in such a diverse atmosphere the above is but a partial listing.

Visitors are welcome but please observe the following principles of etiquette:

- Please walk quietly through the preserve.
- Be especially careful during the breeding season (May-June). Do not stay long within the territory of a singing male, disturb nests or keep adult birds from access to their young. Please don't leave the trail to look at a nest, as a mammalian predator may follow your scent and raid the nest.
- Please use caution when exploring the preserve. The combination of rocky cliffs, open water and beaver trenches makes vigilance necessary. Because the climate of the area is moderated by Flathead Lake, ice on the marsh is not stable in the winter. It is not wise to travel alone through the preserve.
- Please do not disturb any stakes or poles on the preserve. These markers may be part of the MAPS survey, Point Counts and plant studies.
- The Conservancy does not own all the land surrounding the marsh. Please respect the privacy and property rights of private land owners.
- Please report unusual wildlife observations to the Tribal Wildlife Management Program at: P.O. Box 278, Pablo, MT 59855, 675-2700.

To reach SHMP from Polson, at the south end of Flathead Lake, take US 93 northwest for a half mile. Turn right on Rocky Point Road and go four and a half miles to King's Point Road. Turn right. Go a mile and a half to the east and look for a gravel turnout on the north side of the road next to a fence marked with yellow Conservancy signs.

Barred owl

Crown Butte Preserve - Simms

Just south of Simms, Crown Butte juts 900 feet above the prairie, the sort of mega hedron so dominates the landscape one can hardly miss it. The Conservancy notes, "Comprised of igneous rock, never cultivated or heavily grazed, the butte serves as an outstanding example of undisturbed native grassland. Four main grassland habitat types are grouped according to dominant plant species: bluebunch wheatgrass/blue gramma (on west-facing slopes and on the crest of small knolls); rough fescue/bluebunch wheatgrass (on slightly more moist sites); rough fescue/Idaho fescue (the most productive climax plant community on the butte); Idaho fescue/bluebunch wheatgrass (found less frequently, usually on west-facing slopes, and includes needle-and-thread grass and thread-leaf sedge)." The view from up top is quite spectacular with the Front Range out there jutting up cathedral-like from the relatively flat plain.

The Conservancy says the butte is a "...laccolith; formed by intrusions of molten (igneous) rock, called dikes, which flowed between layers of shale and sandstone laid down as marine deposits about 80 million years ago. The weak overlying layers bulged upward as the molten rock (magma) intruded, creating the lens-like body of the laccolith. Some of the dikes are visible to the west of Crown Butte, and the soft underlying layers of shale and sandstone are seen at the mouth of the canyon to the south.

"After the magma cooled, it formed the resultant rock called shonkinite. Shonkinite is a distinctive rock that contains the glossy black mineral augite, which appears as small stubby crystals. Upon cooling, the rock contracted, causing vertical fractures that formed the towers and columns. While this weather-resistant rock still protects the underlying sedimentary rocks, the surrounding layers have eroded, exposing the butte. Laccoliths are rare formations, particularly ones with exposed dikes. Crown Butte is one of the finest examples of a laccolith in central Montana and most likely the world."

The butte itself attracts a wide array of wildlife. The most obvious are mule deer. Birds of prey abound: American kestrels, Cooper's hawks, great horned owls, prairie falcons and golden eagles in particular. Visitors might want to check out the rocky remains of an eagle catch located at the southeast corner of the butte, a circle of stones where Indians once hid under branches baited with meat. The idea was to lure eagles to the bait whereupon the hunter reached up and grabbed it by the legs. And woe is the hunter who should miss one leg, eh?

Crown Butte is 30 miles southwest of Great Falls. You can reach the preserve from Simms on MT 200, just north of the butte, take Simms-Cascade Road south; or from Cascade on I-15, north. A small parking area is located outside the fence at the south slope of the butte. From the parking area there is a one-mile trail (foot travel only) along the west side of the butte. Look carefully along the trail—the circles of stones are teepee rings. Elevation gain to the butte's base is gradual, from there it is considerably steeper to the top, a quarter mile more distant. Ascending or descending, visitors are warned to exercise caution; in warm weather watch for rattlesnakes, which are common; no fires, no camping, no mountain bikes or pets allowed anytime.

Mallard (drake)

South Fork Madison Preserve

The South Fork Madison Preserve provides important wetland habitat for fish, waterfowl and furbearers and a variety of songbirds and other wildlife. An essential cog the larger complex ecosystem known as the Greater Yellowstone Ecosystem, the preserve acts as a buffer zone for Yellowstone National Park's many wildlife species that seasonally depend on areas outside park boundaries. Shiras moose winter here depending on the dense willows for food and shelter; in recent winters, park bison wander out to feast on the meadow grasses. In summer grizzlies frequent the upper watershed and occasionally wander down onto the preserve itself. Year round, the river harbors a healthy introduced brown trout and native mountain whitefish population. In spring rainbows and in fall browns run up from Hebgen Lake to spawn. For a time the river served in a since-failed reintroduction site for threatened fluvial Arctic grayling. Once found throughout the upper Missouri River system native grayling today are in a precarious situation; dwindling in numbers and range to a single population in the upper Big Hole River.

In addition, the preserve supports mule deer, the occasional elk, red fox, coyote, river otter, beaver as well as birds of prey including osprey, bald eagle, marsh hawk and great horned owl. Sandhill cranes frequently nest there as do all sorts of waterfowl and songbirds. At times, the air rings with the howls of introduced gray wolves.

To reach the lower watershed, take U.S. 20 approximately five miles west of the town of West Yellowstone and turn north (right) onto the Madison Arm Loop Road.

Shiras moose

To reach the upper watershed, enter the South Fork Road in the vicinity of Black Sand Springs — about two miles west of West Yellowstone. This road follows the South Fork for about seven miles, but may be gated as part the USFS management of the watershed.

Swan River Oxbow
Preserve - Swan Valley

The 392-acre preserve lies between the Swan Range to the east and the Mission Mountains to the west; the Swan River flows through it. The brochure explains: "Established in 1986 and named for what used to be a long, curving oxbow of the Swan River the preserve is a diverse wetland habitat. Numerous species of birds and wildlife frequent the preserve and plants, some rare such as the threatened Howellia aquatilis—grow almost nowhere else. Historically, portions of the preserve were homesteaded and supported such activities as farming, logging, grazing and even a muskrat farm. Today it serves as place for understanding and protecting the mosaic of land and water, interconnected wildlife and plant communities."

Most of the preserve lies within the delta formed by the Swan River as it flows north to Swan Lake. According to preserve literature,

"The water table remains high throughout thanks to consistent spring floods due the typically heavy snow pack in the surrounding Swan and Mission ranges and reliable, perennial springs and seeps dominate the eastern border of the preserve. In spring and early summer, high water charges the oxbow pond and water from Lost Creek radiates into the limestone till beneath; combined the several sources maintain the wet meadows, marshes, forests and recharge the spring. Spruce forest predominates along the southern boundary. A complexity of sedge fen and birch carr communities lies adjacent to the springs. To the west, cottonwood forest dominates the aquatic oxbow. In addition, much of the northwest portion of the preserve is covered by marsh, which remains flooded throughout most of the growing season. All told a most remarkable wetland community.

Five rare plant populations and two rare lichens have been identified within the variety of wetland communities. Round-leafed pondweed (Potamogeton obtusifolious) grows in the oxbow and adjacent ponds. Northern bastard toadflax (Geocaulon lividum) inhabits the wet spruce forest. Buchler fern (Dryopteris cristata) is found where carr vegetation and spruce forest intermingle. Small yellow lady's slipper (Cyprepedium calceolus) grows on the preserve. In addition the Federally listed threatened species, water howellia (Howellia aquatilis) is especially significant. Howellia is thought to be extinct in California and Oregon and is threatened in Washington, Idaho and Montana. On the preserve howellia grows in the marshy areas next to the oxbow. An annual plant with white flowers, howellia requires very specific conditions for its survival. The plant has flaccid stems and must be submerged in water to grow and reproduce. Its seeds, however, will not germinate under water. Therefore, howellia only grows and reproduces in ponds that are flooded in the spring, but become dry by late summer or fall. Given these and other habitat requirements, howellia is sensitive to periods of prolonged climatic extremes. If conditions are too wet, the seeds will not germinate. In drought conditions the plant will not grow. Though howellia populations fluctuate with changes in the climate, it is estimated the Preserve supports approximately 5,000 plants, thanks in part to the different drying regimes found throughout. This population, however, is extremely sensitive to climatic change, soil conditions and disturbance."

Situated more or less midway between the Swan and Mission Mountains the preserve serves as a natural travel corridor for grizzlies and other migrating wildlife, such as black bear, moose, elk, mule and whitetail deer. Bears, both grizzlies and blacks are frequent visitors in early fall when the many thorn apples in the area ripen. Bald eagles and osprey both nest within the preserve and are commonly seen soaring above and hunting the river.

On a recent visit we checked off numerous waterfowl including several common loons on the lake, mallards, blue-wing and cinnamon teal, ring-necked ducks, numerous common goldeneye and common merganser, several great blue herons and countless spotted sandpipers to name just few.

The brochure states, "Since 1989 the Preserve has been the site of a bird banding station. Under the Monitoring Avian Productivity and Survivorship program (MAPS), volunteers use mist nets to catch and band such neotropical migrants as the western tanager, Swainson's thrush, red-eyed vireo, Lincoln's sparrow and many others."

The Sally Tollefson Memorial Trail winds through it. Not only a pleasant walk but a good way to see the preserve. The trail was made possible by a gift from the Tollefson family and the combined efforts of The Nature Conservancy, USFS, the USFWS and the Montana Conservation Corps.

To insure your visit is a pleasant one the Conservancy recommends:

- Protect yourself against mosquitoes in the spring and summer months.
- Also in the spring and early summer months bring hip boots or waders.
- Bring your bird and plant books, as there is much to see! And the plant identification plaques along the trail will help you.
- Do not travel alone through the preserve.
- Please stay on the trail. This is a sensitive area with special plant communities, an ongoing bird banding project and deep spring holes.
- Warning: "Be Bear Aware" while hiking the trail. Please don't hike the trail between mid-April and mid-June. These are the months when grizzly and black bears are most frequently in the area.
- Please report any bear activity (sightings, tracks, scat) to the U.S. Forest Service, Swan Lake District at 837-5081.

To reach the preserve from Swan Lake take MT 83 south for two and a half miles, turn west on Porcupine Road for a quarter mile; signage will direct you to a parking area and kiosk at the trailhead.

Comertown Pothole Prairie Preserve

In the far northeastern corner of the state is a swatch of native grasslands and shallow potholes; "The result of glacial activity 12,000 years ago. Sometimes referred to as the Missouri Coteau, a low glacial moraine formed at the southern edge of the glacial front." The preserve (1,130 acres) represents the largest unplowed stretch of pothole prairie ecosystem in Montana.

Historically the pothole prairie, as it's sometimes called, extended over much of northeastern Montana, well into North Dakota and into Canada; most has been lost since largely plowed up and converted to small grain cropland.

The preserve comprises a mosaic of lakes, ponds and native grasses, where visitors can expect to see a variety of waterfowl, water birds and other birds. Federally listed birds such as the piping plover, whooping crane, Baird's sparrow and reptiles such as the smooth green snake are frequently sighted. The Conservancy recommends you bring binoculars, spotting scope, bird and plant books, since many species found here are not common elsewhere.

To reach the preserve from Plentywood take MT 16 one mile south, turn east on MT 5 toward Westby. Proceed about 12.5 miles to Comertown Road, turn north for six miles to the town site of now defunct Comertown. Look for the name on the old grain elevator beside the railroad tracks to make sure. This is the south edge of the preserve. There are no facilities. Strictly DIY, tread lightly, take nothing but photographs, leave nothing but footprints.

Mixed waterfowl

Pine Butte Swamp Preserve

Pine Butte Swamp is the largest wetlands along the Front Range. Among other notable attributes, it remains a stronghold for grizzlies venturing from the mountains out onto the High Plains. About 18,000 acres, Pine Butte Swamp is a mix of native prairie grasslands and rocky, forested foothills, and even the Rocky Mountains themselves. Beyond the grasslands limber pine, creeping juniper and spruce fir dominate. The spring-fed swamp itself is intermixed by clear, cold mountain streams and glacial ponds. The preserve houses a number of Montana's rarest plants and animals.

Touted by the Conservancy as, "A large, complex, naturally functioning foothills ecosystem bordering an even larger mountain wilderness area, truly unique and valuable way beyond mere dollars and cents. To the grizzly bear it is the last best place to roam back and forth between the plains and the mountains, relatively uncontested by the hand of man.

"Abutting the Bob Marshall Wilderness, just 60 miles south of Glacier National Park, Pine Swamp Butte is the heart of the largest wild expanse in the lower 48 states. The butte itself, comprised largely of sandstone, rises about 500 feet above the surrounding landscape, was somehow missed during the retreat of last ice age. In spring, grizzlies descend from winter dens high in the mountains to follow the north and south forks of the Teton River to the swamp, to feed, nurture and raise cubs — easy foraging allows adults to regain prime quickly."

Mule deer buck.

Grizzlies, thought to number historically in the tens of thousands, once roamed a wide territory — prairie, foothills, forested mountains — from the Pacific Coast inland to Minnesota and north into sub-Arctic Canada and south into Mexico. In the lower 48 states, following settlement the population crashed to perhaps 500 individuals scattered and fragmented in the few remote spots left. Thanks in large part to our National Parks and to places like Pine Swamp Butte the "grizzled" bear numbers are today on the increase.

The Conservancy brochure states, "Pine Swamp Butte (or fen) is comprised of extensive peat land fed by mineral rich groundwater. It differs from other fens in its proximity to mountains, foothills and grasslands — wetlands to mountain top the elevation changes from about 4,500 to 8,500 feet. The result is a diverse habitat indeed. Rare wetland species such as yellow lady's slipper, Macown's gentian, cotton grass and Craw's sedge; prairie grasslands plants such as shrubby cinquefoil, rough fescue and Montana's state grass, bluebunch wheatgrass; all told some 40 distinct plant communities have been identified on the preserve.

Diverse habitat equates to equally diverse fauna. Forty-three species of mammals, beaver, muskrat, mink, elk, moose, mountain lion, bobcat, lynx, black and grizzly bear, mule and whitetail deer, the largest population of bighorn sheep in the lower 48, 150 species of birds, warblers, waterfowl, waders, shorebirds, raptors and upland game birds, such as mountain and sharp-tailed grouse and last, and in this case least, a tiny, extremely rare hybrid minnow resides wetlands."

The brochure also tells us "Pine Butte is also rich in social, cultural and natural history. Eighty million years ago the preserve was home to vast herds of plant-eating dinosaurs. Eons of geologic folding and erosion have brought thousands of these dinosaurs' bones to the surface. Egg Mountain harbors one of the richest pale-ontological finds of our century: Maiasaura Peeblesorum, the good mother lizard who nested, laid eggs, fed and protected her young. Many nests, eggs, hatchlings and juveniles have been unearthed here. This research has provided more insight into dinosaur behavior than any other site in the world.

"Ancient peoples drawn by an abundance of prey occupied the area off and on for millennia; the Great North Trail brought both animals and people across the Bering Sea land bridge from Asia. Teepee rings suggest heavy use by native people from prehistoric times to the time of white settlement; as do bison jumps and drive lanes to what appears to be a bison mire in the swamp itself. Remains of long abandoned homesteads tell of the hardship and heartbreak early settlers found in the harsh climate — although many of the area ranchers today are direct descendants."

For information contact Pine Butte Swamp Preserve HC 58, Box 34B, Choteau, MT 59422; phone 466-5526. To reach Pine Swamp Butte Preserve, from Choteau, drive north on US 89, five miles, turn west on Teton Canyon Road, 17 miles, turn south, cross the Teton River and proceed straight for three and a half miles to a kiosk.

Lewis & Clark Trails ~ Montana

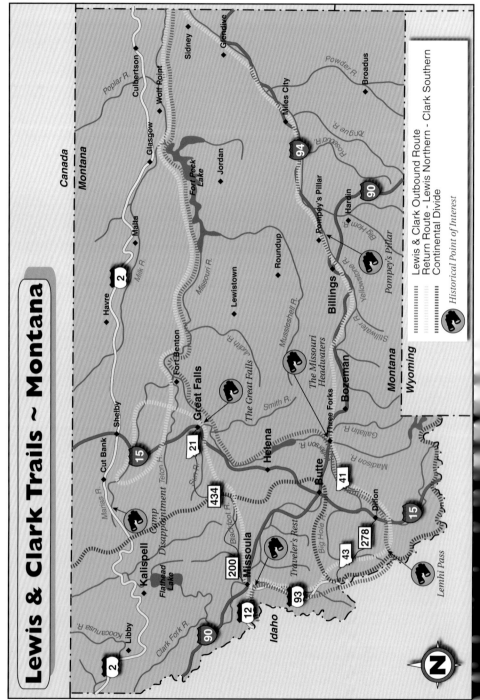

Lewis & Clark Outbound Route
Return Route - Lewis Northern - Clark Southern
Continental Divide

Historical Point of Interest

© 2008 Wilderness Adventures Press, Inc.

Lewis and Clark

In Montana

Meriwether Lewis and William Clark entered Montana on April 25, 1805 on their mission to find an all-water route to the Pacific Ocean. Their trip through Montana, including their return trip, would last well into 1806.

The Corps entered Montana where the Missouri River enters, just west of what would become Fort Union. By June 13, they had made it to what they called the Great Falls, at the present day town of Great Falls. The portage around the falls turned into one of the most arduous ordeals of the entire journey; one Lewis thought would take a week, took over a month; not until July 15 did the Corps resume their journey up river.

By July 27, they'd made it to the headwaters of the Missouri, at present day Headwaters State Park just outside the town of Three Forks. While there, they named the three rivers the Gallatin, Madison and Jefferson rivers.

On August 12, they arrived at present-day Lemhi Pass on the Continental Divide, and the border between Montana and Idaho. After an aborted attempt to run the Salmon River they backtracked and crossed back into Montana, and in late September left Montana again, just west of Missoula via the present-day Lolo Trail, en route to the Pacific.

Upon returning to Montana from the ocean in June of 1806, the Corps reentered where they left and stopped at what they called Traveler's Rest, at which point Lewis and Clark split up – Lewis took the northern route and Clark the southern.

By July 23, Lewis' party had stopped to camp near current-day Cut Bank. They had followed the Marias River to a point where it became clear that it did not reach the 50-degree latitude line, which meant that the Louisiana Purchase was smaller than they'd hoped. Lewis called the site Camp Disappointment.

Meanwhile, on July 25, Clark's party reached what he called "Pompy's Tower" on the Yellowstone River, where he etched his name and the date into the sandstone. The site is known today as Pompey's Pillar.

Soon thereafter, the Corps of Discovery reunited and exited Montana.

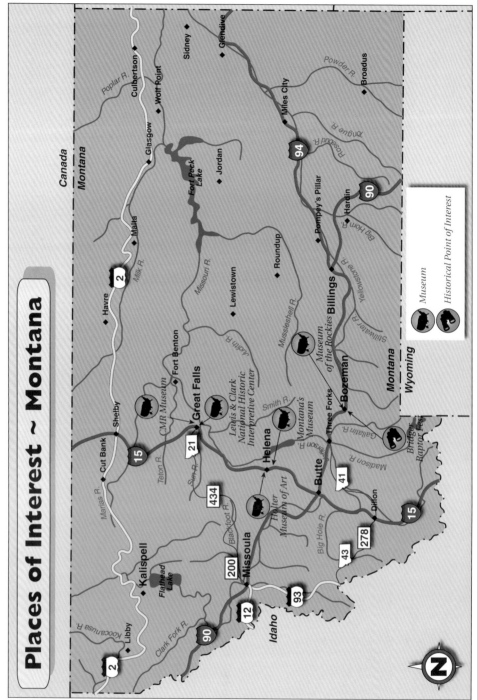

Places of Interest ~ Montana

Canada
Montana

Havre

2

Culbertson

Wolf Point

Sidney

Glendive

Poplar R.

Glasgow

Malta

Milk R.

Fort Peck Lake

Jordan

Powder R.

Broadus

Miles City

94

Tongue R.

Rosebud R.

Pompey's Pillar

90

Hardin

Big Horn R.

Roundup

Musselshell R.

Museum of the Rockies

Billings

Yellowstone R.

Stillwater R.

Lewistown

Missouri R.

Judith R.

CMR Museum

Fort Benton

Great Falls

Shelby

Cut Bank

Marias R.

15

Teton R.

21

Sun R.

Lewis & Clark National Historic Interpretive Center

Helena

Smith R.

Montana's Museum

Bozeman

Montana

Wyoming

Three Forks

Gallatin R.

Bridger Raptor Preserve

434

Blackfoot R.

Montana Museum of Art

Butte

41

Madison R.

Jefferson R.

Kalispell

Flathead Lake

200

Missoula

Big Hole R.

278

Dillon

15

Libby

Kootenai R.

90

12

93

Clark Fork R.

43

Idaho

2

Museum

Historical Point of Interest

N

© 2008 Wilderness Adventures Press, Inc.

OTHER PLACES OF INTEREST

Great Montana Birding and Nature Trail

As the name implies, the GMBNT eventually will cover all of Montana, focus not just on birds but wildlife in general, from mega fauna such as elk, bear, bighorn sheep, moose, and pronghorn, to critters such as pine squirrel, ground squirrel and prairie dog. The first segment of the trail, dedicated in the fall 2004, meanders through the Bitterroot Valley. Twenty-five sites from Lost Trail Pass to Lolo Pass are connected by the theme "Discover the Nature of Lewis and Clark".

Among the many highpoints of the Bitterroot leg is the Lee Metcalf NWR, a birding bonanza. Nesting osprey, American bittern, wood duck, cinnamon and green-winged teal, bald eagle, sora, tundra swan, Virginia rail, Calliope hummingbird, Lewis's woodpecker, marsh wren, raptors galore, including bald eagle, are but the tip of a giant iceberg.

At Lolo Pass (5,235 feet), west of Missoula, and the even higher Lost Trail Pass (7,014 feet), at the southern end of the Bitterroot Valley, you'll find high-country birds such as northern pygmy-owl, boreal owl (rare), three-toed woodpecker, Hammond's flycatcher, gray jay, Clark's nutcracker, American dipper (in Lolo Creek), Townsend's solitaire, Cassin's finch, and red crossbill.

Canyons in the Bitterroot Mountains, west of the river, are home to golden eagle, peregrine and prairie falcons, white-throated swift, western screech owl, red-naped sapsucker, and rock and canyon wrens. At Lake Como, look for pileated woodpecker, olive-sided flycatcher, Cassin's vireo, mountain bluebird, and western tanager.

For Birding Trail Brochures and Information contact: Montana Natural History Center, 120 Hickory Street, Missoula, MT 59801; phone 327-0405; fax 327-0421

Bridger Raptor Festival

The Bridger Raptor Festival, a celebration of the largest known golden eagle migration in North America, is held each year at the beginning of October. Event headquarters is the Bridger Bowl Ski Area. Workshops are held from 9 a.m. to noon. Workshops offer programs on basic raptor identification, binocular use and features, nest monitoring, ecology of raptors and raptor rehabilitation.

Admission is free.

To view the eagle migration requires a physically challenging, approximately two hour hike to the top of the ridge — elevation gain about 2,500 feet in about two and a half miles. Participants should prepare for changeable weather, warm to downright cold, calm to howling wind, clear skies to all-out blizzard, often all in the same day.

Atop the ridge offers an up close and personal look at not only dozens of golden eagles but other migrating raptor species as well — bald eagles, sharp-shinned hawks, peregrine falcons, red-tails, you name it, you might very well spot it.

But goldens are the primary draw and more than 250 have been counted on peak days.

Raptor experts are available on the ridge to assist in bird identification and to answer questions. Beyond the festival itself, peak migration generally occurs between the last weeks of September through mid-October.

To get the most out this, bring binoculars, bird identification books, note pad and pencil.

The Bridger Raptor Festival is a cooperative project among Bridger Bowl, the Gallatin National Forest, Hawk Watch International and the Montana Department of Fish, Wildlife and Parks.

To reach Bridger Bowl, take MT 86 east from Bozeman, follow signs; about 20 miles.

Brochures with information on the raptor migration and assistance with motel reservations are available by calling Central Reservations, 800-???-9600. For additional information, call the Gallatin National Forest, 587-6752 or contact USFS, Bozeman Ranger District, 3710 Fallon, Suite C, Bozeman, MT 59718; phone: 522-2520.

Holter Museum of Art

LOCATED IN HELENA ON LAWRENCE ST., ONE BLOCK WEST OF THE CATHEDRAL; THE MUSEUM IS DEDICATED TO PROVIDING QUALITY VISUAL ARTS EXHIBITIONS

According to museum literature:

"The Holter Museum of Art serves Montana and neighboring states with a quality visual arts exhibition program that includes all media; brings national and international exhibitions into the region; provides a much-needed venue for local and regional artists; and collects, preserves, and interprets significant contemporary Northwest art. Seeking to nurture the creative spirit and to make the arts accessible to all, the Holter is committed to promoting participation by diverse audiences through outreach, innovative educational programming, and collaboration with other organizations."

Located in downtown Helena at 12 East Lawrence St., the museum opened in 1987. The current facility is about 17, 000 square feet and presents on average about 25 different exhibits a year in five separate galleries. In addition it offers art education, artist residencies, lectures and receptions. Considered by many to be the "premier cultural center in the region".

The exhibits are designed to "appeal to a broad and diverse constituency." Exhibits range from historical to contemporary with "the primary focus on contemporary art with twelve exhibitions presented annually". The museum also exhibits the works of about ten local artists each year.

Programs are varied and designed to appeal to visitors of all ages. Lectures, slide presentations, tours, published brochures, catalogues, and wall text help to enhance the experience. Workshops, artist residencies, community collaborations, and school programs round out the museum program.

Fast Facts

Contact Info and Other Pertinent Information: Holter Museum of Art, 12 E. Lawrence St., Helena, MT 59601. Phone: 442-6400; Open all year: Tuesday-Friday 10 a.m. to 5:30 p.m.; Saturday 10 a.m. to 4:30 p.m.; Sunday 11:30 a.m. to 4:30 p.m. Admission is free. Memberships are available.

Getting There: From I-15 exit Cedar St., proceed to North Last Chance Gulch, to intersection E. Lawrence, museum is on right.

Activities: Art exhibits, various programs, call for scheduled events

Lewis and Clark National Historic Trail Interpretive Center

NATIONAL HISTORIC SITE, LOCATED IN GIANT SPRINGS HERITAGE STATE PARK, IN GREAT FALLS

Set on a cliff above the Missouri River the Center provides visitors a virtual window to the past. Focus is of course on the Lewis and Clark Corps of Discovery's remarkable "Voyage of Discovery" but that's just the start. Interpretive displays depict life as it was on the Great Plains both before and after Lewis and Clark — Indians to fur trappers to cowboys to sod busters to early miners; it's all here.

The Great Falls of the Missouri are no longer much in evidence, having long since been inundated by dams. But when Lewis first walked over the hill and heard "...a roaring too tremendious to be mistaken..." and spied the rising mists, he must have instinctively realized hard times lay ahead. He thought it would take a week to portage the 18 miles around the cataracts; instead it took a month — from June 13 to July 15, 1805. Perhaps even tougher going than he had imagined, barely into the ordeal he wrote ". . . They are obliged to halt and rest frequently for a few minutes. At every halt these poor fellow tumble down and are so much fortiegued that many of them are asleep in an instant. In short their fatiegues are incredible; some are limping from the soreness of their feet, others faint and unable to stand for a few minutes, with heat and fatiegue, yet no one complains. All go with cheerfulness . . ."

To make matters worse, the corps was beset by "grizzly bears, rattlesnakes, at least one large mountain cat." Adding to their misery was "mosquetors thick and trublesome," "oppressive heat" and "soreness of their feet." Constantly wet and skewered by prickly pear cactus "the men sewed extra soles on their mocasins to no avail," which only made it more uncomfortable.

The portage route itself is largely across private land with no public access, so visitors must stand back and only imagine the trials and tribulations of such an arduous ordeal — but above the river the landscape hasn't changed all that much and it doesn't take a vivid imagination to feel the pain.

Fast Facts

Contact Info: Lewis and Clark Interpretive Center, 4201 Giant Springs Road Great Falls, MT59405-0900 Phone: 727-8733. The Center is open Memorial Day weekend through September 30 from 9 a.m. to 6 p.m. daily and October 1 through Memorial Day weekend from 9 a.m. to 5 p.m. Tuesday through Saturday and 12 p.m. to 5 p.m. on Sundays. Admission fees: $5 adults (16 and older); $4 scheduled group tours (restrictions apply). Free for children 15 and under; $3 school group programs (reservations required for school groups).

Getting There: Exit I-15 at 10th Ave. South, proceed to the east side of the river, and then turn left on River Drive South proceed to intersection 1st Ave. North; go straight on River Drive North turn left to Giant Springs Rd. to Center.

Activities: The Center conducts a variety of events, year round and self-guided tours anytime.

C.M. Russell Museum

No visit to Great Falls is complete without a visit to the Charlie Russell Museum. Hailed as the "most complete collection of Charlie Russell works and personal objects," and while I'm certainly no expert, I can tell you there is a lot to see here. Museum literature describes the six galleries of "Russell works ... a place where the Old West is still alive. Artist Charles M. Russell captured the landscapes, the spirit, and the culture of the West during the late 1800s and early 1900s. His artwork is part entertainment, part history lesson."

Charles Russell (1864-1926) was a "cowboy, hunter, writer, philosopher, conservationist, and above all, artist." He worked as a Montana cowboy for about 10 years before "retiring" to art. He fostered a life-long relationship with various plains Indian tribes and thus many of his works depicted Indian life. He is considered the "first artist to spend his entire career in the West" and is thought to have completed about 4,000 works.

The C.M. Russell Art Auction (usually in mid-March) is one of the West's best, if not the best period. Check it out; you will not be disappointed.

Fast Facts

The museum is located at 400 13th Street North in Great Falls; to get there exit I-15 at 10th Ave. South, proceed to 15th St., turn left (north) to 5th Ave., turn left. The Museum is two blocks on the left hand side. Phone: 727-8787; Winter to Summer hours vary so be sure to call ahead. Fees: $9 Adults; $7 Seniors and Scheduled Tour Groups; $4 Students; Children under age 5 are free.

Montana's Museum

THE MONTANA HISTORICAL SOCIETY'S MUSEUM IS LOCATED ON NORTH ROBERTS ST, IN HELENA, NEAR THE STATE CAPITOL

The Society's mission statement says: "The Museum collects, preserves, and interprets fine art, historical, archaeological, and ethnological artifacts that pertain to Montana and its adjoining geographic region. Besides caring for the Society's museum collections, in-house staff conducts research and produce a variety of exhibits, sponsor public programs, answer reference requests from the public, and provide technical assistance to other museums and historical societies."

The museum also offers guided tours, school services, conferences, workshops, classes, publications, hands-on activities, and other public events; administers volunteer services within the Society and coordinates two major annual events: the Montana History Conference and the Western Rendezvous of Art.

Established in 1865, the Montana Historical Society is one of the oldest institutions of its kind west of the Mississippi River.

Fast Facts

Contact and Other Pertinent Information: Montana's Museum, P.O. Box 201201, 225 North Roberts, Helena, MT 59620; Phone: 444-2694. E-mail: mhslibrary@ mt.gov. The Museum is open year around: Monday-Saturday 9 a.m. to 5 p.m.; Thursday evening till 8 p.m.; Closed Sundays and Holidays. Admission fees: $5 per adult / $1 per child / $12 per family. Museum/ OGM Combo Passes $8 per adult / $1 per child / $19 per family; Members are free.

Getting There: From I-15 take "Capitol Exit" proceed west on Prospect Ave. to Roberts St., turn left about four blocks to museum (look for large "Herd Bull" statue on lawn). Parking is available in lot on the left.

Museum of the Rockies

LOCATED IN BOZEMAN ON KAGY BOULEVARD ACROSS FROM THE MONTANA STATE UNIVERSITY MAIN CAMPUS.

According to museum literature, "In 1957 the Museum of the Rockies was born as Dr. Caroline McGill's remarkable gift to the people of Montana. Today, the Museum stewards nearly 300,000 objects and 500,000,000 years of history. One of the finest paleontology collections in North America is found under the Museum's roof, along with strong core collections in western history, textiles, Native American artifacts, and photography. The Museum's permanent exhibitions, which tell the story of development in the Northern Rockies over the past 4 billion years, are augmented by changing exhibits representing various facets of cultural and natural history. Indoor exhibitions are complemented by a fully operational, on-site 19th century farm that helps preserve the state's agricultural traditions."

"Our mission is to inspire visitors to explore the rich natural and cultural history of America's Northern Rocky Mountains. In partnership with Montana State University, the museum reaches diverse communities with engaging exhibits, educational programs, and original research that advance public understanding of the collections."

Fast Facts

Contact Info: Museum of the Rockies, 600 W. Kagy Boulevard, Bozeman, MT 59717; Phone: 994-3466; E-mail: wwwmor@montana.edu; open every day except Thanksgiving Day, Christmas Day, and New Year's Day. Winter Hours: 9 a.m. to 5 p.m. Monday to Saturday; 12:30 p.m. to 5 p.m. Sunday, Museum, Store and Planetarium Only. Summer Hours: Museum and Planetarium 8 a.m. to 8 p.m.; Store 9 a.m. to 8 p.m.; Living History Farm and Lewis and Clark Challenge Course, 9 a.m. to 5 p.m. Admission Fees: Winter: Adults, $8; Children 5-18, $4; 4 and under are free. Planetarium Feature: $3; Planetarium laser show: $5; Members: $2.50. Adult Combo, $9.50; Child Combo, $6.50. Summer: Adults: $10; Children 5-18: $7; 4 and under: free; Seniors: $9; All attractions for one price. Memberships are available.

Getting There: Exit I-90 at 19th St. and proceed south to Kagy Blvd. turn left to museum.

Activities: Museum, store, planetarium, living history farm and Lewis and Clark challenge course provide visitors with a wide variety of opportunities and experiences. The exhibits and events are ever changing; call or e-mail for scheduled events and further information.

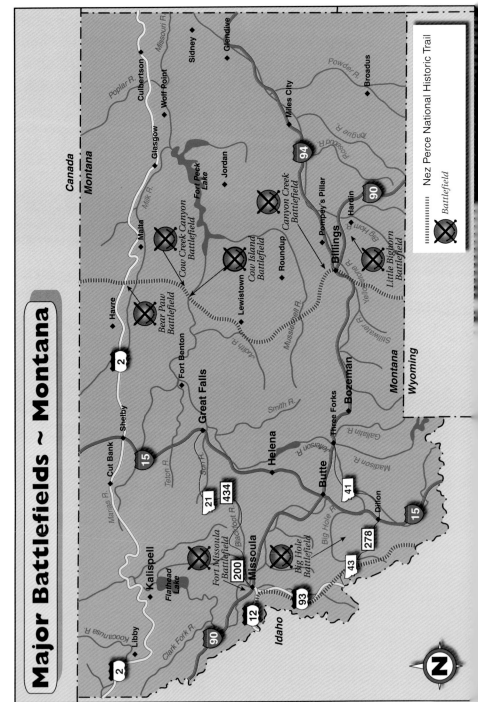

Major Battlefields ~ Montana

Nez Perce National Historic Trail

········· Battlefield

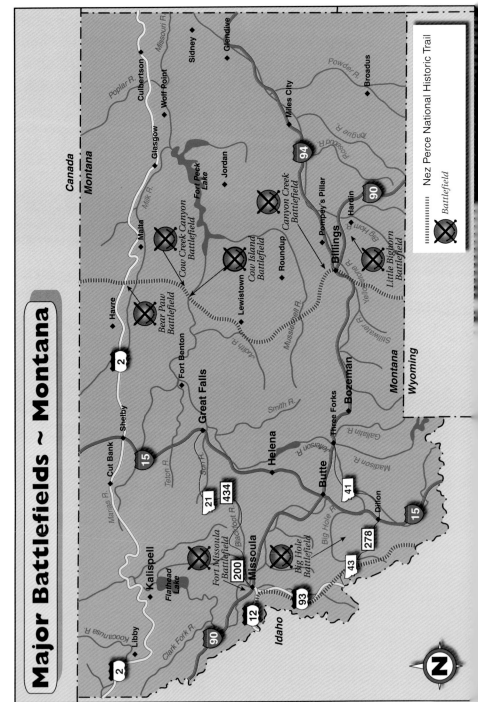

© 2008 Wilderness Adventures Press, Inc

Historic Battlefields

Bear Paw and Big Hole Battlefields

BEAR PAW IS LOCATED IN BLAINE COUNTY, APPROXIMATELY 15 MILES SOUTH OF CHINOOK ON MT 240, IN THE BEARS PAW MOUNTAINS; THE BIG HOLE IS LOCATED IN BEAVERHEAD COUNTY, JUST WEST OF WISDOM ON MT 43

Following a six-day battle, Chief Joseph at last surrendered to Colonel Nelson A. Miles, ending the Nez Perce War of 1877. In one the most often repeated and brief speeches ever, the chief said, "...from where the sun now stands, I will fight no more forever." Ironically the spiel is also among the most disputed ever. But it's hard to argue how fitting considering that by most accounts the Indians weren't so much defeated as just plain worn out. Pure fact or part fiction, the surrender put a dramatic and effective end to a dark and bloody time in Montana history.

Briefly, the "war" began earlier in Washington state when the government attempted to move the Nez Perce onto a reservation. En route, several whites were killed. Chief Looking Glass and several other chiefs (including Chief Joseph) then led the Nez Perce (about 850 men, women and children) on a running fight through Idaho and eventually into Montana (July 26, 1877) — the Indians generally getting the better of the early engagements. Disaster struck however, when a 7th U.S. Infantry detachment under command of Colonel John Gibbon surprised the sleeping Nez Perce encamped on the North Fork Big Hole River, just west the present town of Wisdom and inflicted heavy losses.

The survivors escaped, fled south back into Idaho and then east through Yellowstone Park into northern Wyoming and then north toward Canada. Skirmishes ensued along the way at Birch Creek and Camas Meadows in Idaho and at Canyon Creek in Montana and the tribe was within about 40 miles of their goal when Miles managed to cut them off and eventually ended the fighting for good (September 30 through October 5, 1877).

Fast Facts

Contact and Other Pertinent Info: Chief Joseph is located in a remote spot, with a kiosk, several interpretive signs and an interpretive hiking trail through the battlefield. There are no buildings or personnel, in other words you are on your own. No camping, day use only, hours are from sunrise to sunset; rest rooms and a single picnic table are provided. For further information contact the Blaine County Museum in Chinook. Phone: 357-2590.

The Big Hole Battlefield is permanently staffed by National Park Service personnel. There is an interpretive building, developed interpretive trails and displays, such as several tepees (poles and fire rings only) and a placard on the hill where the army set up a cannon and wreaked havoc amongst the slumbering tribe. Fishing is allowed, no hunting and dogs must be leashed at all times.

Getting There: To reach Chief Joseph, turn south off US 2 in Chinook and follow MT 240 to the battleground. To reach the Big Hole Battlefield from the north turn off I-15 at Divide exit follow MT 43 through Wisdom about 5 miles to the Battlefield. From the south turn off I-15 just south of Dillon at the MT 270 exit, follow 278 north to Wisdom turn left (west) on MT 43 to the Battlefield. From US 93 (Missoula to Salmon, Idaho) atop Chief Joseph Pass (Lost Trail) turn east on MT 43 to the Battlefield.

Activities: Birding, wildlife viewing and fishing (Big Hole Battlefield only)

Hiking Trails: Interpretive trails wind through both battlefields

Little Bighorn Battlefield

LITTLE BIGHORN BATTLEFIELD (AKA CUSTER'S LAST STAND) IS LOCATED EAST OF HARDIN NEAR CROW AGENCY AT EXIT 510 OFF US 212

A National Historic Monument, the Little Bighorn Battlefield is staffed year round by National Park Service personnel. In addition to the battlefield, visitors can browse the National Monument Museum, Custer National Cemetery outside displays, including numerous headstones marking significant battle locations and fallen soldiers. Interpretive trails wind through the battleground providing visitors a glimpse into the past, including how, and perhaps more importantly, why the battle unfolded and ended as it did.

Determined to force Sitting Bull's Sioux (and bands of several other tribes that had thrown in with him) back onto the reservation, the U.S. Army dispatched three columns to the Bighorn River valley. One, the 7th Calvary under command of Lt. Colonel George Armstrong Custer, was ordered to "scout the whereabouts of Sitting Bull," thought to be encamped somewhere either on the Rosebud River or the Little Bighorn, whereupon he was to meet up with the other two columns and proceed from there.

Known as "daring and brave, but lacking sound judgment," true to form, Custer instead drove his men and horses to the point of exhaustion, "riding 60 miles in 24 hours." Spotting what he believed to be the entire Sioux village (although most historians agree he couldn't have seen more than about a third of the hundreds of lodges strung out across some six miles of plains). On Sunday, June 25, 1876 Custer then made what would become the worst "blunder" of his career; one that would lead to the worst single day disaster in U.S. Army history.

Thinking he held the upper hand both in numbers and surprise (actually outnumbered at least three to one and Sitting Bull was anything but surprised thanks to scouts of his own marking every step of Custer's arrival), he divided into three columns and attacked. He ordered troops under Captain Frederick Benteen to shut off any attempt to escape up the Little Bighorn and advised Major Marcus Reno to cross the river and attack the village. Meanwhile, he would lead a charge from the opposite side, and catch the village by surprise in a crossfire.

Things quickly went wrong. First, Reno's column, 175 strong, ran into a veritable horde of angry and well-armed warriors, well short of the village. Surrounded, Reno saw the trap unfolding. A brief dismounted battle ensued before he ordered a retreat to the river. When that position was overrun, the surviving troopers made a run for the hills, whereupon the Indians then re-crossed the river and turned their hostility on Custer's column.

While the Indians were having their way with Reno's crew, Custer's column, 210 strong, was bogged down in a "maze of bluffs and ravines".

Upon finally gaining the river plain, they were quickly overwhelmed and forced to retreat "to a long high ridge to the north". Meanwhile another force, largely Ogallala Sioux under Chief Crazy Horse's command, "swiftly moved downstream, circled and caught Custer in a deadly pincer. Pouring on the gunfire and arrows, the Indians shortly reduced Custer's troopers to just a handful. In a last gasp effort he ordered the men to shoot the horses, stack them to form a wall against the deadly fusillade. Too late, in less than hour it was over".

The lone survivor was a badly wounded horse.

Following the next day's fighting, Reno and Benteen's now united forces escaped when the Indians suddenly broke off the fight, tore down the village and fled.

Fast Facts

Contact: The Visitor Center and battlefield are open year round but times vary seasonally so call first. Phone: 638-2621. Admission fees: $10 per vehicle to visit the Battlefield and National Monument Museum; $5 pedestrian fee. Admission is free to the Custer National Cemetery. Admission is also free Memorial Day, June 25 (battle anniversary) and August 25 (National Parks Day)

Getting There: Off I-90 take Exit 510 east of Hardin onto US 212 approximately three miles east to battlefield

Activities: Hike the various Interpretive Trails, visit the museum, and participate in the many programs presented throughout the year (contact Visitor Center for scheduled events)

Hiking Trails: Interpretive trails wind through both battlefields

Rufous Hummingbird

Beaver Slide - Upper Big Hole Valley

Bureau of Land Management (BLM)

SPECIAL RECREATION MANAGEMENT AREAS (SRMAS) AND EXTENSIVE RECREATION MANAGEMENT AREAS (ERMAS)

The BLM administers about 8 million acres and divides Montana into three Management Districts; within each district are several Resource Areas — 11 total; within each Resource Area are Special Resource Management Areas (SRMAs) and Extensive Resource Management Areas (ERMAs); all are of significant value and interest to the recreationist — hunter, fisherman, birder, wildlife viewer, you name it.

For more information contact the appropriate Resource Area listed below:

Big Dry 232-7000	Great Falls 727-0503	Phillips 654-1240
Billings 657-6262	Havre 265-5891	Powder River 232-7000
Dillon 683-2337	Headwaters 494-5059	Valley 228-4316.
Garnet 329-3914	Judith 538-7461	

Examples of SRMA/ERMA of particular interest to recreationists, their general whereabouts and contact info:

Antelope Walk-In SRMA—near Roundup—contact Billings RA—657-6262.
Bear Trap/Red Mountain SRMA—near Norris—contact Dillon RA—683-2337.
Big Dry ERMA—north Rosebud—contact Big Dry RA—232-7000
Clark Fork River SRMA—near Missoula—contact Garnet RA—329-3914
Great Falls ERMA—near Augusta—contact Great Falls RA—727-0503
Havre ERMA—near Chinook—contact Havre RA—265-5891
Sleeping Giant SRMA—near Wolf Creek—contact Headwaters RA—494-5059
Judith River SRMA—near Winifred—contact Judith RA—538-7461
Moorehead SRMA—near Moorehead—contact Powder River RA—232-7000
Little Rockies SRMA—near Landusky—contact Phillips RA—654-1240
Valley ERMA—near Hinsdale—contact Valley RA—228-4316

The above are but the tip of a very large iceberg—there are at least 40 more such areas within the state.

Wilderness Study Areas

In addition to the already-mentioned Wilderness Study Areas (WSAs), the BLM administers 39 other WSAs comprising about 450,000 acres. While not all WSAs are roadless by definition all have been found to have wilderness characteristics— naturalness, outstanding opportunities for solitude and/or outstanding opportunities for primitive and unconfined types of recreation, are at least 5000 acres in size or of sufficient size as to make practicable its preservation and use in an unimpaired condition and/or comprise unique values.

For the birder or wildlife viewer looking more for a unique experience rather than say to check off a specific species WSAs have much to offer. While access to many WSAs is easy, others fall into the category: Must really want to get there. The best way to find out is to contact one the several BLM regional offices and ask. For the do-it-yourselfer contact the BLM, Montana State Office, 5001 Southgate Dr., Billings MT 59101; phone 406-896-5037 and request WSA information packet—State of Montana Wilderness Status Map shows the location of all designated Wilderness and WSAs; the list of Montana BLM Wilderness Study Areas gives size, county location and the administering regional office for each; the BLM Montana Statewide Wilderness Study Report offers an overview of the process.

Below is a regional list of Montana WSAs and general directions to get you there:

Billings Field Office

WSA 067-205—Burnt Timber Canyon—Carbon and Bighorn Counties
WSA 067-206—Pryor Mountain—Carbon County
WSA 067-207—Big Horn Tack On—Carbon and Bighorn Counties
All three are located south of Billings, near the Wyoming line, generally east of Warren, MT and west of the Big Horn Canyon. Rugged and remote, act accordingly.
WSA 067-211—Twin Coulee—Golden Valley County—Access north of Ryegate via MT 238.

Butte Field Office

WSA ISA-003—Humbug Spires (see Region 3)— Silver Bow County

WSA 075-111—Sleeping Giant/Sheep Creek—Lewis and Clark County—North Helena via I-15, exit 209 (Gates of the Mountains)

WSA 075-115—Black Sage—Jefferson County—North Cardwell via MT 69 approximately 12 miles, turn east

WSA 074-133—Yellowstone River Island—Park County—Access by boat, downstream of Livingston, upstream of US 89 bridge

WSA 075-114—Elkhorn—Jefferson County—Access I-15 north Boulder, generally southeast of Jefferson City

Dillon Field Office

WSA 076-001—Ruby Mountains—Madison County—Access east of Dillon, west of Alder via a number of gravel roads

WSA 076-002—Blacktail Mountains—Beaverhead County—Access south of Dillon via I-15 turn east; via Blacktail Deer Creek road turn west

WSA 076-007—East Fork Blacktail Deer Creek—Beaverhead County—Access via Blacktail Deer Creek road approximately 30 miles, turn east

WSA 076-022—Hidden Pasture Creek—Beaverhead County—Access via I-15 south Dillon to Dell, take Big Sheep Scenic Bi-Way west to Muddy Creek Road

WSA 076-026—Bell/Limekiln Canyons—Beaverhead County—Access via I-15 south to Clark Canyon Reservoir, turn west to Horse Prairie, turn south Medicine Lodge road.

WSA 076-028—Henneberry Ridge—Beaverhead County—Access via MT 278 north from Dillon to Bannack, WSA lies east of Bannack-Horse Prairie Road

WSA 076-034—Farlin Creek—Beaverhead County—Access via MT 278 north from Dillon to Polaris-Grasshopper road; WSA lies east of the road at the base of Baldy Mountain

WSA 076-069—Axolotl Lakes—Madison County—In the Greenhorn Range, access via Axolotl Lakes Rd. from Virginia City or south of Ennis near Varney Bridge

ISA- 002—Centennial Mountains—Beaverhead County—Access via I-15 south of Dillon to Monida turn east toward Red Rock Lakes National Wildlife Refuge, ISA lies south of road near the refuge

WSA 076-063—Tobacco Root—Madison County—East of MT 55 (Twin Bridges to Whitehall) in the Waterloo area

Lewistown Field Office

WSA ISA-004—Square Butte—Choteau County—West of MT 80 between Stanford and Geraldine

WSA 068-250—Stafford—Choteau and Blaine Counties—North side Missouri River, north of Winifred via MT 236, east of highway

WSA 068-253—Ervin Ridge—Blaine County—North side Missouri River, north Winifred—difficult in dry weather, impossible when wet

WSA 066-256—Cow Creek—Blaine and Phillips Counties—Generally north and west of Fred Robinson Bridge (US 191) north of Lewistown, south of Malta—good luck

WSA 068-244—Dog Creek South—Fergus County—South side Missouri River north of Winifred via MT 236

WSA 068-246—Woodhawk—Fergus County—Northeast of Winifred

WSA 075-110—Beaver Meadows—Lewis and Clark County—Located just north of where the Dearborn River exits the Scapegoat Wilderness

WSA 075-107—North Fork Sun River—Teton County—Located north of Sun River Canyon, south of Castle Reef (196 acres)

Malta Field Office

WSA 065-278—Burnt Lodge—Phillips and Valley Counties—Located in the southern Larb Hills southeast of Sun Prairie, difficult in dry weather, impossible when wet

WSA 065-266—Antelope Creek—Phillips County —North Missouri River, west US 191 borders the CMR

Miles City Field Office

WSA 024-633—Billy Creek—Garfield County—Northwest Brusett, borders the CMR on south side of the Missouri River

WSA 024-657—Seven Blackfoot—Garfield County—Northwest Brusett borders Billy Creek WSA

WSA 024-675—Bridge Coulee—Garfield County—East side Musselshell River, north of Sand Springs

WSA 024-677—Musselshell Breaks—Garfield County—East side Musselshell River, north of Sand Springs, south Bridge Coulee WSA

WSA 024-684—Terry Badlands—Prairie County—Borders Yellowstone River generally north and east of Terry

WSA 027-701—Zook Creek—Powell County—Northeast Birney south of Northern Cheyenne Indian Reservation

WSA 027-702—Buffalo Creek—Powder River County—East of Moorehead and the Powder River

Missoula Field Office

WSA 074-150—Wales Creek—Powell County—Northwest of Helmville south of Ovando, in the Garnet Range

WSA 074-151—Hoodoo Mountain—Powell County—Southeast of Helmville, east of Nevada Lake in the Garnet Range

WSA 074-155—Quigg West—Granite County—West of Phillipsburg in the Rock Creek Special Recreation Management Area (SRMA)

Wilderness Montana

10 National Forests—Beaverhead-Deer Lodge, Bitterroot, Custer, Flathead, Gallatin, Helena, Idaho Panhandle, Kootenai, Lewis and Clark and Lolo--within the state comprise about 18 million acres of which about 6.5 million acres are designated roadless; a little more than half, or 3.5 million acres, comprise 16 designated Wilderness Areas. The biggest is Bob Marshall, the smallest is Medicine Lake.

Wilderness restrictions include no motorized vehicles; no vehicles; no new roads; and no new structures. Activities allowed include most non-motorized recreation, horseback riding, hunting, outfitting, wheelchairs, grazing (allotment permitted prior to designated wilderness), maintenance of range developments, new range improvements (to protect a resource), existing mining and mineral leases, mineral exploration (where compatible), natural fires and rescue equipment. Leave no trace is highly encouraged but not mandatory in most places.

USFWS Wilderness Areas

Medicine Lake—11,366 acres
Red Rock Lakes—32,350 acres
U.L. Bend—20,819 acres

BLM Wilderness Areas

Bear Trap—6000 acres

USFS Wilderness Areas

Lee Metcalf—248,288 acres
Cabinet Mountains—94,272 acres
Great Bear—286,700 acres
Bob Marshall—1,009,356 acres
Scapegoat—239,936 acres
Mission Mountains—73,877 acres
Rattlesnake—32,976 acres

Welcome Creek—28,135 acres
Selway-Bitterroot—251,443 (MT)
  1,039,017 (ID)
Anaconda Pintlar—157,993 acres
Absaroka-Beartooth—920,343 acres
  (MT) 23,283 (WY)
Gates of the Mountains—28,562 acres

Confederate Salish and Kootenai Tribes

Mission Mountain Tribal Wilderness—100,000 acres

Montana Bird List

This state bird list is provided courtesy of the Montana Audubon Society. To view updated lists or to purchase a copy of Montana Bird Distribution, log on to www.mtaudubon.org.

ANSERIFORMES

ANATIDAE (Waterfowl)

Anserinae (Geese and Swans)

Greater White-fronted Goose	*Anser albifrons*
Snow Goose	*Chen caerulescens*
Ross' Goose	*Chen rossii*
Brant	*Branta bernicla †*
Canada Goose	*Branta canadensis*
Cackling Goose	*Branta hutchinsii †*
Mute Swan	*Cygnus olor*
Trumpeter Swan	*Cygnus buccinator*
Tundra Swan	*Cygnus columbianus*

Anatinae (Ducks)

Wood Duck	*Aix sponsa*
Gadwall	*Anas strepera*
Eurasian Wigeon	*Anas penelope*
American Wigeon	*Anas americana*
American Black Duck	*Anas rubripes*
Mallard	*Anas platyrhynchos*
Blue-winged Teal	*Anas discors*
Cinnamon Teal	*Anas cyanoptera*
Northern Shoveler	*Anas clypeata*
Northern Pintail	*Anas acuta*
Garganey	*Anas querquedula †*
Green-winged Teal	*Anas crecca*
Canvasback	*Aythya valisineria*
Redhead	*Aythya americana*
Ring-necked Duck	*Aythya collaris*

Greater Scaup	*Aythya marila*
Lesser Scaup	*Aythya affnis*
Harlequin Duck	*Histrionicus histrionicus*
Surf Scoter	*Melanitta perspicillata*
White-winged Scoter	*Melanitta fusca*
Black Scoter	*Melanitta nigra †*
Long-tailed Duck	*Clangula hyemalis*
Bufflehead	*Bucephala albeola*
Common Goldeneye	*Bucephala clangula*
Barrow's Goldeneye	*Bucephala islandica*
Hooded Merganser	*Lophodytes cucullatus*
Common Merganser	*Mergus merganser*
Red-breasted Merganser	*Mergus serrator*
Ruddy Duck	*Oxyura jamaicensis*

GALLIFORMES

PHASIANIDAE (Upland Fowl)

Phasianinae (Old World Fowl)

Chukar	*Alectoris chukar*
Gray Partridge	*Perdix perdix*
Ring-necked Pheasant	*Phasianus colchicus*

Tetraoninae (New World Grouse)

Ruffed Grouse	*Bonasa umbellus*
Greater Sage Grouse	*Centrocercus urophasianus*
Spruce Grouse	*Falcipennis canadensis*
Willow Ptarmigan	*Lagopus lagopus †*
White-tailed Ptarmigan	*Lagopus leucura*
Blue Grouse	*Dendragapus obscurus*
Sharp-tailed Grouse	*Tympanuchus phasianellus*
Greater Prairie Chicken	*Tympanuchus cupido †*

Meleagridinae (Turkeys)

Wild Turkey	*Meleagris gallopavo*

GAVIIFORMES

GAVIIDAE (Loons)

Red-throated Loon	*Gavia stellata* ††
Pacific Loon	*Gavia pacifica*
Common Loon	*Gavia immer*
Yellow-billed Loon	*Gavia adamsii* ††

PODICIPEDIFORMES

PODICIPEDIDAE (Grebes)

Pied-billed Grebe	*Podilymbus podiceps*
Horned Grebe	*Podiceps auritus*
Red-necked Grebe	*Podiceps grisegena*
Eared Grebe	*Podiceps nigricollis*
Western Grebe	*Aechmophorus occidentalis*
Clark's Grebe	*Aechmophorus clarkii*

PELECANIFORMES

PELECANIDAE (Pelicans)

American White Pelican	*Pelecanus erythrorhynchos*
Double-crested Cormorant	*Phalacrocorax auritus*

CICONIIFORMES

ARDEIDAE (Herons)

American Bittern	*Botaurus lentiginosus*
Least Bittern	*Ixobrychus exilis* ††
Great Blue Heron	*Ardea herodias*
Great Egret	*Ardea alba*
Snowy Egret	*Egretta thula*
Little Blue Heron	*Egretta caerulea* ††

Cattle Egret	*Bubulcus ibis*
Green Heron	*Butorides virescens* †
Black-crowned Night Heron	*Nycticorax nycticorax*
Yellow-crowned Night Heron	*Nyctanassa violacea* †

THRESKIORNITHIDAE

Threskiornithinae (Ibises)

White-faced Ibis	*Plegadis chihi*

CICONIIDAE

Wood Stork	*Mycteria americana* †

CATHARTIDAE

Turkey Vulture	*Cathartes aura*

FALCONIFORMES

ACCIPITRIDAE (Hawks and Allies)

Pandioninae (Ospreys)

Osprey	*Pandion haliaetus*

Accipitrinae (Hawks and Eagles)

White-tailed Kite	*Elanus leucurus* †
Mississippi Kite	*Ictinia mississippiensis* †
Bald Eagle	*Haliaeetus leucocephalus*
Northern Harrier	*Circus cyaneus*
Sharp-shinned Hawk	*Accipiter striatus*
Cooper's Hawk	*Accipiter cooperii*
Northern Goshawk	*Accipiter gentilis*
Red-shouldered Hawk	*Buteo lineatus* †
Broad-winged Hawk	*Buteo platypterus*

Swainson's Hawk	*Buteo swainsoni*
Red-tailed Hawk	*Buteo jamaicensis*
Ferruginous Hawk	*Buteo regalis*
Rough-legged Hawk	*Buteo lagopus*
Golden Eagle	*Aquila chrysaetos*

FALCONIDAE

Falconinae (Falcons)

American Kestrel	*Falco sparverius*
Merlin	*Falco columbarius*
Gyrfalcon	*Falco rusticolus*
Peregrine Falcon	*Falco peregrinus*
Prairie Falcon	*Falco mexicanus*

GRUIFORMES

RALLIDAE (Rails and Gallinules)

Yellow Rail	*Coturnicops noveboracensis* †
Virginia Rail	*Rallus limicola*
Sora	*Porzana carolina*
Common Moorhen	*Gallinula chloropus* †
American Coot	*Fulica americana*

GRUIDAE

Gruinae (Typical Cranes)

Sandhill Crane	*Grus canadensis*
Whooping Crane	*Grus americana*

CHARADRIIFORMES

CHARADRIIDAE (Plovers and Allies)

Charadriinae (Plovers)

Black-bellied Plover	*Pluvialis squatarola*
American Golden Plover	*Pluvialis dominica*
Snowy Plover	*Charadrius alexandrinus* ††
Semipalmated Plover	*Charadrius semipalmatus*
Piping Plover	*Charadrius melodus*
Killdeer	*Charadrius vociferus*
Mountain Plover	*Charadrius montanus*

RECURVIROSTRIDAE

Black-necked Stilt	*Himantopus mexicanus*
American Avocet	*Recurvirostra americana*

SCOLOPACIDAE

Scolopacinae (Sandpipers)

Greater Yellowlegs	*Tringa melanoleuca*
Lesser Yellowlegs	*Tringa flavipes*
Solitary Sandpiper	*Tringa solitaria*
Willet	*Catoptrophorus semipalmatus*
Spotted Sandpiper	*Actitis macularius*
Upland Sandpiper	*Bartramia longicauda*
Whimbrel	*Numenius phaeopus*
Long-billed Curlew	*Numenius americanus*
Hudsonian Godwit	*Limosa haemastica* ††
Marbled Godwit	*Limosa fedoa*
Ruddy Turnstone	*Arenaria interpres*
Black Turnstone	*Arenaria melanocephala* ††
Red Knot	*Calidris canutus*
Sanderling	*Calidris alba*

Semipalmated Sandpiper	*Calidris pusilla*
Western Sandpiper	*Calidris mauri*
Least Sandpiper	*Calidris minutilla*
White-rumped Sandpiper	*Calidris fuscicollis*
Baird's Sandpiper	*Calidris bairdii*
Pectoral Sandpiper	*Calidris melanotos*
Sharp-tailed Sandpiper	*Calidris acuminata †*
Dunlin	*Calidris alpina*
Curlew Sandpiper	*Calidris ferruginea †*
Stilt Sandpiper	*Calidris himantopus*
Buff-breasted Sandpiper	*Tryngites subruficollis †*
Short-billed Dowitcher	*Limnodromus griseus*
Long-billed Dowitcher	*Limnodromus scolopaceus*
Wilson's Snipe	*Gallinago delicata*
American Woodcock	*Scolopax minor †*
Phalaropodinae (Phalaropes)	
Wilson's Phalarope	*Phalaropus tricolor*
Red-necked Phalarope	*Phalaropus lobatus*
Red Phalarope	*Phalaropus fulicarius †*

LARIDAE

Stercorariinae (Skuas)	
Pomarine Jaeger	*Stercorarius pomarinus †*
Parasitic Jaeger	*Stercorarius parasiticus †*
Long-tailed Jaeger	*Stercorarius longicaudus †*
Larinae (Gulls)	
Laughing Gull	*Larus atricilla †*
Franklin's Gull	*Larus pipixcan*
Little Gull	*Larus minutus †*
Bonaparte's Gull	*Larus philadelphia*
Mew Gull	*Larus canus †*

Ring-billed Gull	*Larus delawarensis*
California Gull	*Larus californicus*
Herring Gull	*Larus argentatis*
Thayer's Gull	*Larus thayeri †*
Glaucous-winged Gull	*Larus glaucescens †*
Glaucous Gull	*Larus hyperborus*
Great Black-backed Gull	*Larus marinus †*
Sabine's Gull	*Xema sabini*
Black-legged Kittiwake	*Rissa tridactyla †*
Ivory Gull	*Pagophila eburnea †*

Sterninae (Terns)

Caspian Tern	*Sterna caspia*
Common Tern	*Sterna hirundo*
Arctic Tern	*Sterna paradisaea †*
Forster's Tern	*Sterna forsteri*
Least Tern	*Sterna antillarum*
Black Tern	*Chlidonias niger*

ALCIDAE

| Long-billed Murrelet | *Brachyramphus perdix †* |
| Ancient Murrelet | *Synthliboramphus antiquus †* |

COLUMBIFORMES

COLUMBIDAE (Pigeons and Doves)

Rock Pigeon	*Columba livia*
Band-tailed Pigeon	*Patagioenas fasciata †*
Eurasian Collared-Dove	*Streptopelia decaocto*
White-winged Dove	*Zenaida asiatica †*
Mourning Dove	*Zenaida macroura*

CUCULIFORMES

CUCULIDAE (Cuckoos and Allies)

Coccyzinae (New World Cuckoos)

Black-billed Cuckoo	*Coccyzus erythropthalmus*
Yellow-billed Cuckoo	*Coccyzus americanus* †

STRIGIFORMES

TYTONIDAE (Barn and Grass Owls)

Barn Owl	*Tyto alba*

STRIGIDAE (Typical Owls)

Flammulated Owl	*Otus flammeolus*
Western Screech Owl	*Megascops kennicottii*
Eastern Screech Owl	*Megascops asio*
Great Horned Owl	*Bubo virginianus*
Snowy Owl	*Bubo scandiacus*
Northern Hawk Owl	*Surnia ulula*
Northern Pygmy Owl	*Glaucidium gnoma*
Burrowing Owl	*Athene cunicularia*
Barred Owl	*Strix varia*
Great Gray Owl	*Strix nebulosa*
Long-eared Owl	*Asio otus*
Short-eared Owl	
Boreal Owl	*Aegolius funereus*
Northern Saw-whet Owl	*Aegolius acadicus*

CAPRIMULGIFORMES

CAPRIMULGIDAE (Goatsuckers)

Chordeilinae (Nighthawks)

Common Nighthawk	*Chordeiles minor*

Caprimulginae (Nightjars)

Common Poorwill	*Phalaenoptilus nuttallii*
Whip-poor-will	*Caprimulgus vociferous* †

APODIFORMES

APODIDAE (Swifts)

Cypseloidinae (Tropical Swifts)

Black Swift	*Cypseloides niger*

Chaeturinae (Spine-tailed Swifts)

Chimney Swift	*Chaetura pelagica*
Vaux's Swift	*Chaetura vauxi*

Apodinae (Typical Swifts)

White-throated Swift	*Aeronautes saxatalis*

TROCHILIDAE

Trochilinae (Typical Hummingbirds)

Ruby-throated Hummingbird	*Archilochus colubris* †
Black-chinned Hummingbird	*Archilochus alexandri*
Anna's Hummingbird	*Calypte anna* †
Costa's Hummingbird	*Calypte costae* †
Calliope Hummingbird	*Stellula calliope*
Broad-tailed Hummingbird	*Selasphorus platycercus*
Rufous Hummingbird	*Selasphorus rufus*

CORACIIFORMES

ALCEDINIDAE (Kingfishers)

Cerylinae (New World Kingfishers)

Belted Kingfisher	*Ceryle alcyon*

PICIFORMES

PICIDAE (Wrynecks and Woodpeckers)

Picinae (Woodpeckers)

Lewis's Woodpecker	*Melanerpes lewis*
Red-headed Woodpecker	*Melanerpes erythrocephalus*
Red-bellied Woodpecker	*Melanerpes carolinus* †

Williamson's Sapsucker	*Sphyrapicus thyroideus*
Yellow-bellied Sapsucker	*Sphyrapicus varius* †
Red-naped Sapsucker	*Sphyrapicus nuchalis*
Downy Woodpecker	*Picoides pubescens*
Hairy Woodpecker	*Picoides villosus*
White-headed Woodpecker	*Picoides albolarvatus* †
American Three-toed Woodpecker	*Picoides dorsalis*
Black-backed Woodpecker	*Picoides arcticus*
Northern Flicker	*Colaptes auratus*
Pileated Woodpecker	*Dryocopus pileatus*

PASSERIFORMES

TYRANNIDAE (Tyrant Flycatchers)

Fluvicolinae (Typical Flycatchers)

Olive-sided Flycatcher	*Contopus cooperi*
Western Wood-Pewee	*Contopus sordidulus*
Eastern Wood-Pewee	*Contopus virens* †
Alder Flycatcher	*Empidonax alnorum*
Willow Flycatcher	*Empidonax traillii*
Least Flycatcher	*Empidonax minimus*
Hammond's Flycatcher	*Empidonax hammondii*
Gray Flycatcher †	*Empidonax wrightii*
Dusky Flycatcher	*Empidonax oberholseri*
Cordilleran Flycatcher	*Empidonax occidentalis*
Eastern Phoebe †	*Sayornis phoebe*
Say's Phoebe	*Sayornis saya*
Vermillion Flycatcher	*Pyrocephalus rubinus* †

Tyranninae (Kingbirds)

Ash-throated Flycatcher	*Myiarchus cinerascens* †
Great Crested Flycatcher	*Myiarchus crinitus* †
Cassin's Kingbird	*Tyrannus vociferans*
Western Kingbird	*Tyrannus verticalis*
Eastern Kingbird	*Tyrannus tyrannus*
Scissor-tailed Flycatcher	(*Tyrannus forficatus*) †

LANIIDAE

Loggerhead Shrike	*Lanius ludovicianus*
Northern Shrike	

VIREONIDAE

White-eyed Vireo	*Vireo griseus †*
Yellow-throated Vireo	*Vireo flavifrons †*
Plumbeous Vireo	*Vireo plumbeus*
Cassin's Vireo	*Vireo cassinii*
Blue-headed Vireo	*Vireo solitarius †*
Warbling Vireo	*Vireo gilvus*
Philadelphia Vireo	*Vireo philadelphicus †*
Red-eyed Vireo	*Vireo olivaceus*

CORVIDAE (Corvids)

Gray Jay	*Perisoreus canadensis*
Steller's Jay	*Cyanocitta stelleri*
Blue Jay	*Cyanocitta cristata*
Western Scrub Jay	*Aphelocoma californica †*
Pinyon Jay	*Gymnorhinus cyanocephalus*
Clark's Nutcracker	*Nucifraga columbiana*
Black-billed Magpie	*Pica hudsonia*
American Crow	*Corvus brachyrhynchos*
Common Raven	*Corvus corax*

ALAUDIDAE

Horned Lark	*Eremophila alpestris*

HIRUNDINIDAE

Hirundininae

Purple Martin	*Progne subis*

Tree Swallow	*Tachycineta bicolor*
Violet-green Swallow	*Tachycineta thalassina*
Northern Rough-winged Swallow	*Stelgidopteryx serripennis*
Bank Swallow	*Riparia riparia*
Cliff Swallow	*Petrochelidon pyrrhonota*
Barn Swallow	*Hirundo rustica*

PARIDAE

Black-capped Chickadee	*Poecile atricapillus*
Mountain Chickadee	*Poecile gambeli*
Chestnut-backed Chickadee	*Poecile rufescens*
Boreal Chickadee	*Poecile hudsonica*

SITTIDAE

Sittinae (True Nuthatches)

Red-breasted Nuthatch	*Sitta canadensis*
White-breasted Nuthatch	*Sitta carolinensis*
Pygmy Nuthatch	*Sitta pygmaea*

CERTHIIDAE

Certhiinae (Typical Creepers)

Brown Creeper	*Certhia americana*

TROGLODYTIDAE

Rock Wren	*Salpinctes obsoletus*
Canyon Wren	*Catherpes mexicanus*
Bewick's Wren	*Thryomanes bewickii †*
House Wren	*Troglodytes aedon*
Winter Wren	*Troglodytes troglodytes*

Sedge Wren — *Cistothorus platensis*††
Marsh Wren — *Cistothorus palustris*

CINCLIDAE (Dippers)
American Dipper — *Cinclus mexicanus*

REGULIDAE (Kinglets)
Golden-crowned Kinglet — *Regulus satrapa*
Ruby-crowned Kinglet — *Regulus calendula*

SYLVIIDAE

Polioptilinae (Gnatcatchers)
Blue-gray Gnatcatcher — *Polioptila caerulea*††

TURDIDAE (Thrushes)
Eastern Bluebird — *Sialia sialis*
Western Bluebird — *Sialia mexicana*
Mountain Bluebird — *Sialia currucoides*
Townsend's Solitaire — *Myadestes townsendi*
Veery — *Catharus fuscescens*
Gray-cheeked Thrush — *Catharus minimus*††
Swainson's Thrush — *Catharus ustulatus*
Hermit Thrush — *Catharus guttatus*
Wood Thrush — *Hylocichla mustelina*††
American Robin — *Turdus migratorius*
Varied Thrush — *Ixoreus naevius*

MIMIDAE (Mimics)
Gray Catbird — *Dumetella carolinensis*
Northern Mockingbird — *Mimus polyglottos*
Sage Thrasher — *Oreoscoptes montanus*
Brown Thrasher — *Toxostoma rufum*

STURNIDAE (Starlings)
European Starling — *Sturnus vulgaris*

PRUNELLIDAE (Accentors)
Siberian Accentor — *Prunella montanella*††

MOTACILLIDAE (Wagtails and Pipits)

American Pipit	*Anthus rubescens*
Sprague's Pipit	*Anthus spragueii*

BOMBYCILLIDAE (Waxwings)

Bohemian Waxwing	*Bombycilla garrulus*
Cedar Waxwing	*Bombycilla cedrorum*

PARULIDAE

Golden-winged Warbler	*Vermivora chrysoptera* †
Tennessee Warbler	*Vermivora peregrina*
Orange-crowned Warbler	*Vermivora celata*
Nashville Warbler	*Vermivora ruficapilla*
Northern Parula	*Parula americana* †
Yellow Warbler	*Dendroica petechia*
Chestnut-sided Warbler	*Dendroica pensylvanica*
Magnolia Warbler	*Dendroica magnolia*
Cape May Warbler	*Dendroica tigrina*
Black-throated Blue Warbler	*Dendroica caerulescens* †
Yellow-rumped Warbler	*Dendroica coronata*
Black-throated Gray Warbler	*Dendroica nigrescens* †
Black-throated Green Warbler	*Dendroica virens* †
Townsend's Warbler	*Dendroica townsendi*
Blackburnian Warbler	*Dendroica fusca* †
Yellow-throated Warbler	*Dendroica dominica* †
Pine Warbler	*Dendroica pinus* †
Prairie Warbler	*Dendroica discolor* †
Palm Warbler	*Dendroica palmarum*
Bay-breasted Warbler	*Dendroica castanea* †
Blackpoll Warbler	*Dendroica striata*
Black-and-white Warbler	*Mniotilla varia*
American Redstart	*Setophaga ruticilla*
Prothonotary Warbler	*Protonotaria citrea* †
Ovenbird	*Seiurus aurocapilla*
Northern Waterthrush	*Seiurus noveboracensis*

Kentucky Warbler	*Oporornis formosus †*
Connecticut Warbler	*Oporornis agilis †*
Mourning Warbler	*Oporornis philadelphia*
MacGillivray's Warbler	*Oporornis tolmiei*
Common Yellowthroat	*Geothlypis trichas*
Hooded Warbler	*Wilsonia citrina †*
Wilson's Warbler	*Wilsonia pusilla*
Canada Warbler	*Wilsonia canadensis †*
Painted Redstart	*Myioborus pictus †*
Yellow-breasted Chat	*Icteria virens*

THRAUPIDAE

Summer Tanager	*Piranga rubra †*
Scarlet Tanager	*Piranga olivacea †*
Western Tanager	*Piranga ludoviciana*

EMBERIZIDAE

Green-tailed Towhee	*Pipilo chlorurus*
Spotted Towhee	*Pipilo maculatus*
American Tree Sparrow	*Spizella arborea*
Chipping Sparrow	*Spizella passerina*
Clay-colored Sparrow	*Spizella pallida*
Brewer's Sparrow	*Spizella breweri*
Field Sparrow	*Spizella pusilla*
Vesper Sparrow	*Pooecetes gramineus*
Lark Sparrow	*Chondestes grammacus*
Black-throated Sparrow	*Amphispiza bilineata†*
Sage Sparrow	*Amphispiza belli †*
Lark Bunting	*Calamospiza melanocorys*
Savannah Sparrow	*Passerculus sandwichensis*
Grasshopper Sparrow	*Ammodramus savannarum*
Baird's Sparrow	*Ammodramus bairdii*
Le Conte's Sparrow	*Ammodramus leconteii*

Nelson's Sharp-tailed Sparrow	*Ammodramus nelsoni*
Fox Sparrow	*Passerella iliaca*
Song Sparrow	*Melospiza melodia*
Lincoln's Sparrow	*Melospiza lincolnii*
Swamp Sparrow	*Melospiza georgiana †*
White-throated Sparrow	*Zonotrichia albicollis*
Harris's Sparrow	*Zonotrichia querula*
White-crowned Sparrow	*Zonotrichia leucophrys*
Golden-crowned Sparrow	*Zonotrichia atricapilla †*
Dark-eyed Junco	*Junco hyemalis*
McCown's Longspur	*Calcarius mccownii*
Lapland Longspur	*Calcarius lapponicus*
Smith's Longspur	*Calcarius pictus †*
Chestnut-collared Longspur	*Calcarius ornatus*
Snow Bunting	*Plectrophenax nivalis*

CARDINALIDAE

Northern Cardinal	*Cardinalis cardinalis †*
Pyrrhuloxia	*Cardinalis sinuatus †*
Rose-breasted Grosbeak	*Pheucticus ludovicianus*
Black-headed Grosbeak	*Pheucticus melanocephalus*
Blue Grosbeak	*Passerina caerulea †*
Lazuli Bunting	*Passerina amoena*
Indigo Bunting	*Passerina cyanea*
Painted Bunting	*Passerina ciris †*
Dickcissel	*Spiza americana*

ICTERIDAE

Bobolink	*Dolichonyx oryzivorus*
Red-winged Blackbird	*Agelaius phoeniceus*
Western Meadowlark	*Sturnella neglecta*
Yellow-headed Blackbird	*Xanthocephalus xanthocephalus*

Rusty Blackbird	*Euphagus carolinus*
Brewer's Blackbird	*Euphagus cyanocephalus*
Common Grackle	*Quiscalus quiscula*
Great-tailed Grackle	*Quiscalus mexicanus †*
Brown-headed Cowbird	*Molothrus ater*
Orchard Oriole	*Icterus spurius*
Hooded Oriole	*Icterus cucullatus †*
Bullock's Oriole	*Icterus bullockii*
Baltimore Oriole	*Icterus galbula*

FRINGILLIDAE

Fringillinae (Fringillid Finches)

Brambling	*Fringilla montifringilla †*

Carduelinae (Carduelid Finches)

Gray-crowned Rosy Finch	*Leucosticte tephrocotis*
Black Rosy Finch	*Leucosticte atratus*
Pine Grosbeak	*Pinicola enucleator*
Purple Finch	*Carpodacus purpureus*
Cassin's Finch	*Carpodacus cassinii*
House Finch	*Carpodacus mexicanus*
Red Crossbill	*Loxia curvirostra*
White-winged Crossbill	*Loxia leucoptera*
Common Redpoll	*Carduelis flammea*
Hoary Redpoll	*Carduelis hornemanni*
Pine Siskin	*Carduelis pinus*
Lesser Goldfinch	*Carduelis psaltria †*
American Goldfinch	*Carduelis tristis*
Evening Grosbeak	*Coccothraustes vespertinus*

PASSERIDAE

House Sparrow	*Passer domesticus*

† - fewer than 20 records

Montana Wildlife List

Amphibians

Boreal Toad	Pacific Chorus Frog
Great Plains Toad	Western Chorus Frog
Woodhouse's Toad	Northern Leopard Frog
Western Toad	Columbian Spotted Frog
Great Plains Toad	Bullfrog
Great Basin Spadefoot	Wood Frog
Great Plains Spadefoot	Woodland Salamander
Tailed Frog	Giant Salamander
	Newts

Mammals

Yuma Myostis	Idaho Pocket Gopher
California Myostis	Northern Red Pocket Gopher
Fringed Myostis	American Beaver
Little Brown Myostis	Western Jumping Mouse
Long-eared Myostis	Meadow Jumping Mouse
Long-legged Myostis	Yellow Pine Chipmunk
Western Small-footed Myostis	Least Chipmunk
Big Brown Bat	Uinta Chipmunk
Hoary Bat	Redtail Chipmunk
Townsend's Big-eared Bat	Hoary Marmot
Silver Haired Bat	Yellow-bellied Marmot
Eastern Red Bat	Unita Ground Squirrel
Spotted Bat	Thirteen-lined Ground Squirrel
Pallid Bat	Richardson Ground Squirrel

Columbian Ground Squirrel	Moose
Wyoming Ground Squirrel	Wapiti or Elk
Golden-mantled Ground Squirrel	Mountain Goat
White-tailed Prairie Dog	Bighorn Sheep
Black-tailed Prairie Dog	American Bison
Eastern Fox Squirrel	Preble's Vole
Eastern Gray Squirrel	Masked Vole
Northern Flying Squirrel	Dusky or Montane Vole
Red Squirrel	Vagrant Vole
Great Basin Pocket Mouse	Water Vole
Olive-backed Pocket Mouse	Merriam's Vole
Hisbid Pocket Mouse	Hayden's Vole
Ord's Kangaroo Rat	Dwarf Vole
Deer Mouse	Arctic Vole
Northern Harvest Mouse	Pygmy Vole
Northern Grasshopper Mouse	American Pika
White-footed Mouse	Mountain Cottontail
Bushy-tailed Wood Rat	Eastern Cottontail
Muskrat	Desert Cottontail
Norway Rat	Pygmy Rabbit
Southern Red-backed Vole	White-tailed Jackrabbit
Water Vole	Black-tailed Jackrabbit
Meadow Vole	Snowshoe Hare
Long-tailed Vole	Grizzly Bear
Heather Vole	Black Bear
Montane Vole	Fisher
Prairie Vole	American Marten
Sagebrush Vole	Least Weasel
Northern Bog Lemming	Ermine
House Mouse	Long-tailed Weasel
Common Porcupine	Black-footed Ferret
Pronghorn	North American Wolverine
Mule Deer	Northern River Otter
White-tailed Deer	Mink

American Badger	Red Fox
Bobcat	Swift Fox
Lynx	Common Raccoon
Mountain Lion	Striped Skunk
Gray Wolf	Western Spotted Skunk
Coyote	Feral Horse

Reptiles

Common Garter Snake	Western Hognose Snake
Gopher Snake or Bullsnake	Smooth Green Snake
Racer	Milk Snake
Rubber Boa	Painted Turtle
Western Rattlesnake	Snapping Turtle
Western Terrestrial Garter Snake	Spiny Softshell Turtle

Montana Specialty Bird List

Below is a list of birds, not necessarily rare in Montana (though some are) but rather not seen every day, every where; in other words either you get lucky, or you do your homework, pay your dues and then get lucky.

Anna's Hummingbird	Canyon Wren
Baird's Sparrow	Cassin's Finch
Black-chinned Hummingbird	Chestnut-backed Chickadee
Black-headed Grosbeak	Chestnut-collared Longspur
Black-throated Sparrow	Clark's Grebe
Blue Grouse	Clark's Nutracker
Brewer's Sparrow	Common Poorwill
Bullock's Oriole	Cordilleran Flycatcher
California Gull	Ferruginous Hawk
Calliope Hummingbird	Grey-crowned Rosy Finch

Harris's Sparrow	Ruffed Grouse
House Finch	Sage Sparrow
Le Conte's Sparrow	Sage Thrasher
Lewis's Woodpecker	Say's Phoebe
McCown's Longspur	Sharp-tailed Grouse
Mountain Bluebird	Smith's Longspur
Mountain Chickadee	Spotted Towhee
Mountain Plover	Spruce Grouse
Nelson's Sharp-tailed Sparrow	Townsend's Solitaire
Pileated Woodpecker	Trumpeter Swan
Pinyon Jay	Western Bluebird
Prairie Falcon	Western Grebe
Pygmy Nuthatch	Western Screech Owl
Red-bellied Woodpecker	Whooping Crane
Red-naped Sapsucker	White-headed Woodpecker
Red-shouldered Hawk	White-tailed Ptarmigan
	Williamson's Sapsucker

MONTANA OWL WATCH

Late April is prime to observe and listen for owls in northwest Montana: Flathead, Mission, Swan, lower Clark Fork, Thompson and Kootenai River valleys and surrounding forests. Montana boasts the largest number of breeding owl species of any state in the United States. Fifteen species of owls occur in Montana, of which 14 species breed: Flammulated owl, northern pygmy-owl, northern saw-whet owl, boreal owl, eastern and western screech-owls, burrowing owl, northern hawk owl, long-eared owl, short-eared owl, barn owl, barred owl, great horned owl, and great gray owl. Snowy Owls are regular winter visitors.

Optics and Gear

While I suppose you can play the birding and wildlife-viewing game without optics, binoculars and spotting scope, I can't imagine it. And not just any old optics either; for if ever there was truth to the old adage, "You get what you pay for," binoculars and spotting scopes are it. Trust me; there is a world of difference between top of the line binoculars, such as Leica, Zeiss and Swarovski, and El Cheapo Brand X. That said, do you need the best? No. Is there good glass out there doesn't take a second mortgage? Yes. There are many good binoculars out there in the $200 to $400 price range. But there are no really cheap options worth squat — period, end of discussion. Ditto for spotting scopes, but first let's discuss binoculars. For a review of binoculars, Google "best binoculars" or check out http://birds.cornell.edu.publications/livingbird/spring99/binos.html.

Beyond price, the obvious first question is: What do those numbers mean?

Binoculars regardless of price or brand name are labeled: 7X32, 8X42, 7X50, and so forth. The first number denotes the magnification: 7 equals seven power, or 7 times the magnification of 1 power; 10 equals ten power, 10 times the magnification of 1 power. The second number — 32, 42, 50 — denotes the size, in millimeters, of the objective lens (the one farthest from the eye, closest to the subject). All things equal (quality of glass, etc.) the bigger the objective lens the more light gathered (transmitted to the eye)—the better, clearer your view of the subject and the lower the light level in which you will be able to use it effectively — better earlier at dawn and later at dusk, when wildlife is most active. But, bear in mind, a bigger objective lens translates into more weight; there is a big difference in weight between 7X32 binoculars and 7X50s.

Which brings us to the Porro Prism versus Roof Prism debate. Porro prism binoculars are best described as wide at the front (objective lens end) and skinny at the back. Roof prisms are essentially two parallel straight (slightly wider front to back) tubes. Most of today's quality binoculars are roof prism designs. Again, all things equal, roof prisms tend to be much lighter than porro prism models.

Okay, which one?

We own several roof prism binoculars — Nikon and Pentax — all fall in the above price range and all do the job for us. They are 8X42 and 10X42. Gale likes the 8X42s best, smaller, more compact, lighter. I, however, go for the 10X42s, every time. I have heard the argument 10 power "wiggles too much" but I don't find that a problem, maybe you would. Best advice, test drive before plunking down the cash.

That is one thing I don't think there is much argument about. Unless you are in love with the porro prism design, choose a roof prism design, the best you can afford. As pointed out above, good (not necessarily best) quality works; any well-known, recommended brand in the power and objective lens size best suits you and your needs.

For a really up close and personal view, nothing beats a good quality spotting scope mounted on a sturdy tripod.

The same rules apply as for binoculars, choose the best you can afford. Top end ($1,500 or more) trumps middle of the road ($500 plus or minus) every time but there are a bunch of good scopes out there that won't break the bank. Again check out the reviews, see what the experts have to say. One thing to consider is straight or angled eyepiece — for my money I'll take the angled jobs every time, thank you. I also want a big objective lens 60 to 80 mm and zoom capability, at least 45X and preferably 60X magnification. Lighter is better but I'll gladly compromise weight for superior optics and increased light gathering. As with binoculars there are El Cheapos out there but why waste your money when, for just a few dollars more, you can enjoy good quality; test drive first.

While this book is pretty comprehensive in the where to go category, you won't find bird or mammal descriptions. To properly identify your subjects, get a good book, get several good books...hell, build a whole library of good books. To aid in identifying, it helps to recognize individual bird songs; bird song also helps to locate often reclusive, elusive subjects. Good bird books usually attempt to convert bird songs to human language — might work for you but sort of leaves me baffled. Instead, get a CD or tape. If it works for tone-deaf me, it will work for anyone. Taking good notes is also a good idea, but we've found the best way for us is to snap a picture. But bird/wildlife photography is an art in itself and opens up a whole other can of worms. A bit beyond the scope of this discussion let me say this: You won't get much done with a throw-away box camera. A point and shoot, film or digital, no matter what the optical zoom, might get you in the ball park but don't expect a box seat sort of view. Serious bird/wildlife photos call for serious camera equipment — especially lenses — 400 mm minimum and 600 to 1,000mm works a whole lot better. Film or digital is still a matter of choice but watch out for bargain basement type lenses, they are almost always junk, hardly worth the price of postage or gas to retrieve them. Again, if you want to take bird/wildlife photos, check out the zillion reviews and advice available in photo magazines and online.

Beyond the above essential and exotic items, buddy up with an expert and I guarantee you will learn far quicker than you can ever learn on your own.

Birding and wildlife viewing, by its very nature, usually means stepping outside; where it might be raining, snowing, cold, blistering hot, dry, you name it. There might very well be biting bugs and brambles and, heaven forbid, fanged serpents, and who knows what else to make life miserable. Weather changes out here faster than you can read this sentence. Elevation change affects weather big time; 60 degrees and calm in the valley, wind howling and subfreezing a few hundred feet up. Rain, snow, sleet, and subfreezing temperatures can and do occur at any season, any month of the year. Be prepared. NEVER leave home without a rain jacket; I know it sounds weird but you WILL be surprised how often it rains like hell on days that start out sunny and not a cloud in the big blue sky. Dress in layers; remember, you can always take it off but you sure can't put on what you left in the truck, the house, or the motel room a couple hours away.

While you can get to most of the places in this book in a two-wheel drive, low clearance passenger car, trust me, there are a bunch where you will wish for more ground clearance, more traction, etc. Often it is a matter of going or not...your call. It is not unusual to find high-country roads blocked by snowdrifts well into June or July, so checking locally is always a good idea. All across the state, but especially in the eastern two-thirds, wet, even damp, means the road might not be passable; don't screw with gumbo, if it's wet, turn around and come back when it's dry.

Enough said.

Index

A

Agate 11
Alaudidae 386
Alcidae 382
Anaconda 76, 105
Anseriformes 375–376
Apodiformes 384

B

Baker 323
Bear Paw and Big Hole Battlefields 361–362
Photo 362
Bears Paw Mountains 361, 367
Beartooth Wildlife Management Area 134–139
Photo 134, 137, 139
Beaverhead County 10, 361
Beaverhead-Deerlodge Forest Headquarters 130
Belt Creek 179
Benton Lake Bird List 153–156
Benton Lake National Wildlife Refuge 3, 150–157
Benton Lake Bird List 153–156
Photo 150, 157
Bighorn Basin 215
Big Lake Complex 207
Billings 11
Bitter Creek Wilderness Study Area 282–285
Bitterroot Canyons 73–74
Bitterroot River Fishing Access Sites 75
Black Coulee National Wildlife Refuge 3, 238–240
Photo 238

Black Eagle Falls 165
Blackfoot-Clearwater Wildlife Management Area 58–61
Photo 59
Blackleaf Wildlife Management Area 140–158
Photo 140, 145, 149
Black-spotted Cutthroat Trout 10
Blaine County 239, 361, 367
BLM Wilderness Areas 374
Bluebunch Wheatgrass 11
Bowdoin Bird List 233–237
Bowdoin National Wildlife Refuge 228–237
Bowdoin Bird List 233–237
Photo 228, 237
Bridger Raptor Festival 354–355
Bridger Waterfowl Production Area 194–199
Central Plains and Island Mountain Ranges Bird List 195–199
Photo 194
Brush Lake State Park 248–251
Photo 248, 251
Bureau of Land Management 370
Bynum 141

C

Canyon Ferry Amphibians 97
Canyon Ferry Birds 95–97
Canyon Ferry Mammals 97
Canyon Ferry Reservoir 91
Canyon Ferry Wildlife Management Area 90–97
Canyon Ferry Amphibians 97
Canyon Ferry Birds 95–97

Canyon Ferry Mammals 97
  Photo 90, 93
Caprimulgiformes 383
Cardinalidae 391
Cathartidae 378
Central Plains And Island Mountain Ranges
  Bird List 195–199
Certhiidae 387
Charadriiformes 380
Charles M. Russell National Wildlife Refuge
  3, 203, 252–267, 257–272, 262–277,
  267–282
  Map 262
  Photo 252, 257, 262, 267
Chief Joseph And Big Hole Battlefields
  Photo 368–369
Chinook 361, 367
Choteau 142, 159, 168
Ciconiidae 378
Ciconiiformes 377–378
Clark Fork River, I-90 East 72–73
C.M. Russell Museum 357–358
Colter Falls 165
Columbiformes 382
Columbus 207
Comertown Pothole Prairie Preserve 347
  Photo 347
Confederate Salish And Kootenai Tribes 374
Conservation Reserve Program 3
Coraciiformes 384
Cottonwood Creek Natural Area 129
Council Grove State Park 68–70
  Photo 69, 70
Coyote Coulee Trail 74
CraNe 331
Creedman Coulee National Wildlife Refuge 3,
  241–242
  Photo 241
Crooked Creek Valley 215
Crooked Falls 165
Crow Agency 365
Crown Butte Preserve - Simms 342–343
Cuculiformes 383
Custer's Last Stand 365

D

Dagmar 249
Dahl Lake 31

Dancing Prairie Preserve 338–339
  Photo 339
Deer Lodge 105
Dillon 127, 130
Duck-billed Dinosaur 11

E

Ear Mountain Outstanding Natural Area 141,
  158–163
  Photo 158, 161, 163
East Glacier 19
East Pryor Mountain 216
Ekalaka 323
Elk Island Wildlife Management Area
  290–295
  Photo 290
Emberizidae 390
Essex 17

F

Fairfield 168
Falconidae 379
Falconiformes 378
Flathead County 30
Flathead National Forest 18
Flathead Waterfowl Production Area 32
Fort Peck Reservoir 297
Fort Union Trading Post 286–287
  Photo 287
Fox Lake Wildlife Management Area 284–285
Freezeout Lake Wildlife Management Area
  10, 168–177
  Freezeout Lake Wma Bird List 174–176
  Photo 169, 172, 177
Freezeout Lake Wma Bird List 174–176
Fringillidae 392

G

Galliformes 376
Gaviiformes 377
Giant Springs Heritage State Park 164–167
  Photo 164, 167
Glacier National Park 14–28
  Photo 14
Glasgow 282
Glendive 317
Great Falls 135, 141, 150, 159, 165, 168
Great Montana Birding And Nature Trail 354

Greenough Park 72
Grizzly Bear 10
Gruidae 379
Gruiformes 379

H

Hailstone National Wildlife Refuge 3,
    202–205, 207
  Photo 202, 205
Halfbreed National Wildlife Refuge 3, 206–209
  Photo 206, 208
Harlem 239
Havre 241, 246
Haymaker Wilderness Management Area
    200–201
  Photo 201
Helena 11, 135
Hell Creek State Park 296–298
Hewitt Lake National Wildlife Refuge 3,
    243–245
  Photo 243, 245
Hill County 241, 246
Hinsdale 282
Hirundinidae 386
Historic Battlefields 360–369
  Bear Paw And Big Hole Battlefields 361–362
  Little Bighorn Battlefield 364–366
  Map 360
Holter Museum Of Art 355–356
House Bill 526 3
Humbug Spires Wilderness Study Area
    98–103
  Photo 98, 101
Hysham 299

I

Icteridae 391–392
Isaac Homestead Wildlife Management Area
  Issac's Homestead Wma/Howery Island
    Area Bird List 305
  Photo 300, 303
Issac's Homestead Wma/Howery Island Area
    Bird List 305

J

Jocko River 38
Jordan 297

K

Kalispell 15, 19, 26, 30
Kelly Island Fishing Access 71
Kiwanis Park, Hamilton 74

L

Lake Como 74–75
Lake Mary Ronan State Park 26–29
  Photo 29
Lake Mason National Wildlife Refuge 3, 207,
    210–213, 211
  Photo 210, 213
Lake Thibadeau National Wildlife Refuge 3,
    246–247
  Photo 247
Lambert 284
Lamesteer National Wildlife Refuge 3,
    306–314
  Photo 306, 315
Laniidae 386
Laridae 381–382
Lee Metcalf National Wildlife Refuge 3, 62–67
  Photo 62, 66–67
Lewis And Clark 350–351
  Map 350
Lewis And Clark National Forest 141
Lewis And Clark National Historic Trail
  Interpretive Center 356–357
Lewistown 203
Lindbergh Lake Pines - Swan Valley 338
Little Bighorn Battlefield 364–366
Lolo Creek 64
Lolo Pass 73
Lost Creek State Park 76–79
  Photo 77, 79
Lost Trail National Wildlife Refuge 3, 30–35
  Photo 35
Lovell 215

M

MacDonald Creek 17
Maclay Flat Trail 71
Makoshika State Park 316–321
  Photo 316
Malta 229
Maverick Basin 129

Medicine Lake National Wildlife Refuge 3, 272–281, 276–285
  Medicine Lake Nwr Bird List 308–314
  Photo 272, 276
Medicine Lake Nwr Bird List 308–314
Medicine Rocks State Park 322–325
  Photo 322
Middle Fork Flathead River 17
Migratory Bird Conservation Act 3
Miles City 327
Milk River 244
Mission Creek 38
Missouri Headwaters State Park 112–115
  Photo 112, 114
Montana Bird List 375–392
  Alaudidae 386
  Alcidae 382
  Anseriformes 375–376
  Apodiformes 384
  Caprimulgiformes 383
  Cardinalidae 391
  Cathartidae 378
  Certhiidae 387
  Charadriiformes 380
  Ciconiidae 378
  Ciconiiformes 377–378
  Columbiformes 382
  Coraciiformes 384
  Cuculiformes 383
  Emberizidae 390
  Falconidae 379
  Falconiformes 378–379
  Fringillidae 392
  Galliformes 376
  Gaviiformes 377
  Gruidae 379
  Gruiformes 379
  Hirundinidae 386–387
  Icteridae 391–392
  Laniidae 386
  Laridae 381–382
  Paridae 387
  Parulidae 389
  Passeridae 392
  Passeriformes 385
  PelecanIformes 377
  Piciformes 384–385
  Podicipediformes 377
  Recurvirostridae 380
  Scolopacidae 380–381
  Sittidae 387
  Strigiformes 383
  Sylviidae 388
  Threskiornithidae 378
  Trochilidae 384
  Troglodytidae 387
  Vireonidae 386
Montana Natural Heritage Program 282
Montana's Museum 358
Montana Wildlife List 393–395
Mount Haggin Wildlife Management Area 104–111
  Photo 104, 111
Mount Jumbo 72
Mourning Cloak 11
Museum of the Rockies 359

N

National Bison Range National Wildlife Refuge 3, 36–41
  Photo 36
Nature Conservancy Sites 336
  Comertown Pothole Prairie Preserve 347
  Crown Butte Preserve - Simms 342–343
  Dancing Prairie Preserve 338–339
  Lindbergh Lake Pines - Swan Valley 338
  Map 336
  Northern Prairies of Montana 337
  Pine Butte Swamp Preserve 348–349
  Safe Harbor Marsh Preserve - Flathead Basin 340–341
  South Fork Madison Preserve 344–345
  Swan River Oxbow Preserve - Swan Valley 345–346
Ninepipe National Wildlife Refuge
  Photo 43
Ninepipe Wilderness Management Area 44
Northern Prairies of Montana 337
Northwestern Glaciated Plains Section 283
Notch Cabin 128

O

Optics and Gear 397–399
Other Places of Interest 352–360
  Bridger Raptor Festival 354–355
  C.M. Russell Museum 357–358

Great Montana Birding and Nature Trail 354
Holter Museum of Art 355–356
Lewis and Clark National Historic Trail Interpretive Center 356–357
Map 352, 353
Montana's Museum 358
Museum of the Rockies 359

P

Pablo National Wildlife Refuge 46–49
Photo 46, 49
Painted Rocks State Park 80–81
Paridae 387
Parulidae 389
Passeridae 392
Passeriformes 385
Pattee Canyon 73
Pelecaniformes 377
Piciformes 384
Pine Butte Swamp Preserve 348–349
Photo 348
Pirogue Island Bird List 329
Pirogue Island State Park 326–329
Photo 326
Pirogue Island Bird List 329
Pleasant Valley 30
Plentywood 249
Podicipediformes 377
Polson 47
Ponderosa Pine 11
Pryor Mountain/Bighorn Canyon Bird List 221–225
Pryor Mountains Wild Horse Range 214–225, 215
Map 217
Photo 214, 219
Pryor Mountain/Bighorn Canyon Bird List 221–225

R

Rainbow Falls 165
Rapelje 203, 207
Rattlesnake National Recreation Area 71
Recurvirostridae 380
Red Rock Lakes Bird List 125

Red Rock Lakes National Wildlife Refuge 3, 116–119
Map 118
Photo 116, 121
Red Rock Lakes Bird List 125
Region 1 12–56
Lake Mary Ronan State Park 26–28
Lost Trail National Wildlife Refuge 30–35
Map 12
National Bison Range National Wildlife Refuge 36–41
Pablo National Wildlife Refuge 46–49
Wild Horse Island State Park 54–55
Region 2 56–87, 57–88
Blackfoot-Clearwater Wildlife Management Area 58–61
Council Grove State Park 68–70
Lee Metcalf National Wildlife Refuge 62
Lost Creek State Park 76–79
Map 56, 57
Painted Rocks State Park 80–81
Photo 57
Warm Springs Wildlife Management Area 82–87
Region 3 88–132
Canyon Ferry Wildlife Management Area 90–97
Humbug Spires Wilderness Study Area 98–103
Map 88, 89
Missouri Headwaters State Park 112–115
Mount Haggin Wildlife Management Area 104–111
Photo 89
Red Rock Lakes National Wildlife Refuge 116–119
Robb-Ledford/Blacktail Creek Wildlife Management Area 126–131
Region 4 132–191, 133–192
Beartooth Wildlife Management Area 134–139
Blackleaf Wildlife Management Area 140–149
Ear Mountain Outstanding Natural Area 158–163
Freezeout Lake Wildlife Management Area 168–177
Giant Springs Heritage State Park 164–167

Map 132, 133
Photo 133
Sluice Boxes State Park 178–181
Sun River Wildlife Management Area
    182–185
War Horse National Wildlife Refuge
    188–191
Region 5 192–226
    Bridger Waterfowl Production Area
        194–199
    Hailstone National Wildlife Refuge 202–205
    Halfbreed National Wildlife Refuge 206–209
    Haymaker Wilderness Management Area
        200–201
    Lake Mason National Wildlife Refuge
        210–213
    Map 192, 193
    Photo 193
    Pryor Mountains Wild Horse Range
        214–225
Region 6 226–287
    Black Coulee National Wildlife Refuge
        238–240
    Bowdoin National Wildlife Refuge 228–237
    ush Lake State Park 248–251
    arles M. Russell National Wildlife Refuge
        252–282
    edman Coulee National Wildlife Refuge
        241–242
    t Union Trading Post 286–287
    Lake Wildlife Management Area
        284–285
    vitt Lake National Wildlife Refuge
        243–245
    226
    dicine Lake National Wildlife Refuge
        272–281, 276–285
    end National Wildlife Refuge 268–271
    7 288–335, 289–336
    sland Wildlife Management Area
        290–295
    reek State Park 296–298
    teer National Wildlife Refuge
        6–314
    ika State Park 316–321
    , 289
    Rocks State Park 322–325
    9

Pirogue Island State Park 326–329
Seven Sisters Wildlife Management Area
    330–335
Richland County 284, 291
Riverfront-Kim Williams Trail 72
Robb-Ledford/Blacktail Creek Wildlife
    Management Area 126–131
Photo 126, 129
Rocky Mountain Elk Foundation 129
Roosevelt Fault 18
Roundup 211
Ruby River 130
Running Rabbit Mountain 18

S

Safe Harbor Marsh Preserve - Flathead Basin
    340, 341
Photo 341
Sapphire 11
Savage 291
Scolopacidae 380–381
Selway-Bitterroot Wilderness 64
Seven Sisters Wildlife Management Area
    330–335, 335–340
Photo 330, 335
Seven Sisters Wma Wildlife List 334,335
Sidney 284
Sioux Indians 165
Sittidae 387
Sluice Boxes State Park 178–181
Photo 178
South Fork Madison Preserve 344–345
Photo 344
Strigiformes 383
Sun River Specialty Bird List 185
Sun River Wildlife ManagemEnt Area
    182–185
Photo 182, 184
Sun River Specialty Bird List 185
Swan River National Wildlife Refuge 49–52
Photo 51, 53
Swan River Oxbow Preserve - Swan Valley
    345–346
Sykes Ridge 216
Sylviidae 388

T

Teller Wildlife Refuge 74
Teton County 141, 159, 168
Three Forks 113
Threskiornithidae 378
Tillet/Burnt Timber Ridge 216
Townsend 91
Treasure County 299
Tribal Trust Lands Of The Confederated
    Salish And Kootenai Tribes 47
Trochilidae 384
Troglodytidae 387
Turner 239
Two Dog Flats 17

U

UL Bend National Wildlife Refuge 3, 268-271
    Photo 268, 271
Upper Missouri Breaks National Monument
    186-187
USFS Wilderness Areas 374
USFWS Wilderness Areas 374

V

Valley County 282
Vireonidae 386
Virginia City 128

W

Walton Goat Lick 17
War Horse National Wildlife Refuge 3,
    188-191
    Photo 188, 191

Warm Springs Wildlife Management Area
    82-87
    Photo 82, 85, 87
Waterton Lakes National Park 16
Western Meadowlark 10
West Glacier 19
Wibaux 307
Wilderness Montana 374
    BLM Wilderness Areas 374
    Confederate Salish and Kootenai Tribes
    374
    USFS Wilderness Areas 374
    USFWS Wilderness Areas 374
Wilderness Study Areas 371-373
    Billings Field Office 371
    Butte Field Office 372
    Dillon Field Office 372
    Lewistown Field Office 372-373
    Malta Field Office 373
    Miles City Field Office 373
    Missoula Field Office 373
Wild Horse Island State Park 54-55
    Photo 55
Willow Creek 211
Wisdom 361, 367

Y

Yellowstone River 327, 331